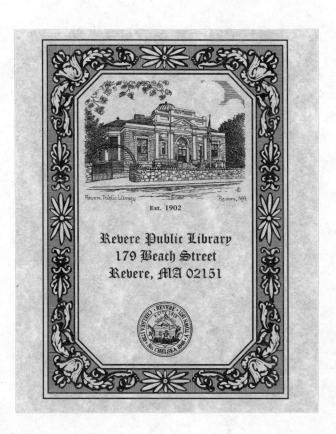

Beating the Adoption Game

Beating the Adoption Game

Revised Edition

Cynthia D. Martin, Ph.D.

A Harvest/HBJ Original
Harcourt Brace Jovanovich, Publishers
SAN DIEGO   NEW YORK   LONDON

This book is designed to educate and inform you about various
aspects of adoption. No single book can address all the legal and other
issues you may be faced with, and the counsel of an appropriate
professional may be advisable in a given situation.

Library of Congress Cataloging-in-Publication Data
Martin, Cynthia D.
    Beating the adoption game.
    "A Harvest/HBJ book."
    Bibliography: p.
    Includes index.
    1. Adoption — United States.   I. Title.
HV875.M369   1988   362.7'34   87-12022
ISBN 0-15-610930-1 (pbk.)

Designed by Francesca M. Smith
Printed in the United States of America
First Harvest/HBJ edition 1988
B C D E F G H I J

To my very special family

. . . David for his strength to be himself
and his love and understanding
which allows me to be myself.
. . . Scott, Dru, Nohl, Shaine, and Anthony,
our natural children both adopted and nonadopted,
for enriching our lives.

Contents

Preface

I HAD HOPED THAT BY THE TIME THE NEW EDITION OF *BEATING THE Adoption Game* was published, the title would be inappropriate. Unfortunately, adoption remains a game. However, the number of people who are winning the adoption game is growing. When I hear people say, "There are no babies available," I feel compelled to reply, "Not true!" Babies are available for adoption.

People successfully adopting today are learning and using creative, legal, and individualistic methods. Those who come to me for adoption counseling continue to teach me new ways to relinquish and new ways to adopt. The flexibility and open minds of both the birthparents and the adoptive parents reaffirm my faith in people. These individuals comprise many of the case studies presented in the book. As adoptees share with me their feelings about the adoption process, I continue to expand my perspective. Adoption statistics tell little about the very human needs of those trying to find a child. For them this book is written.

I owe thanks to the many adoption agencies throughout the United States who supplied information for this book. Their cooperation was an essential ingredient in completing this project. As I hear from individuals who have been referred to this book by adoption agencies and from adoption agencies who have begun to open up their adoption practices, I grow encouraged that change within the system might be possible.

Other people, too, helped in special ways. My children have each helped in their own ways to contribute to the book and to my understanding of adoption. My friends, Cindy and Charles Tillinghast, who originally suggested I write the book, have continued to encourage my writing. Dr. Warren Baller, who read the original manuscript and taught me a great deal about research, added significantly with his many suggestions. My editors, John Radziewicz and Martha Lawrence, who showed friendship and caring in their editing, were a significant help in many ways. Leona Heth's positive view and warm hugs greatly encouraged me.

My deepest appreciation goes to my husband, David, who helped me learn about adoption and then helped me write about it. His suggestions, confidence, and hard work were essential in completing this project. His patience was magnificent and certainly essential.

Books are written not by individuals but by groups. The group that helped me on this one has been absolutely wonderful.

*And a woman who held a babe against her bosom said, Speak to us of
  Children.*
And He said:
Your children are not your children.
They are the sons and daughters of Life's longing for itself.
They come through you but not from you.
And though they are with you yet they belong not to you.
You may give them your love but not your thoughts.
For they have their own thoughts.
You may house their bodies but not their souls,
*For their souls dwell in the house of tomorrow, which you cannot
  visit, not even in your dreams.*
*You may strive to be like them, but seek not to make them like
  you.*
For life goes not backward nor tarries with yesterday.
*You are the bows from which your children as living arrows are set
  forth.*
*The archer sees the mark upon the path of the infinite, and He
  bends you with His might that His arrows may go swift and
  far.*
Let your bending in the archer's hand be for gladness;
*For even as He loves the arrow that flies, so He loves also the
  bow that is stable.*

—Kahlil Gibran, *The Prophet*

All the incidents used as examples throughout this book are true. The people cited are real, but their names and identifying data have been changed.

Beating the Adoption Game

A Few Words Before You Begin

YOU CAN GET A BABY. YOU CAN GET A BABY EVEN IF YOU CANNOT GET pregnant and even if you are turned down by the adoption agencies. You don't need a lot of money or a fancy house. You can get a baby if you are overweight, old, handicapped, or even if you are single. There is a baby somewhere for you if you are willing to try some new ways to obtain one.

Babies are available. Actually it is quite a simple matter. The people who want babies and cannot make them need to meet either people who are good at making babies or medical people who are good at fixing reproductive problems. These are the only options. The means to take advantage of them are varied.

If you want a baby, you must look at the choices and then look at yourself. There is no right or wrong choice or direction, but there is a right way for you.

Adoption Options

You need to explore which ways of seeking a baby are comfortable for you. At first glance, some of the methods may seem inappropriate for you, but think about them. You may need to try familiar approaches first; later, if you have had no luck with the familiar ways, you may become more comfortable with some of the newer or riskier ways. Part of making your choice of alternatives is to understand your limits and whether you can stretch those limits.

For some people, the traditional modes of obtaining a baby are the only ones they have ever considered and the only ones with which they would be comfortable. Go through the routine medical test for infertility. If a medical problem is discovered that cannot be corrected and you reach some level of acceptance of your infertility, you may choose to contact an adoption agency to ask for a baby. Assuming you are accepted by the adoption agency, you follow the set process until the exciting day you are called about your baby or child. You raise your family just like any other normal family, and soon no one knows you are different at all. This procedure has been followed by thousands of people. For many people today, however, this method will not lead to a baby.

This traditional approach sharply contrasts with the risk taken by a couple who had the same goal: a baby. After the initial medical exams, John and Debbie learned she could not get pregnant. While thoroughly and openly discussing their feelings about Debbie's infertility, the couple discovered it was important for them to have a child that was genetically, if only partly, theirs. They decided to find a surrogate mother to carry John's child, and placed an ad in a national magazine. Risky? Of course. However, sixteen months later they had their baby. They took the risks and won.

For others, the need to explore all the medical possibilities in order to have a child of their "own" is a critical factor. England's baby Louise, the so-called test-tube baby, was one couple's way. Hundreds of other couples wait to try this or even more radical methods.

Adoption may be considered by these couples, but only after trying every reasonable medical remedy for their infertility. Some would say these people are disturbed or poor risks for adoption because they have been unable to resolve their feelings about their infertility. Others would admire the perseverance and willingness of these people to pursue advances that seemed improbable a short time ago.

The desperation of some couples drives them to utilize a source currently considered illegal . . . the black market. People are willing to pay $25,000 or more to get a baby. Most people are shocked that a couple would elect to *buy* a baby. However, if you really want a baby and have been thwarted in every way, and someone tells you that for $25,000 you can have a baby about to be born, what would you do? Patty and Jim, a couple in their late thirties who had been turned down by the adoption agencies, had that chance and took it. To them, it was a bargain!

Who are the people willing to seek babies in nontraditional ways? Are they different from "normal" couples who get pregnant or who adopt by traditional means? Yes, definitely. They are desperate. They want a baby and cannot get one the regular way. Their choices are to be creative and risky, or to be childless. They take the risks.

Some will find it hard to identify with these people and their search. Others may tell them to fill their lives in alternate meaningful ways, like taking in foster children, raising some nice pets, or becoming teachers. While these substitutes may be enough for some people, they do not provide a baby to love and be loved by. There is no substitute for your own baby.

I strongly support and encourage those willing to take risks . . . you, if you are searching for a baby. I know there are children available. Open up to new ways to find a baby. Create new ways to find one. Think, explore, search, try. You *can* find a baby!

Consequences of Infertility

Infertility journeys are always painful and frequently private. Few people totally understand your personal response to not being able to have a baby when you want one. The emotional issues of infertility dominate the couple's lives and put strains on them as a couple and as individuals. At times the strains show to the world, and it underscores the struggle.

In some ways, not having a child "proves" to the world an individual's deficiency. If we are poor, financial inadequacy may or may not show to the world. If we are insecure, the world may not necessarily know. But if we are childless, our sexual deficiency is exhibited for all the world to view. To understand the emotional consequences of infertility is to understand the plight of feeling inadequate.

Sexuality still remains so blurred and confusing to most people that fertility is one of our primary means of demonstrating our sexuality. Our society headlines the older male who fathers a child. In southern California, an old lion at one of the animal parks was eulogized for fathering so many lion cubs late in his life. Shirts with his picture on them were printed in admiration.

Young people, too, brag about sexual conquests to bolster their feelings about sexuality. Roger was sixteen and had few friends. He felt very unsure of himself in most situations. He told his school counselor and a few acquaintances about getting a girl pregnant at church camp. Everyone started to listen to him a bit more, so he related that the girl gave birth to their daughter. Then he told how his girlfriend's parents made them get married. Now a lot of people knew about Roger. He told his counselor he had gotten her pregnant a second time and wasn't sure what he should do. The counselor suggested he seek legal help, but Roger did nothing. The counselor then learned, from Roger, that the girl had stepped out in front of a car and had been killed, and her parents had given him his baby for him to raise. Everyone knew about Roger's story by now. His story had been told at school for over a year. He had added prestige with his peers, and he felt more confident about dealing with people who knew of him. He spoke positively about his daughter to the counselor, who was impressed with his strong commitment to the child.

Then one day, someone from the school office contacted Roger's home and found out from Roger's mother that Roger didn't have a baby. Roger hadn't caused anyone to become pregnant. Roger didn't even have a girlfriend. In fact, Roger had never been sexually active at all. Roger had made up the entire story. He needed to have the same kinds of stories, or better ones, to tell the guys in the gym. He needed to have people see him as a sexual creature who knew what he was doing sexually just like he thought others knew what they were doing. Roger couldn't feel comfortable doing the same things others did to "establish" their sexual identities, so he made them up.

Our sexual identities are frequently very fragile. Early sexuality may be an attempt to "prove" adequacy for some uncertain reason. Lots of sex is another way of proving sexuality. Frequently, men seek to improve their sense of sexuality by the number of climaxes they can achieve or the number of women with whom they have had sex or the frequency of their intercourse. Number of children is another way of proving sexuality. Contraceptive clinics in low-income areas have frequently failed because too often the identity of low-income groups is based on how many children they have. They may be poor, but they are "good" parents because they have lots of children.

With so much emphasis on demonstrated sexuality, infertile

couples are obviously in some trouble. They are forced into feelings of inadequacy. In order to survive emotionally as complete persons, they have to learn how to handle feelings of deficiency, since they are unable to establish their sexual identity by producing a child as others do.

The couple experiencing infertility must first come to grips with how this factor affects each of them individually. Each individual must grope for new ways to establish a firm sexual identity. The person who is sure of his or her sexuality will be less affected than the person who is less sure. If you are sure of your sexuality, demonstrating it to yourself or your friends or the world becomes less important. Generally, the woman who is doing other things in her life places less emphasis on her fertility as her only means of viewing herself as a woman. The man who is successful in other areas of his life is less concerned about his lack of success in impregnating his wife. Basically, the more "together" the person, the easier time he or she will have accepting his or her infertility . . . easier, but still not too easy.

The couple experiencing infertility must also face the strains it puts on their relationship. All major problem areas—a new job, a new home, the woman beginning to work outside the home, someone being fired, a relative coming to live with them, the death of a relative, an injury to one of the partners—cause shifts and changes in the marital relationship. Sometimes the changes are for the better and sometimes for the worse. How the relationship bounces back determines where the couple goes from there; these are vulnerable periods in marital relationships. Infertility may be one of the most significant experiences a couple will ever have.

Couples, at this time above all, need to communicate openly. To harbor feelings of blame toward your sterile spouse can cause long-term, irreparable damage to the relationship. Scheduled sexual relations and the stress of medical tests put severe strains on any relationship. If this is coupled with hidden hostility and unspoken blame, the couple will have difficulty overcoming the strain of infertility. They may end up not only without a child, but also without a partner.

Attitudes of relatives and friends may be a significant problem for the infertile couple. Relationships with others are filled with references to the couple's infertility. The potential grandmother has her advice to give. The potential aunts and uncles, going through their own period of child-rearing, are quick to offer tips concerning your childlessness. Baby showers where people say, "You're next" become ordeals and alter your relationships with your friends.

Society, with no knowledge of your pain, views you with confusion and skepticism. You are likely to be pictured as selfish in not wanting children—which is ever so far from the truth. Even if you are viewed as childless not by choice, society is likely to offer little sympathy, because people with children have difficulty identifying with your infertility plight. People openly sympathize with mourning couples whose child has been lost through death; people fail to comprehend the mourning of the couple whose child is lost through infertility.

At times, outsiders will view you in your childlessness as neurotic or immature. Newspapers and magazines you read may relate your childlessness to your frigidity and sexual immaturity. In this time of overpopulation, your problems will be viewed as insignificant and lacking in substance.

As the desire for pregnancy supersedes most things in your life, you need to find adequate and acceptable ways to handle your feelings about infertility. The primary way to deal with these feelings is to talk with people . . . especially your partner. Express your feelings to sympathetic listeners, if you have feelings of guilt or deficiency. Talking with others helps to eliminate the irrational feelings you have about your infertility problem. If you have difficulty finding someone to talk with, seek professional help from a psychologist or psychiatrist.

A second means of coping with your feelings is to redirect your energies. For months you may have been engrossed with fertility tests, temperature charting, medical appointments, and scheduled sexual activities. Infertility has dominated your existence. At some point you have to accept the fact that there is no solution to your infertility that will produce a pregnancy. So now what are you going to do? You need to change directions. One new direction may be trying to find a child to adopt. It may be toward a different kind of creative approach to life. A change in direction, however, is critical.

Don't expect the feelings you have to go away immediately. You need to be prepared for a period of mourning. This might be called mourning for the child you couldn't have. Expect this period to last at least six months. You will find your feelings of depression, anger, and anxiety decreasing with time, with redirection of your energies, and by talking openly about your problem.

The emotional consequences of infertility are surmountable. The individual dealing openly, honestly, and thoroughly with his or her feelings of inadequacy and anger is much more likely to overcome these emotions than the person who pretends everything is fine when in fact it isn't. The lack of babies available for adoption makes it even more critical that your feelings about infertility are resolved and not simply denied. Your options, now that you are certain of your infertility, take strength to pursue. If you remain handicapped by the discovery of your infertility, you will be less likely to be able to pursue effectively the options you still have to obtain a baby.

Options to Infertility

Many ways exist to meet your need for a child. Some are direct means of getting a child, and others emphasize a redirection away from parenting. People will choose different options. As in many areas we are discussing, there is not a right or wrong way; there is a way with which you are likely to feel more comfortable. You may pursue several options before you find the one that best suits you. You may eliminate an option now that later on might suit you better. Meet your needs in your own way.

• *Adoption*

If you choose not to pursue the more elaborate or experimental techniques of reproduction, or if you have pursued them unsuccessfully, adoption may be the option you choose to attain parenthood. The many avenues to finding children are discussed in this book. Find the one that best meets your needs.

Both private and agency adoptions should be considered when you are thinking of adopting a child. They each have advantages and disadvantages that will be discussed in detail later in this book.

In order to seek a child through the process of adoption, you should first know that reasonable medical corrections of your infertility problem have been attempted. If these are tried and you have allowed yourself some time to digest the fact of your infertility, adoption can be almost or just as meaningful as producing a child biologically.

• *Foster Parenting*

A different kind of parenting possibility exists through becoming a foster parent. This can be a rewarding opportunity to participate in the raising of a child.

At times people confuse foster parents with adoptive parents. There are very few similarities. Foster parents are usually temporary parents. Foster parents do not have legal custody of the child. The child can be taken from the foster home at any time. Foster parents are paid for the care of the child. Adoptive parents, on the contrary, provide permanent homes; the parents have legal custody of the child. In adoptive homes, the parents are legally responsible for the upbringing of the child and receive no pay for this responsibility.

The foster care system in this country has come under considerable attack in recent years. Agencies running foster care programs are often adoption agencies. Not all, but many, of these agencies have been accused of deliberately keeping potentially adoptable children in foster care because the state pays the agencies for each child it keeps in the foster care system. If these children are placed in adoptive homes, the agency no longer receives funds from the state. Critics of the system say the agencies are being supported by state funds and therefore have no incentive to place these children in adoptive homes. The state cost of raising a foster child from early childhood to age eighteen can be several hundreds of thousands of dollars. This tremendously expensive parenting system is not only a burden on the taxpayers, but it also offers little stability for the child raised in these "temporary" facilities. It is estimated that as many as 500,000 children are currently in foster care.[1] The average stay will be between four to six years. Representatives of the Health, Education and Welfare Department estimate that between 50 and 85 percent of the children in foster care will remain there through the age of eighteen.[2] This type of permanent-temporary home situation causes tremendous confusion to the child who belongs nowhere.

None of these criticisms negate the great good being done by foster parents who willingly offer temporary homes to children in need. The ideal foster parent is one with an ability to love without having to feel the relationship will go on forever. This is not an easy kind of love for many people to offer, so there is often a lack of good foster parents.

With this scarcity of foster homes, little screening of potential foster parents may actually occur. As a consequence, large numbers of foster parents are not truly involved with their foster children. At times, the primary reason people become foster parents is to have the income from caring for the foster children. Some homes have large numbers of foster children as a means of having a significant income.

Children in the foster care system come from one of three groups. The first group are children who are waiting to be placed in adoptive homes. These are usually the most temporary children in foster homes. Older children waiting to be adopted are frequently kept in foster homes for a long period of time to make certain the correct type of home is found. The second group are children whose parents are temporarily unable to care for them but who do not want to place them for adoption. This is a temporary situation that allows the parent to maintain contact with the child while the parent stabilizes his or her life. Some of these children are voluntarily placed by their parents; at other times the court system has intervened because the parent has not adequately cared for the child. The third group of children are the ones whose parents have little contact with them. These children are likely to remain in foster care through their eighteenth birthday. The Child Welfare League of America maintains that children whose parents do not take the child back within a year and a half probably never will. As with the previous group, these children are placed in foster care both voluntarily and by the courts.

Cases have recently been publicized of foster parents being allowed to adopt their foster children. In the past this was strictly forbidden by the adoption agencies. Although more cases are occurring, foster parents must go to great lengths to be accepted as the adoptive applicants for their foster child. This is not a very sure way to find a child to adopt. Adoption agencies, I believe, should consider the foster parents first if a specific foster child they are raising does become adoptable. Some states are beginning to recognize the value of considering foster parents as the parents of first choice in situations where the placement has been long-term. The home the child knows should be the first one to be considered permanent.

A new type of adoption has recently emerged. It is called fost-adopt. The theory is that parents seeking to adopt can have the child before the child has been fully released from the custody of the birthparent. In most cases the relinquishment is fairly firm, so this is a way of beginning the adoption process earlier. Obviously there are greater risks that a birthparent will not sign the papers relinquishing the child and may choose to take the child back. These risks are made clear to the adoptive parents considering fost-adopt.

This is especially important since the parents who are being considered for fost-adopt situations are people seeking to adopt, and not foster parents who understand the temporary nature of the placement. Information is not yet available on how successfully these programs are working. They do seem to be a step in the right direction.

• *Substitute Parenting*
Some people will choose to remain childless but will find themselves intimately involved in parenting vicariously. There are many means of being a substitute parent.

One of the ways to be a substitute parent is with the children of relatives. Some aunts or uncles are extremely involved with their nieces and nephews. They take them places, spend time with them, travel with them. They are involved in their holidays and in their other joyous events. They are able to participate in these children's growing years.

Other childless people, wanting to participate in child-rearing, seek out close relationships with children in the neighborhood or do extensive baby-sitting. Other people become Big Brothers or Big Sisters for children who do not have an adult of their sex in their lives. These people find that part-time parenting meets some of their needs for contact with children.

Another way people become substitute parents is by teaching children. Becoming a teacher or helping in a nursery school will sometimes substitute for not having children. The teacher spends four to six hours a day with lots of children. That may be far more hours of parenting than many actual parents spend.

The people who choose substitute parenting are saying it is important to them to have children in their lives. They are not actually remaining childless. They simply have children who are slightly more "borrowed" than those who adopt or who have foster children. All our children—the ones we produce, the ones we adopt, and the ones we merely nurture for a while—are borrowed. No one *owns* a child.

• *Childlessness*
One of the options to infertility is to remain childless—an option that is chosen far more frequently than is generally believed. Figures on how many childless people have actually tried to become

pregnant and failed are impossible to find. It is difficult to determine how many people are childless and how many people are childless but not by choice.

Childlessness has only recently been studied. It is known that greater numbers of couples have not had children during certain periods of our history, such as the Depression. Explanations for the decreased fertility rates are purely speculative.

A resurgence of childlessness was seen in the seventies and continues—while not as strong—into the eighties. Organizations advocating childlessness received large amounts of publicity for a period of time. Today this issue seems to be less positively regarded. The advocates for childlessness have undoubtedly increased the acceptability of nonparenting as a viable alternative open to couples.[3] Support groups are sometimes available in local communities. They generally have speakers who are available to publicize their cause. It is worthwhile to contact them if you wish to know more about childlessness.

Studies have been undertaken only recently to assess why people are childless and how this affects their lives. Results have found that the childless couples were just as satisfied with their lives as those who had children.[4] The common assumption has been that the childless couple will be lonely in later life and that life will have held no meaning for them. This assumption appears invalid.

Another group of studies published in the fifties focused on the failed marriages of childless couples. The results were presented to the childless as a further reason to have children: If you don't have a baby, the marriage is more likely to fail. In recent years, these same studies have been shown to be invalid. Early divorces are frequently childless by nature of the length of these marriages. Assessing the effect of having children on the failure of the marriage becomes impossible.

So where does this leave people who remain childless not by choice? Is there a negative effect on their marriages or on their lives in general as a result of their childlessness? What can people do to minimize any negative effect that remaining childless might have on them?

Marriages are not held together by babies for long. The quality of a marriage is most directly related to the commitment and work of the two people involved. Open communication can help any couple surmount a specific difficulty encountered. Marriages neither succeed nor fail solely because of children or the lack thereof. The *primary* means of making sure your life is fulfilling is not necessarily having children.

Children may or may not add to your feelings of satisfaction with life. If you decide to remain childless, it is important to have other means to feel good about yourself. A satisfying job is one means. Doing worthwhile things in your life is another. If you feel good about yourself, you won't need a child to prove your worth. Validation from others or from society in general based upon your parenting or nonparenting becomes less important to you. You know you are worthwhile . . . you feel it . . . no one needs to tell you that you are okay.

• *Experimental Methods of Reproduction*
Some people will try to go further than others to correct their infertility problems. More extraordinary help is available in the area of fertility studies than ever before in history. Yet there are some problems with pursuing this option.

You have already spent several years trying to become pregnant. Your life has been thoroughly absorbed by this primary goal. It is likely that the strain of the pursuit is showing in your relationships with spouse, family, and friends.

Find out from your physician what your chance of success is before you decide how far to go with extraordinary medical procedures. Look at the costs; they too can be extraordinary. Only in this way can you evaluate how worthwhile it might be to continue. As in many areas of life, you are playing the odds; you want to calculate the costs, emotionally and financially, versus the possibilities of the payoff.

Many people and sources are out there to help you to solve and accept the problems you are experiencing. This very emotional issue is difficult to handle alone. Seek out the support you need. Seeking help from loved ones or from professionals is not a sign of weakness—it's a sign of intelligence.

Sterility hurts. It makes people cry, it makes them angry, it makes them feel incomplete. It's hard to determine and it's hard to accept. It's clinical and it's emotional. It can dominate your life and yet it is painful to know when to let it go. Only the strong should suffer sterility.

Basically, these are the options to infertility. You may elect to try some of the options simultaneously. You may try new, experimental ways to get pregnant, while trying to find a child to adopt. You may elect to go from one option to another. You may try being very active with children as a substitute parent and decide later that it isn't what you want. Then you may decide to pursue medical remedies further or to pursue adoption.

Nancy and Warren are a good example of a couple trying many options to their infertility. They went through infertility studies and found Warren had a low sperm count that probably was the cause of their infertility. They decided it was "no big deal" and went ahead to adopt two children. Everything was going along fine until they began to have marital problems. As they came closer and closer to a divorce, they realized that the unexplored and undiscussed areas of Warren's sterility were a significant factor in the hostility Nancy was feeling. As this came more to the foreground, they saw that many areas of concern revolving around their infertility had been ignored or denied. With the discussion came improvement in the marriage. What had started out to be a dissolving of the relationship ended up with their deciding to resume their fertility work to see if they had gone as far as they needed to in trying to produce a child. After some additional tests, they decided to try artificial insemination; it didn't work. As a result, they discovered that Nancy, too, was part of the infertility problem. They decided to adopt another child while continuing their medical possibilities. Nancy and Warren exemplify the multiple attempts and changes a couple can experience while they seek an acceptable alternative to their infertility.

Try what sounds best to you. Don't hesitate to say, after a time, that the option you chose is the wrong one and you want to try another one. Life changes and so can you.

Unplanned Pregnancies: A Source of Babies

While you suffer the pains of infertility, another person suffers from a pregnancy she doesn't want. Why would a woman who says she doesn't want to be pregnant get pregnant? Why would a woman not take the necessary precautions to prevent an unwanted pregnancy? Why does fate treat each of us this way?

Since you are trying to find the woman who is unhappy about her pregnancy, it is important for you to understand who she is and how she arrived at this position in her life. Your understanding of her helps you find her and empathize with her once you have found her.

Some women will get pregnant because of contraceptive failures. Other women believe the risks or the disadvantages of taking the necessary contraceptive precautions are too great, and they would rather take a chance on an unwanted pregnancy. Some will also fit into another group of women who experience unplanned pregnancies—women who at some deep level desire to be pregnant.

• Contraceptives Available

The current state of our knowledge about contraception is far more sophisticated than before. Just about everyone, no matter what his or her age or socioeconomic status, knows about contraception. Most large cities have free contraception available upon request.

Fear of pregnancy prevented women from being sexually active in the past. Most women need not have that fear any longer if they choose to use contraceptives or have their partner use contraceptives. Even with our knowledge of how to prevent a pregnancy, the availability of this knowledge to most people, and the advantages derived from this ability to control unwanted conceptions, women still get pregnant. Several explanations account for these pregnancies:

1. Contraceptive failures account for some unplanned pregnancies.

2. Some contraceptive techniques are not easily used, which discourages their faithful or effective use.

3. Contraceptive availability does not offset a woman's deliberate, although unconscious, exposure to an unwanted pregnancy.

4. Some women don't care if they get pregnant because they view abortion as an easy way out.

Contraceptive availability sounds like an easy preventative to unplanned pregnancies. It would be, if only people weren't so complex. For the couple who desperately seek a child because they cannot become pregnant, it is difficult to understand that many people become pregnant accidentally and easily. Yet understanding unplanned pregnancy will help you with your adoption.

• Unconscious Desire to Be Pregnant

One reason unplanned pregnancies occur is that many women, at some unconscious level, desire to be pregnant. The fact that contraception is available, but not being used, substantiates the possible existence of this unconscious desire. If you *really* don't want to get pregnant, you do something to prevent it. The woman who cannot find any methods of contraception that are acceptable to her may be saying she doesn't want to find any methods to prevent a pregnancy. The woman who is a sometime contraceptive user is one who sometimes may want to be pregnant.

Women who have had abortions as a means of resolving an unwanted pregnancy at times find themselves deliberately exposing themselves again to the same predicament. The woman's stated desire not to be pregnant must seriously be questioned if she keeps putting herself in a position to get pregnant. These women, who may have some strong underlying reasons for wanting to be pregnant, are a source of babies who might be available for adoption. For that reason, we have to look closely at the factors that cause a woman to expose herself to a pregnancy when she says she doesn't want to be pregnant.

Pregnancy means a lot of different things to different women. For some women, especially the adolescent woman, pregnancy is a means of establishing her identity as an adult. The adolescent's primary psychological task is her search for a firm sense of who she is—her identity. The adolescent girl struggles to find her identity as a woman, not as a girl; or an adult, not as a child; and as an individual, not as an extension of her parents. Seeking to find her unique identity, she may use her developing sexual behavior as a form of saying, "Look, I am an adult, too!"

For some adolescent girls, having sexual feelings and the recognition of their developing bodies adds enough to their sense of identity. For other girls, further proof of their adulthood is needed and is achieved through active sexual behavior. Still others, unsure of who they are, need a pregnancy to prove to themselves that they are women. However, bearing the child or mothering the baby may not be essential in developing their female identities. Some of these young women with a need to be pregnant would be good candidates for allowing their pregnancies to go full term and placing their babies for adoption.

Another reason a woman might expose herself to an unwanted pregnancy is to maintain a relationship with a man. Perhaps the relationship is deteriorating and she seeks pregnancy as a way to maintain it. But babies make poor cement. In fact, in most cases, accidental pregnancies cause the breakup of nonmarital relationships. Historically, this tactic may have prompted many marriages, but this result is no longer as common. The woman's reason for exposing herself to an unwanted pregnancy may have left her; however, her pregnancy does not leave that easily. Again, women in these circumstances might be good sources of adoptable children.

People help others who are in trouble. At times this well-intentioned help might in itself lead to a pregnancy, as it did with Sharon. She was a lonely nineteen year old who had few friends. She had difficulty talking to people. In fact, she said that sometimes it was easier to go to bed with a guy than try to talk to him. Not surprisingly, she got pregnant. Agencies opened their doors to her. Volunteer counselors spent time with her whenever she needed them. People, new "friends," helped her get to and from the agencies. Sharon said it was the best time of her life. Then she had an abortion and was back where she was before her pregnancy. The "friends" were no longer there. Her next pregnancy was not much of an accident. She needed help, and the second pregnancy gave her that opportunity even though it was short-term abortion counseling. Sharon needed professional counseling to avoid unwanted pregnancies and to help her solve her personal problems. If she had considered carrying her pregnancy to full term and placing the baby for adoption, at least she would have received longer-term counseling.

At times a pregnancy may result from an attempt to compensate for a previous abortion. The woman, feeling the unresolved loss of the previous pregnancy, is likely to get pregnant again. She may inadvertently expose herself to an "accidental" pregnancy to "undo" her abortion. For this woman, carrying the child to term in the first instance may be a better choice. She may feel better about herself if she allows herself to complete the pregnancy, and she would provide another child for adoption.

Fears of sterility can motivate women toward an unwanted pregnancy. A doctor told Evelyn, who was adopted as an infant, that she was unlikely ever to get pregnant. To prove her womanliness to herself she became pregnant at an early age. Evelyn typifies the woman who gives birth to satisfy her fears of infertility. She may also have to reject abortion since she owes her existence to her natural mother's choice not to abort.

Some women deliberately keep their lives in a constant negative state. Jennifer was one. She had a late abortion that made it a difficult, laborlike procedure. She was in labor for over fourteen hours and left the hospital angry with the staff and with the father of the child. Her primary way of relating to people was through the negative things that were "happening to her." She saw herself as a victim. The new man in her life did not treat her as she deserved. She was angry that he did not pay for her birth control pills, so in spite she quit taking them. Unable to take responsibility for her own actions, Jennifer was a victim of her own making, paying for her anger with another pregnancy. She *was* a victim in her own unhappy way. At one of these pregnancy crisis points in her life she might consider placing the baby for adoption as an alternative to abortion.

These women are some of the over one million women each year who have unwanted pregnancies. Counseling services seldom pinpoint these reasons. They arrange for abortions—the cheaper, the better. Some of these women who are given quick abortions might be better off giving up their babies for adoption; many of them may have never considered adoption as an alternative.

Dilemma of Unwanted Pregnancies

No matter what the reasons for an accidental pregnancy, contraceptive failure, or unconscious desire to be pregnant, once the woman is pregnant she faces a new dilemma. She is no longer involved in risk-taking—she is on her way to having a baby. Whether she is single or married, she has only three choices open to her:

1. She can have the baby and raise it.
2. She can have the baby and place it for adoption.
3. She can terminate the pregnancy with an abortion.

If she doesn't want a baby, all the choices are difficult and she chooses the least offensive.

She is now about to be bombarded by all the people who would like to have input in her decision-making process. She begins with her own view, which involves her feelings about herself and her relationship to others—the father of the child, parents, siblings, and friends. Her personal view of what to do is influenced by her religious and moral feelings. Her view of herself as a woman and as a "maybe" mother enter into the decision. She is usually filled with ambivalence and confusion.

There is in each woman a view of herself as a potential mother. The ambivalence between the feelings of childlessness and motherhood is viewed with alarm by the woman who is not sure that she wants to be pregnant. She resents the child's intrusion on her life, while at the same time fantasizing about her new life with a baby. She immediately begins to form a view of herself as a "mother," no matter what decision she makes about the baby she carries.

In this moment of great uncertainty, many others have their say in an unplanned pregnancy. The father of the child has his say, even though it is quite limited legally. He has no legal right to prevent or to force termination of the pregnancy. Jeff, age fifteen, found this out the hard way. He had convinced Sue, aged sixteen, that they should "get rid of the baby" the first time she was pregnant. A friend told her if she took a lot of birth control pills she would miscarry—she did. (Probably not because of the pills.) The second pregnancy in the same year found her more reluctant. Jeff convinced her to get an abortion. She delayed as long as possible, then finally aborted twins. Jeff insisted to no avail that she use the pill or something. She never remembered. Her third pregnancy, at seventeen, which she decided to complete, surprised him. He tried to convince her to abort the pregnancy, but she refused. He was responsible financially for the baby boy she later delivered. Jeff is only seventeen now, but if Sue chooses, he will be forced to support his son for quite some time.

The unmarried father has no legal right to prevent the pregnant woman from placing the child for adoption; however, he does have a legal right to be considered as the appropriate home for the child. Amy was faced with a problem because of this new legal right for fathers. Amy was an active student in high school when she became pregnant with Kevin's baby. Her parents, mindful of their community involvement and social standing, were appalled. They made plans for her to visit relatives in another state until she delivered and could quietly place the child for adoption. Everything was so clear until Kevin's parents said they wanted him to keep the baby and they would raise it. His parents were willing to go to court to get the baby if Amy relinquished it. Amy was unwilling to deal with this, so she kept the child she had wanted to place for adoption.

The influence of the father greatly depends on the relationship he and the mother have. Although his rights are limited, they are increasing.

No one else has legal rights in the mother's decision-making about the fate of her unborn child. The impact of others is likely to be felt, but cannot be sustained in a court of law.

Everyone *knows* what she should do. Everyone tells her what she should do. Parents, siblings, friends—all give her their opinions on the subject. And all she gets is more confused. It's a comparatively easy decision for a thirty-five-year-old woman with three children who, through contraceptive failure, becomes pregnant. She doesn't want the child and decides to get an abortion. It's an equally easy decision if you have been married for a year and want to wait a bit longer to have a baby. You accidentally got pregnant, so you merely change your time plans a bit. The decision isn't as difficult when all the indicators point the direction for you. It's hardest when the pressures go in all different directions.

At this point the woman, confused and hurried by time pressures, needs to look objectively at all available alternatives. There are advocates, not necessarily equally represented, for each of the alternatives. Unfortunately, it is difficult to find someone who advocates exploring all the alternatives.

In recent years, the pro-abortion counseling groups have become the loudest. Abortion as a legal choice is fairly recent in the realm of options. Over one million abortions per year are being performed in the United States alone. Today, most young women finding themselves pregnant consider only abortion or keeping the baby. That is what their friends did, and those are likely to be the only choices they consider.

The choice to raise the baby, if the mother is not married, has only recently been viewed as an option by other than special minority groups. At one point, the single mother was viewed with alarm. Now, with single mothers merging with the serially married mother, society barely takes a second glance. Celebrities who have elected to remain single while carrying a child actually glamorize this choice as an alternative to unplanned pregnancies. The romanticism and independence of having a baby and handling it on one's own also encourages single parenting. From time to time, even adoption agencies put their seal of approval on single parenting by placing children with singles. Like abortion, single parenting has an advocacy group.

Adoption has no effective advocates. The adoption agencies' workers are not a visible group. Outreach programs and searches for potential biological parents to place children for adoption are unheard of. We do not recruit babies! I don't know why not. With advocates for two of the three alternatives available to the unhappily pregnant woman, the need for greater publicity of the adoption alternative is clear. "Pregnancy counseling," as it is popularly offered, is a deception. All the alternatives to a pregnancy are not presented in an unbiased manner. Each group that does "pregnancy counseling" has something to advocate—to sell. Most groups are selling a philosophy: zero population growth, abortion is murder, or women's liberation. Other groups are selling a product: adoptable babies or abortions. The concept of advocacy by any group might be acceptable if each group were equally represented. This, however, is not the case. If you open your newspaper, you are likely to find classified ads for "pregnancy counseling" under the personal heading. The young woman who turns to the "counselors" for help is trying to make a good decision about her unborn child. Unfortunately, she seldom has a chance to explore equally all the alternatives open to her.

A few years ago I called a number of agencies in one area and told them about my "fifteen-year-old friend" who was pregnant and did not know what to do. The responses were astounding.

One agency, with the little information I had given, told me to bring her in the next day—she could have an abortion and be out by noon. I asked where they did the abortion . . . in the office, or where? The worker-counselor told me they were working on that, but for now they went to a nearby hospital. She said they didn't have women doctors, but they hoped to soon because sometimes male doctors "treat you like a hunk of meat." I told her that my friend thought she might get married or place the baby for adoption. The worker said, "Oh, she is too young to get married, and the adoption agencies are a bunch of crooks." My fifteen-year-old friend might have had difficulty exploring alternatives with this group.

The bias of this agency was blatant, but not singular. I called another agency about the same friend. The volunteer indicated the agency had "trained counselors" who would help her through her abortion. Again, I said my friend was uncertain as to whether she would be better off keeping the baby or even getting married. The woman said they would talk to her about her choices. I asked about adoption. The worker said they had a number for her to call if that was what she wanted. I asked her whose telephone number it was, but she did not even know whose number she was distributing.

The fact that the major source of revenue for many volunteer pregnancy counseling agencies is "kickbacks" given by hospitals that perform referral abortions cannot help but influence the counseling they provide. Some agencies are on quota systems, which means they guarantee a certain number of abortion referrals per month to a specific hospital. Although these innovative approaches have significantly lowered abortion costs, they have been at the expense of women who deserve to know *all* the alternatives to their pregnancy. The sad part is that the unsuspecting woman, usually young, does not even realize she has not explored all her options. She believes she has had pregnancy counseling in order to make the best decision. Women who have truly explored all the alternatives might consider adoption. Women who have not even considered adoption represent a virtually untapped source of babies for people seeking a child to adopt.

Conflict Between the Fertile and the Infertile

The conflict between the fertility extremes is marked. Some women get pregnant too easily, and others get pregnant not at all. This underlying difference causes problems throughout the adoption process.

Adoptive couples frequently are unable to understand how a birthmother could possibly give up her child. Wanting so much to have a child prevents the infertile couple from being able to place themselves in the position of the birthmother and can even create some alienation. It increases their fears that the birthmother will change her mind, and it may even cause them to look down on her. Adopting couples need to view the dilemma of an unwanted pregnancy from a perspective that has grown foreign to them in their struggle with infertility.

Put yourself in a different place as you begin your search. Attempt to understand how someone who doesn't want to be pregnant might still risk a pregnancy. (You may have even been there at another time in your life, before you discovered you couldn't get pregnant.) Look at the complexities of pregnancy from the perspective of one who accidentally gets pregnant. (You certainly are able to understand the complexities of pregnancy from the perspective of one who cannot get pregnant.) You are doing two things by trying to change your perspective: learning places to explore in your search for a baby, and learning to understand and accept the birthmother of your child.

Come to grips with the angry feelings you have about someone who can so easily do that which you cannot do. Without this understanding, you may create problems with the adoption you so much want.

The woman who is unhappily pregnant might not have considered adoption because she does not understand the current scarcity of babies available for adoption. She simply doesn't know how many people would like to have the child she is carrying. Even today, the pregnant woman is likely to view her child as unwanted. The need to change this misconception is evident. In reality, the woman carries within her a valuable person desperately wanted by thousands of people. Perhaps the fact that her unborn child is in great demand could help effect a decision that offers the best solution for herself, the child, and some potential parents. She needs to feel she can do something beneficial with her baby.

With fewer babies available today than ever before, adoption is a viable, healthy alternative to unwanted pregnancy and needs to be promoted. It is time to try new, open, and different approaches to adoption. It is time to advocate adoption as an alternative to unwanted pregnancy. It is time to make adoption a desirable, known alternative the pregnant woman might consider.

If you, the adopting couple, understand the reasons women use or do not use contraceptives, you will learn the best places to search for women who might place a child for adoption with you. An understanding of some women's unconscious motivation to become pregnant might give you additional clues in your search. Knowing the inadequacies of the counseling system open to the pregnant woman gives you an additional source of potential babies to explore. Understanding your own feelings, even angry feelings, about the ease of fertility the birthmother has, and you don't have, will help in your dealings with her. If you know where the babies have gone, it helps you to understand where they might still be found.

Adoption: A Personal Issue

For each participant in adoption, the issues are personal. Each person needs to attempt to understand the positions of the others. Each person needs to attempt to understand his or her own position on adoption.

Adoption rules and procedures are set up to accommodate groups. Adoption studies and statistics report the tendencies of *most* people. Yet adoption is an individual, personal issue. Personal issues must be pursued personally. Others don't have quite the circumstances in their lives that you do. Your accumulated life experience puts you where no one else has been. No one can tell you the best way for *you* to adopt a child. This book is a guide to options—various methods of finding a child—options for beating the adoption game.

Adoption is personal for me also. The options have increased over the years. Choices I believed were open to me at one time in my life have changed, and others have appeared.

I know, and have known for some time, that being a mother is very important to me. It is a role I wanted to have, and I always thought it would be easy to achieve. I grew up, got married, but the next step—children—did not happen. Being a product of my time, I had a hard time accepting the fact of infertility that confronted my husband and me. At times, I could minimize where a child would fit in my life; at other times, my insides would not allow this pretense.

We adopted three children in the next eleven years. Our first two, Scott and Dru, were adopted through adoption agencies. Our third child, Nohl, was adopted independently. When Nohl was four, for some reason I got pregnant. Our jokes over the years about how I would get pregnant when I was forty weren't too far off. Our fourth child, Shaine, was born the week before I turned thirty-eight.

Our first two children were easy to adopt. Our third child was adopted at the time children were becoming hard to find, so we were fortunate to find her. Our fourth child, our surprise, was truly unplanned, but after the initial shock and disbelief, she was, and is, a most welcome addition.

Almost as surprising was the recent addition of our fifth child. We were sure that our family was complete until we heard about Anthony. Because he was older (seven), and from a racially mixed background, and his birthmother did not want him to spend any time in foster care, finding a home for him was difficult. When we heard about him we thought he would fit nicely into our family, especially because of his closeness in age to our youngest child. After consulting with the younger children, we decided we wanted to meet him. The next day he came home with us. It has amazed us how well we have adapted to a new family member. He, too, has added immeasurably to our feelings about adoption and to our lives.

Adoption for our family is something very special. It is not important for us to have the children look like us. Our blond, blue-eyed daughter is a sharp contrast to our dark-skinned, curly-haired son. Each one looks and acts differently from the others. Adoption is not the same as having children biologically. It is neither more nor less satisfying, but it is different—and special.

My views on adoption have changed considerably since we first adopted, but then so have my views on life. One thing remains the same: I know, no matter how hard it might be to adopt a child, I would find one to adopt.

Purpose of This Book

An event as important as adopting a child should never be delegated completely to another person to handle and solve. You need to understand the adoption process and the different options open to you within that process. If you want to beat the game, you need to understand the rules. The players who have control and understand the game thoroughly are the ones most likely to win— to get the child they want. That is what this book is all about— getting the child you want.

A passive approach to adoption may work. Maybe someone will find you and give you a baby. Maybe an adoption agency will open the door for you to form your family. No question about it, this is the easiest way to adopt a baby. For some people this will work.

For others, this passive approach will fail. They will not be able to get a child from an adoption agency. Perhaps it will be their looks, a simple statement they make, their income, their rigidity, their age, or their view of life. Not being sure of what the adoption agency wants, they may do or say something "wrong" and may fail the adoption agency's entrance examination. They may never know why they were rejected. Without admittance to the system, they cannot get a child from the adoption agency.

Others will reject the adoption agency. The couples who cannot tolerate the adoption agency system must seek children in another way or remain childless. People who have negative feelings about the adoption agency system are likely to be rejected by that system, even if they continue to work within it.

This book is written for the potential losers in the adoption agency game who want to know the rules before they start, in order to increase their chances of winning. It is also for those who have been turned down by adoption agencies and for those who want to know other ways to find a child to adopt. This book is written for the adoption agency worker—the decision-maker in adoption—who needs to look at adoption in a more creative and flexible way. It is also written for me, because I believe it is time to change the adoption process, and I want to be a part of that change. I want adoption to be possible for many kinds of people because *adoption is special and it shouldn't be a game.*

A Time for Needed Change

We are living in a time of rapid changes in the world—environmental changes, technological changes, and social changes. In order for people to cope emotionally with the changing world, they too must change. The next level of change that must be made is in the institutions that serve the people. When we find that institutions serving people are not working, we are discovering institutions in need of revitalization—institutions in need of change. Adoption is one of these institutions.

The institution of adoption is theoretically designed to help all the people involved in adoption. Yet cries of dissatisfaction are heard from each of the adoption participants. Potential adoptive parents are being turned away by adoption agencies for inconsequential or unproven reasons. The emphasis in screening applicants seems to be on how people can be eliminated rather than on how they can be helped. The reasons for rejection are seldom given to the applicants, and there is no recourse within the system. "Different" people who seek to adopt a child have little chance of getting through the established system.

Parents who have already adopted children from agencies are beginning to wonder and ask if they were told as much about their children as the adoption agency knew. The secretiveness surrounding adoption brings fear of some negative information that for some reason must not be revealed. The secret side of adoption creates stress and suspicion in the adoptive home.

Birthparents complain of agency pressure to relinquish their children and the harshness of the procedure. They deplore the lack of financial aid from the adoption agencies that purport to help in this stressful time. Birthparents wanting a more flexible approach to this difficult process have a tough time trying to get the adoption agency to bend its procedures. The suddenness and finality of adoption for the birthparents allows little room for their grief.

Adoptees object to the sealed records that prevent them from knowing about their backgrounds. They feel cut off from their past, with no recourse. The dissatisfaction of the adoptee, for whom the entire institution of adoption is currently created, indicates that something is wrong with the system.

Something is drastically wrong when so many people express unhappiness with the current process of adoption. Institutions should be molded to fit the people who use them. Adoption needs to change to serve those who want to adopt, those who want to place children for adoption, and the adoptees themselves. People will remain disgruntled if they are forced to suit the adoption agency.

The suggestions in this book on how to work within the adoption system are in reality a compromise. Ideally, the institution itself will change and develop new, creative ways to serve its clients. Because most people can't wait that long, this book explains how the adoption system operates and provides options for making a defective system work for them.

About the Book

Adoption is a beautiful way to have a family. It is beautiful, however, only if it works. If you can't adopt, the disappointment can be overwhelming.

With a thorough understanding of the system and the options you have, you can try new approaches that you have never imagined. Ideally, your new approaches will lead you to the baby you want, because I am sure that babies are available.

The stories in this book of people who have succeeded in adoption, and even of those who have failed, will, I hope, cause you to consider new approaches to adoption. They will help you rehearse what you might have done in the same circumstances. They will prepare you for the many different situations that might confront you as you begin this process. They are not meant to show you how to do it, but to help you learn what you are capable of doing.

Most people simply need the information and the courage to find a baby. If you really want a baby, go out and find one. *Be creative, be flexible,* and *be assertive.* If you really want to find a child to become a part of your family you can. The very avenues you might have considered before may be the ones that enable you to beat the adoption game.

The Adoption Agency Game | 1

A NEW BABY IS A JOYOUS EVENT. A BEAUTIFUL NIGHT . . . AND NINE months later, the pregnancy is complete. The infant wriggles into the world and a new life begins.

The simplicity of this scene contrasts sharply with the arrival of an adopted child. Medical test after medical test is needed to prove infertility, followed by interviews and endless questions to "qualify" for becoming a parent. Clouding the entire process is a veil of secrecy and evasion. The couple necessarily approaches the process of adoption filled with ambivalence. Feelings of inadequacy and fulfillment, fear and joy, anticipation and anxiety, distrust and determination are emotions experienced by the participants in the adoption picture. Adoption is *not* like having a baby.

Twenty years ago, if you wanted to adopt a baby, you merely gave your name to the agency of your choice, did what they told you to do, and as long as you weren't blatantly inadequate, you obtained the baby you requested. Of course, you had to be able to play the adoption game, but the rules were not hard to follow. The game plan was apparent because there were lots of babies available. The agencies needed you.

Today the picture is markedly changed. Few babies are available.

The sought-after blond, blue-eyed girl is seldom available. Agencies are looking for couples who will accept a wide range of children. To be too specific about your desires as a potential adoptive parent—you want an infant or a child without any physical disabilities, or a child who is not from a mixed racial background—may very likely spell your elimination from the agency's waiting list. Agencies' emphasis is on how to eliminate applications, not on how to serve couples wishing to adopt a child.

Waits of three to six years are now common in adoption agencies. Many couples are judged unacceptable for parenthood by the agencies' unstated and unknown criteria. Adoption agencies seek ways to trim down the ever-lengthening list of adoptive parent applicants. Consequently, couples have four choices: rely on being accepted, tell the agencies what they want to hear, abandon hope for a child, or look elsewhere. Looking elsewhere includes alternative methods of pregnancy, private adoptions, and black market adoptions.

Adoptions through agencies, if performed properly, are potentially the most advantageous kind of adoptions. I do not mean adoptions as they are currently being administered by the agencies, but as they *could be*. Adoption agencies have the greatest number of babies and children, adoptive parents, trained workers, and facilities to get the job done really well. The entire set up for healthy, open adoptions exists within the current adoption agency structure; however, it isn't being utilized to the advantage of all the parties concerned. Since these agencies do have what prospective adoptive parents want, it is critical to understand how they work, what they are looking for, and how to work with them.

The Agency Process
Assuming that you are going to start with adoption agencies, as most people do, how do you begin? If you understand the process thoroughly, you will significantly increase your chances of being one of the chosen parents.

Most adoption agencies work in similar ways. You call the agency, and they tell you of a group meeting coming up for prospective parents. Anyone wishing to consider adoption is encouraged to attend. This means you *must* attend.

The meeting deals with the lack of available children and the general time period couples should expect to wait before a baby might become available for adoption. The social worker discusses

the types of children available and explains the sequence of interviews with couples seeking to adopt. The fees of the agency and its
general requirements are outlined.

*The meeting sounds fairly innocuous. It isn't. Listen carefully,
because the worker at this point is telling you exactly what this
particular agency is looking for in each couple it examines. At no
other point in the adoption process will the agency provide you
with this specific information.*

If you decide to continue after hearing the general information
regarding the agency, you will be asked to fill out an application
and set up an appointment with a social worker. Remember, the
agency has not said it will accept your application, but that you
may submit one. At the point when the agency officials meet with
you for the initial individual interview, your entire case is on the
line. Many agencies will screen you in or out on the basis of this
one interview and your application. Be careful.

A flexible attitude is one of the single most important characteristics that agencies seek in prospective parents. You will be asked
in general what you want in terms of adoption. If your answer is
"a Caucasian infant under four months with no physical problems," you're in trouble. The reason is clear. The agency has approximately fifteen couples for each child. They need to select a
couple who will accept just about any of the children they have.
The couple far more likely to get on the waiting list will say they
want a child under eight, the younger the better, and they are willing to take a child with physical or emotional problems. If you
don't get on the list, you have no chance. You may not even get
another interview. Most people don't know this, but if you don't
make it through the first interview successfully, that is your last
interview and the agency is finished with you, period.

Does this mean you should show no preferences? No, not exactly. It means you should be careful not to show too many preferences. Does this mean you will get an eight-year-old mentally
retarded child of mixed racial background? Not necessarily. It means
you have kept the door open and have at least gotten far enough so
that the agency will take your application. You still have a lot of
other interviews ahead of you.

If you pass the initial interview, the agency will accept your application and your application fee. All this means is that you are
doing all right so far. It doesn't necessarily mean the agency will
give you a child.

After the initial interview, the agency usually asks for medical histories and doctors' reports dealing with the couple's infertility. Most agencies will no longer place infants with couples who do not have a fertility problem.

Letters of recommendation on how you would be as a parent are usually expected. It is obvious, as in all letters of recommendation, that you should get the right people to send them. People who meet lots of other people, like ministers, who can make comparative judgments, are usually good references. People who have seen you with children and who can comment on your ability to deal with children are good references. Do not hesitate to tell people what to put in their letters. If you often see a couple with children, make certain you tell them to write about your good interaction with their children. Letters of recommendation are important—select them carefully.

Some letters of recommendation will not help you, even if they should. Usually it is unwise to have your therapist send in a letter. In fact, you probably should not tell the agency you have had any psychotherapy unless you are certain they would accept this information positively. If you do tell, first make certain that your therapist will send a positive letter concerning your qualifications for parenting.

Another interview with you as a couple is usually scheduled after your application has been accepted. At this point, questions are geared again toward what you will accept in a child, but now the social worker is likely to get into your experience with children, your acceptance of the infertility problem, your marital strengths and weaknesses, and your current support system of friends and relatives. Ideally you will come across as a couple who loves and accepts children, even those who are not yours. You should present an image of a couple who wish they could have had biological children, but who have come to accept infertility. Your marriage should appear sound but not unrealistically perfect. Your friends and relatives should seem important, but not people upon whom you are unduly dependent for your emotional well-being. In general, you want to appear normal—whatever that means. You want to present a picture of a couple who is emotionally stable and secure.

The next step is to interview each member of the couple alone. The intent of these sessions is to make certain that both partners are in agreement. The worker is checking to see if the less verbal partner believes the same things as the more verbal partner. A final interview is then conducted, usually in the prospective adoptive parents' home. The worker will not go into drawers and check for dirt in the corners. The worker will be seeing how you live and what arrangements you have made for a potential child. The house that appears too perfect is just as suspect as the house that is a shambles.

After your final interview, you will receive notice that your home study is complete; you now enter the waiting stage. The time varies, but for everyone it seems long. For some it means forever, because even though they have been approved, the "right" child never comes along. Most agencies, after a long wait, will suggest the couple drop off the list, since no child is available. One of the reasons this may happen is that many agencies now allow the biological mother a chance to read several histories, or to hear about several families of potential adoptive parents, and to choose the one family for her child. It is possible that no mother will choose you. It is also possible that you will just get "shuffled around" and that after a period of time you will be somewhat forgotten. If you haven't heard from the agency in two or three months, demonstrate your continuing desire to adopt by calling them.

At times, part of the sessions will involve group meetings. This is especially true if couples are considering special needs children.

Some agencies are currently involving prospective parents in a self-evaluation. Since this is a relatively recent technique, it is hard to say how these evaluations will be used. The theory is excellent if they are indeed used to help all applicants determine with which kind of child they could best be paired. On the other hand, it may be a way of screening out potential parents who have little hope that they will ever receive a child.

If you are finally selected to receive a specific child, you are called into the agency to see if you like the background of the child the agency has chosen for you. The worker will tell you about the child and the history of the natural parents. If you find anything objectionable in the background information you hear, the worker will want to discuss it at this point. This is your opportunity to discuss anything you have been told that may prompt questions. Perhaps you are confused about the father, or perhaps you want to know more about the evaluation of the child's physical health. If your questions do not clear up your hesitation at this point, the worker may choose not to go any further in placing this specific child with you. However, if you hear about the child and everything meets with your approval, you will be allowed to see the child. Seldom will the agency let you take the child home at this point. Most frequently they will give you until the next day to allow time to change your mind or to prepare for your new child, now that you know the age and sex of the child.

If you are selected to receive an older child, more emphasis is placed on your reaction to the child and that of the child to you. Several meetings may occur before an actual placement is made. At times, a temporary placement is made to see how readily everyone is able to adjust to the new situation.

Assuming you are the winner of a child, you still continue to be scrutinized by the worker from the adoption agency. Remember the child is not yours until you go to court to finalize the adoption. This usually takes at least six months from the time a child is placed. During this period you have visits from the social worker, who sees how you, your spouse, and the child are adjusting. Ideally, these visits should be a chance to explore any difficulties you have encountered, but the specter of the agency still being the guardian of the child is real. The child belongs to the agency, not to you.

The Wilsons found this out. They were the ideal couple the adoption agency cited in its introductory group interview for prospective adoptive parents. They were both professional people who had ample money and two previously adopted children who seemed very happy and adjusted. Dan, the husband, was exceptionally involved with the children, far more so than most fathers. Ellen presented a beautiful combination of the traditional mother mixed with a moderate approach to working outside the home. They luckily had a third child placed with them. After five months, their marriage had some problems and they considered divorce. Because they believed what the agency had said about calling if they ever needed help, they told the agency of their marital difficulties. The worker was understanding and said it was no problem and they would give Dan and Ellen time to work out their problems. One month later, when all of their problems had not been resolved, they were told the agency wanted the child returned. All their pleas notwithstanding, the child was taken back. Dan and Ellen had no recourse because they had no legal rights to the child. Seven months later they had reconciled, but there was lasting trauma over the loss of the child they had loved and nurtured for almost six months. The trauma extended, of course, to the two previously adopted children, who had to cope with their own fears of their possible return to the agency. The adoption agency is definitely in control until the child is legally adopted.

After the six-month waiting period is completed, you obtain a lawyer and go to court for the finalization of the adoption. This is a step in the process that warrants celebration. The court appearance is not a very elaborate process; in fact, a letter stating that the adoption is final would be sufficient, at much less cost to all concerned. However, the event is one to be heralded. The child is yours . . . no one can take it back!

Roughly, then, this is how adoption progresses with an adoption agency. There are basically three ways you can approach this process. You can be absolutely truthful and revealing, holding back nothing. You can be selective in the amount and content of the information you provide. Or, you can present yourself in a way that is most likely to get you the child you want.

The first approach—being honest, open, and forthright—should be the ideal approach. This should be an opportunity to explore all your feelings about what you bring to this potential parenting experience. You should be able to discuss your limits with respect to the child you want to adopt, and your potential for extending them. You should be able to explore flaws in your marriage in the hope of gaining insight into how to better deal with the problems. You should be able to reveal your resolved and unresolved feelings about your inability to have a biological child and in the process understand and live with them more comfortably. You should be able to deal honestly with the support systems you wish you had but do not have and to make the adjustments necessary to remedy whatever difficulties exist. You should feel the agency is one hundred percent behind your efforts and is working with you toward your parenting goal. This is how adopting through an agency should be and could be. Unfortunately, this is not the way it usually works in the real world of adoption agencies.

Your second option, and probably the most frequently used option, is to be selective in what you say to the adoption agency. You are well aware that the adoption agency has the "prize" you want, so you do some cautious and judicious editing. You neglect to tell the interviewers of your husband's anger when he comes home tired. You decide not to tell them about your mother-in-law, who believes that "illegitimate babies come only from lower-class people and are basically inferior." When they ask you how you feel about your infertility, you decide it isn't important to tell them that you still cry each month when you have your period. You take a basically honest approach, but you remember that these workers are judging you to see if you fit into their preconceived ideals.

The third choice is a further extension of the previous option. However, this time you seek to find out what the adoption agencies are looking for and you give it to them. You find out as much as possible about their methods of selection and their reasons for turning people down, and you act in response to this information. Of course, adoption workers are appalled at the mere suggestion of acting in this way. They would obviously say the first option of honesty and openness is the only way to approach the process. For them, it would be. For you who want a baby, I'm not sure. If you really want a baby, you go about getting a baby in the best way you can. If you know you will be eliminated if you tell them that you, the wife, love your job and want to work throughout the new child's growing years, what do you do? You might choose to say that you intend to stay home with the child and do so until you go to court and finalize the adoption. After that, the agency has no say in how you lead your life. If you know you will be eliminated if you tell the agency that you really would have great difficulty having a child of a mixed racial background, what do you do? Again, you might choose to say that you are open to the possibility of accepting a child from a mixed racial background and hope that it never comes to the point where you have to say no to a child that is offered to you. You don't have to take any child they offer. Obviously, you lessen your chances when you turn down a child, but at least you have a chance as long as you are being considered for a child by the adoption agency.

What approach would I suggest? I don't know. I believe the way you approach the process of adopting through an agency must be thoroughly, thoughtfully, and individually considered. I believe that the more you know about the procedures of the agencies and all the alternative means of obtaining a child, the better you can choose among the alternative approaches to adoption.

Criteria for Selecting Adoptive Parents

Now that you are familiar with the general procedures for adopting a child through an agency, it is important to look at the specific criteria the adoption agencies say they are looking for in prospective parents.

• *Financial Status*

The primary factor the adoption agency looks for when examining potential parents' financial status is stability. All things being equal, the agency would obviously prefer that the adoptive parents be in the best financial situation possible. Fair or not, the more money and job stability you have, the better your chances are to win a baby.

More and more subsidized adoptions, especially for children with special needs, are available. Adoption by foster parents, at times, is made possible through subsidies, especially if the child is a hard-to-place child. As long as the parents remain foster parents, they receive state aid. The moment they adopt the same child, they lose all state support. Some families would be unable to handle the financial burden this might involve, especially since the medical expenses of some of these children are very high.

Most agency adoptions are not subsidized, so the agency is looking for couples who demonstrate financial stability. At times the agency will look for adequate housing as a means of determining financial security. Checking out employment records also helps to determine the stability of the family's financial situation. Agencies look for a couple whose income allows one of the parents to remain at home with the child.

Many agencies maintain sliding fees as a means of providing adoption for people of modest incomes. Yet private agencies are limited in the percentage of their cases where lower fees can be allowed. Money cannot be a stated criterion, yet there is no question that it is. The family in financial difficulty at the time they seek a child is a poorer risk than a financially sound family. In the war between love and poverty, poverty usually wins. Poverty causes so much anxiety that even good marriages rarely survive. This is not the home environment the agencies want for their adoptive families.

• *Age*

Recent court cases involving age have significantly changed the adoption agencies' ability to use age as a criterion for acceptance. Some agencies admit that they still use age as a factor. Some say you must be over twenty-one, others say over twenty-three, some say over twenty-four, and others over twenty-five. Obviously, no one knows which minimum age is the "correct" one.

The primary concern of agencies is on the other end of the age spectrum. While unstated by many of the agencies because of the violation of federal civil rights, most agencies will place children with adoptive parents who would be the "normal" age for parents of the child who is placed with them. Generally, this would be less than a forty-year difference between the parent and the child. Some agencies believe it is permissible for the father to be older. Currently, with older children needing homes, older applicants would be considered.

As in all of the requirements put forth by the adoption agencies, people in the middle range of the requirements stand the greatest chance of selection. If you are about forty, you have less chance of adopting through an agency than a couple of thirty, if all your attributes are equal. Linda and Sam found out about age as a deterrent to adoption. Sam had been married and divorced after having two children. He married Linda when he was forty-two and she was thirty-eight. She had never been married, nor did she have children. When she was not pregnant after eighteen months, they sought to adopt a child through their local adoption agency. They were unsuccessful. The reason for their rejection by the agency was her age, but even more important was the fact that at her age she had never had any children. The agency was concerned about her adapting to a child, even an older child, at such a late period in her life. Sam and Linda were told they should consider being foster parents.

Age, as with other factors the agencies use to discriminate among potential parents, will not be specified as a reason for refusing your application. In fact, agencies at times are adamant that age is not a criterion used for selecting adoptive parents. The truth, however, is in the placements. Agencies are *not* placing children with people they believe are beyond the "normal" age difference between parents and children. Despite the recent increases in the age difference between parents and the children born to them now, agencies have not allowed that change to influence their dated placement procedures.

• *Educational Background*
Educational level is not usually stated by adoption agencies as a criterion. Its influence is more subtle. While some agencies state

that they want their parents to be the kind who "will provide a stimulating environment" or who "will provide a positive cultural environment," few will go any further.

However, education in our society is highly valued. Since all the social workers share a college background, it is not surprising to find that a college background is an asset in your application. The higher the degree the better, especially if the man is the highly educated one; the woman's high degree (M.D. or Ph.D.) at times causes the agency to question her commitment to children as a high priority in her life. Martha and Charles found that education was a door-opener for them with the adoption agencies. Martha and Charles had a fairly distant relationship in their marriage and that was fine for each of them. They were both bright people who had a tendency to be very intimidating to many people they met. While the agencies noticed their aloofness, the fact that he was a physician made a big impression. Agency workers, like many other people in our society, can be awed by physicians. The verbal ability of both Martha and Charles made a good impression on the agency. His financial ability was also viewed very positively. They received a baby with little difficulty. Soon after, Charles became involved with another woman and Martha found out. She was enraged and blamed his infidelity on the new child. Their aloofness allowed them to get by this period until they went to court, without the agency knowing of their marital difficulties. Their personal qualities were not the kind the agencies say they want in their adoptive parents. In fact, many of their acquaintances were surprised they even got a child from the agency. The primary factor that set them apart from others was that he was a physician; so they got a baby. Education makes a difference.

• *Medical History*
A medical history of each potential parent is required in virtually all adoptions. The results are expected to indicate that each person is in good physical health except in terms of the infertility problem.

Infertility is an asset. In fact, most agencies will not consider your application without a fertility problem. The irony of this stand is that it has become increasingly difficult to know with assurance that you have exhausted your means of achieving a pregnancy before you look at adoption. Medical advances continue to expand the potential of a biological child for the infertile couple; the couple who may have waited until their late twenties or early thirties to have a baby may now spend so long pursuing every alternative of infertility treatment that time runs out for them. To be totally sure you have exhausted every possibility of becoming pregnant and to be absolutely sure you have resolved your feelings about your infertility before you consider adoption may be unrealistic today.[1] The goal may be to become resolved about the unsureness of your infertility, rather than its absoluteness. Many couples proceed with agency adoption without telling the agency they are continuing with their fertility work. They are content with the concept of adopting and perhaps becoming pregnant within a close period of time. The adoption agency wants you to have resolved your feelings about your infertility; pursuing getting pregnant does not indicate to the agency you have resolved these feelings. Saying that you are continuing to attempt a pregnancy will probably cause you to be eliminated.

Health does not fit neatly into good or bad, so how does health fit in as a criterion for becoming a parent? The answer to the question depends on which agency and which social worker you are asking. In general, the more serious the medical problem, the more it will affect your chances to adopt.

Since children have become more scarce, people who weigh more than average have had difficulty being approved for adoption by the agencies. With thirty percent of the population of the United States overweight, this obviously places greater restrictions on the overweight person who also happens to want to adopt.[2]

Barbara and Gordon Ray gained considerable notoriety in the media over the refusal by the Wisconsin State Department of Health and Social Services to allow them to adopt a child because they were overweight.[3] The Rays were told to lose weight or no child. They sought help from their state senator in getting a child. The agency contended that the refusal was based on insurance companies' preferred height and weight charts. The Rays objected to this discrimination because their doctors certified that they were in good health. There was no proof that a health problem existed, but it was difficult to get the agency to change its stand. To deny someone a chance to adopt a child because they have a weight problem is unfair, but the agencies make the rules; it's their game.

To my knowledge, smokers and drinkers whose appearance does not reveal any problem have not experienced the same discrimination as have overweight people. However, an applicant who is an alcoholic or even a reformed alcoholic might be rejected if the agency knew of the problem. It is unlikely that the smoker, whose life span may be significantly shortened, will be given any special scrutiny. An exception to this might be the chain-smoker. The worker who sees this behavior might feel that the smoking is a symptom of great stress, which might work against the couple's adopting a child.

Serious illnesses can affect the agencies' decisions. Kathy felt her problems with cancer were behind her when she had passed the five-year non-active time limit. The agency, however, denied her application. Her doctor's protests that Kathy was no more likely than anyone else to develop cancer at this point did not help her.

Physical handicaps are seldom included in the list of criteria used by adoption agencies. Mostly they are ignored, at least verbally and in writing. An adoption agency would have to be quite naive legally to state that the reason a couple has not been accepted is because one of the parties has a handicap. A lawsuit would be immediate.

Sally and Matthew ran into an agency's subtle discrimination after they applied to adopt a child. Sally met Matthew after he became a quadriplegic, having been wounded in Vietnam. When they married, she knew he could not father any children and she just assumed they would adopt. After they were married for six months, they approached the adoption agency. They were told they would have to wait until they had been married two years before they could apply. So, they waited the specified time, then applied and were turned down. No one from the adoption agency said it was Matthew's confinement to a wheelchair, but everyone who knew how much they both wanted a child knew that his handicap was the reason for the denial. I remember being very moved by Matthew when he said, "I can hold a baby and I can love a baby . . . I just can't play ball with a child." I believed him. The adoption agency, faced with a choice between many healthy fathers, may have reasoned, "Why choose one with limited fathering capacities when we can simply choose someone else?" I understand the reasoning; I just can't accept the solution or delaying these people for two years when they had no chance to be accepted as adoptive parents.

• *Race and Nationality*
As with other criteria I have mentioned, race and nationality cannot legally be stated as a method of selecting potential adoptive

parents. Legally, however, these factors have been used as justification for denying a child's placement in a specific home. Timothy is a case in point: partly black, he had been raised in a foster home from one month until two-and-a-half years old. At that point his foster parents sought to adopt him and were denied by the adoption agency because they were white. The foster parents fought to keep Timothy, but lost their legal appeal on the grounds that "adoption agencies have a right and responsibility to take racial questions into account when matching a child with prospective parents."[4]

Black social workers have taken a strong stand against black children being placed in white homes. They believe, as do many blacks, that a white family cannot help a black child identify with his or her cultural heritage. However, at times, the needs of black women who want to place children for adoption are sometimes not met; black women are at a distinct disadvantage if they wish to place their child for adoption.[5]

A judge in Pennsylvania agreed that race should be a consideration in adoption, but for an absurd rather than intellectual reason. The judge said he would no longer allow white families to adopt black children because "it's great when they're little pickaninnies. They're cute and everybody is a do-gooder. But what about when they're children?"

Large groups of parents who have adopted children of other races and nationalities believe these adoptions have been successful. But adoption agencies, mindful of the position of the black social workers, discourage many couples from adopting children of a race that is different than their own.

• *Religion*

Most adoption agencies do not have specific requirements for religion unless they are private religious agencies. The religious requirement from these specific agencies is obvious. Catholic and Jewish agencies are the most common among religiously oriented agencies.

At times, the biological mother has specific religious criteria she sets forth. In that case, the adoption agency is likely to honor her request. Her request may be quite general, such as "I want my child to be raised by people who believe in God," or "I want my child to be raised in a home where religion is a significant part of the family's life." Some mothers may want their children specifically raised Catholic or Methodist. Since the biological mother may know the histories of several families seeking to adopt, her religious preferences may enter into her decision.

Religions that prevent a child from receiving medical care are viewed skeptically by adoption agencies. Agencies do not specifically prevent people of any faith from adopting children, but under circumstances where religion affects the medical care, the agency will consider the case separately. Again, since it does not fall into the "normal" range sought by the agencies, a less popular religion is likely to be considered a disadvantage in a prospective adopting family.

• *Marital Relationship*
Length and strength of marriage are criteria used to select most adoptive parents. The length of the marriage is easy to measure; strength of a marriage presents some real difficulties.

Some agencies specify how long a couple must be married before they will consider that couple's application for adoption. Most agencies require between one and three years of marriage. Usually this requirement has three purposes. One is to ascertain the stability of the relationship. The second reason is to preserve the stability of the relationship by not having a child placed too early. (This reason has much less validity now that there is such a long wait to have a child placed after the application is accepted.) The third reason is to determine with certainty that a fertility problem does exist. Sometimes the stress of trying to have a baby will cause fertility problems that go away without treatment. Almost anyone can tell the story of a friend who got pregnant right after adopting a baby. This is not as common as it seems, but it does happen.

Some adoption agencies have a different requirement for the marriage if one of the partners was previously married. Any couple who has a history of a previous marriage is given extra scrutiny. Despite the large numbers of people in our society who have been divorced, it is still viewed negatively by most adoption agencies. The agencies are unlikely to eliminate you for that single factor alone, but it is one more mark that works against you.

When the adoption agencies attempt to determine strength and stability in the marriage, they work from a precarious position. Who knows what makes a good marriage? Some marriages that people would evaluate as strong and secure are relationships I would not, under any circumstances, consider satisfactory for me—yet for them they work. Our society doesn't have one good kind of marriage;

but for some reason, if you are seeking to adopt a child, your marriage has to meet a certain set of criteria.

Characteristics exemplifying marital strength vary with the agency. The agencies are usually positively influenced if the marriage seems to show "communication between the partners," a "sharing relationship," or "being committed to the marriage." One agency looks for a "growing" marital relationship. I certainly think that all these marital characteristics are worthy, but they cannot be reliably assessed by the agency. Even if an adoption agency could measure whatever criteria they feel create a good marriage, it is obvious that some marriages can and do work successfully without all these factors present or maybe even without any of them present.

• Employment of the Mother

Adoption agencies have fluctuated on how critically they view the adopting mother who works. When babies are plentiful, employment of the mother has been more acceptable. With the current scarcity of babies, most agencies want the mother to stay home. Some agencies specify that one parent must remain home. While more and more people are recognizing that the male is quite capable of being the primary parent, it is a rare case where an adoption agency will place a child in a home where the father is to care for the child. Again, this does not fit into the "normal" pattern. Strong questions would be raised about the adoptive mother's ability to mother, which would lessen a couple's chances of having a baby placed with them.

Other agencies have criteria stating that "acceptable arrangements be made for the care of the child." Marie and John found that this sounded better than it turned out to be in reality. Marie was a doctoral candidate in chemistry and very excited about lots of things in life. She was thirty-two and felt she had to go ahead immediately if they wanted to adopt. She also loved her work and had several exciting professional opportunities coming up. To pass them up now was to pass them up forever. She wanted it all and she had the energy and drive to do it all. John fully agreed. The adoption agency didn't. Their application was denied. For the agency it was either baby or work. Despite large numbers of working mothers in the United States, the agencies want it the way *they believe it should be* . . . a full-time mother. With few exceptions, any other arrangement does not qualify. Agencies have the babies and they make the rules.

• *Involvement with the Adoption Agency*
Many agencies look for potential parents who have "an ability to work with the agency." I am sure this helps the agency, although I have difficulty seeing how this indicates potential parenting qualities. This very fact, however, may account for the reason that more adopted than nonadopted children are seen by mental health professionals for psychological problems. After working with the medical profession on infertility problems and the adoption agency worker on getting a baby, these people are accustomed to asking for help and admitting problems. The adoptive parent sees a problem and tends to assume that professional help is needed in solving it.

At times adoption agencies become quite competitive. I recently heard from a social worker in one adoption agency that if a couple tells their agency that they had previously applied to another adoption agency, this alone will eliminate them from consideration. This particular agency wanted complete loyalty and dedication to their agency and no other. Perhaps the feeling is that if the couple was not good enough for another adoption agency, then they are not good enough for this one either.

On the more positive side, the agency is also trying to generalize. If people cannot work with them, can they work with others in their lives? How do these potential parents get along with others? How do they relate to the people in their lives?

• *Flexibility*
A flexible attitude on the part of parents is a characteristic that entered the selection process only as children replaced babies and scarcity replaced abundance. This characteristic—flexibility—is the single most frequently mentioned characteristic agencies cite in looking for prospective parents.

Flexibility primarily concerns what type of child you can accept. Adoption agencies are seeking people who are willing to take older children as well as infants. These agencies are screening in people who will take physically handicapped children and screening out people who want only physically healthy children. They are eliminating people who would not consider an emotionally disturbed child in favor of those people who would. The agencies are searching for potential parents for children of mixed racial backgrounds and are reluctant about people who will consider only Caucasian children. The more demands you place on the agency for what you want, the more your chances for a baby decrease. The less flexibility, the less chance of adopting through an agency.

• *Personality Factors*
If you describe an emotionally stable and mature person, you have just included the personality factors the adoption agencies are seeking in their potential adopting parents. Statements the agencies use to describe the people they choose for parents include the following:

- —Is emotionally mature
- —Is stable
- —Has sense of humor
- —Is warm
- —Deals well with others
- —Is loving
- —Expresses affection
- —Is sensitive and caring
- —Is accepting
- —Is committed to whatever he or she undertakes
- —Has problem-solving ability
- —Is secure within self
- —Has good self-image
- —Succeeds with struggles
- —Is optimistic about life
- —Has ability to cope with stress and change
- —Can handle whatever comes along
- —Is well integrated
- —Is open
- —Is able to accept responsibility
- —Is wholesome
- —Is understanding
- —Is able to see small gains and not take everything personally
- —Is empathetic
- —Is realistic in expectations
- —Admits imperfections in self and can handle them
- —Is self-aware
- —Has ability to delay gratification
- —Has common sense

—Is motivated
—Handles frustration and anger
—Has character
—Has ego strength
—Is able to relate positively and grow
—Is sharing
—Establishes meaningful relationships
—Is able to turn to others for assistance if needed
—Does not need neighbors or friends for self-worth
—Has support of extended families
—Has high expectations of life, of self, and of others
—Has stable relationships
—Is aware of each individual's dependency needs

What then does this lengthy list of characteristics tell us? It means if you have everything really together, the adoption agency will consider you "normal" and will see if it has a child for you.

• *Parenting Skills*
Parenting skills, as with the other abstract criteria, are extremely difficult to predict and to evaluate. The best predictor of parenting ability is "successful" parenting, but the agency is usually evaluating people without children. Evaluating what constitutes quality parenting is like evaluating what makes a good marriage. We do not have the knowledge to say that, if you do this, your child will turn out well-adjusted. We simply do not know what makes good parents.

Given these rather serious limitations, the agencies set out to do exactly what no one has shown they can do: to evaluate what will make a good parent. While their task is impossible, their intentions are admirable.

With this goal in mind, they search for potential adoptive parents who can "love and accept a child they did not produce." They want "parents who can be open about the biological parents" and who can be "understanding of their adoption decision." "Respect for the biological roots of the child" and "a willingness to discuss the child's adoption with him or her" are some of the ingredients they seek to find.

Beyond the adoption issue of parenting, the agency looks for the basic skills of raising children. They want parents who can allow a child to grow to his or her own potential, who are able to give and receive love from a child, who can meet the needs of a child, who have a realistic approach to parenting, who are accepting, nurturing, supportive, understanding. Basically the agencies seek parents with good, healthy child-rearing skills.

The adoption agency uses several criteria in evaluating these skills. What the potential parents say, what experience they have had with children, and what experiences they have had in the homes in which they were raised are all part of the parenting skills evaluation.

The agency listens carefully to the statements of the people seeking a child. The prospective parents must convey their *strong* desire for a child to the agency's social worker. The agency has to believe that having a child is exceptionally important . . . a high priority in these people's lives. Without this intense feeling being conveyed, they won't get a baby. The Brunsons were a good example. Bob and Eileen Brunson were quiet people who were not very demonstrative or expressive. They each came from homes where self-sufficiency, not vulnerability, was valued. They had not responded with outward emotion to Eileen's fertility problem, nor did they respond with any intensity in their desire for a child. They knew they wanted a child; their lack of intensity in expressing this desire did not lessen their wish. Their low-keyed, quiet approach to life was interpreted by their social worker as meaning that a child was not very important to them. They were rejected because their inability to fully express their desire to have a child left their adoption worker unconvinced that it was really a critical goal for them.

To evaluate your experience with children, the worker will want to know all of your contacts with babies and children—the more the better. If you have had none, the adoption agency will feel that you lack the skills necessary to parent. Search your background. Remember every baby-sitting experience, the Christmas with your sister's family, including her three children, the day at the zoo with the neighbors and their children, your airplane ride and discussion with the four-year-old who ended up in the seat next to you. You are proving parenting skills to the agency worker.

The other criterion used to determine your potential for parenting is what kind of parenting you had. The agency wants to know about how you were raised because that frequently predicts how you will parent. When Lori and Scott went to adopt, they did not know that their childhoods would be evaluated. They were both proud of the fact that Scott had overcome a very difficult childhood. He had been badly neglected as a child and was eventually sent to live in a boys' home at age twelve. He had really pulled himself up on his own and had established a close and loving relationship with Lori, whom he married when he was twenty-five. When Lori and Scott were turned down by the adoption agency because Scott lacked the proper parenting model it was a great blow to them. After the rejection, they knew they'd made a mistake in telling the agency about it at all.

The agencies, seeking the best possible homes for their limited number of adoptable children and trying to make the best placements possible, have an extremely difficult job. They necessarily work in the dark because no one knows which homes will be the best homes for the available children. Unfortunately, many fine people are turned down by adoption agencies because they do not adequately fit the agencies' undocumented criteria for becoming good parents.

Fighting the Adoption Agency's Rejection
If you go through part or all of the adoption agency process and are rejected, is that it? Are there ways to fight the agency's decision; is there a chance you can be reconsidered?

The place to begin trying to reverse an adoption agency rejection is to find out the cause of the rejection. This sounds easy but is not. Many times the agency will be vague, saying they simply have too many applicants for the number of children they have to place. For some reason you were eliminated, so there is some cause for this rejection. Try to get the agency to be specific but be tactful; you are still trying to work within its system.

Annie and Ed decided to fight the rejection they received from one agency. They were a fine young couple who seemed as though they would be ideal parents, but they made several tactical errors with the agency. They waited until they had been married nine years to seek a child, so the agency felt this indicated a child was not too important to them. Annie worked as a teacher and loved it, but the agency felt this could be a problem if she decided to go back to work. Annie and Ed thought they could ask for a baby, since that was their first choice, but the agency believed this demonstrated their lack of flexibility. They led a busy, active life, but the agency felt it would be difficult for them to incorporate a child into their life-style. So the agency said no baby. They were crushed. They went back to find out the reasons for their rejection and if the agency would reconsider. Of course, this effort alone indicated to the agency a greater desire for a child than the agency had previously believed. So the agency, knowing Ed had a very powerful position with a television station in the community, decided to allow them to be evaluated by an agency psychologist for their potential parenting ability. Ed and Annie were bright enough to know you do not let the person who has rejected you send you to his or her colleague for a second opinion. They asked if they could have a private evaluation from another psychologist and the agency agreed. Their own psychologist gave them a glowing evaluation, which they well deserved. The agency reconsidered their rejection and within six months they had a darling baby boy. They fought and won.

Marian and David fought the agency in a different way. They were an older couple seeking an older child. They had been approved for adoption, but waited and waited and waited. After two years they were not even being contacted by the agency. When they questioned the agency, the adoption agency worker suggested that they withdraw their names from the agency's waiting list, but they refused. They could not understand how articles could appear in the local newspaper about the older children in need of homes that were not available. They were available and they wanted one of those children. In fact, they would even take older siblings as well as only one child. They called the newspaper and questioned the validity of the agencies' "propaganda" about the children needing homes. The newspaper, recognizing a controversial, newsworthy story, interviewed them and published their plight. The agency has not contacted them since their story appeared in the newspaper. The likelihood that they might get a child or children from that agency is very slight.

At the same time Marian and David were not making headway with the adoption agency, two young children, aged four and six, were being evaluated by a committee to decide what was in the best interest of this older brother and sister who had just been made available for adoption. The committee consisted of a psychologist, two social workers from the adoption agency, and the supervisor of the local center that screens problem children. It was decided that these two children, who had been together since birth and who represented the only stability they had ever known in each other's lives, would be put into separate homes because there was no one who would want to take both of them at the same time. The protest of the psychologist that this would seriously harm the two children was ignored because it was "impossible" to find a home that would take both of these children.

Your chances of fighting the adoption agencies and winning after you have been rejected are not good. However, it's better to fight than to do nothing. Remember, the people who get the children today are those who really know how to go after them. They know how to work within the system and they know how the system works.

Creative Flexibility Needed Within the Agencies
Everything is changing and the adoption field is no exception. In order to keep abreast of the needed changes, adoption agencies need to look at their deficiencies from a position of hope, not from a position of defense. The areas in which the agencies are weak are areas that should become alive with change.

The adoption agencies have been able to respond with a vital, creative approach to change before. When the supply of available infants diminished, the agencies put additional emphasis on the "special needs" child. Partly this was altruistic, partly it was for the agencies' survival. An adoption agency must provide children to adopt if it is to remain in business. The adoption agencies, in a positive response to the lack of children, found themselves in the unique position of at last being able to place children who were previously unadoptable. They developed new criteria for parent selection and moved right along with the trend.

In placing children with special needs, the agencies conducted group parent meetings after the adoption placements. The agencies knew there was a need for broader support systems for the families that adopted "special needs" children. They responded to this newly created need.

Also, since special needs children are frequently more expensive to raise, the adoption agencies approached the problem creatively. Frequently, financial assistance is given to families that adopt children whose medical costs alone might have prevented their adoption.

The adoption agencies are beginning to respond to the potential opening of the adoption records as the adoptee becomes an adult (see Chapter 9). While some adoption agencies fought and continue to fight this possibility, others are making constructive plans for its eventuality. Some agencies are asking birthmothers at the time they sign relinquishment papers to indicate their wishes about these

records being opened to the adult adoptee. Letters from biological
parents are being enclosed in the records of adoptees in case the
adoptee wishes to know, on a more personal level, the biological
mother or father. Some adoption agencies are currently taking an
active role in reunions between adoptees and their biological parents. The role of the adoption agency sometimes has been that of
communicator between the biological parents and the adoptive
parents, without identities becoming known. Some adoption agencies have shown that they are able to respond to the needs of all of
the people involved in adoption.

The needs of the biological parents have become more important
as the supply of infants has dwindled. The biological parents have
a "product" the adoption agencies want, so the parents have more
negotiating power. In response to this shift in power, adoption
agencies are allowing the biological parents to have more say in
the placement of their child. The biological parent, usually the
birthmother, is allowed to read case histories of several families
being considered for her child. She then can choose the family she
likes the best. This is a marked departure from the past. The process could become even more responsive to the wishes of biological parents through direct parent-to-parent contacts without names.
There is no question that this is a creative step for adoption agencies.

Adoption agencies have also exhibited delayed creativity. While
delayed creativity is not as desirable as timely creativity, it at least
indicates a willingness to try new approaches. And new approaches
remain to be tried.

In the peak years of baby availability, adoption agencies did not
know how to cope with the overabundance of children available
for adoption. At the end of this period, when there were fewer babies, the agencies finally utilized the powerful medium they had
so long neglected . . . television. In limited numbers, children who
were hard to place were shown on television; the response from
the public was extremely positive. (You still hear on television or
radio or read in newspapers of the children who are available. Since
the supply of children is so limited, it seems we should now be
advertising *the waiting parents* who are now so abundantly available.)

For years adoption agencies bemoaned the fact that blacks adopted
fewer babies than were available. Frequently, blame was placed on

the black culture for their nonacceptance of adoption as a means of parenting. For too many years adoption agencies failed to look at what they could do to improve the situation. As the agencies developed more outreach programs and hired more blacks, the black community responded positively and increased the number of babies they adopted. The predominantly white agencies finally began to meet the needs of the black community.

These examples of creative responses clearly demonstrate that agencies can make changes when necessary. Since these changes have been instituted, agencies have continued to use and slightly modify them, yet the response time is still too slow. The agencies need to scrutinize carefully the ways they are not meeting the needs of adoption participants today. To continue mechanically what was innovative yesterday is to be inflexible today.

The adoption agencies have, for some reason, chosen not to participate in some other innovative concepts that have emerged from related helping professions. One of the most remarkable changes in recent years has been the advent of free or low-cost medical care and counseling through community outreach programs. It is clear that minorities and especially young people have not felt welcome or comfortable in the normal, organized health care settings. As a result, free clinics developed. These clinics, staffed primarily by volunteers, have become the direct health service provider for a significant segment of our society. The facilities are not glamorous, in fact they are often austere. The volunteers are not bejeweled members of the auxiliary society. Instead they are young people, blacks, or Chicanos with whom the individuals seeking services can identify. The professionals who participate in the free-clinic movement are a special group who also identify with the needs of the community they serve. Adoption agencies who once provided service to youth and minorities have found their client base eroding. Many women undergo pregnancy tests and counseling concerning unwanted pregnancies at a free clinic from volunteers who know little about adoption. Abortion and keeping a child are freely discussed, but seldom is adoption even mentioned. A significant number of potentially adoptable children have been lost to adoption agencies and to people seeking to adopt as a result of the failure of the adoption agency system to participate actively in the free-clinic movement.

Because adoption agency workers have no contact with free-clinic workers, there is no exchange of information. The adoption agencies may be losing a significant source of potential clients due to their hesitant approach to change.

Power of the Adoption Agencies

Social workers from the adoption agencies, as with all helping professionals, have a difficult problem to surmount. They offer to help people, but frequently they exercise control over those they seek to help. Social workers suffer from the power they wield and the godlike feelings that power engenders.

There is no question of the power that the social worker has over all the people involved in adoption. The biological parents are at the mercy of the social worker, who controls the destiny of their child. Based upon how the biological parents present themselves to the social worker, the future of the child is cast. The judgment of the worker extends most profoundly to the potential adoptive parents. The social workers from the adoption agencies decide if you will or will not be chosen to get a child based on how positive an image you present.

Unfortunately, at the point when social workers become fully aware of their power, they become less effective in helping their clients. Their emphasis switches from helping others to controlling others. Adoption workers need to help their clients, not to be their judges.

The only possible reason to trust a worker from an adoption agency is if you believe he or she is working for you. Social workers who are seeking ways to eliminate people cannot possibly be working for you. To even pretend that the social worker is there to help you is a misrepresentation.

The only client the agency says it is seeking to serve is the child. The agencies make it abundantly clear that the "best interest of the child" is their primary concern. This single representation is truly unfortunate. There is no reason that the agency would be in any conflict if they sought to serve the biological parents, the adopted child, and the adopting parents equally. Serving one segment of the adoption triangle does not preclude serving all segments.

To thoroughly serve the biological parents, the social workers from the agency should seek to clearly understand all the ways they can help either of the biological parents. While in most cases the biological father is not as involved as the mother, all the suggestions I make are applicable to him as well as to her. The agency needs to meet her needs of knowing about the family with whom her child will be placed. At times she may want to meet the new parents. Fine—if it's agreeable to both biological and adopting parents, then why not? The agency needs to set up a regular communication system with her if for no other reason than to update medical records. It is possible that she might wish to keep up with the child's progress. Again, if it is acceptable to everyone involved, the role of the agency should be to facilitate these requests. If the biological parents are open to contact with the child when the child becomes an adult, the agency should help in whatever manner makes it easiest for all the people involved.

The agency should seek also to serve the adoptive parents in whatever way possible. This should include trying to find a child for them. The agency would then be involved in recruiting babies to help serve the people who wish to adopt them. If the interest of adoptive parents were a high-priority item for the agencies, the problems and concerns the adoptive parents encounter with infertility, with parenting, and with raising an adopted child could be freely explored. The adoption agency would be there to serve, not judge, the potential adoptive parents.

To thoroughly serve the child who has been adopted means to provide service after placement. This can be done only if all parties are openly served by the adoption agencies. Now the primary emphasis is on the child's placement, but the child is done a disservice by the agency's lack of concern for the other parties involved. The child and/or the adoptive parents who are having difficulty soon after placement cannot consult with the adoption agency for fear it might indicate weakness and jeopardize the legal adoption. This is not in the best interest of the child or the adoptive parents. The older, adult adoptees who seek information about biological parents are not served by the agency that tells them there is no way it can help and that they should be grateful for the adoptive parents they have. Even the teenage child who seeks information about his or her adoption could benefit from some careful counseling, taking into account the current concerns being expressed. To thoroughly serve the child necessitates updating of the medical records so that newly found medical problems of the biological parents can be communicated to the adoptive parents. In this way the health of the growing child is protected. Adoption is healthiest for the child when the needs of the child are given a priority equal to those of all the people involved in the adoption picture.

Adoption agencies have a long way to go to make adoption a healthy, viable alternative for those involved: the biological parents, the child, and the adoptive parents. The base is there . . . the potential is there. In this time of scarcity of adoptable children, the goal should be to serve all those who have a need for help in the adoption process. This is not a time for defensive retrenching on old lines, but for new, creative, open approaches that take into account everyone's importance.

Summary

People who want babies are going to find them somewhere, somehow. They will find children even if they would be unfit parents or even if they are seriously disturbed. To work with these people and all the people who really want a child within the framework of an organized adoption setting would increase their potential for raising happy, healthy children. To force these people out of the system only causes them to look elsewhere and to lose the support system that could exist through the adoption agency.

Many advantages are available to those people who work within the adoption agency system. The biological parents usually receive more prerelinquishment counseling under this system than anywhere else they may give up a child. If the birthmother or birthfather wishes not to be identified, he or she has the greatest chance of anonymity in the adoption agency system. The biological parents know the child they relinquish to the agency has a greater choice of homes than if they place the child privately. Frequently the biological parents become involved in a group counseling session where they share a common bond with others in the same predicament.

Advantages to going through the adoption agency system exist for the adoptive parents also. The adoption agency system offers the greatest source of children available for adoption. By going through an agency, the adoptive parents know the child they receive has been fully relinquished before they receive the child. They can be confident that the child has been medically screened and that known medical problems are evident to all. The adoptive parents are aware that the child placed with them probably has been screened for suitability to their particular home life.

The adopted child also gains advantages by being adopted through an agency. The child has the chance of being placed in a home that most fits his or her needs. For instance, a child whose biological mother and father had demonstrated superior intelligence might experience great difficulty being adopted into a home with parents of less than average intelligence. The child with special needs will best fit in a home that can accept his or her limitations.

While the advantages to adopting through an agency are significant, they have the potential for becoming far more significant. This means greater advantages to everyone if the adoption agencies can make the necessary and timely alterations of the adoption agency system. But for now, no matter how great the advantages might be, if you aren't accepted by an agency you have to choose another direction.

The best way to increase your chances of winning the adoption game with the adoption agencies is to thoroughly understand their method of operation. It is important that you understand who their primary client is and where you fit in the current adoption picture. If you understand what the adoption agencies are looking for in the parents they choose, then you stand the best chance of getting your baby. I wish you luck!

Your Own Game

2

HORROR STORIES ARE TOLD AND RETOLD OF PRIVATELY ADOPTED babies being taken back by their birthmothers, being sold to be sexually abused by those who adopt them illegally, and being removed from the adoptive homes by judges lacking compassion who say the adoptions were illegal. These tales frightened people from private adoptions. But similar tales that have occurred in agency adoptions are rarely heard.

At the same time, terms such as "gray market adoptions," "black market adoptions," and "agency adoptions" are bantered about in the adoption scene. Exactly what these terms mean and what is legal or illegal in the process of adoption are not always clear. In actuality, there are no private adoptions; there are private placements of children followed by the normal adoption process, which involves a state designated agency. All adoptions, even most illegal baby placements, ultimately become agency adoptions. The one exception occurs when children are adopted from other countries.

In the United States, there are three alternatives to agency adoptions. Each alternative is considered a private adoption, since an agency did not place the child in the adoptive home:

1. Private adoptions (independent adoptions)

2. Family adoptions (stepparent adoptions, grandparent adoptions)

3. Black market adoptions (illegal adoptions, baby-selling)

After a couple has the child, they usually then complete the formal adoption process through some state-designated adoption agency. *Private adoptions are legal adoptions in most states,* although some states have specific provisions that must be met for the adoption to be legal.

Confusion exists about the difference between black market adoptions and private adoptions that are sometimes called gray market adoptions. The primary difference is in the exchange of money that takes place. The law regarding the exchange of money in adoption cases varies from state to state, and many people circumvent the law. What expenses can be legally paid in a private adoption are sometimes difficult to define. In a regular private adoption no money is paid to have a child placed. However, the line between black market babies and gray market babies is not at all distinct.

Private Adoptions

Private adoptions are legal in most states, despite attempts to make them appear shady or illegal. Most private adoptions fall into the category where no one receives money for the child being placed for adoption; therefore, they are not black market adoptions and are legal. Most private adoptions go smoothly, with no problems.

Adoption agencies over the years have attempted to have private adoptions ruled illegal; in most states they have been unsuccessful. The agencies maintain that private adoptions should be illegal to protect the welfare of the child. The adoption agencies say these adoptive homes have not been investigated prior to the child's placement and, therefore, might be inappropriate or unsatisfactory. (Could this be carried to the extent that the state would license married couples to allow them to conceive and raise children?)

If the adoption agencies could clearly demonstrate a higher quality of parenting in agency-chosen homes, they might have some reason to advocate only agency adoptions.[1] But no research has shown that agency adoptions are any more or less "successful" than private adoptions. An English writer points out the difficulties of evaluating potential adopting parents and states that they have not been shown to be effective; he feels evaluation ought to be replaced with preparation for parenting.[2] This same writer indicates that since it is impossible to detect unsuitable parents, agencies seem to have substituted education and economic factors to indicate suitability for parenthood. Certainly with all the screening that occurs in agency adoptions, they should be more successful; yet they are not.

Another reason adoption agencies want private adoptions stopped is because they decrease agency business. Many adoption agencies across the country have closed because the commodity they deal with, namely children, is no longer available in sufficient numbers to pay for the adoption agency's expenses. A child placed privately might have been, under other circumstances, a child placed through an adoption agency. Sometimes, birthparents deliberately choose private adoptions so that they can be intimately involved in choosing the home into which their child goes. At other times, a birthmother might decide how she wants her child placed more on the basis of who talks with her first.

The adoption agencies maintain that the interests of all the people are not met in a private adoption. They claim that anyone who has been rejected by an agency, with all its wisdom, can still go out and adopt privately. They claim that counseling is not provided the woman relinquishing her child and that the child is a pawn in the process. At times these criticisms are justified. However, the same criticisms can properly be directed toward adoption agencies as well.

There are several advantages to using an adoption agency to find a child to adopt. First, agencies may not have many babies, but they have more than any other single place. The second advantage in going through an agency is that most of the legal problems of adoption are taken care of by the agency. The third reason to go through an agency is if you feel you would be uncomfortable with the exchange of names that usually occurs (but not always) in a private adoption. With the possibility of records becoming open to all adult adoptees (see Chapter 9), the emphasis on maintaining anonymity becomes less valid. The fourth reason is that there can be a closer matching of qualities of the child with the adoptive parents because an agency has a greater number of both available.

Despite these advantages, many people still adopt privately—some people because they are rejected by the adoption agencies; others because they believe that the advantages of private adoption outweigh the risks. Frequently people adopt privately because they believe it is faster method to get a child.

Before you become involved in private adoption, learn the difference between private adoption and agency adoption. You should clearly understand how a private placement works. It is also important to understand the advantages and the risks of adopting a child privately.

• *How Private Adoption Works*
All private adoptions are similar . . . even those that involve monetary transactions, as in black market adoption. You need a general understanding of what goes on so that your next step will be an informed one.

Making Contacts
In order to adopt privately, you have to find someone who has, or who knows about, a child available for adoption. This is the main difference between private and agency adoptions . . . *you* have to find the contact who can provide the child.

Historically, the primary contacts for potential children to adopt outside of adoption agencies have been physicians and lawyers. This is still probably true, but these groups, like the agencies, have seen the availability of children decline in recent years.[3]

Many other potential contacts are available for the resourceful person who tries to find a child. These potential sources are discussed in detail in the next chapter. *You* are the only limit on the number of possible contacts. Children are available for adoption if you search long enough and thoroughly enough.

With each contact you make, tell people about your situation and about how they might be of help to you. Find other leads from everyone you contact, so that even if they don't personally know of a child for you, they can suggest someone else who might. You are attempting to contact many people in the hope of finding one child. The more people who know of your situation, the greater the chance of finding the one child you want.

Once you begin your search, you have to be prepared for what happens when you find a contact that pays off. What do you do when someone says, "I heard about this baby I thought you would be interested in knowing about"? Are you prepared?

Contacts with attorneys are sometimes easier than other contacts. They know the next steps (or at least they should know), so it is a bit easier for you to proceed if an attorney is the one who tells you about a baby. In no way does this mean you should limit your contacts to attorneys. You can and should hire an attorney to handle the legal side after you have found a child . . . you don't necessarily have to have one to *find* that child.

Hiring a Lawyer

After you have found a possible adoptable child, you need to find an attorney immediately. Preferably, you should look for an attorney while you are looking for the child.

All lawyers are not equal. If you have a legal problem related to a business contract, you want a lawyer who has expertise in business contracts. If you are planning to adopt a child, you want a lawyer who knows something about private adoptions. Some lawyers know little or nothing about adoption . . . you don't want to hire one of those.

To assess the level of knowledge of your potential lawyer, you need to interview several lawyers to find the one who seems best for you. Ask the lawyer how many private and agency adoptions he or she has handled. What have been the outcomes of those adoptions? The legal side of agency adoptions is far simpler than the legal side of private adoptions. What are the laws under which you will have to operate in your area? In general, you are trying to figure out if the attorney knows what he or she is talking about. As you interview several attorneys, you will see very quickly which ones know most about the subject.

If you don't know where to begin to find a lawyer, call any lawyer you know and ask for a suggestion. If you have read about any controversial adoption proceedings in your local area, find out who represented the parents. If someone teaches classes on adoption, ask the instructor for recommendations. If none of these suggestions work, call your local bar association and ask for names of lawyers who know something about adoption. You still need to interview them to make certain they know enough to handle your case. You want to be sure.

Your lawyer must know adoption law, agree with your philosophy about adoption, and represent you positively if the birthmother desires contact with him or her. The Ridgeways learned how important their lawyer was after their potential adoption fell through. They had been searching for about eight months when they heard from a cousin of a woman in Illinois who wanted to place her unborn child for adoption. They immediately wrote to her, sending her a picture, telling her about themselves, and asking her to contact them or their lawyer. She chose to contact the lawyer. But she and the lawyer did not get along. The Ridgeways heard from the cousin that the birthmother did not like the cold, legal tone of the lawyer, who made the process seem so much like a business. The Ridgeways had hired a lawyer who did not represent them in a way that helped them in adopting the baby they wanted. Lawyers can help and they can hinder.

Matt and Kate's situation was a bit different. They went out to interview lawyers from their area and found huge differences among lawyers' philosophies about adoption and adoption costs; even facts were presented in a different manner. They found one lawyer who said that if anything other than doctor's bills were paid, the adoption was in the illegal area and he would not represent them. They went to another lawyer who totally disagreed. He maintained that the same state laws allowed for the woman to receive counseling paid by the prospective adoptive parents, maternity clothes, car payments when she couldn't work, and her dental work. Both these lawyers were ethical and responsible members of their profession who did adoptions regularly. It was important for Matt and Kate to choose the lawyer whose philosophy most closely resembled theirs.

After you have settled on a lawyer, you need to be positive that you are going about this adoption in a legal way. Your lawyer should be able to tell you exactly what is legal in your state. The laws pertaining to adoption and their degree of enforcement in your state may vary; your lawyer should be able to answer any questions you may have about these laws.

Even if this book were longer, it would be difficult to clearly state specific laws from state to state so that you could know exactly what you might encounter. Some laws in each state are not enforced, while other states with less specific laws may enforce them far more stringently. The law is not known for its consistency of application.

Five general trends and documents seem to be setting legal precedent in adoptions: (1) More states seem to be encouraging adoption through agencies rather than private adoptions. (2) Frequently the states are looking at the Revised Uniform Adoption Act as a guideline, though few states have adopted the act in total. (3) The United States Senate hearings on baby-selling have had considerable impact on the interpretation of adoption laws. (4) The Supreme Court in *Stanley v. Illinois* ruled that all parents, legitimate or otherwise, are entitled to a court hearing before their children are taken from them. This has had a strong legal impact on the rights of birthfathers. (5) Another document that has had considerable impact on adoption is a book called *Beyond the Best Interests of the Child*[4], which has set the precedent for what is termed the "psychological parent." The informed potential adoptive parents who are considering private adoption should be familiar with each of these items, as should their attorney.

The legal aspects of private adoption are critical. It is imperative that you choose an informed, competent lawyer to advise you on what is or is not possible within your area. No lawyer can decide if you should go ahead with adoption placement or not, but a lawyer should be able to tell you exactly what the potential legal risks are. Then you should be able to choose whether or not to proceed with adoption.

How great a legal risk would you be willing to take in order to adopt a child? That question is difficult for anyone to answer with certainty, but it is something you may need to decide. If you have had great difficulty finding a child and you are strongly motivated, you might be willing to take a reasonable risk if a child were available. Most people who really want a child will take some legal chances rather than give up a child. Only the potential adoptive couple can decide whether and how far they should privately challenge unclear adoption laws.[5] Obviously adopting couples need the best legal help they can find.

• *Determining the Amount of Contact*
One of the primary deterrents for couples seeking a child is the potential contact they might have with the birthmother. Without question, you are more likely to have contact with one or both birthparents in a private adoption than in an agency adoption. How much contact you might have will vary from situation to situation. The contact may be as minimal as an exchange of names or the contact may exist as long as you raise the child. Examples of different levels of contact are given in Chapter 10.

The amount of contact you might have is difficult to predict. At times, you start out with one amount of contact, but the birthmother, who is usually in control, may decide to change the amount.

Wendy and Mickey found this out. They had waited a long time for a child. They were delighted to hear about a pregnant woman who wanted to privately place her child for adoption. They agreed to pay medical and other expenses incurred in the pregnancy in exchange for the child. The birthmother was satisfied with the arrangement and chose not to have any direct contact with them. She wanted to know a lot of details about the adoptive parents from the intermediary, but she did not want to meet them. That was fine with Wendy and Mickey, who kept their fingers crossed each day of the pregnancy. At last "their" baby boy arrived. Everything was great. The birthmother never wavered in her decision to let them have the child, but after her son arrived, she decided she wanted to meet and talk with Wendy and Mickey. The news of this meeting was met with great uncertainty by Wendy and Mickey . . . they were scared. What if, after finally getting this close, she changed her mind? What if she didn't like them? However, the birthmother had what they wanted, "their" baby, so she could make the rules, and they arranged to meet her at the hospital. Wendy and Mickey left that meeting without the anxiety they came with. They were thrilled about the meeting; they really liked the birthmother and felt she liked them. They had a long, meaningful talk and left feeling grateful that they had met her. The birthmother, too, felt that way. She said any previous doubts were gone after meeting the couple. She said that she felt she was doing something that was important and that made her feel really good about herself. She felt her baby was going to have an excellent home, and she was absolutely certain that she had done the right thing in meeting Wendy and Mickey.

While most experiences are good, some cause more anxiety. Many people wish for no contact with the birthmother, but that option may not be possible. In a private adoption you have to remember that the birthmother is pretty much in control until the legal adoption process has been completed. You will probably have to do it her way because you want her to give you the baby. For many considering adoption, this concept of having contact with the birthparent is new. Suzanne Arms in her book *To Love and Let Go*[6] takes the reader through the process from the viewpoint of both the birthmother and the adoptive parents, which may help to familiarize you with the advantages of this type of adoption.

Some adoptive parents maintain contacts with the birthparents throughout the entire growing-up period of their child. Jim and Barbara regularly send pictures of their daughter to her birthmother. They also tell the birthmother about the child's development and interests, and they are not greatly worried about the contact. Since they have two other children, they make a point of sending a family picture each time a picture of their daughter is requested; they want the birthmother to think of their daughter as part of a family. Another couple, Patty and Andrew, take their son to the park so that the birthmother can watch the growth of the boy she placed for adoption. The birthmother never makes contact with the boy, but she is able to see for herself how well he progresses in his family.

Previously, if you could maintain anonymity in an adoption, it would make it difficult for the birthmother or for the adopted child to ever make contact. If no one knew the other's name, no contact would be possible. The illusion that this was an "ordinary" family could be maintained. Now, this illusion is recognized as just that . . . an illusion. This is not a regular family. This is a special family that stays together by its history, not by its blood. This in no way lessens the family ties. At some point the child becomes an adult and may seek to know more about his or her blood relatives. The trend is toward making identifying information available to the adult adoptee, and thus anonymity has become impossible and less important. Contact between the two sets of parents seems less ominous.

• *Paying Pregnancy Costs*
The main difference between black market adoption and legal private adoption is the financial arrangement. In a private adoption no one makes a profit from the transfer of a child from the birthparent to the adoptive parent. The medical costs of the pregnancy, other expenses resulting from the pregnancy, and legal costs are the only expenses allowed in a legal, private adoption. Some states require a full disclosure of funds that the parties have exchanged in relation to the adoption.

Medical costs related to the pregnancy include prenatal care, delivery, and hospital costs. You can reasonably expect to pay costs for prenatal vitamins or other tests necessary for the pregnancy. You can also pay a reasonable legal fee. Other expenses are questionable. Counseling or psychotherapy for the pregnant woman is permissible in most states, especially since one of the major criticisms of private adoptions is that the pregnant woman does not receive adequate counseling concerning her decision. Dental care also might be related to the pregnancy. Cost for food to make certain the woman is adequately nourished is probably acceptable. Expenses can add up rather readily. However, in most adoptions you don't cover all of the possible expenses. Each adoption is different and private adoptions are not necessarily expensive.[7] Because expenses can vary a great deal, it is not always easy to determine if the fees being charged are legal. Don't hesitate to ask for itemization of all monies paid. Inflation quickly dates money figures; but in general there are some guidelines you can follow. Adoptions that cost over $15,000 are likely to fall into the questionable category. One can expect medical costs of several thousand dollars. In deliveries where there are complications, these expenses could easily double. Legal costs should usually not be more than $2,000, but may be slightly more if the lawyer also makes the placement arrangements. The variability in fees charged by attorneys makes it worthwhile to ask before you hire your attorney.

The fact that a baby is being sold on the black market will not be identified to the potential adoptive parents. No one says, "Do you want to buy a baby?" Adoptive parents must be able to identify the circumstances that would make a black market adoption.

Allison, a single woman, wanted a baby, and she wanted it legally. A friend told her about a lawyer who knew of a woman about to deliver a child. She had her friend call the lawyer to find out some of the details. The friend asked what kind of costs were involved. The lawyer said it would be $18,500. The friend gasped and asked why so much. He said it was $7,000 for the medical costs, $3,500 for psychotherapy because the woman had been raped, $4,000 for expenses for the woman to "relocate," and $4,000 for the legal fees. The longer they talked, the more uncomfortable the lawyer became with Allison's friend's comments and questions. He finally said, "I think you're right . . . this sounds too sticky and I don't want to be a part of it." They hung up. Allison then had her own attorney call the lawyer with the baby. It was apparent that the lawyer with the baby still did want to be involved. The total fee was the same although the itemization was different from the day before. The lawyer told Allison's attorney to act quickly because several people were considering this child. As you can see, the lawyer made the fees seem reasonable. Someone would consider this baby even though they would not consider an illegal adoption. It is not as obvious as the situation where a baby is offered for $40,000— an unmistakably illegal proposition.

In one recent case, a black market adoption was far less expensive than many adoptions. A woman calling herself Hilda called a couple she heard were looking for a Hispanic child. She told them about an expectant birthmother who wanted to place her baby for adoption for $5000 and who would sign a paper that promised she would never bother them again. According to Hilda, the birthmother didn't want to meet the couple and wanted the money, in cash, to be paid to Hilda. Two days later, the baby was born, and Hilda wanted the money paid to her before the baby would be given to them. The couple, unwilling to take the chance of being involved in a black market adoption, declined the offer; these arrangements were clearly illegal.

Private adoptions may be more or less expensive than agency adoptions. It is worthwhile to formalize in the early stages exactly what expenses you, the adoptive parents, will pay; it is very difficult to say no as the delivery of the child approaches. You also need to have an agreement as to what happens financially if the birthmother changes her mind and does not relinquish the child for adoption. This is a very sensitive area. It is also important to understand that most agreements would not be legally binding even if the agreement were made. For this reason, few people will be repaid the money they have paid in an adoption that doesn't work out. Knowing this ahead of time will help you to be cautious about how you proceed.

• Securing Medical Consent Forms

One of the first things you should do if you adopt privately is to have the birthmother sign a medical consent form so that you can legally have medical treatment for the child. This is the type of document you don't have to be concerned with in an agency adoption; the agency obtains this for you. In a private adoption you should be cautious about taking the baby until this document is signed.

Usually, the hospital will have the birthmother sign this type of document before they will release the baby to you. If they do not have such a document you can ask the birthmother to sign a medical authorization, which you must provide or your lawyer can prepare. When possible it is worthwhile to have the document notarized, although this is not always critical. The most important thing is that the birthmother sign it.

If for some reason the form is not available, should you not take the child? Again, this is your choice. You increase your risks, but you also have the child. It is better to have the medical consent *and* the baby.

• *Working with the State Agency*

After you have a child placed with you in a private adoption, you need to begin the formal proceedings of adopting the child. In most states, a court representative, or an agency delegated by the state, investigates you and your adoptive home and makes its recommendation to the court.

This investigation is usually conducted by a social worker meeting with you to understand your background and see your home. Stories of social workers going through drawers and checking for cobwebs in the room are not true. That doesn't mean this meeting is not an investigative meeting, but dirt in the corners is not what they are looking for. They want to understand who you are, your relationship within your family, how you will discipline the child, how you got the child, what money you paid the birthmother, what arrangements you have made for future contacts with the birthmother, and how the child is doing. They will go over what papers are needed to send to the state in order for them to complete the home study.

The emphasis in the state's study is far different from, and more superficial than, the home study done by adoption agencies to determine if they will place a child with you. In some cases, the state worker assigned to you will have less training than a social worker doing agency adoptions. The state is merely trying to make certain you can provide a fit home instead of trying to decide if you are the best home available. The burden of proof is on them, not on you.

Even though you are in a position of strength, don't underestimate the agency. Two examples illustrate the control that agencies continue to try to exert in private adoption placements.

Thelma decided to place her racially mixed child for adoption after raising him until he was eight years old. She saw her son being raised on the street. His leadership and ability were going to waste as he performed poorly in school and was becoming a problem at home. Her attempts to provide guidance were unsuccessful as she felt her own needs to have a life filled with things other than children. After much soul-searching, she finally approached the adoption agency. She was shocked to learn that he would be placed in foster care for an indefinite period of time. That concerned her, so she delayed her decision until she learned of private adoption as an alternative. She heard of a potential adoptive couple who sounded perfect for her son. They had two older, racially mixed, adopted children who seemed to be doing well even though the parents were Caucasian. The couple and their other children were excited about adopting another child. Everything proceeded as the couple had anticipated. Hank, their new son, flourished in his new environment. After the usual testing, he responded well to the guidance that came from his new family. His grades in school soared. Everyone was pleased with the pronounced progress. The social worker, however, was skeptical. When Thelma went in to sign the papers, the worker told her she was sure that Hank must be having a difficult time despite the glowing letters of recommendation about the couple and Hank. The social worker felt a placement with Caucasian parents was inappropriate and would cause him problems (even though she had never asked one question of the adopting couple about the racial issue). She doubted that he would adjust to the adoption because of the implied rejection by his birthmother. Thelma was angry. She knew the couple and of Hank's progress; she felt certain he was doing well. She was sure she knew more about the progress he was making than the social worker did, and she resented the implication that it was wrong to have placed Hank for adoption. After expressing her anger toward the worker, she insisted on signing the adoption relinquishment form and stormed out of the social worker's office.

The Kents learned the hard way about working with the agency in their private adoption. They didn't know a lot about adoption when they heard about a woman wishing to place her racially mixed child in their racially mixed family. They jumped at the chance, and soon Eliza was a part of their family. They had agreed to certain things with the birthmother before Eliza was given to them: pictures would be sent yearly through an intermediary, and Eliza would be told about the adoption throughout her life so that it would not come as a shock to her. The couple had mixed feelings about these requests from the birthmother, but agreed.

In their first meeting, the social worker indicated to the Kents that private adoption was a poor way to adopt and she thoroughly disapproved of it. After hearing that the birthmother had asked for regular pictures of Eliza, the social worker told them that many couples initially agree to provide pictures but few actually do. The Kents were surprised but thought perhaps they also wouldn't need to send pictures. The social worker sensed their unsureness and continued to question their knowledge of adoption issues. Since Eliza had become theirs so easily, they really hadn't decided some of the issues about adoption. They had spoken with a counselor who told them about the availability of Eliza, but now they felt she might have been wrong on how she suggested they proceed. Their confusion showed. After telling the Kents that everything was fine at the end of the interview, the social worker wrote a negative report about them that was given to the birthmother.

The birthmother was distressed to learn that the agency was recommending against the adoption. She asked the counselor who had assisted her in placing Eliza to intervene and set up a meeting with the adoptive parents to discuss the situation. They again reconfirmed their commitments to each other to provide information about Eliza as she grew up and to keep a positive and open relationship between them. The birthmother, over the objection of the social worker, strongly requested the adoption proceed. She wrote letters of protest to the social worker's supervisor expressing her displeasure on how her case had been handled. She felt the original agreement with the Kents had been significantly undermined by the social worker's "meddling" and felt that her case had not been handled in a professional manner and not "in the interest of anyone involved in the adoption." The adoption was completed despite the social worker's disapproval.

Social workers who disapprove of private adoption should not be working with couples who adopt privately; however, such a person might be assigned to your adoption case. Certainly there is a need for some investigation about the suitability of people adopting a child, but the goal of that investigation should be clear. Hostility toward birthparents, adopting parents, and private adoption should not be a part of the agency process.

One adoption agency in Ohio is using a cooperative approach with prospective adoptive parents who are undertaking private adoption. If an adoptive family locates a potential child for adoption, this agency will do the investigative, counseling, and legal steps. This increased involvement of an adoption agency with private adoption cases has some excellent possibilities. Seldom is this level of cooperation seen.

Your involvement with the agency is not over until you go to court. The usual six-month probationary period that started at the time your attorney filed the petition to adopt is used to complete these visits. Your visit must take place before the agency will arrange an appointment with the birthmother to sign the relinquishment form. Your visit with the social worker takes place first so that she can report to the birthmother how she viewed your home and you. She will also be making certain that your story of how this adoption was arranged is the same as the birthmother's story.

• *Signing Relinquishment Papers*
The signing of the relinquishment or consent-to-adopt papers is the crucial point in the adoption process. In agency adoptions, the relinquishment papers are usually signed *before* the child is placed in an adoptive home. In a private adoption, the relinquishment papers are usually signed *after* the child has been placed with the new adoptive family. In neither case do the adoptive parents obtain the consent to adopt from the birthparents. In an agency adoption, the agency obtains relinquishment; in a private adoption, usually a state-designated agency obtains the relinquishment. The consent or relinquishment is the major legal problem involved in adoption.

Actually, consent of the adoptive parents is also obtained in an adoption. They give their consent by filing the petition to adopt. It is possible that adoptive parents can be unhappy with the child placed with them or feel that they were not fully told about the child's background or medical history. They, like anyone unhappy with the adoption, can ask to have the proceedings stopped before the finalization of the adoption, or declared void after the adoption is finalized if they can prove fraud occurred.

The consent of the child may also be necessary if the child is over eleven years old. Usually this consent is given at the court hearing for finalization of the adoption. At this time, the judge will ask if the child agrees to the adoption.

In some states, the consent of the foster parent is recognized in the adoption process. The foster parents' rights have increased in recent years. Occasionally foster parents are allowed to contest the adoption if they believe it is not in the best interest of the child.

The critical person involved in consenting to the adoption is the birthmother. In the case of unmarried birthparents, the birthmother, even if she is a minor, must consent to the adoption. The only exceptions would be if (1) the birthmother is legally incompetent and therefore unable to give consent, (2) the birthmother has had her legal rights to the child terminated because of abandonment, or (3) the birthmother has already relinquished the child to an adoption agency.

The laws governing the consent of the natural father are less clear and less consistent in cases where the child is illegitimate. The landmark Supreme Court decision in 1972 in the case of *Stanley v. Illinois* has had a significant impact on the rights of the unmarried father. The court ruled that all parents, legitimate or not, are entitled to a court hearing before their children can be removed from their custody. This decision was based on the case of a man and woman who had lived together out of wedlock for a long period of time. They had several children, but after the woman died, these children were taken from the father on the grounds that he had no rights to his illegitimate children. The major impact of the court's decision was that it was based on the man's rights as a father and not on the basis of the family unit that had been established.

With this decision, adoption procedures changed how the relinquishment of the child was obtained. Before, the father's consent, if he was not married to the mother of the child, was usually not considered necessary when a child was relinquished for adoption. As a result of this court decision, some states established what is called the Uniform Parent Act. This, in effect, says the father must be notified before the child is adopted. The father must deny paternity, sign consent forms for the adoption, or be legally deprived of his parental rights. Some adoption agencies publish notices of a pending adoption in the newspaper, stating that the father should claim the child if he wishes to exert his rights. If no one comes forth to acknowledge fatherhood, the father's legal rights are legally terminated and the adoption can proceed without the father's consent.

In contrast, the 1978 Supreme Court upheld a Georgia law that said the consent of a father is not a requirement for adoption. This decision indicates that perhaps the *Stanley v. Illinois* decision was interpreted too broadly and that the consent of the unmarried father may not always be necessary. Reading through the tremendous variety of state legal decisions leaves one feeling the courts are inconsistent in how they view the right of the unmarried father and at what point the father has or does not have parental rights.

It is important to understand exactly how your state operates and to act within the law in obtaining the consent of the birthmother and/or birthfather. One of the few reasons for courts nullifying or voiding an adoption is when it can be proven that the consent of the birthparents, especially the birthmother, was obtained fraudulently. Some states will not allow birthmothers to sign relinquishment papers until at least three days after the birth of the infant; this is to avoid the criticism of pressure or of too hasty a response in an unusually emotional time. On the other side of the picture is the situation in South Carolina, where adoption relinquishments are immediately obtained from the birthmother and adoptions take only a few days.[8]

Some states do not look favorably on private adoptions even though they are legal within the state; they will pay particular attention to the consent of the birthparents. The courts want to make absolutely certain that no coercion was involved in obtaining the consent. These states, to have the utmost control, frequently insist that the relinquishment be obtained by an authorized service agency representing the state.

Usually, once a consent has been signed, it may not be withdrawn without the approval of the court. If the birthparent can prove that the consent was obtained by fraud, misrepresentation, or coercion, the court may decide to cancel the consent. If the parent has merely changed her or his mind, the case will depend on the individual circumstances. The overriding factor in these decisions is what the judge deems to be in the best interest of the child. The longer the child has been in the adoptive home, the less likely the child will be removed. More and more the courts are recognizing the concept of the psychological parent. This concept is clearly spelled out in legal precedents. At times the circumstances of relinquishment are less important than the length of time the child has been with the adoptive parents, thereby reinforcing the concepts of psychological parenting and bonding.

Even in cases where fraud was involved in obtaining consent of the birthparents, they must act within a "reasonable" length of time in order to have the adoption rescinded. The same is true if the adoptive parents believe they were not fully informed of pertinent facts at the time of the adoption. The courts expect people to act promptly if they believe a problem exists.

In most private adoption cases, the consent of the birthparents is rather routinely obtained. Some state laws specify that the relinquishment must be obtained within a certain length of time, for example, forty-five days after the petition to adopt has been filed. This is worthwhile, and when done it minimizes the risk of the birthmother's changing her mind. At the time she placed the child, she believed that what she was doing was in the best interest of the child. Therefore, to obtain timely relinquishment of the child is beneficial for all persons in the adoption. Relinquishments are not always obtained in a timely fashion so it is important that you have the best legal advice possible. Your lawyer should be able to tell you how to best proceed if there is any question that comes up about the legal relinquishment of the child.

• *Going to Court*
States vary in the manner that court proceedings are conducted in adoption cases. Some adoption proceedings are conducted in superior courts, others in circuit court, surrogate court, domestic relations court, county court, orphan's court, and so on. Your lawyer knows the court in which your adoption will be conducted.

All people involved in consenting to the adoption must be notified of the court hearing. Again, your lawyer will know how this notification must be made.

The actual court appearance will probably be in a judge's chambers or in a private session with the judge. The hearing is a legal formality but in a friendly informal session. Usually the adoptive parents and the child, especially if the child is older, will appear for the hearing. Sometimes the lawyer must attend. Some states do not require anyone to be there. It is a jubilant time for the adoptive parents because it means the child is now theirs legally as well as psychologically.

In some states the court hearing is merely a probationary hearing that declares the home is now open to be investigated. At other times, if there is some question about the fitness of the adoptive parents, the judge may require a probationary period to examine their qualifications.

The role of the state-appointed agency that has conducted the home investigation is important in this court hearing. If the agency says the adoptive home is not a good home for the child, the judge will probably not approve the adoption at this time. The weight of this agency's recommendation is important. If the judge has questions about the home, it is usual to have a longer investigation of the adoptive home. Remember though—the agency must prove your unfitness. The investigation is seldom thorough and rarely recommends against the adoption.

Following the granting of the final adoption decree, an amended birth certificate is issued for the adopted child. The new birth certificate lists the adoptive parents as the parents of the child and the child's surname as that of the adoptive parents. In some states, the adoptive parents may request deletion of the birth city and county of the adopted child. These are details you need to be aware of so that you can decide how you want them handled. Your law-yer should be able to keep you advised before you face each of these steps in a private adoption.

Basically, this is the general framework in which a private adop-tion operates. The person who enters the process understanding what to expect makes the fewest mistakes. The importance of the legal help you hire cannot be overestimated, especially in an adoption where there are any unusual circumstances.

• The Advantages of Private Adoption

The biggest single advantage to adopting privately is that this may be the only way you can get a baby. Currently, many people who adopt privately are people who cannot, or believe they cannot, adopt through an agency. The supply of infants available through agen-cies is seriously limited; the primary children being placed for adoption by the agencies are older children and children with spe-cial needs.

Even if it is possible to adopt an infant through an adoption agency, the waiting period is likely to be several years. In all likelihood, the waiting period will be much less in a private adoption.

The immediate placement from birthparents to adoptive parents is an extremely significant advantage in private adoptions. Agency adoptions emphasize the conservative approach; placements usu-ally do not occur until all relinquishment papers have been signed. This approach may offer the greatest legal safeguard, but it is defi-nitely not in the best interests of the child or of the adoptive par-ents. The importance of the early bonding between parents and child cannot be overestimated—*it is critical*. In some private adoptions, the adoptive parents are allowed to spend time with the newborn within hours after birth. Psychologically this is a distinct advan-tage to the adopted child and to the adoptive parents. It is also to the advantage of the birthmother concerned about the child easily fitting into the new family.

The lack of prying by the agency is considered an advantage by many people who select to adopt privately. The forced counseling for birthparents and for adoptive parents may be considered intru-sive by some people. Control of the process in a private adoption is also an advantage for both the adoptive parents and the birthpar-ents. The adoptive parents are actively involved in finding a child to adopt. They are involved with making the contacts and the actual search for the child. The birthmother and perhaps the birthfather can be directly involved in the placement of their child. As one woman stated, "I could never just give my child away to an agency; I want to know exactly where and with whom she is or I would be uncomfortable for the rest of my life."

Another big advantage in private adoption is the personal knowledge adoptive parents and birthparents can gain about each other. While some people talk of the disadvantages of meeting the birthparents, this can be a most important advantage. To be able later to tell an adopted child personally about his or her birthparents can be extremely positive for all concerned. For the birthmother to have personal knowledge about the people who will be raising her child makes the letting-go easier. *You can learn many facts about each other if you go through an agency to get your child. But if you personally meet one another, you know each other.*

Private adoptions have their risks (see Chapter 5) and they have their advantages. You need to consider them to see if the advantages outweigh the risks. You also need to consider your options. The fewer options you have for obtaining a child may make the risks of private adoption seem less monumental and the advantages seem more compelling.

Many of the alarmist views and negative statements about private adoptions come from adoption agency representatives. In actuality, adoption agencies are the newcomers to the adoption scene. As the agencies have become larger, the only method of supporting their programs has been to have a bigger segment of a continually diminishing supply of children. One of the ways they seek to get this larger segment is by initiating state laws to drive the private adoption competition out of business. Giving an adoption monopoly to the agencies would solve the agencies' problems while accomplishing no demonstrable benefit for anyone in the adoption process, except the adoption agencies. Unfortunately, proponents of private adoption are not organized to demand the legal right to adopt privately.

Private adoption keeps the proper checks and balances on the adoption agencies. It puts an appropriate amount of pressure on the adoption agencies so that the latter will examine the relevancy of their methods in today's society. It also offers a choice to people who would have difficulty working within the often rigid system the agencies run. Private adoption offers another way that is neither better nor worse than adoption through an agency—it is merely a different way!

Family Adoptions
The primary focus of this book is not on family adoptions, but they complete the picture of the kinds of available adoptions. Half of all adoptions are by relatives and present little difficulty. As long as the adoption is agreed upon by all the individuals, it is relatively simple. Usually no home study of suitability for parenting or probationary period is involved. While the same consent forms are necessary, the courts at times waive restrictions that otherwise might be imposed. However, even in this type of adoption, it is worthwhile to hire a lawyer to make certain that you proceed in a legal manner. Adoption is too permanent to let anything be overlooked.

The main concern in family adoptions is the potential for fights over the child. To have an aunt and uncle or grandmother and grandfather raise the child sometimes sounds good to the birthmother until she sees her relatives being "parents" to her child. Legalization of the new family arrangement prevents the relatives from moving the child about, following family feuds.

The other form of adoptions by relatives is stepparent adoption and where divorce has become common, there has been a significant increase in this type of adoption. The primary requisite in stepparent adoption is obtaining consent of the parent abdicating his or her parenting rights; generally, this is the father. In California, if the parent who does not have custody of the child fails for one year or more to pay child support or to visit the child, his or her consent to the adoption is no longer required.

Black Market Adoptions
Of the several kinds of adoptions available, no other kind elicits more emotional response from the public than the concept of babyselling. These are the adoptions that cause people to question the entire idea of private adoption. These are the adoptions where large sums of money are exchanged for a baby.

Black market adoptions are not legal. In every state there are laws against people profiting unduly from the placement of children for adoption. We have no way of really knowing how many babies are placed in this manner. It is estimated that 5,000 to 10,000 babies are placed this way each year.[9]

Why would any couple pay $30,000 or $40,000 for a baby when they could go to the local adoption agency or find another child privately at a fraction of the cost? Why would anyone risk getting involved in an illegal arrangement to get a baby? The answer to both of these questions is, they wouldn't. Couples would go to an adoption agency if they could. Illegally obtaining a child is not the way they would choose the situation to be, but this is their reality. These are couples who probably can't adopt from an agency, not because they are unfit or wouldn't be good parents, but rather because they don't fit the image of a parent the adoption agencies are seeking.

Black market adoptions thrive under certain conditions. Those conditions exist right now. There is a scarcity of infants available for adoption. There is a need for someone who cares about supplying what these couples dearly want—a baby. The current adoption agency system does nothing to remedy the scarcity, nor does it do anything about taking care of all of the potential adoptive parents' need for a child. As a consequence, a different group has emerged to handle these unmet needs . . . people who sell babies.

• *Why Not Sell Babies?*
Selling babies would not work if there were not a need and demand for these services. People are quick to criticize the people involved in selling babies, but the ones who would come to their defense, those who have obtained children from them, are necessarily quiet. Why are people upset about baby-selling? If it is meeting a need and no one is hurt, why not sell babies? Is it the profit being made by the intermediary? Does baby-selling sound like slavery? Will selling babies cause women to become pregnant just for the money? Are babies more of a commodity this way than through an adoption agency? Are we concerned that the birthmother is being taken advantage of or do we object to the birthmother making a profit from her nine months of labor? Just exactly what upsets us about black market adoptions?

The profit being made on black market adoptions seems to be the main concern for some people. They argue that intermediaries or baby brokers shouldn't profit from people's miseries. That sounds right, but in reality many people profit from other people's miseries. The surgeon operates on you for a fee, the dentist charges you for the tooth he or she pulls, the mortician profits from the death of your loved ones, the psychotherapist charges you for listening to your problems. Even adoption agencies make enough money in their "nonprofit" organizations to have nice facilities, good salaries, and pleasant working conditions. Our society is set up in such a way that you pay for the things you want, even when you need them very badly. We obtain these services only if we cannot provide them ourselves. Many people in our society profit from the needs of other people, but for some reason, to do this by selling babies really upsets people.

If the profit is what most upsets us in black market adoptions, perhaps the way to solve the problem is to figure out how to decrease the profits. One of the age-old ways to decrease profits is to allow supply and demand to equalize. Currently there is a great demand for babies. If we remove the legal restrictions from people profiting by selling babies and allow the supply to meet the demand, the cost of buying a baby would go down radically, and the profits would be cut drastically. Perhaps all the legal restrictions we put on baby-selling are creating the very problem we deplore— large profits in the selling of babies.

Many people believe it is horrible that an unwed mother became pregnant in the first place and bad enough that she would consider giving the baby away; and for her to make a profit is, in their view, deplorable. Perhaps the reason people are so against the mother making a profit is that they really want the mother punished. If we pay her for her transgressions, aren't we rewarding evil? But are intercourse and pregnancy really evil? She may not be doing a good thing for society but she certainly is doing a fantastic thing for the childless couple who has been stopped at each turn from finding the child they want so much.

Perhaps we fear that the birthmother will be exploited. Will the offer of money for her baby keep her from doing the right thing for herself? Maybe she should have an abortion or maybe she should keep the baby. Maybe she needs counseling to decide what is best. If there is any possibility that she is being exploited, it is most likely to occur while this process remains illegal and underground. If a woman felt she was doing something worthwhile in placing her child for adoption, she could freely choose which alternative would be best for her. Yet if the prevailing attitude is to punish her for what she has done, even in subtle ways, she is much more vulnerable to being exploited. All businesses, even baby-selling, are easiest to regulate if they are not driven underground. Prohibition taught us this most vividly.

The criticism that baby-selling is a form of slavery is difficult to substantiate. Perhaps all forms of parenting are types of slavery. (I'm not certain for whom: the parents or the child.) Certainly, any form of adoption could be subject to this same criticism. It would be difficult to say whether more slavery is involved when a child is bought for $35,000 from a baby broker or for $3,000 from a social worker.

Another complaint raised by critics of black market adoptions is that the fitness of the parents who are seeking to adopt has not been verified. Sex perverts and child abusers can obtain children by this unscrupulous means. Why any sex pervert or child abuser would go to all this trouble is beyond me . . . especially when it might be easier for such persons to have their own children and not have to pay so much for them. No one makes us pass any tests for parenting unless we want to adopt a child. Just about anyone, no matter how unfit for parenting, can have a baby. *Only the infertile must offer proof of fitness for parenthood.*

Another objection raised about black market babies is that they take away potentially available babies from legal adoption sources. An opposing criticism is raised when some say that young girls are hired to get pregnant so that large profits can be made from the babies they produce. Obviously if this second criticism is true then the first one is not. If it is possible to take potential children from adoption agencies because of the profit to the mother when she sells her baby, then we should examine how we can learn from this. Should we offer greater incentives, better living conditions, a financial allowance, and consequently, fewer feelings of guilt to the birthmother who elects to place her child with an adoption agency? Again, instead of expecting penitence from her, let us demonstrate to the woman that her pregnancy is not such a terrible thing. Someone is going to benefit from her possible mistake and inconvenience.

People will respond that the approach just described would encourage women to have babies for profit. The feelings of remorse that are an inherent part of placing a child for adoption and the length of time it takes to produce a child will ultimately limit and discourage this practice. However, if someone is really good at making babies and can make them for others who are not, then why not?

One of the most poignant arguments against black market babies came from a pregnant woman about to give up her baby for private adoption. She said she could never sell her baby because she was sure that someday her child would find her. How then could she explain selling her baby? As long as making a profit on giving up a baby for adoption is so condemned, she is right. Ultimately, the birthparent and child may realize that, regardless of money, the most worthwhile situation occurred—a loving mother and father raised a loving child. That should be the focus in the debate over selling babies.

Another argument used against high-priced black market adoptions is that they discriminate against poor people who cannot afford to participate. This argument is a strong one only if you believe that black market adoptions are worthwhile. Again, if supply meets demand, the cost of buying a baby will be more affordable to people with less money.

Obviously, the stand I am taking on black market adoptions is not widely accepted. One writer on adoption boldly stated, "Baby-selling is abhorrent to all civilized people."[10] I believe we should consider changing current adoption laws to allow the mother and those involved with arranging adoptions to make a profit. I take this stand for several reasons. I have known the pangs of infertility. I have known the intensity of the desire to have a child. I have met couples who desperately wanted a child they could not find. I have known women who loved being pregnant, but who did not want to be mothers. I have seen poor women struggle financially with a pregnancy that would eventually become an adoption, fearful of taking any money because it might look like a black market adoption. Somehow there should be a way to accommodate all these people in their times of need.

People will say, "What of the abuses?" But the abuses will always be there. They are there now in parenting by birth, and in adoption through adoption agencies, private adoptions, stepparent adoptions, grandparent adoptions, and black market adoptions. The abuses are least likely to occur when the system can be scrutinized . . . the system can be scrutinized when the system is legalized.

• *Problems with Black Market Adoption*
A person should be very careful about getting involved in black market adoptions. As in all illegal business, unscrupulous people

can be involved. Illegal business is unfamiliar to most of us, so we don't know our way around in the system.

The biggest single risk in black market adoptions is the possibility that the adoption decree might be set aside if the illegality of the procedure is discovered. As a consequence, people adopting in this way live in fear for years with the thought that someone can take their child from them. Of course, this fear diminishes over time. At some point, even if it were found out that you had paid $35,000 for your child, the judge is unlikely to take your child of five years away from the only home he or she has ever known. Living with this secret for years, however, is bound to take a toll on you. It also makes you vulnerable to threats of blackmail.

The financial risk in black market adoption, as it is currently practiced, is significantly greater than that incurred in adoption through an adoption agency. The first figure quoted to a couple may not be the final cost. As with private adoptions, it is important to have an agreement before you begin. After you have agreed to pay $25,000 and you have paid it, it is difficult to say forget it when the baby-seller says he or she needs $5,000 more. You can't say, "That's not fair" or "I am going to report you." Remember, the law does not look upon your baby transaction with favor.

Another problem with obtaining a baby through black market is that when you go to court to finalize the adoption, you have to commit perjury. When the court requests a recounting of the expenses involved in the adoption, you obviously cannot tell the truth. The lie you tell, if discovered, could cause the adoption to be set aside.

As black market adoptions are currently conducted, the rights of the father are frequently ignored to expedite the adoption. If the birthmother indicates the father is unknown when he is really known, she is depriving him of his rights to his child. If this is later discovered, once again, the adoption could be set aside.

At times in black market adoptions, the woman first agrees to place the child for adoption and later changes her mind. In a reputable adoption process, whether through an adoption agency or a private adoption, the adoption proceedings should stop at this point. In a black market adoption, the woman might be pressured into continuing with the adoption. Threats of having to pay back money already paid toward prenatal care or "damages" to the adopting couple who are waiting for her baby might intimidate the woman into signing relinquishment papers she would not otherwise have signed. If it can be proven to the satisfaction of a judge that the woman was coerced into signing consent forms, the finalized adoption can still be nullified and the baby returned to the coerced birthmother.

At times in black market adoptions, the birthmother enters the hospital and registers in the name of the adoptive mother. When the birth certificate is filed, the adoptive parents are listed as the birthparents. Obviously, this is illegal, and it, too, is grounds for taking the child from the adoptive parents; it has not been legally adopted.

One other technique used in black market adoptions may in fact be the primary way of legalizing this process. A child is born in the United States, bought by a couple, flown to Mexico, and adopted legally in Mexico. The birthmother may be represented by an attorney who formally acts in the interests of the mother in relinquishing the child.

As you can see, there are definite risks in black market adoptions. Because of the risks and mostly because these adoptions are illegal, I do not recommend adopting a child in this way. On the other hand, there is much to be learned from the success of these black market adoptions. If this type of adoption were legal, I see nothing wrong in people making a profit from meeting a definite need that currently exists in our society.

Very few differences, other than those already mentioned, exist between private adoptions and black market adoptions in relationship to the adoptive parents. The primary difference is how you obtain the baby. You need to make contact with someone who knows about a baby that is available for adoption for a sum of money. After that, the investigation and the legal process are usually the same. Most black market adoptions go rather smoothly, and most of the children adopted in this manner remain in the home of the adoptive parents just as in any other adoption.

Black market babies are a response to an unmet need in our society. Emotional arguments against this form of adoption fail to explore why this type of adoption exists and why black market adoptions elicit such a strong negative response. Perhaps it is time to overhaul antiquated laws that might be creating the only negative side to profitmaking by meeting a need: baby-selling.

Summary

Adoptions that involve children being placed privately constitute the majority of adoptions in the United States each year. Most are legal adoptions by single people, married couples, and relatives. Some are children adopted through the black market, where money is exchanged.

An infertile couple seeking a child would probably choose agency adoption if that choice were open to them. Agency adoptions are easier, may cost less, involve less legal knowledge, and offer the greatest choice. But too many couples are eliminated by the agencies' rigid rules, arbitrary requirements, and noncreative approaches to adoption. The second choice of most couples is a private adoption. The biggest difficulty here is making the contacts that will produce a child (see Chapter 3). Sometimes, searching privately for a child, a couple will encounter an opportunity to buy a child. A couple who has been rejected by the adoption agencies and who has been having difficulties finding a child to adopt through regular private means is likely to consider a black market adoption. Black market adoption is not a good way to seek a child, but it is all that is left for the desperate. It is difficult to find fault with the people who are driven to this point by the inability of our adoption system to allow them the child they so much want.

Private adoptions, no matter how the placements occur, offer a choice. The need for the choice is apparent by the number of people who adopt in this way. Private adoptions and intercountry adoptions are the only opportunities left for the people whom the adoption agencies see as less fit for parenting. In no way does this make these people lesser parents. It only makes them parents by a different method because the adoption agencies chose not to help them become parents.

Looking Elsewhere and Everywhere | 3

YOU SAY YOU WANT A BABY. HOW MUCH TIME, EFFORT, AND CREATIVITY are you willing to put into finding your baby? One test of your desire for a child is how far you are willing to go. It's one thing to go to an adoption agency and wait for them to give you a child; it's a whole different matter to go *find* your child.

Many people have never considered *finding* a baby. The approach is radical; it may be necessary for some people and impossible for others. The only way for you to evaluate its merits for your own use is to study its advantages and risks. How does it feel to you? Are you uncomfortable? If so, why? New approaches may take some testing before they fit well into your life. Look back on ideas about which you were intolerant a few years ago and see how familiarity has changed your attitude toward them. In the same way, consider some of these approaches, discuss them with others, become familiar with them, and *then* see how they seem to fit for you.

Searching for a baby takes time, lots of time. The more time you spend, the greater the likelihood of your success. The more people you inform, the more people there are who know of your desire to find a baby. You may be lucky and learn about an adoptable baby after a contact or two. You may have to talk to dozens of people before you get even a trace of a lead.

Patience is a critical ingredient in a baby search. Many leads will turn up nothing. But remember, you are looking for only one baby, so don't give up . . . be patient. It is easier to be patient when you are actively working on a problem. You are not waiting for a call from the adoption agency that may or may not come. You are an active participant in deciding your fate.

Skill is also important in your search. You need to know what you are doing. You need to understand why you should approach this group or that person. You need to know who gets pregnant and why, in order to understand where you are most likely to find a baby.

Develop your creativity as you begin. There are all sorts of innovative approaches to finding a baby. With an understanding of who accidentally becomes pregnant, you can then figure out how to reach them. We are all creative in a pinch. You need to develop that creative approach because, right now, you are in a pinch.

Openness is essential in searching for a baby. If you would have difficulty contacting the biological parents or knowing anything about them, you will have difficulty with this approach to parenthood. The more open you can be, the greater your chances of success. You need to be open with lots of people about your feelings of being childless. You need to be open to suggested leads and to where these leads might take you.

Above all, in a baby search you must be bold. Believing that there is a child out there for you, you must be willing to venture forth to find him or her. Timidity will leave you childless. The people who will find a child are those who boldly go after one.

All these qualities are within each of us. You may not see yourself as creative and bold but try it—maybe you really are. The desire to have a baby is very powerful. The strength of this desire may cause you to discover characteristics you don't think you have. Give it a try. What's the worst thing that can happen? It is simply that you may end up without a baby, and that's where you are right now.

Potential for Finding a Child

Before you begin your baby search, you have to believe that there is a potential for success. If you don't believe the potential is very great, you won't put your heart into the search. There are several reasons why I strongly believe that a child is out there for you now.

America is a society influenced by fads and cycles. The world of fashion is an example. Fads and cycles also exist in family size, sexual behavior, contraceptive practice, unwanted pregnancies, and babies available for adoption. Over the years the pendulum swings back and forth.

The figures I have received from adoption agencies across the country indicate a slight trend toward more children being placed for adoption than five years ago. Part of this increase is attributable to fewer agencies handling more babies as others close. It is possible that we are now going to see an upswing in the number of adoptable babies.

The increased negative publicity given to abortion as a solution to unwanted pregnancy argues positively for adoption as an alternative to abortion. The number of abortions has leveled off in recent years and may be beginning a downward trend. Fewer abortions does not necessarily mean fewer pregnancies; it could mean that more women are keeping their babies or placing them for adoption.

Statistics can be very misleading. Adoption agency statistics indicate huge numbers of people waiting to adopt, but anyone wishing to adopt has also consulted with every agency in town. They are probably being counted two, three, or four times. We really don't know how many people are trying to adopt. Every doctor and lawyer you approach has a list of people who would like a baby, but again these lists overlap and recount people many times. I know of dozens of people waiting right now for a baby, but if I had a baby available today for adoption many of these people might no longer be looking for one. Some would have moved, some would have recently obtained a child, some would not want this particular child because they would not like his background, some would want only a girl and this is a boy, and some would simply be scared off when actually confronted with a specific child. Therefore, my list is much shorter than it seems.

A number of "accidental" pregnancies may at some unconscious level be deliberate. Some women want to be pregnant and therefore purposefully allow themselves to be exposed to an "accidental" pregnancy. If these same women knew of someone who really wanted to adopt their baby, they very well might choose adoption, not abortion. If women really don't want to be pregnant today, they have the means to prevent it. If they choose not to use these means, it is possible they really *do want* to be pregnant.

Adoption is not a well-known or common choice for women who become "accidentally" pregnant. If you can reach women in these circumstances, you reach an entirely new group. These are women from whom the adoption agencies should be recruiting babies. Lisa represents this untapped source of biological mothers. Lisa is a bright young woman who knew about contraceptives but found them "inconvenient" to use. She came in to make plans for her second abortion. She was nineteen. I asked her if she had considered adoption and she said she hadn't. She reasoned very clearly, though incorrectly, that there were already too many unwanted children in the world and she wouldn't want to contribute another. She was not at all aware of the current lack of adoptable babies.

Supporting the contention that babies are available out there for those who search is the changed attitude of young people toward openness. Today, many young women would not consider placing their child with a monolithic and impersonal institution such as an adoption agency. Adoption agencies and their aloofness are looked on with disfavor by large numbers of young people who want to be personally involved with the event. To give a baby up to an adoption agency would not be comfortable for them, but to give a baby up to "real people" would be worth considering.

Amy was going to have an abortion until she heard about a couple who desperately wanted a child. The more she learned about their long wait and their strong desire for a child, the more sure she became. She said she could never give her child up to an adoption agency where she "wouldn't be sure what happened to it." So she chose private adoption over abortion because she believed she was "doing something significant for society" by helping this childless couple. It gave her a reason to feel good about herself and her decision about her unborn child. The personal details about the couple who wanted the child gave her positive involvement with adoption as an alternative. Amy needed personal knowledge about those involved in the adoption in order to fully consider it.

Another reason I strongly believe babies are available is the phenomenal success I have seen from the couples I have worked with in trying to find babies to adopt. The amazing thing is that everyone seems to find a baby. I have never seen a couple who has searched vigorously who has not found a child. At times, when a birthmother comes to me and I go through my files of people seeking children, I am amazed how many of the couples have already found a child to adopt.

All these reasons support the theory that babies are there—you just need to find them. But any search needs a plan. Where does one begin a baby search?

Beginning Your Baby Search

You believe you are capable of trying to search for a baby; you have looked within yourself and believe you have the patience, the openness, the boldness, and the creativity to find your own baby. You also believe that there is a distinct possibility you can find one. Now you need an understanding of how to approach your undertaking.

• Limits on Your Search

Everyone has limits on what he or she will accept. Before you begin to search for a baby in a random manner, it is essential that you understand your own limits. If you definitely don't want a child from a Mexican background, don't approach Mexican people with your plight. If you would find it extremely uncomfortable to have the birthmother live with you prior to giving birth to the child you want to adopt, make certain this doesn't occur. If you would have difficulty meeting the biological parents, know this so that it does not become an issue; you can use an intermediary. Each limitation you put on yourself also limits the options open to you, but limits are important in making the situation comfortable for you.

One area of limitation is in the amount of contact you are willing to have with the birthparents. Some people would feel comfortable in having knowledge about the biological parents, but would want no contact. Other people would feel that it is extremely desirable to meet the biological parents.

Maura and Jon, who had previously adopted through their local adoption agency, were extremely open to contact with the biological parents. In fact, they felt it would be beneficial for all of them, including their four-year-old adopted son, to become more personally involved with the biological mother and/or father of the second child they were seeking to adopt. They met Stacey, who at nineteen was getting ready to have her second abortion. Maura and Jon really liked Stacey and expressed their desire to raise her child if she would let them adopt it. Stacey was flattered at their interest in her. She also liked many things about both of them. However, she was confused about what to do because her boyfriend, the father of her unborn child, wanted her to have an abortion. Maura and Jon told her she could come to live with them until the baby was born. They told her how good it would be for their adopted son to see a mother who really loved her baby and who would place it for adoption. Stacey wavered and said she would love to do that if only she could convince her boyfriend. She tried, but to no avail. He stood firm and told her that he would never see her again if she placed his baby for adoption. Through tears for both Stacey and Maura, it was confirmed that Stacey would have an abortion. Maura and Jon both supported her decision. Soon thereafter, Stacey broke up with her boyfriend, but at the time of her decision he was too important in her life for her to ignore his wishes. Maura and Jon continue to have contact with Stacey because they shared a very important time in each other's lives.

A similar issue confronted a couple who became closely involved with a birthmother they had met. Julia and Howard were a friendly and caring couple; they loved people. In some ways, the hardship they had experienced in trying to have a child had brought them very close with the people they knew. When they met Dawne, this warmth showed immediately. Dawne felt they would make great parents. The four months Dawne had with Julia and Howard before the baby arrived brought them exceedingly close. As the delivery neared, Julia realized she could not go through with this adoption. She had become so close to Dawne that she could not risk losing her friendship with Dawne by taking her baby. Howard agreed. The three of them found another home for Dawne's baby. Julia and Howard found another baby to adopt, but this time they limited their contact with the birthmother so the contacts could cease after the baby arrived. Dawne has loved remaining in their lives as a friend as Julia and Howard enjoy their new baby boy.

Some people would limit their baby search to areas where they could be sure of no legal difficulties. Others are more willing to take legal risks. Carly and Jake did not feel threatened by the possibility of legal difficulties when they had a chance to adopt. Carly and Jake were at the older limits of the age group that the adoption agencies were willing to accept. Coupled with this was the fact that this was a second marriage for each of them, and Carly had a strong desire to continue working. They knew they had little chance with the adoption agencies long before they were given their rejection. They were disillusioned because they sincerely felt they would be good parents, but they were undeterred in their search. They sought help, advice, ideas, and directions from anyone who might possibly help them. One of their contacts heard about a twenty-three-year-old pregnant woman who wanted to place her baby for adoption privately. Carly and Jake decided to approach her, despite the fact that she might change her mind. Additionally, the father of the child was considering fighting for custody of the child in court. Carly and Jake decided they had to take some major risks if they were to achieve their desired goal. They knew they could lose any financial support given to her during the pregnancy; but at the very least they would have served society by helping this woman with her prenatal and birth expenses. Their open manner was of prime importance to the biological mother, who strongly disliked secrecy and red tape. She occasionally tested their support by making additional demands, but they were unwavering in helping her in every legal way possible. Their limit to getting a child was that it had to be legal; they would not waver on this issue. They were willing to face the father of the child in court and to take the risk that he might even win. Ultimately, the biological father did not go to court. Carly and Jake stayed in touch through an intermediary trusted by the biological mother. They found out many positive things about the way the mother cared about the child she was carrying. The adoptive parents felt they would be able to discuss the birthmother with their daughter in the coming years because she had loved and planned for her child, even though she could not keep her. This was what the birthmother wanted. She won, they won, and the little girl won.

One of the limitations that couples have at times is the possible drug involvement of the biological mother. People seeking babies at times become alarmed over the potential drug use of the biological parents and how it will affect their newly adopted child. If you want a child whose mother has never experimented with drugs, you might find yourself very limited in today's drug-oriented culture. On the other end of the spectrum are mothers who are addicted to heavy drugs like heroin. You probably would know about heavy addiction before the child was born. In fact, the greater the contact between you and the biological parents, the more likely you are to know this kind of personal information. You are certainly in as good a position to find out this information as any social worker with an adoption agency. I think prospective adoptive parents should seek information about drug use, alcohol use, and tobacco use, all of which may be harmful to the child. Would you eliminate a child from consideration if you discovered that the mother used marijuana regularly? Would you not accept that child if the mother smoked a pack of cigarettes a day while she was pregnant? Two packs a day? I don't know what your limits are, but you need to know what they are. You will also find that they change with time and disappointment.

Intellectual limitations are another factor. If you feel it is extremely important for you to have a child who is likely to be bright, how can you go about searching for that kind of child? As with all limitations in what you can accept, this also limits the potential for finding a child. On the other hand, if you feel strongly about it, you should limit where you search for a child. Maybe you should seek a child from a woman in college. You should also make it clear to those you contact that this is an important criterion to you. This doesn't assure you that the child will be bright—neither does having your own biological child. This merely increases the chances of your child being bright.

Some kinds of situations that might produce a child for you are predictable and you know they will be acceptable. These are easy to define ahead of time. You won't be able to anticipate every situation, but if you are comfortable about your ability to solve problems as they arise, unexpected situations won't become major problems for you.

Mary Lou and Greg were delighted when they heard from a physician about a young girl who just had a baby and would be willing to give it to them. They tried to keep calm by talking about their "maybe baby" in case the whole deal fell through. They did not want their other adopted child to be too disappointed if the plans did not work out. They entered the situation very confident of their ability to handle an independent adoption. The biological mother wanted to nurse the child for a couple of weeks before she gave it to them. This was nice for the baby, but caused fear for Mary Lou and Greg, who worried that the bonding might cause the birthmother to change her mind. Then the biological mother became ill and she asked them to come early to get the baby. Naturally, Mary Lou and Greg were more than willing. They drove 150 miles in a state of joy. But as the end of the journey approached, the pending meeting with the biological mother began to concern them. What if she didn't like them? What if she changed her mind? What would they talk about? They finally reasoned that the only way to solve their fears was to confront them. The biological mother had something they wanted, a baby, so she was in a position to call the shots. They decided they would just have to take whatever came.

After meeting the biological mother and their "maybe baby," they wanted to grab the baby and run. Instead, they handled the situation with what appeared to be relative ease. When they heard that the mother had named their baby boy they said nothing, because that could be dealt with later. When the biological mother offered them numerous items for their new son, they graciously accepted them even though they wanted nothing but their child—everything else seemed to make their son more hers. They handled each unanticipated event smoothly, much more smoothly than they thought they could. They did not anticipate a visit from the maternal grandparents the second week they had their son at home, but they weathered that potential crisis also. They found the limits that they had set were helpful in many ways, but many issues they were forced to confront were unexpected.

Later, as Mary Lou and Greg reflected on their son's adoption, they said that some aspects made it better than their previous agency adoption. The secrecy was gone. Everyone felt good about everyone else. The weaning process for the biological mother seemed healthier for her than immediately having to give up the baby to an agency worker. The magnitude of the emotional response from the grandparents seemed lessened by their chance to meet the people who would be raising their first grandchild. The biological mother knew what kind of a home Mary Lou and Greg had, knew the town her child would be raised in, knew about the sister her child now had, and she could feel comforted in her knowledge.

People ask Mary Lou and Greg how they would feel if the birthmother stopped their son some day after school and told him she was his birthmother. They answer that their son would be curious but it would not be any big issue, because he already knows about her and he knows his "real" mom and dad are the ones who adopted him. They are secure in their relationship with him. They don't feel they own him; they just have had a fantastic opportunity to borrow him and raise him. They feel very fortunate. They are.

One of the primary advantages of having significant interaction with the biological parents is that you grow to know them. One mother of two adopted children, one a private adoption and the other an agency adoption, discussed what this interaction had meant to her. She said she knows more specific details about her first child, a son adopted through the adoption agency; she knows all sorts of medical and historical information about his family. But she knows far more about the parents of her daughter who was adopted privately because she met them. This adoptive mother says, "I can tell my first child facts about his parents, but for my second child, I can really tell her about her parents because I know them as people and I can pass on feelings about them to her. I wish I could give this same advantage to my son."

Most of us know we can significantly improve the health and maybe even mental state of our child if we can control certain pre-natal factors. Nutrition is one essential ingredient in the health of an unborn child. If you could choose the mother of your child, I am certain you would hope that she eats properly during her pregnancy. If, however, you have to choose between a child whose mother ate poorly during her pregnancy and not having a child, which would you choose? If you had to choose between a child whose mother did not receive any prenatal care and not having a child, which would you choose? If you must choose between a child whose mother was under great stress and duress during her pregnancy or not having a child, which would you choose? Your choices are limited. Compromise is essential. Compromise only as far as you are reasonably comfortable, but strict limitations, no matter how well placed, are limitations on your finding a child.

• *Establishing Priorities*
Establishing priorities in your search is essential. As you go down your priority list, you are likely to enlarge and expand the kinds of situations you are willing to experience to find a child.

People set priorities for different reasons. Priorities may be set by how likely a particular area of search is to yield a child, or it may be related to how likely you are to get a specific kind of child. Again, you have to decide what you want, which then determines how and where you start to look.

In setting priorities, you set up what it is you most want if you could choose. Then you work down the list until you are not comfortable with any of the choices left.

One of the areas discussed later in this and the following chapter is kinds of places to search for children. In order to begin your search, you need to determine which of these suggestions are the best ones for you. You can begin, once priorities are established.

• *Presenting Yourself*

Now you know what you are looking for, how far you will go, and what you would most like in a child. The next step is to prepare something to leave with each of the contacts you make: an information sheet about yourselves.

Resumés have been proven effective in employment searches. There is every reason to believe they would also be helpful in a search for a baby. A resumé or personal information sheet not only shows the people who are evaluating you how serious you are, but it also serves to remind the evaluators of who you are. The same logic applies if you want a baby. You want the people to remember who you are and to have some way to contact you if they hear of any potential children. Your contacts might also choose to pass your resumé along to others, which of course would enlarge your number of contacts.

Ideally, your resumé will have a picture of you on it. Let the picture truly represent you. The formal picture represents a formal person. The serious picture represents the serious person. Choose your picture carefully, keeping in mind how you want people to remember you as well as how you would best come across to the pregnant women to whom you are trying to appeal.

To leave a document like this with numbers of people obviously destroys your chances of remaining anonymous. On your information sheet you should have your name, address, and phone number. You should indicate your willingness to receive collect calls. You see how vulnerable you are becoming. Be prepared for some calls you may not like. You can, if you wish greater protection, leave the number of an intermediary. Lawyers, for a fee, are willing to do this, but this could turn off some good sources.

Your resumé should include something about your interests. Do you ski? Is traveling an important thing in your life? Do you play the piano? Do you like camping? What do you do for a living? How much education have you had? Do you own your home? Do you have a cat or dog or horse? What was your major in school? Where did you grow up? You won't want to mention everything I have listed, just the items that would portray you most advantageously. Again this argues for understanding the population group you are trying to convince to place a child with you—usually young people.

If you have relatives in Minnesota, make certain you mention those relatives when you send your resumé to Minnesota. When you send your resumé to Virginia, don't forget that you went to school in Virginia or when you were stationed there in the service. When you send your resumé to Boston, mention the fact that you are in the process of restoring an old Victorian home. You are trying to find the many ways the birthmother can identify with you and feel comfortable with you.

Worth reporting on your resumé is how long you have been searching for a child, how important this is to you, or why you can't become pregnant. You are trying just a bit to tug at the birthmother's heartstrings. You want to consider her emotional side and convince her that as a pregnant woman she would be doing a service for the world or for you by giving her child to you. Don't be maudlin, but don't be too aloof. People open their hearts to other down-to-earth people in our society.

Since the resumé is such a critical part of the process, I have included several examples of what I believe are effective resumés. (See Appendix A at the end of this book.) Your resumé is most effective if it accurately reflects who you are. Remember, this resumé is like a brief picture of you, so individualize your letter and make it you. You should be very pleased with your resumé.

Some people will ask that you send additional information, so be prepared to respond in lengthier form to someone who wants to know more about you. One example of the kind of letter that might be asked for by the birthmother is in Appendix B. Letters detailing some things about your life should be friendly but in far more detail than your original resumé. The resumé, however, is the first step.

With this resumé in hand, you are ready to begin making contacts. Emphasis so far has been on the fact that someone out there has something you want. Remember, though, that you too have something important. You have love and a home to offer to a child.

Contacting Everybody
Now your work begins, but this can also be fun. You are about to meet many new people in a way you are unlikely to have met people ever before. You are about to boldly ask a lot of people to help you with your problem.

Everybody you meet is a potential contact for a baby. Everywhere you go, you need to figure out a way to bring this subject into your conversation. Everytime you talk to someone, you should leave your resumé with them; just because they don't have an immediate suggestion for you doesn't mean they won't have one in a week or two. Everyone you talk to is a source of other contacts. Ask people for suggestions of others to contact.

While any of these random contacts might possibly result in the lead you need, there are some specific places that you are most likely to find a baby. These are not presented in any special order, rather, you should put them in the order that seems appropriate to you and your priorities and limitations. The places suggested are where you may have contact with young people, pregnant women, women in trouble, and women with financial problems. These are the places you are most likely to find a woman who will consider your proposal to adopt her child. Remember, the more contacts you make the better chance you have of finding the one you need. One attorney who is very successful in helping couples locate children suggests that couples send out 4,000 letters. While I have never met anyone who has sent out that many, I believe it is worthwhile to realize the magnitude of the work that is there for you.

• Physicians

Historically, physicians, especially obstetricians and gynecologists, have been sources of potential adoptable babies. This has significantly changed in recent years; rather than place their children for adoption, today's women tend to handle unwanted pregnancies by either aborting or keeping their babies.

The fact that there are fewer babies available through physician contacts should not eliminate them as sources in your search for a baby. You are looking for only one baby. Any potential source is worth exploring.

The best way to approach the physician is through a personal contact. Certainly if you know any physicians, tell them your story. Ask them to talk to their physician friends. Ask your friends to mention your adoption desires to their physicians. Basically, any way to make the contact personally increases its effectiveness for you. You probably can't contact every single physician in your city in a personal way. Contact as many as possible personally and just write to others. Go as far as you can.

If you live in a large metropolitan area in a progressive state, physicians may not be a very helpful source because many people are looking for infants to adopt.[1] However, physicians in more rural areas may not have had many contacts from people looking for babies to adopt. Remember, attitudes toward unplanned pregnancies and single mothers differ from rural areas of sparsely populated states to metropolitan areas.

With each of your contacts, be sure to leave your resumé. If your contacts mention that they might know of someone they could speak to about your case, leave them an extra copy or two. Ask them if they would suggest anyone else whom you might contact. Ask for their help.

• *Lawyers*

Lawyers are basically in the same category as physicians. Many of them used to know about adoptable babies. With the decreased supply of babies for adoption, they have found themselves much less involved in adoption placements. However, from time to time, a lawyer may still have a child for whom the biological parents say they want a lawyer to find a home. Some lawyers specialize in adoption; they would be better sources of babies than lawyers in general.

Again, the personal approach in making contacts with lawyers is the best way. Contact every lawyer you know. Try to make personal contacts with as many others as possible. You should be certain to contact any lawyers you hear about who have been involved in any adopted children placements. Some lawyers in larger cities specialize in adoption, and they will have more adoption contacts than the ordinary lawyer. As people have become more successful at finding children to adopt, more lawyers have begun to develop this as a specialty. Try to find the names of lawyers who work a lot with the groups with whom you are trying to make contact. Lawyers giving seminars on college campuses, lawyers serving in free clinics, lawyers who work with poorer people—these are the lawyers most likely to hear about a child who might be available.

Tell each of the lawyers you contact of your circumstances and ask them to help. Ask them to pass the word along so that they can make contacts for you also. Be sure to leave your information sheet with them.

Some lawyers will have suggestions about adoptions that sound more like black market transactions than legal adoption procedures. This is an area you will have to explore cautiously.

Besides being a potential source of contacts about babies to adopt, lawyers are always involved in adoption; at the point the adoptive parents go to court to finalize the adoption, they are represented by an attorney. The involvement at that level has nothing to do with contacting a lawyer to find a child.

As with any of the contacts mentioned, the more the better. Your information sheet, mailed to many of the local attorneys, may be all it takes to find the baby you want.

• Groups of Adoptive Parents

While it doesn't seem that adoptive parents would be a source of adoptable babies, they certainly can be.[2] People involved with adoption seem to remain involved. People who have gone through the agony of infertility studies and shared the excitement of getting a child through adoption seem to be eager to help others in the same situation.

Virtually all major metropolitan areas have "parents of adopted children" groups. These groups usually meet regularly as a social group to offer a support system for adoptive parents. You can get names of these groups from your local adoption agencies. At times these groups are specialized, like the Open Door Society, a group of parents of children from mixed racial backgrounds.

"Parents of adopted children" groups will be one of the most understanding of all the groups you might contact . . . they know the desire to have a child. They will be able to tell you of contacts they have found helpful. They also have an exceptionally large, informal network. Adoptive parents have a great deal of information on adoption.

Be sure to leave your resumé with strategic members of the group. Ask if you can check back with them from time to time. The groups change, so each meeting may be attended by a different group of people. At times the groups will have speakers on topics pertaining to adoption. These speakers are also potential contacts for you.

• Infertility Groups

Most infertility groups would not be a good source for children to adopt; they are, however, a good source of information. They are also a good source of support for people experiencing difficulty accepting their infertility.

You can locate infertility groups in your area in several ways. Sometimes the adoption agencies will know the names of people who are active in infertility groups. RESOLVE, Inc. (5 Water Street, Arlington, Massachusetts 02174) is a national group with local chapters throughout the United States. If you write them they will tell you of groups in your area. Large metropolitan areas are likely to have groups, like the Infertility Association of San Diego. You can even contact your local medical association and get the names of doctors working in the area of infertility or ask your own doctor if any groups of people experiencing infertility meet regularly in your area.

Not everyone in an infertility group is in competition with you to adopt a baby. Some people who experience infertility will choose to attempt to correct the problem or they will remain childless. They do not necessarily consider adoption. The primary reason for contacting an infertility group would be to enlarge your contacts. The more people who know of your desire, the greater your chances of finding a baby. Leave your resumé with some of the group members. Don't hesitate to call again to let them know how important this is to you.

• *Free Clinics*
One of the best available sources for potentially adoptable children is the free clinic. Free clinics are a relatively recent health care delivery service designed to appeal to groups of people who might not use the regular health services provided by private physicians. The free clinics are used especially by young or poor people—likely candidates to consider placing a child for adoption.

I use the term "free clinic" as a concept of health care; not all of the groups are called this. Included in this large group would be Planned Parenthood, Birth Control Institute, Birthright, women's clinics, and feminist clinics. Each town has a different list of groups that provide contraceptive information, pregnancy testing, pregnancy counseling, vasectomies, venereal disease testing, pelvic exams, Pap smears, alternative life-style counseling, general health care services, and counseling to young people, minority groups, and poor people.

You can find out the names of similar individual groups in your town by checking several sources. Young people know the names; they may be their source for the pill. Check local newspapers under the personal section—frequently you will find ads for free pregnancy tests or birth control information. A third source of information to identify these local clinic groups is the newspapers aimed toward young people. College newspapers or counterculture papers frequently have advertisements or articles about these groups.

All these groups are similar, and they are usually staffed by volunteers. Since they use volunteers, especially for the information and counseling services they provide, they have a significant turnover and numerous part-time staff members. Their survival depends on bringing in large numbers of people as volunteers. A lot of information is shared from one group to another. In some areas they have interagency council meetings to share what they are doing; this further increases their similarities.

Few of these agencies understand the difficulties encountered by the couple wishing to adopt a child. The volunteer workers have a tendency to view adoption as a bleak alternative to an unwanted pregnancy—a much more difficult and time-consuming path for a woman to follow than having an abortion. As a result, the volunteers seldom mention adoption to the woman who says she wants an abortion. The volunteer tends not to even think about adoption as an alternative. This is the attitude you need to change.

You need to talk personally to as many volunteers in each agency as possible. Tell them about your problem. Inform them about adoption. Let them know personally of someone who desperately wants a baby. Then the next time they give an unhappily pregnant woman her positive pregnancy test results, they can discuss with the woman this wonderful couple they met the other day who has been searching everywhere trying to find a baby to adopt.

It will help to have the supervisors in these groups learn about adoption and about you. But to really make the potential contacts, you need to talk directly with the workers dealing with the pregnant women.

Planned Parenthood is probably the best known of these types of groups. I have talked with many of their volunteers who never even thought about adoption as an alternative to an unwanted pregnancy. Yet they are providing pregnancy counseling daily for thousands of women with unwanted pregnancies.

As you finish talking with each worker, leave your resumé with him or her. The worker can help spread the word for you. Many of these volunteers are young people themselves, so they become "double contacts." Your sheet may be given out to the next pregnant woman they counsel, or it might be taken home to their roommate.

Of all of the untapped sources of finding a baby, I think groups like the free clinic provide the greatest potential for success. This is especially true if you are the kind of person who would appeal to young people or if your story is especially appealing. Check out the local groups in your area and spend some time there.

• Ministers, Priests, and Rabbis

Ministers, priests, rabbis, and other religious advisors are occasionally consulted by the unhappily pregnant woman to help her decide what is the best thing for her to do about her unwanted pregnancy. They can frequently be of help to you also. These contacts are most helpful if you have a strong religious background yourself, but consider them no matter what your religious affiliation. Your chances may be less if you are not a member of this certain faith, but not necessarily.

If you and your spouse are Catholic, you have a special appeal to other Catholics who oppose abortion; religious affiliation is especially important to emphasize in your resumé.[3] In addition to your personal emphasis, there are more pregnant women to whom you can appeal who want their children raised in Catholic homes.

Don't rule out other religious affiliations as possible sources. In one area of the south, a higher percentage of Baptist birthmothers relinquish children for adoption than any other religion.[4] Religious factors influence people's adoption decisions.

• High Schools

Many pregnant women are young. It is worth your time to contact even junior high schools, but pregnant girls are more likely to be found in high school.

The schools may or may not be aware of the numbers of their students who are pregnant. Certain staff members, those who relate well with young people, are most likely to know. Schools are under considerably greater restraint than free clinics in dealing with matters such as pregnancy. How openly pregnancy and other personal matters are handled greatly depends on the individual staff members of the school. I remember one school counselor who said he would never let a pregnant girl leave his office until she had called her parents and told them of her predicament. He probably did not confront this problem often because pregnant girls would learn this and never come to him. What you need to find out is to whom the young people in the specific school talk. One way to find out who these staff people are is by asking some of the students who the best teachers and counselors are. The school personnel they tell you about are excellent contacts.

Besides the people the students talk to when they are in trouble, other school staff members are sometimes in a position, by nature of their specific assignment, to know of pregnant girls. Physical education teachers are frequently the first ones to realize a young girl is pregnant. Make contact with the physical education department in as many schools as you can. The school nurse knows about most students who get sick, even with morning sickness. She is worth contacting. These are both sources found at any high school.

Another source worth checking is the high school pregnant minors program. These are special programs (usually held at only one school in each district) that are designed to keep the pregnant girl attending school rather than dropping out. Young girls who have elected to abort their pregnancies will not be in these programs; most of the young women in the programs are planning to keep their babies. Occasionally, a pregnant girl may be planning to place her child for adoption, or else a "keeper" may change her plans.

The teacher in this kind of program is usually specially selected for the ability to work with these young women. The school, recognizing that these young women are very prone to drop out of school, tries very hard to find teachers who relate well with youngsters in trouble. These are certainly teachers worth talking to about your problem.

At times teachers invite couples in to speak with their classes about trying to find a child to adopt. The teachers are usually careful to balance these presentations with talks by young women who keep their children. These presentations are made to help all the pregnant women in the class consider fully the alternatives. Some women will change their minds as they continue with a pregnancy. They may change their minds after they hear about someone who wants a baby; maybe they will change their minds after they hear about the problems of raising a child while still in high school. The fact that this important teacher knows about you, or the fact that this young pregnant woman heard you talk in her class, might result in your getting a child. You are trying to be in the right place at the right time.

Teachers of these programs vary as much as any other kind of teacher. You may find some who are unwilling to take your resumé or even talk with you. Don't let that discourage you from contacting another teacher of another pregnant minors program.

A source similar to pregnant minors programs is the continuation high schools that many school districts have. These are schools where students are sent who are not doing well in the regular high school. Usually each school district has one continuation school. The staffs of these schools are also selected to work with students who have problems and who, without special treatment, are likely to quit school. These teachers and other staff members are good people to contact. Since the classes in these schools are very small and frequently are run on a one-to-one basis, the teachers usually know the students very well. They not only know how the students are doing academically, but they also know a lot about the students' personal lives. The teachers often know about pregnancies. Students are likely to seek out teachers they know on a personal basis to discuss their problems and to seek advice.

You are telling each of your contacts in the schools not only about yourself, but also about the whole adoption picture. These school personnel who are sought out by pregnant students need to know about adoption if they are to talk knowledgeably about pregnancy alternatives. You are helping them to understand the current picture of adoption through a personal perspective.

Schools are a potentially great source of contacts for you if you get to the right people. Some members of the staff would be of no help to you. The teacher who hid his own niece for the last five months of her pregnancy is unlikely to be a good contact. The teacher who believes that school personnel shouldn't be involved in a student's personal life and that school is only a place to learn is unlikely to be a good contact.

One teacher I encountered while on a publicity tour for the first edition of this book was enraged at my suggestion that people contact schools; she said she "would never help a couple . . . it would interfere with her responsibility to the student and the parents at the school." I have no difficulty with people who view the situation in this manner. But don't be discouraged by them. They are simply not the people you need to be contacting at school.

The place to start to make contacts in the schools is not at the top. Don't contact the superintendent or the principal to ask permission to do something they would rather not know about. Contact individuals, not schools. Maybe they can give you the name of the next teacher you should talk with or maybe they know a minister or doctor to call. Remember, this is a personal matter between you and another individual. No one needs to approve or disapprove of your conversation. If you go to the superintendent for permission, you will be refused because this is not a matter in which the schools want to be involved. If the school finds out what you are doing, they may tell you to stop. Fine, stop, but hopefully at this point you will have contacted several people.

With each of your personal contacts at school, leave your resumé. They need something by which to remember you. It is not enough for them to remember your story . . . that's easy. If they have a potential child for you, you want them to have your name and phone number or some way to contact you. *Remember to ask everyone to keep your resumé.* A note on the sheet would help, like "Please don't throw me away."

• *Colleges*
Working with the staffs of higher education institutions is slightly easier than working with high school staffs. These people are no longer working with minors and are less restricted by parents and fear.

Work in the same way as you would with the high schools. Find the staff members who talk to students on a personal level. Being over seventeen does not preclude students from seeking help from their teachers.

Colleges also have counseling staffs. If the pregnant woman doesn't know where to go, she may seek help from the counseling staff. This, as always, varies with how good a job the specific counselor does . . . the word passes quickly on every campus.

One new contact possibility in colleges is the health services center. The high school has its nurse who is limited to providing a place for the sick student to rest. At the college level, some of the health services are extensive—some colleges administer pregnancy testing and counseling right on campus. Of course, these are valuable people to contact.

Tell each of your contacts your story, enlist their help, get new names for further contacts and leave your resumé. You are getting this down to a science. None of the individual contacts takes a long time to make, but making all your contacts can be very time-consuming. Don't give up . . . all you are looking for is one contact to succeed.

• *School-Age People*
While contacting school employees is a good way to find out about pregnant young women, so is contacting young people directly.

Young people tend to be very open. Subjects that adults may hesitate to talk about are casually discussed between young people who barely know each other. Young people can also be very open with adults, too.

Talk to any young people you know. Ask them if they know about anyone who is pregnant. Tell them about your problems finding a child to adopt. Enlist their help. You can find young people to talk to all around you. Besides the ones you know well, extend yourself and talk to those you don't know very well. Talk to the adolescents or the twenty-year-olds who live on your street. Think of which of your relatives have children who fall into the right age category. Talk to your friends' teenage baby-sitters.

Go to specific places where young people are likely to be. Go to some of the concerts that appeal to young people and try to talk with the people who sit next to you. Go to the ski movies or the surfing movies and be friendly with those around you. When you eat, go to the restaurants frequented by adolescents or young adults. The ice-skating rink, the billiard center, the video arcade, the youth-oriented dress shop, the used clothing shop are all potential sources of contacts.

Another potential source is female hitchhikers who are the right age. You have the advantage in this situation of talking on a one-to-one basis with a young woman who might give you a lead. (Of course, bear in mind that picking up *any* hitchhiker can pose a safety risk to you.) The open response might surprise you. When I was doing a study of teenagers' emotional response to their abortions, I regularly stopped to give young, female hitchhikers a ride, and asked them if they knew of anyone who had had an abortion. I told them about my study and how I wanted to interview teenagers who had obtained abortions and to talk to them about their responses to the procedure. Without hesitation, I got names. When I called these complete strangers and told them what I was doing and how I heard about them, every one of them was willing to be interviewed. I was really surprised. I found that I was more reluctant to ask them to help than they were to respond.

Again, be sure to leave your information sheet with each person. If they don't know anyone who is pregnant now, ask them to keep it in case they hear of someone later.

Those most likely to succeed in this approach are people who can readily talk with young people. If you feel this is impossible for you, try to find someone who would be willing to make some of the contacts for you. That isn't quite as effective as doing it yourself, but it is far more effective than not doing it at all.

One million young women between the ages of fifteen and nineteen get pregnant each year.[5] You are trying to get your information and your story to one of these women at the right time so she will consider adoption as an alternative to her unwanted pregnancy. One of these million babies is all you are trying to find.

• *Friends, Neighbors, Acquaintances, and Everyone*
Now, if you have exhausted the method of direct contact with young people, it is time to begin to check with friends, relatives, and acquaintances. Here you are probably aiming at the parents of pregnant girls more than the pregnant girl herself.

Many times the mother of a pregnant girl is very involved with her daughter and her pregnancy decision. To find out that a daughter is six months pregnant would be startling to most parents. At that point, the parents may inform their pregnant daughter that they will not raise her child for her. The daughter, who may have been counting on this arrangement, may now consider adoption.

You are trying to make contacts with parents or friends of a pregnant woman. This means that contacts with lots of people have the possibility of paying off. Talk to everyone. Your neighbors are contacts. They have relatives and friends to whom they will spread the word. People you meet at the coffee shop or at the bus stop are contacts. The clerk at the maternity shop where you are shopping with your friend is a contact. Your grocery clerk and the person bagging your groceries should all hear about your efforts. The lady with the little girl who sits next to you on the airplane—tell her how cute her daughter is and how much you are hoping to find a child. If nothing else, you will find people fascinated to hear how you are going about trying to find a baby, and they will also learn about the current state of adoption. Ideally contacts will also lead you to a child.

In Southwestern communities bordering Mexico, there is a large Mexican population that at times knows of available babies. For people wanting to adopt children with a Mexican background, this can be an excellent source. The fact that most Mexicans are likely to be Catholics who disapprove of abortion makes this group a likely place to hunt for a child to adopt. Mexican women may know of people who have chosen not to abort but who are financially unable to raise a child. You may be just the right solution for someone's pregnancy problem. To hear of the right people at the right time might work out to everyone's advantage.

Friends or strangers, it doesn't matter; you need to spread the word about your search. Leave your information sheet and your personal story with people. Any contact has the possibility of being the one you need. Since these contacts are all so varied, you have to modify your approach depending upon whom you are contacting. Perhaps it is clearer now why it is important to start with a knowledge of your own capabilities, limits, and priorities before you begin your search. Knowing where you are on a search gives you the basis to know whom to approach and how to approach them—it is your framework for looking everywhere.

Advertising

Advertising for a baby may seem like a radical approach to find a child, but is it really? You are trying to contact as many people as possible. The media is one method of doing this. Fifty years ago you hung a notice in a conspicuous place and everyone for miles around knew exactly what you were hunting for. Today it would be almost impossible to personally contact everybody in a radius of so many miles. As a result, newspapers, radio, and television seek to inform people. Had we not modernized our methods we would not be able to communicate effectively. All advertising is a means of communicating. You are trying to tell people in a specific area what you want, so you advertise.

If you want money for your business, one way to get it is to advertise. If you want a new partner to come into the business with you, you might find one by advertising. If you want a wife, you might find one by advertising, and if you want a baby, you might find one by advertising.

There are many forms of advertising you might use. You can type a card and put it on the bulletin board at a supermarket or laundromat; they will let you keep it there for a specific length of time. (I know a couple that found a baby through just such an ad at the laundromat.) You can take out an ad in the local newspaper or in a specialty advertising supplement that is mailed to every house in a certain area. You can have flyers printed and distribute them to sources you think might lead you to a child. You can advertise in magazines that have national distribution.

If you want to advertise for a baby, some states have specific laws about how it may be done. You should check out the laws in your state. Some states will allow written or typed advertisements that are personally placed as long as they are not in printed form; other states have no objections to the concept of advertising as long as you do not become involved in "buying" a child. Currently it is legal to advertise in about half of the states: Arizona, Arkansas, Colorado, Florida, Georgia, Hawaii, Iowa, Kansas, Louisiana, Maine, Maryland, Montana, Nebraska, New Hampshire, New Jersey, Oklahoma, Oregon, Pennsylvania, Rhode Island, South Carolina, Texas, Utah, Vermont, and Washington. At the same time, be aware that the laws pertaining to advertising for children are not always clear-cut, nor are they always enforced.

Two couples in one area of California elected to advertise for a child. Their methods were different and so were their results. Pat and Ray had two adopted children and were told by both of their local adoption agencies that they would not be accepted to adopt another child. Pat and Ray were both very open to having contact with the biological parent(s). Pat was a school counselor who had a lot of experience talking with young people, and she felt she would be at ease interviewing women who might be the birthmother of a child she could adopt. So they decided to advertise for their baby. They chose the local university as a place to put their ad because they reasoned that it could increase the chances of finding a child from bright parents. The university newspaper unhesitatingly accepted their ad. The couple placed their ad after a long vacation period when they felt more young women were likely to be pregnant. Their ad ran for only one week and they heard nothing. In the meantime, one of their other contacts paid off. They canceled their ad and never found out whether it would have gotten them a child. They still believe it eventually would have been successful.

Another couple, Heidi and Joe, had a different response. They too were turned down by both of the local adoption agencies. They also had circumstances they felt could appeal to young people, so they placed the following ad:

> PARALYZED VIETNAM VETERAN AND HIS WIFE REALLY
> WANT TO ADOPT A BABY. WOULD YOU CONSIDER
> HELPING US? CALL HEIDI OR JOE.
> PHONE NUMBER — — - — — —.

They chose an advertising supplement sent to all homes in a given area. Within the week they received a call about a baby from

Mexico. Within three months they had legally adopted a newborn baby boy. Right after they received their call about the Mexican baby, they received a second call. This call came from one of the supervisors who had turned them down when they applied at one of the local adoption agencies. She called to tell them that to advertise for a child was illegal and to query why they didn't apply for a child through legal channels by contacting an adoption agency. Heidi told her of their experience with the agencies. The supervisor told them that even if they had been rejected, they could not legally run printed ads for a child and so must stop. Heidi told her they would. Their ad, however, still got them their son.

Another couple in Florida recently published the story of their successful experience in advertising for and obtaining a baby. They pointed out the problems of crank calls they had to deal with and enduring the long days (not months or years) of waiting. They discussed their fears that it wouldn't work until the time they actually held their new baby. At that point, of course, the adoption agencies became involved in the legal proceedings, but the couple had their baby. All they then needed to do was to go through the formal adoption process. They took a chance because they felt they had no other choice.

Advertising is simply a way to get people who want a child together with someone who has a child they don't want or can't keep. Some people would feel comfortable advertising for a child and others wouldn't. Would you advertise? You should do what you feel is right for you. There is no one effective way to advertise for a baby; this is a new method that few people have used, so you must set up your own rules. You must be sure of yourself and your goal as you break new ground, because some people will be critical of your method.

Summary

Most people who want children would not as a first choice elect to go out and find their own child. Your first choice would undoubtedly be to simply become pregnant. Your second choice would probably be to go to an adoption agency and have them give you a child. But if neither of these choices is open to you, you need to find another choice that is open, and that choice is to find your own child to adopt. Despite the fact that finding your own child is probably your choice of last resort, there are some extremely positive benefits for you in adopting this way.

What a fantastic story to tell your child as he or she grows up! You could share with her how far you went to fulfill your tremendous desire for a child. You could share with him how much you gained from meeting and learning from others and from finding him. You would really have a special story to share.

Obviously there are risks involved in seeking a baby in this way. You run the same risks anyone has who is involved in a private independent adoption. You run the risks of being contacted by people who are upset with your method of adopting. You run the risk of not finding a child. You have to evaluate these risks versus the potential results. Not everyone should try this method. I don't know whether you should. I do believe that searching for your own child is a method seriously worth considering. It may be the only way you will get a child.

Along the way you will find people who say you can't do this. Maybe you can't. If that is the case, stop. If you go out looking for all the things you can't or shouldn't do, you will find your options limited. Don't let others set your limits, at least not initially. Go as far as you want and if someone says you shouldn't go that far, you may have to revise your plan. Your other option is to not go very far at all. You may avoid all possible criticism . . . but you may miss your chance to find a baby.

What | 4
to Do
When the
Telephone
Rings

SO NOW YOU HAVE DONE ALL THE THINGS YOU NEED TO DO TO HELP
you find a baby. Your resumé is widely distributed, you have an
attorney who agrees with your philosophy, you know how private
adoption works, and now you are waiting for the call. You still
have a few things to do to be totally prepared for what can happen
at any time now.

Before you get that call, you need to do some emotional preparation for what is coming. You need to do some reflecting on how
you would ideally like to guide a potential adoption to make it
work well for everyone involved. You also need to reflect on how
you will react if the process falters or fails along the way.

In any adoption, each of the required steps needs to be carefully
and realistically considered. In an agency adoption, you will be
guided through the steps. In a private adoption, you need to be in
charge. The payoff for this careful consideration is a successful
adoption, with some other significant additions to your life, such
as increased communication with your spouse, heightened self-
understanding, expansion of your limits, taking control of your life
in meaningful ways, and being involved in an emotional experience that will forever change your life.

Preparing for the Call

Some people say that they are ready for the call from anyone who says they have a baby for them. This is not always true.

Cecilia and Henry were really excited when they got a call from a birthmother who was responding to their letter to a gynecologist in the Midwest. They felt they were in complete agreement as they sought a baby to adopt. But Cecilia's view of how willing she was to have contact with the birthmother was not at all what Henry's view was. Henry wanted the birthmother to have adequate counseling and assistance, but he wanted minimum contact with her personally. Cecilia wanted to be involved in every way possible. She wanted to take the birthmother to the doctor, attend natural childbirth classes with her, shop for clothes with her, have her stay with them until the delivery, and be at the delivery. Henry and Cecilia had talked about adoption, but in general phrases: "for the good of all concerned," "want it to be a healthy adoption," "to be open," "contact is fine." It sounded fine, but they didn't actually communicate fully with each other. When the birthmother called, Cecilia and Henry really weren't ready.

To be fully prepared for the call, the specific issues about adopting need to be discussed in detail. Each partner has the chance, maybe the responsibility, to delve into some very personal values. Each partner needs to talk about feelings! These discussions—personal, deep, and often emotional—can result in a healthy, happier, and more intimate relationship for the partners. Since adoption can be a difficult process, it's nice that it can have positive benefits for the couple.

You each need to share how *you* would ideally program the adoption process. Then you need to understand and communicate how much you are willing to compromise your ideals. Your partner needs to be open to listening to how you feel so you both can discuss which points need compromise. Some areas are easier to give in to than others; the compromises are to stretch you, not break you. It's all right to have plans on which you won't compromise or to talk about how painful they would be for you. Perhaps just talking about the pain will lessen it and allow you to go further than you ever imagined.

Some areas will be quickly dealt with, and others may take hours of discussion. Some of the topics that should be explored are:

Who will be better at relating with the birthmother (husband or wife)?

What shall we ask her about herself? What shall we ask her about the father of the baby?

Would we be willing to meet her? Where would we meet her?

How frequently would we be comfortable having contact with her before and after the adoption?

Exactly what costs should we pay? What other costs would we be willing to pay? Does our lawyer agree?

What should we tell our friends and family about the birthmother? What questions will we answer? What questions will we not answer?

Could we accept her staying with us during the pregnancy? What problems would that pose for us and our relationship?

Where else could we have her stay while she is pregnant?

Would we want her to come home with us after the baby is born? Can we bond as easily with the baby if she is here? Will she feel that we took the baby and ran if we have her stay elsewhere?

What if she is only a few months along? Should we meet her someplace long before it's time for the baby to be born? Should we have her come to meet us or go to meet her?

How would we handle it if she changed her mind after the delivery? What about after a couple of weeks or after five or six months?

What if she needs counseling?

What if we get more than one reply?

If she is young, are we willing to meet other family members? What if the contact comes from her mother, not from her?

What if the baby has a problem? What if the baby has a major defect of some kind?

How much would we really like to know the birthmother? Would we rather not know about her?

What if someone approaches us about a child of a racial background different from ours? How do we find out if the racial background is different from ours if we are talking on the telephone?

How will we answer questions about religion that she may ask?

How difficult will it be for us to raise a child born to someone

*else? Should we have examined artificial insemination or other
means of becoming pregnant?*

*How important is the birthmother and birthfather's intelli-
gence? How can we measure that?*

*What are we going to tell our child about his or her birthpar-
ents? How open are we willing to be?*

*How much time and effort are we willing to put into this pro-
cess? Which of us will be doing the work? How will the other
support the effort?*

*Which of us wants a baby most? (Someone almost always wants
to have a baby more than the other one.) How will that affect
our adoption?*

How much can we afford for adoption?

Why are we adopting?

What if someone calls tomorrow? Are we ready?

Asking these questions won't cover every alternative that may occur, but it certainly is a good start on communicating with your
spouse and preparing for the call. Remember that listening is half
the process. Don't be panicked with your partner's response on any
area you choose to explore; the process is just that—an exploratory
process. You will discover your views changing and softening, and
somewhere at the end you will be closer to what is true for you
and your partner. In that way, the call you receive will not be as
likely to catch you mentally and emotionally unprepared.

Making Meaningful Contact

After having counseled many people planning to adopt, I have come
to the conclusion that the best advice I can give you before you
have contact with a birthmother is to be yourself. If you have presented yourself in the resumé as someone you are not, it is likely
to come out at this point. If you have not done the internal search
we have discussed, the birthmother will sense your indecisiveness
and perhaps think you are not interested in or prepared for her baby.
If you and your spouse do not hold the same views on what is
about to occur, your discord will probably show.

Ideally, through the readings you have done, you have an appreciation of the birthmother's plight. Certainly you have some understanding of where you are in this process. While keeping in mind

both sides of this adoption picture, be yourself as you make contact with the woman you hope will give you a child to raise.

Maria and Jim taught me the most about being oneself. Maria was happy but anxious about meeting the birthmother. She debated what to say, what to wear, and what to ask to make everything go well. She called me before the interview (which I would attend) to ask what she should wear. I told her whatever she felt comfortable wearing to meet a seventeen-year-old pregnant girl and her mother. She finally said she thought she would wear her "job interview" dress. I said that sounded fine. She asked if she could bring pictures of their house, their relatives, and their cats. I said fine, whatever she thought. (In my mind, I thought I wouldn't do that but if she wanted to, it would probably be all right.) Maria arrived on time and uptight. Jim was more laid back.

We all sat down to talk, the five of us. As Jayme, the birthmother, asked several questions about Jim and Maria, the tension decreased. We discovered that Jim's occupation was similar to what the birthfather was studying, and we laughed together about the coincidence. As the mood began to shift, Maria brought out her pictures to show Jayme and her mother. They seemed interested, but when Jayme got to the pictures of the cats she was impressed. Jayme loved cats also. Everyone felt more at ease. Then Jayme threw out a question that was a bombshell. She asked Maria and Jim how they would feel if the baby was born with a defect. Maria and Jim were really shocked. We all knew what the right answer was supposed to be. Then Maria told Jayme, "In all honesty, I have to tell you this is likely to be our only child. It would be really hard for us to have our only child defective, so I'm not sure what I would say." After her answer, it wasn't long before the meeting came to an end.

Maria and Jim left knowing their answer was not what Jayme wanted. I spoke alone with Jayme and her mother. They spoke positively about Maria and Jim and loved their warmth and openness. I asked Jayme about Maria's reply to her question about the child's being defective because I knew this was one of the prime questions Jayme wanted answered. She told me she liked their answer on this because it seemed genuine and honest, and she felt they would make great parents for her baby. Jayme told them herself that she wanted them to have her baby. She also indicated to them that, after the baby was born, she did not want to remain in contact with Maria and Jim and that she knew her baby would be in good hands. The baby is now a happy, healthy, and actively talking five-year-old boy. Pictures of cats and total honesty helped them get their son.

Prospective parents who have sent out their resumés frequently ask what they should do if the woman calls or a meeting is arranged. While I believe you should be yourself, I also think there are some guidelines on how to handle first contacts.

Be open and listen carefully. You want to hear the birthmother because she has information you need to have. As a general rule you want to ask questions of her that give you a chance to hear who she is. If she is terribly shy, you may have to do more of the talking to keep the situation from becoming awkward.

The questions you ask should encourage her to talk. For instance, you might say, "Can you tell us a bit about yourself?" or "What are you looking for in the people you want to adopt your baby?" Of course, there are going to be specific questions you want to ask, but if the conversation sounds like a third degree interrogation you won't seem like very caring people.

Leaving lots of loose ends after the initial contact is fine. If there are areas the birthmother asks about and you aren't certain how to answer, it is fine to say, "I'll have to think about that," or "Let me talk that over with my husband and get back to you on that issue." If she isn't certain about meeting you or how a meeting might work for her, leave that open also. The primary goal of the first contact is to learn something about each other and to like each other at this point.

Before ending the conversation or meeting, talk about the next step. The next step is determined by what has happened so far. If the birthmother seems to be in doubt, give her time, perhaps suggest some counseling, or acknowledge her hesitation and see if meeting again might help her to decide a direction. If she seems absolutely certain she wants to move ahead, you can talk about meeting a second time to set up the details or perhaps have her contact your attorney. Know what details need to be discussed at that second meeting.

No one can tell you how to handle the contact with the birthmother. I know that I can only heighten your anxiety by saying that this is probably the most important interview you will ever have. Be prepared for it. Find out who she is and how she might fit into your life. Be patient, warm, open, and try to listen rather than to talk too much. She is in charge whether she knows it or not, and you need to know what she wants, needs, and requires of you if she is going to choose you to be the parents of her child. Then it is up to you to see if her needs fit with your needs.

Setting Up the Arrangements

After the birthmother has agreed to give you her child, the process isn't finished. You have to continue to make the adoption work. The next step toward a successful adoption is to set up the details on how everything is to be handled. Again, the birthmother is the leader to a great extent. To the point of letting you know what she needs, she is in charge. However, when you decide how you will respond to her needs, you are in charge. Don't let her dictate something that is impossible for you to accept, but be willing to compromise.

How you approach one area of adoption may affect your plans in other areas. The situation confronting the Phillips was a good example. They had sufficient money to embark on a private adoption but not enough money for an expensive adoption. For them to help a birthmother with any living expenses, they would have to find a birthmother who either had significant medical insurance or who would be eligible for Medi-cal. When they heard about Alicia they were delighted. Alicia's mother was in the military service, and all of Alicia's medical expenses and most of her counseling expenses would be paid for by insurance. As a result, they were able to help pay for Alicia's living expenses and maternity clothes. They were also able to pay for a dieting program after the baby was born to help Alicia lose the significant weight she had gained during the pregnancy.

The Settlemeyers had a similar situation. They knew that Melinda was going to have her baby by cesarean. Since the costs involved in a birth by cesarean are significantly higher than in a normal delivery, the Settlemeyers felt they would be less able to help Melinda with other expenses. This was clear to Melinda from the very beginning. Because she liked the Settlemeyers and felt they would be a perfect home for her baby, she was willing to live with a good friend of theirs until the baby was born and then she would return to her home in another part of the country. They still felt counseling was a critical item, and they let the therapist who would work with her know ahead of time of their limited funds. It was decided that she would have four sessions with the therapist before the baby was born, one time at the hospital, and three sessions after the baby was placed for adoption. That was agreeable with Melinda, who felt the counseling was very helpful. Melinda and the Settlemeyers all knew that to make the adoption work best, they would have to compromise.

These examples illustrate how the factors to consider in adoptions are not always as separate as they seem. In most cases you consider the entire process to determine what you are going to do on each detail.

When you first make a contact with a birthmother, you need to be prepared for some ambiguity. Uncertainty and ambiguity surrounded you as you went through your infertility studies and then again as you attempted to find a birthmother. Similar feelings will continue until the adoption is legally completed. But they do end.

• Medical Care

You need to know how much prenatal care she has had. Many women have not seen a physician, so that needs to be taken care of first. You need to help her select a physician. If you will be taking her to the physician, then you might have a stronger view about whom she should select. If she will go alone or with someone else, that might influence the physician she would choose. Some birthmothers have already started prenatal care and want to continue with their physician. This is an important arrangement. Some physicians are more supportive of birthmothers than others, so your selection is important.

• Living Arrangements

Some birthmothers remain in their own homes until the delivery. If she lives in another state or is trying to keep her pregnancy a secret, she may need to move before she begins to show the pregnancy. What you do on this is based very much on how much contact you choose to have with each other. Some adoptive couples have elected to have the birthmother of their child live with them. Others would prefer to make arrangements to have her live with a friend. Still others provide an apartment for her until the baby arrives and for a brief time after the baby is born until she can resume her life in her own home. Here again, the arrangements cannot be totally decided ahead of time, but you can think of alternative plans before you know of the birthmother's specific needs.

• *Financial Arrangements*
The financial arrangements you make will be based on the individual situation you encounter. Some birthmothers are very specific about what expenses they expect to be paid by the prospective adoptive parents. Expenses may include medical costs, dental care, living costs, counseling, clothes, food, rent, or car payments while the birthmother is unable to work. All these could be legally covered in most states. Other birthmothers would possibly incur very few birth expenses. A birthmother may be qualified to go on welfare to cover medical costs, make do with very few clothes, and live with friends or relatives during the pregnancy. Sometimes it would be appropriate to have the expenses paid through your attorney, but at other times the birthmother may resent dealing with an intermediary. Listen to her and you will know what would be most comfortable for her. Once again, the expenses should be discussed ahead of time between you and your spouse, but you won't know what the birthmother expects until you speak with her about these details. You need to have thought this through.

• *Hire an Attorney*
If you have not already hired an attorney, you should when you have been selected by a birthmother. That doesn't mean he or she has to be involved in these specific arrangements other than on an advice-giving basis, but it is important to have someone ready to file the petition to adopt as soon as the baby is born. In many cases, the hospital will ask for a letter of intent from the attorney of the adopting couple, to be certain that someone will pay the bill. The attorney will also need to have information given to him or her about the birthmother and birthfather, any marriages for the adopting couple and for the birthmother, the name of the hospital, the name of the child as it appears on the birth certificate, the date of birth, the name of the attending physician, and names, addresses, and birth dates for each of the parties involved. In order to expedite the proceedings, you will want the attorney to have as much of that as possible before the birthmother even enters the hospital.

• *Counseling*
I believe counseling is an extremely important part of healthy independent adoptions. The birthmother should be able to find someone with whom she can speak about her hesitations and concerns. It is probably the greatest insurance policy you can have that she

will really know what she wants to do with her baby. If she is indecisive she may not know whether to keep the baby, perhaps have her mother raise it, or place it for adoption. It is important that the counseling be with someone who knows something about adoption (especially private adoptions) and is aware of the normal reactions a woman is likely to experience going through an adoption. Without knowledge of independent adoption, a counselor may be shocked at the way you are going about your adoption, in much the same way the general public has been. You may need to educate the counselor before you send the birthmother for counseling. Having someone the birthmother can talk with also minimizes any dependence that she may develop with you. Of all the areas most frequently criticized about independent adoption, the lack of counseling is the major one.

• *In the Hospital*
The birthmother's stay in the hospital also needs to be arranged. However, you may not need to discuss this until she is close to the delivery date. As you get to know her, you will have a better idea of how appropriate it will be for you to be involved with her when she is in the hospital. More and more adoptive parents are involved in the actual birth of their adopted children. This is the direct result of adoptions being more open.

Whether you are in the delivery room or not, the hospital will expect financial arrangements be made. You will also need to have a pediatrician examine the baby in the hospital. Another unexpected area confronted by some adopting parents is the issue of circumcision. You need to be cautious about this area because the birthmother must consent to any medical procedure. Don't neglect to involve her. Sometimes the birthmother will not want to have any contact with the baby in the hospital, so here again, accommodate her wishes to help make the process as easy as possible for her. If you are to be there for any of the feedings of the baby or to spend time with the baby while in the hospital, you need to make certain the hospital staff is aware of this. Many times the hospital staff needs to be educated about adoption alternatives, and your way of conducting this adoption may be new for them.

After the baby is born, the birthmother will be asked to fill out the birth certificate for the child. She may use the first and middle names you have picked out, or she may use whatever she chooses. Hopefully, you will have spent enough time with her that you will know ahead of time what she will do. It is helpful to know exactly what name she gives the baby on the birth certificate, since your attorney will ask for this information.

Arrangements for taking the baby home from the hospital also need to be made. Most hospitals will have her sign a release giving the hospital permission to have you take the baby home. This release also allows you to be responsible for the medical care of the baby. It is the only legal document you have as you leave with the baby. Few hospitals will even ask her to sign this release until she is ready to leave. Some hospitals will release the baby to you as soon as the child's condition is stable enough. Others will release the child only after the birthmother is ready to leave. Handle as many of the details as you can before the birthmother is admitted.

• *After the Hospital*
After the baby is born and everyone is ready to go home, it is important to have plans about where the birthmother is to go. Some adoptive parents bring her home with them. Others feel this is the time for them to bond with the baby and that they need this time alone with their child. The important factor is to not let the birthmother feel that she is being abandoned now that she has delivered the baby. Make certain you have made the arrangements and she is comfortable with them. Don't let this become a problem. The adoptive father usually should be the one who takes the birthmother to where she is going to stay. Call her frequently to make certain she is all right. If she has been in counseling, it will be important for her to continue at this point. It is in your best interests for the birthmother to be with people who care about her at this time. If she has to travel some distance to her home, help her with the arrangements. If she feels you don't care about her at this time, she will question your caring all along. She will already be feeling lonely now that the baby is gone; she will have even more difficulty if you, too, totally leave her.

• *Continuing Contact*
How much contact you will continue to have with the birthmother is as individual as each of the other areas we have considered (see Chapter 10). It will greatly depend on the amount of caring and trust that has developed between you. Until you go to court, she can call the shots to some extent, but it shouldn't be coercion that determines the contact, it should be the best inter-

ests of all involved. Some birthmothers will want to have no contact after the child is placed with you. Other birthmothers will want letters from time to time. Others may want to have some regular contact and meetings over the coming years. There is no one way to handle this. Once she resumes her life after the adoption, she may desire less or no contact regardless of how she felt before the baby was born. Find a solution that is acceptable to all of you and that might be renegotiated at another time.

• *Signing the Relinquishment*
The department of adoption in your specific state is the agency that obtains the consent from the birthmother for the adoption. You need to know ahead of time how this department operates in your state so that signing the relinquishment can be handled easily. If the birthmother is returning to another state, you need to determine how this will be handled for her. Some areas make the procedure very easy; others make this step an agonizing process. Know ahead of time how your area operates. You might also discover ways to simplify this process.

• *Birthfather's Involvement*
Some birthmothers will have the birthfather involved in selecting the adoptive parents with her. Some birthmothers feel very punitive toward the birthfather and do not want him to know of the pregnancy or adoption. Some birthmothers will still be working out their relationship with the birthfather and he may be involved occasionally.

The birthmother needs to decide for herself how she chooses to handle this situation. You may feel strongly that you want to meet him in order to decide if you want this baby. That's fine; however, she may also feel strongly that she doesn't want him involved in anything other than signing papers or denying paternity. You need to decide if you are willing to jeopardize this adoption if what she wants to do is not in accord with your wishes. It is also easy to not hear what she is saying about not wanting the birthfather involved in the process if you want it to go your way and have him involved. Listen to what she is saying or you may find yourself without this potential adoption.

The birthmother is the one to decide if she will list the birthfather on the birth certificate. It is important that she understand the legal implications of how she lists the birthfather, but it remains her decision. If there is any question about how this is to be handled, get her the legal advice she needs to make a good decision that will not cause the adoption to be held up in court.

• *Special Issues Involving American Indian Babies*
Some unique issues present themselves when either the birthmother or the birthfather is all or part American Indian. If the baby you are going to adopt is more than one-eighth Indian, the baby falls under the 1978 Indian Child Welfare Act. As a result, the consent of the tribal court is necessary for the child to be adopted.

While this usually is a formality, especially as the percentage of the Indian blood becomes less or if the ties to the reservation are remote, it does cause the adoption to be a more prolonged experience. Don't turn down the baby just because there is some Indian blood, but at the same time know that adoptions involving American Indian babies are more complex. Knowing ahead of time about these complications helps make them seem more manageable.

• *Help with Adoption*
The details in an adoption are important and it is in your interest that they be done correctly. I believe that the best way to handle the process is for you to be involved in each step along the way. The more you know about what needs to be done and do it, the more likely you are to understand how to avoid or solve any problems that develop. However, I certainly know many people who would make very good parents who feel overwhelmed by the number of steps that need to be considered. As a result of this need, more people are becoming involved in adoption. More lawyers and psychologists are specializing in adoption, as private adoption has become more frequent. Groups that provide counseling and live-in facilities are emerging to provide service to couples after the couple has found a birthmother—emerging at such a rate, in fact, that it is difficult to judge how helpful they are. It is important before you decide to use any services that you determine the costs, what services are provided, who provides the services, and the quality of the services provided. The more you turn this process over to someone else, the more cautious you need to be.

Remember that the adoption process is not over until you go to court. In some ways it is never over but after you go to court you know the legal process is complete. However, adoption contacts or questions or searches can go on for the next twenty or thirty years.

Conduct the entire process well, and you can be reasonably assured of its outcome.

Adoption is an interesting process filled with many unknowns and unexpected changes. You can never be sure exactly where the process is leading you. You know the goal is to find a baby, and the route that you take to find that baby should leave you feeling good about yourself. You need that feeling in order to be able to share this process with the child you will be raising. You don't want to feel that anyone is a victim in adoption. Adoption can and should be a healthy process for everyone involved. While you are looking for your child and making the arrangements for the adoption, you have a chance to contribute significantly to the adoption process by steering it in a healthy direction.

Putting it All Together

It might be helpful to explain how several people put all of the pieces together, to get an overview of what happens in a specific adoption. In this manner, you can put yourself in a situation before you actually answer the phone and need to set up all of the arrangements.

The need for adaptability was evident in the Ritters' adoption. They heard from an attorney about Penny, who was seven-and-a-half months pregnant. She had read their resumé and liked them. She wanted to meet them.

They met in the attorney's office and arrangements were made for them to have her baby. Penny had applied for welfare after arriving in the state. She was living with her sister, who was helping her until the baby arrived. Obviously the costs of this adoption would not be high. But Penny had been experiencing problems, including a traumatic breakup with her boyfriend, being kicked out of her home when her parents discovered she was pregnant, being uprooted from school in her senior year, and moving to a new state to have a baby. All agreed that since there had been so many changes recently in Penny's life, there was a need for some counseling. The Ritters agreed to pay for those costs. They also agreed that some of the counseling should involve some vocational help, since Penny was due to graduate from high school and had no idea what to do after that.

Penny's sister called the Ritters after Penny went to her new physician. Penny did not like him and was very upset. Now the Ritters were also upset. They knew it was important for Penny to feel comfortable with her physician. Since they had a very friendly and comfortable relationship with their own doctor, they decided to have Penny go to him rather than to have the child on welfare. They felt the health and well-being of their child was at stake as well as their concern for Penny.

Penny liked her counselor. The woman obviously knew a great deal about adoption and was able to discuss what was ahead for Penny. During the course of the sessions, the problem Penny was having with her weight was frequently discussed. After working with the counselor on dealing directly with the Ritters, Penny decided to ask the Ritters to help her go to a diet center after the baby was born to help her regain her shape. It wasn't easy for Penny to do this since she did not want to ever feel she was selling her baby. The Ritters felt this was a reasonable expense they might have incurred if they had given birth to the baby themselves and were willing to pay for this. Their attorney agreed.

Penny wanted her sister and the Ritters with her for the delivery. They all went to the Lamaze classes with Penny. This was really a family affair. Penny included them in visits to the doctor and at times, Mrs. Ritter went with Penny to help her buy maternity clothes. Penny never asked to go to the Ritters' home, and the Ritters felt that was up to her. The relationship was extremely adaptable based on whatever came up. The Ritters felt a trust in Penny and Penny in them.

The delivery went well. Penny referred to the baby as the Ritters' from the moment their baby boy was delivered. The experience amazed the staff at the hospital, who learned a great deal about how healthy adoptions can be.

Penny had originally decided not to see the baby after she went home from the hospital. Then, three weeks after the baby was born, she asked to see the baby. She had spoken with the Ritters several times on the phone before asking to see the baby, so it worried the Ritters. As they discussed this, they decided there was no reason to believe that Penny had changed her mind. Nothing she had said would indicate any change from before. In some ways, it seemed she wanted to put some closure on the adoption before she returned to her home state. She may have wanted the Ritters to see how much weight she had lost since the baby arrived. The meeting was set up for two weeks from then so that it would coincide with the end of her semester and just before she left for her home state.

They met in a neutral place where all could be at ease. But tension was evident, until Penny reassured them that even though the baby was darling, she was glad he was with them and that she wasn't a single mother. They were able to talk with her about their fears, and she told them there was nothing to worry about and that she was very pleased with how well he seemed to be doing. It amazed Penny how different he looked. It was almost like she really didn't feel he was her baby anymore. The meeting had proved to be very helpful for Penny. She was able to return home feeling good about what she had done and good about where her son was.

Another example illustrates the complexity of some of the situations a couple can get into. The direction the adoption may proceed may be difficult to determine when you first begin. Be prepared for the unexpected. Your adaptability will be important.

Mat and Glenda heard about several potential leads before they finally met Kim. Since none of their previous leads had worked out, they were much more accommodating than on the first contact. They were also concerned about being older and felt they didn't have a lot of time to waste.

An adoption counselor called them to say that she knew of a nine-month-old baby girl who might be available for adoption. Were they interested? "Absolutely" was their unhesitating reply. That was the kind of answer that was needed in a situation like this because things were going to happen rather quickly. The counselor told them she was going to set up an interview with them and the birthmother, Kim, and the sister of the birthmother. This was rather important since Kim was deaf.

The adoption counselor called them back in about thirty minutes to say that a meeting was planned for the next day at 11:00 A.M. That wasn't the best time for Mat and Glenda, but they made it possible. By then the counselor knew a little bit more about the potential adoption. The birthmother was twenty-three, unmarried, deaf from German measles, and in need of reimbursement for expenses she had incurred for this child, roughly calculated at $3,500. The baby girl, Marissa, seemed to be normal and there was no evidence of deafness. The father of the child was also deaf; the cause of his deafness was unclear and he was not available. With that little bit of information and with great anticipation, Mat and Glenda spent a sleepless night.

There were many unknowns for Mat and Glenda. Was this child going to be deaf? Would they be chosen? How would it be to have a child who was already nine months old? Where was the birthfather? How would they communicate with Kim? Why was she placing her for adoption now? Would she change her mind? Would the birthfather agree? How had she calculated the $3,500? When would that be paid to her? When could they get the baby if Kim would let them have her? They had a favorite baby girl's name—would they have to keep "Marissa" if they wanted to use their own name? How long would the interview take, since they had a family picnic at the same time? With these and many other questions, it was difficult to do anything except think about a baby that might be theirs.

Sunday arrived slowly. They were to meet with the counselor who would be at Kim's sister's house. They were nervous, anxious, excited, and scared. The counselor told them that Kim was a very pretty young woman who seemed quite bright. The living conditions at Kim's sister's house were marginal, and they should be prepared for a rather upset household. Kim's brother-in-law seemed like a very angry man who wanted very much to be in charge of the adoption proceedings. Glenda and Mat not only needed to win over Kim, but also her sister and her brother-in-law. Nothing seemed to indicate a problem with Marissa's hearing. She was not clean and in dirty clothes, but she was very cute.

The brother-in-law tried to dominate the discussion. The counselor kept trying to keep things centered on Kim and the couple; that helped a great deal. Many questions were asked and information was exchanged. Glenda and Mat explained that Mat owned his own computer business in a nearby town. He had majored in business administration in college, and they were doing very well financially. They owned their own home in a family-type neighborhood. They had ample room for a baby. They explained that Mat had been married before and had two boys from a previous marriage. Glenda and Mat had been married for six years. They brought a picture album showing their home and their relatives. Kim really liked being able to see some of their life-style. They indicated their willingness to talk about the money with Kim and to try to work out an agreement with her. Kim did quite well lip-reading, so she understood much of what was said. At times her sister would help by repeating what had been said and also by using sign language with Kim. Kim's sister offered them coffee, which they took but they really didn't want, given the lack of hygiene in the house; this certainly wasn't the time to be fussy. Time wore on but no one wanted anything left out.

As the discussion continued, the counselor saw that Kim was ready to give them the baby. The counselor asked to speak with Mat and Glenda for a few minutes outside. She told them she felt that if they wanted the baby they should strongly indicate it. Glenda said she felt funny taking the baby from her mother and just didn't know how to do it. She said she really wanted Marissa but was somewhat overwhelmed that it was happening so quickly. Mat said he thought they should act swiftly and see if Kim would let them have the baby immediately.

Inside the house, the counselor asked if Mat and Glenda were the kind of couple Kim was looking for, and Kim strongly indicated they were. She said she wanted her baby to go to college and to live in a regular house. She liked it that Glenda would be staying at home with Marissa. Kim said she couldn't be a good mother because many times she couldn't even tell when Marissa was crying. Her sister indicated that Kim had learned few domestic skills from their mother and that she was totally unprepared for motherhood. Kim and her sister had both decided this baby should be placed for adoption, even though they felt the baby's grandmother would not like it. They both seemed sure that it was better for the baby to be with a couple rather than with the grandmother.

Talk now began to focus on making the switch of Marissa to Glenda and Mat. Quickly the car was loaded with all of Marissa's clothes, food, and car seat. Phone numbers were exchanged, hugs were given, reassurances were spoken about the care Marissa would receive, and expressions of gratitude for this marvelous child were genuinely and generously given. Kim walked them to the car and kissed Marissa and did not shed a tear. The counselor encouraged Glenda and Mat to leave and told them she would talk with Kim, her sister, and her brother-in-law for a few more minutes. They left with their new baby daughter, twenty-four hours after hearing about her.

That same night, the counselor spoke with Glenda and Mat on the phone. They were somewhat shocked by the conduct of Kim's brother-in-law and the general home environment. They were very impressed, however, with Kim and Marissa. Although relieved to have left with Marissa, they were concerned that their anxiety had not subsided since the meeting. They took their new daughter to the family picnic after they left. They stopped at a local store and bought her some new clothes and some wash towels. After cleaning her up, they took her to meet her new relatives, who were rather amazed. The usual cautionary words were expressed by those who couldn't understand why anyone would get involved in something like this. However, Marissa was a charmer. Concerns faded as they watched her smile. By now Marissa was already known to everyone as Marissa, so the issue of what to name her became decided. (When things finally calmed down, they gave Marissa their favorite name as a middle name, but she continues to be known as Marissa.)

They spoke about the difficulties of having a nine-month-old baby as opposed to a newborn. The counselor encouraged them to spend time alone with Marissa and to know her better before they tried to share her with anyone else. They needed to become bonded with Marissa and make her their own. They needed to become a family.

The following week the counselor met with Kim at her home where she was living with a boyfriend. Kim's dislike for her brother-in-law came through as she told the counselor she wanted nothing more about the adoption to involve him or her sister; she still felt it was best that her mother not know about her placing Marissa.

Her boyfriend's parents, who were obviously very involved with this young couple, arrived during the meeting. Kim's ability to handle money had always been a problem, so they advised that the money be given out in monthly installments over a period of time to best help her. They discussed the problems Kim had with Marissa, and how the landlord had once called Child Protective Services since Kim was not responding to the baby's crying. Kim had been experiencing difficulties as a mother no matter how hard she tried. Kim was unprepared for having a baby and she knew it. She felt relieved in placing the baby with Mat and Glenda, and she felt good about it. She sent many things with the counselor to give to Mat and Glenda—Marissa's baby book, medical records, a favorite toy, some additional clothes, and a note for Marissa when she was older.

Two more appointments were arranged between the counselor and Kim, just to make sure she remained comfortable with the adoption. Mat and Glenda also had several appointments with the counselor; adjusting can be a problem when a new child has a strong personality and is quite mobile sometimes. Adjusting to an adoption that happens very quickly also creates problems for adopting couples; Mat and Glenda's adoption of Marissa had certainly gone quickly, but they were the kind of people who were willing to get the help they needed to make certain everything would go smoothly and positively.

Mat and Glenda's attorney filed the adoption papers for the routine adoption this seemed to be. The attorney was not happy with the financial arrangements, but felt they would be acceptable.

Everything seemed fine until eight weeks later, when the counselor got a call from an angry Mrs. Broderick—Kim's mother. She wanted some answers, and Kim had suggested her mother call the counselor. Glenda and Mat were worried about the effect the grandmother might have on Marissa's adoption.

The counselor met with Mrs. Broderick and Kim the following Wednesday. Mrs. Broderick was unwilling to go to the counselor's office for the meeting, or for the communication to occur between Kim and the counselor using the special telephone device for deaf people unless she could see the messages. It was obvious she was extremely angry with and untrusting of the counselor; she was set on being in charge of how this meeting would be handled.

Kim and the counselor went over the details of when she placed Marissa. The question Mrs. Broderick continued to come back to was why hadn't she been consulted. The role of Kim's brother-in-law seemed to take on greater complexity as the animosity between him and Mrs. Broderick became apparent. Mrs. Broderick asked many questions about Glenda and Mat. Kim explained who they were and why she felt good about placing Marissa with them. The fact that they were a "good Christian family" helped Mrs. Broderick feel more comfortable with Kim's choice. A note the counselor had asked Glenda and Mat to write for Mrs. Broderick also helped considerably. The more Mrs. Broderick talked with the counselor, the more it became clear that she, too, felt Kim was not a competent mother. Her biggest concern was losing contact with Marissa. The counselor spoke with her about the possibility of maintaining some contact with the adopting couple. That seemed attractive to Mrs. Broderick and significantly changed the direction of the meeting.

After a two-and-one-half-hour meeting, the counselor left. The meeting ended on a positive note. Mrs. Broderick wanted to meet with Kim, Glenda, Mat, and the counselor. She also wanted Marissa at the meeting, but the counselor said she felt that would be inappropriate because it might prevent the group from being able to concentrate on the issues that needed to be resolved. It was important in the relationship with Mrs. Broderick that the counselor took a strong stand against some of Mrs. Broderick's demands. Everything couldn't be on her terms and that needed to be demonstrated. Perhaps the counselor's show of strength coupled with compassion for each person's position in this adoption is why the meeting was successful.

The counselor informed Mat and Glenda of the meeting. They were willing to meet with her; they actually had little choice. They hadn't planned on having to sell themselves to Grandma as well as Kim, her sister, and brother-in-law, but if that was what was necessary, they were willing. The possibility of maintaining some ongoing contact between them and Mrs. Broderick was discussed. Glenda and Mat both indicated they felt they could handle that, as long as it wouldn't be weekly meetings with her and that there was no question of their parental rights.

If the one-night wait to meet Kim and Marissa had been long for Glenda and Mat, a two-night wait to meet Mrs. Broderick was agony. In the two months they had had Marissa, they had become extremely attached to her. She was a very loving child and responded quickly and warmly toward them. They decided how far they would be willing to go to try to make this adoption work. Any differences between them were solved by long talks. Glenda knew from speaking with the counselor that the primary burden would be hers for having the contact and making things go smoothly with Mrs. Broderick. They talked together about how Mat could help by being supportive of any stress this might put on her. They each knew they would be able to handle some contact and it might even have some advantages. However, they knew at some point they would be unwilling to compromise their entire life in order to make the adoption work. They understood their limits before they went to the meeting. That was critical.

The meeting began with considerable anxiety, as one might imagine. While everyone understood that Mrs. Broderick didn't have the legal power to stop the adoption, she did have the influence over Kim to have Kim stop it. Without this ever being said, everyone knew that was the issue.

Through the lengthy discussions Glenda and Mat had, they decided to present themselves just as they were. Whatever happened would happen. They brought pictures of their families and their home, letters of reference, and a friendly, apparently relaxed manner to the meeting. All of these paid off. Mrs. Broderick liked them. The questions she had about being able to maintain contact with Marissa were satisfactorily answered by Mat and Glenda. It helped that another meeting was planned where she could see Marissa.

While this was the most difficult part, other unforeseen hurdles remained. The first time Mrs. Broderick visited Glenda and Mat at their home was not easy. Nor was the first time Kim came to visit them. The birthday cards that came signed "Love, Grandma" weren't easy to explain to Glenda's mother who was also Grandma. But Glenda and Mat were open, shared their thoughts and concerns, loved each other, and were committed to making this work. They also strongly believed that what they were doing would ultimately be in everyone's best interest, so it was worthwhile to solve the problems now.

After they had Marissa for four months, Mrs. Broderick approached the counselor and indicated that she was uncomfortable with the strain she felt her contact generated with Glenda. She couldn't understand why Glenda wasn't comfortable with her reference to Kim as mother number 1 and Glenda as mother number 2. There was obviously a need to have a meeting between at least Glenda and Mrs. Broderick with the counselor present.

During that meeting, Glenda beautifully described her feelings about wanting to be a mother for such a long time. She went through her infertility history and the joy she felt when Kim handed her Marissa. She explained she couldn't be mother number 2 . . . she had to be mother number 1. Mrs. Broderick could be Grandma Broderick and everyone could handle that because we are all used to more than one grandmother in the family. But mother number 2 just would not do. Mrs. Broderick seemed to understand when it was discussed in this manner. She too had something to gain by solving this problem: She wanted to be able to have healthy contacts with Mat and Glenda; they needed to be able to be honest with her if these contacts were to continue. Everyone agreed on the new labels. Kim would be Kim; Glenda would be Mommy. Glenda assured Mrs. Broderick that contacts would be able to continue and appreciated her understanding of how important the mother issue was for her. Communication had been effective. The compromises had been made. The meeting was a success, the problem solved.

This is the way adoption works. You don't really know how all of the details work until you are actually into the process. You can make a lot of plans but nothing will take the place of being responsive to the needs of everyone involved.

Summary

One of the most exciting times in your life is when the phone rings to tell you that someone might know of a baby for you. Anything this important needs thorough planning, discussion, and understanding. Be ready for this exciting moment.

The adoption process will then have entered another phase. You have not yet arrived, but you are now ready to make the necessary arrangements, set up meetings, figure out financial and living arrangements, plan for counseling, and prepare for the delivery of your baby. This is a working stage, and the preparation is crucial if the arrangements are to go well for everyone involved.

During the process, considerable flexibility and adaptability are required to make adoption a success. The complexity of the issues cannot be shown by looking at each individual item that must be dealt with; the drama of adoption is how it unfolds. It is important to be prepared. There are many issues to be considered while you wait for the telephone to ring.

Problem Solving | 5

(and some problems that can't be solved)

ADOPTION, LIKE MOST EVERYTHING IN LIFE, DOES NOT COME WITH guarantees. You are not sure if you will find a child to adopt, if the birthmother will choose you, if the child will turn out the way you had hoped, if the child will want to find his or her birthparents, or if the child will love you the way you want. The unknowns in adoption are abundant. Looking directly at the unknowns perhaps can help you avoid some of the pitfalls that cause problems.

We all know stories of failed adoptions. These are the stories that are interesting to tell. Who wants to hear the stories of successful adoption? Our sense of drama is not touched with the everyday. But are the negative stories enough to cause us to reject adoption as a way of having a family? I don't think so.

Some adoptions may falter and others may fail. Some adoptions can be saved. Sometimes it is the birthmother who causes the problem; sometimes it is the adopting parents. It may even be just bad timing, slight changes in luck, a grandmother's intervention, the birthmother disliking your friend, or other small details over which you may have no control. But many times you will have the ability to control the course of the adoption by your behavior.

Problems arise in adoption sometimes inadvertently but sometimes purposefully. Compromises alone might solve the problem. Solutions may or may not be found. There are also problems that will remain unsolved and the only solution may be our acceptance of that fact. Problems, compromises, solutions, and acceptance may sound negative. Yet many of these can be handled if we approach adoption openly, honestly, carefully, and knowledgeably. This chapter is meant to be a realistic opportunity to see how you can avoid mistakes others have made.

Risks of Private Adoption

Yes, there are risks in private adoption, probably greater risks than in agency adoption. But how great are the risks? Are you willing to take the risks? How can you avoid the risks or at least minimize them? Are there red flags that someone considering adoption should look for?

After having worked in adoption for years, I find I am extremely reassured about how small the risks are in private adoption. According to my experience, about 12 percent of private adoptions get into some kind of trouble. Of that 12 percent, half of the problem cases are easily resolved, and could have been prevented by each party listening more carefully, being more responsive, and not becoming alarmed so easily. Of the remaining six percent, I believe half the problem adoptions can be solved with a lot of work. These would be adoptions that need some outside intervention such as therapeutic assistance, to aid in communication and assess ways of solving specific problems. The remaining three percent of troubled adoptions are probably unsalvagable. These are the adoptions that do not succeed; the birthmother or the adopting parents change their minds and the adoption is "aborted." To me, these statistics are reassuring, especially since most private adoptions occur with people who know little about the adopting process.

The other amazing thing about adoptions that get into trouble is that in most of the cases the clues—the warning signs—were there from the beginning. I have seldom seen an adoption fail that didn't have warning signs. However, many adoptions with warning signs do not fail.

No one can tell you whether or not you should take the risks of private adoption. It may be helpful for you to have someone else look at the situation with you to see how you can minimize the risks, even if you decide to pursue a risky situation. Consult an attorney who does a lot of work in adoptions; speak with a counselor who works in adoptions. The advice of someone who knows nothing about adoptions is not helpful. In fact, they are likely to tell you most situations are too risky because they don't know enough about adoption to understand that all adoptions necessitate a risk.

It is important to realize that if an adoption fails, it isn't the end; all is not lost. The pain and grief will be there because of the loss of something very important. You many need to get some help to put the loss in perspective and to make certain it doesn't interfere with your next attempt to adopt. But after you get through the part of the healing, just as with your infertility, you pick up the pieces and start out again. The amazing thing is that once you have experienced an adoption that for any reason has not been completed, people will go out of their way to try to help you. It is almost like you go to the top of the lists of those who are willing to help couples. If you are willing to risk again, you will surely find a baby.

Some risks are different between private and agency adoptions. For some people, the risks in private adoption will cause them to consider the use of adoption agencies whenever possible. However, many people will not be given a child by an adoption agency. The agency, seeking ways to eliminate excessive applicants, is forced to use arbitrary and unvalidated criteria to eliminate some of the people applying to adopt. Therefore, for many couples, no matter how great the risks of private adoption, it is their only potential avenue to a child.

Certainly the investigation of backgrounds is less thorough in a private adoption, whether it be the child's, the birthparents', or yours. In an agency, some attempt to match the child's background or the child's potential to that of the adoptive parents is made. Your opportunity to have the best child selected for you is not available in private adoption. If you hear of a child available privately, that is likely to be the child you will get. There is little selection.

The risk of identities being exchanged is significantly higher in private adoptions. You will probably know the birthmother's name and she, yours. If the birthmother seeks to regain her child, it is much easier for her if she knows who has the child.

The legal risks are significantly higher in a private adoption than in an agency adoption. In an agency adoption, most legal problems are handled by the agency and you won't even be aware of them.

The relinquishment by the birthmother is usually obtained before the child is placed in your home. This decreases the chance that the birthmother will change her mind, even though it delays early placement of an infant into the adoptive home. You also have to anticipate more legal steps in a private adoption. The adoption agency tells you each step you need to take. Your lawyer plays a much more important role in a private adoption: it is more important to have a knowledgeable, competent lawyer if you are adopting privately than if you are adopting through an adoption agency.

The potential risk of having an adoption declared null and void is higher in private adoption than in an agency adoption. This risk is very slight if the necessary legal procedures are followed. The primary reason that this occurs is if the consent-to-adopt forms are not properly signed by the birthparents. Hire a qualified lawyer and you should not have to worry. The biggest single risk in private adoption is that the birthmother will change her mind and ask for her child to be returned. (A similar risk exists in agencies, but it would be the adoption agency that asks for the return of the child.) In an agency adoption, the relinquishment of the child is done fairly early and then the child is in the custody of the adoption agency. In order for a birthmother to regain custody of the child she has relinquished to an adoption agency, she must go through the agency. The birthmother who changes her mind in a private adoption has merely to request the return of the child if she has not signed the relinquishment papers. As mentioned previously, some slight changes are occurring in cases where the birthmother changes her mind after significant bonding with the adoptive family has occurred and can be proven in court. If she has signed the relinquishment papers, it is more difficult for her to regain custody but still possible. Even if she has difficulty in regaining custody, the amount of identifying data she has about you could cause you great concern.

Does this mean the risks in private adoption are too great to take a chance? Definitely not! Most private adoptions, like agency adoptions, are successful and proceed without a problem.[1] As the number of private adoptions increases, undoubtedly more stories will be heard of problem adoptions. However, ways exist to minimize the risks of private adoptions. The important fact to remember is that the adoption is not over when you find a baby. You need to continue to work to make the adoption a success.

What if the Birthmother Changes Her Mind?

The biggest fear for most adoptive parents in private adoption is "What if the birthmother wants the baby back?" Certainly the possibility exists that the birthmother can change her mind sometime between the time she says she will give you the baby and when the adoption is final. While this does not happen often, it can be devastating when it happens. I believe you need to be realistic about the possibility and to know what you can do if you are ever faced with this. A birthmother's request for the return of the baby doesn't necessarily mean that she wants the baby back nor does it mean she will get the baby back.

While no time is a good time for you to have her change her mind, your alternatives for handling her change of heart depend on when and what the birthmother requests. Obviously the easiest time to have her change her mind, and the time you have the fewest alternatives, is before you actually have the baby and have begun to bond with the child. The longer you have the child, the more difficult it would be to have the birthmother change her mind. However, the longer you have the baby, the less likely she is to change her mind and the less likely she is to be able to get the child back. No matter how far you are in the adoption process, this possibility can be very threatening.

Some people question why anyone would even consider taking the risk of losing a baby to a birthmother who might change her mind. But for a couple who cannot have a child without adopting, isn't this small risk worthwhile in order to have a child? At the worst, couldn't you recover from such a loss to adopt another child? Before you actually decide on private adoption, I think it is important to know this risk and how you can have some control.

The greatest risk of the birthmother changing her mind occurs at the earliest stage in the adoption process. She is most likely to change her mind after she really begins to show her pregnancy and can feel the movement of the fetus; the baby she is carrying becomes more of a reality to her. A change of heart can also occur around the time of delivery; the pain and the joy of birth may cause the birthmother to bond with the child so that she is unwilling to proceed with the adoption. Doubts may also occur in the first month after the child's birth; the birthmother may be overwhelmed by loneliness and she may reconsider the adoption. Finally, potential problems may arise at the time the relinquishment papers are signed;

the finalization of the process, legalized and made irreversible, may cause her to reconsider.

Most adoptive couples understand that the birthmother can change her mind at any time before the adoption becomes final. No matter when the birthmother changes her mind, the pain for the adoptive parents may be as strong as when anyone loses a baby.

Birthmothers who change their minds at the time of the delivery are perhaps fewer in private adoption than in agency adoptions. Actually knowing the adoptive parent seems to decrease the possibility the birthmother will change her mind while she is in the hospital. The increased vulnerability of women at the time of birth probably also precludes birthmothers from changing their minds. Usually, when couples have established a meaningful relationship with the birthmother, their emotional support at this time is so essential to the birthmother that she is very unlikely to change her mind. Adoptive parents, however, are very fearful of this time; they have anticipated this moment so much that they sometimes imagine the birthmother is more likely to change her mind than is actually the case.

More crucial seems to be the first few weeks after the baby is born. Here, for the first time, the birthmother realizes how alone she is and how important the child has become now that she is separated from the child. She felt she could get past this period and now finds she is unable to do it. Therefore, she asks the adoptive couple to return the baby to her. At this point, the adoptive couple is on the weakest grounds to say no. They cannot argue that bonding has been so significant that there would be harm to the child. Legally they would have great difficulty preventing her from taking the baby back. The decision at this point is difficult. They wonder what is different in the birthmother's life that now she feels she can take the baby back and raise it. What happened to all her feelings about wanting this child to be raised in a two-parent home or with financial security or with a nonworking mother? All these areas should be discussed openly with the birthmother and certainly they can be if the proper kind of relationship has developed between the birthmother and the adoptive couple. Ultimately, if she continues to want her baby, she probably will be able to get the baby back.

Irene and Phil were confronted with this problem. Three weeks after Joy presented them with a darling baby boy, she called to say she couldn't go through with it. They were shattered. They had had complete confidence in her. They knew their options were limited. However, they asked if she would speak with a counselor about this before she made her final decision. Joy agreed. The counselor spoke first with Irene and Phil to try to learn exactly where they were on the issues. Of course, they were extremely upset. They also said that if Joy were going to change her mind, they wanted to know now so that they would not have to go through the possibility of this happening a second time. They would most want to keep the baby, but they did not want to live in fear for the next six months because Joy really wasn't sure of what she was doing. They were able to express their anger at Joy for letting them down, but they also felt she needed to do what she felt was right.

The counselor then spoke with Joy. Joy was adamant that she wanted the baby back. Her mother had recently reentered the picture and would now be available to care for the baby while Joy worked. Before, Joy had no one to care for the child and her only option had been to go on welfare. The counselor explained that no one was trying to prevent her from taking the baby back but that Irene and Phil had the right to know why she had changed her mind and to know that the baby would be all right since, at this point, they too had an investment in this baby. They had been involved with Joy and the baby for the last four months. Caring goes both ways. Joy felt that was reasonable so she was willing to discuss her changed feelings.

No one tried to change the birthmother's decision; the counselor merely wanted to make sure she had thoroughly considered the issues involved in taking the baby back and in raising the baby. The counselor also wanted to make sure she was not just reacting to the normal feelings of loss that accompany the birth of a child being placed for adoption; in that case, she might only need reassurance that these feelings would pass with time. Irene and Phil insisted that they would return the baby only to Joy. They said that the baby came from Joy and that they would now give the baby back only to Joy. Despite the pain she felt because she liked Irene and Phil, Joy made the arrangements to pick up the baby from them. It was difficult for everyone, but the actual exchange process lent an air of reality and finality. Irene and Phil could have done nothing to prevent this situation. They had done all the right things and it hadn't worked. Sometimes that happens. The miracle in this example was that Irene and Phil heard the next day of another woman who wanted to give them a baby.

In the very early stages of adoption, counseling with the birthmother may save a faltering adoption. However, if the birthmother is certain she wants the baby back after she has considered all of the possibilities, the adoptive couple has little alternative but to return the baby.

Remember, when a birthmother asks for the baby back, it is still possible she will change her mind. As I wrote this chapter, a couple called me about having lost the baby that had been placed with them for one week. Then the birthmother changed her mind and wanted the baby. Their immediate inclination was to be angry and to lash out at the ones who might be responsible. They were angry with the therapist who counseled the birthmother but who was not available to help when this crisis came up. My advice was for them to be cautious since the therapist might still help the birthmother reconsider her decision to take the child back, or she might at least be the only place the birthmother might talk about her doubts about what she had done. This was not the time for the hurt adopting couple to alienate the therapist. They were also angry with the birthmother. I suggested they write to her and express their love for the child and their understanding of the birthmother's desire to have the child back. At the same time they should express how much they would like to have her reconsider and place the child with them again. Often the birthmother is still undecided after taking back the baby, but her indecision may be resolved by the adoptive parents who get angry and terminate the relationship. The birthmother may have to experiment with keeping the child before she realizes she may not be able to handle it. If you have not lashed out at her she might still like you and consider you her best alternative if she can't handle the situation. This might not be a good way for you, but it might be the way the child is returned to you once she experiences the difficulties keeping the child may present to her. It is a long shot but it is worth trying. Many times it works.

Linda and Tom found out about being nice when the adoption looked as if it had failed. When the birthmother, Janice, wanted the baby, they were devastated. They tried to persuade her to change her mind, but nothing seemed to make a difference. They had her speak with a counselor who determined that it was a change in

Janice's circumstances that caused her to want the baby back and not unhappiness with anything they had done. She liked Linda and Tom and felt bad that she was disappointing them. She felt she just had to try to see if she could keep her baby.

Linda and Tom, working with the counselor, decided the best bet and in fact the only choice they had was to give the baby back. They decided they would do it calmly and without anger while trying to convey to Janice that they really wanted the baby. They spoke with Janice about how much the baby had meant to them and wished her the best. They were in no way punitive.

Two months went by before the counselor heard from Janice. She wasn't succeeding. Again she wanted Linda and Tom to have the baby. Would the counselor see if they would take the baby back? She said this time she was sure.

Tom and Linda were obviously shocked. Yes, they wanted the baby. It wasn't an easy decision to make. Fears of her changing her mind again and going through another loss were seriously considered. But this was the only way they were going to have the baby that they felt was truly theirs. They met with Janice and were reassured by her. Now it was her turn to wish them the best as she left and never saw them again.

Undoubtedly this passing back and forth of the baby was not in the baby's best interest. However, it probably had no greater detrimental effects on the child than the child being in foster homes waiting to be placed for adoption.

Even if this method fails you will have made the best attempt to make the situation work. Then it is time to move on. If the basis of good, healthy communication has been established between the husband and the wife, they will help each other pick up the pieces after a difficult event like this. While it seems like the end of the world at this point, it isn't. If you have been successful in finding a child before, there is no reason to believe you won't find one again. It is important to heal the wounds, determine what caused the problem, understand your part in the process, and then move ahead. Don't overreact to what has occurred, by saying you will never meet another birthmother or that you will never deal with a birthmother who wants to see the baby in the hospital. The reason she changed her mind may be totally unrelated to seeing the baby. Assess what happened and react accordingly. Overreacting causes you to cut off potential avenues of adoption for no real reason except that you have been hurt.

The most difficult time to have the birthmother ask for the child to be returned is after the child has been with you for several months. This is usually the period of time it may take before the birthmother is contacted to sign relinquishment papers. Unfortunately, some states delay this process for many months, sometimes for over six months. Rarely will a birthmother then reconsider and ask for the return of the child. But long delays in having her sign the relinquishment may allow problems to develop that otherwise might not have occurred.

Sheila and Nick Callahan had not heard from the birthmother of their son, Michael, in over four months. It was a real shock to hear from their attorney who had arranged the adoption that she was unhappy with the Callahans and did not want to proceed with the adoption. The attorney was equally upset since he had been involved in the process all along to make certain that nothing could upset the adoption. He had monitored each contact, arranged all meetings between them, resisted the birthmother's desire to visit them, and made sure that all calls came through him.

The Callahans were terribly confused because they felt they had done everything that the birthmother wanted. They decided to try to convince her to leave the child with them. They asked if I would speak with her and try to learn the problem. They felt it might help if she talked with a woman who understood adoption. I spoke with her and then with her and the attorney. She was hesitant to talk at first, but opened up as we shared things about birth, adoption, and raising adopted children. It seemed that she was upset because the Callahans had so little to do with her after they received the baby. In fact, she was insulted that they had never invited her to their home. As I listened to her views, it became apparent that the attorney had done just the opposite of what this particular birthmother had needed. The attorney had become a screening agent, but the birthmother wanted more contact.

The Callahans were amazed with the birthmother's concerns. They had no idea she wanted to have more contact, and they were not opposed to it as long as she was willing to sign the relinquishment papers. They set up a meeting for the next week at the Callahans' home. The birthmother did not like the name they had given the child. The birthmother was not Catholic and she didn't like her son having a "Catholic-sounding" name. Again, the Callahans were surprised, since she had said nothing when she learned what they were going to name him. They decided that adding another name that sounded more like the nationality of the birth-mother was the solution; it would make the adoption easier for the birthmother and was a small compromise to make. The birth-mother felt much better after another meeting with the Callahans; she signed the relinquishment papers. The adoptive parents have no hesitation about meeting her in the future. No one wants these meetings to become regular monthly occurrences; they are meant to help both sides keep in touch and know the other people care.

This couple decided to find a way to communicate and compromise with the birthmother to try to save the adoption after the birthmother asked for the child back. Many times, intervention may discover the roots of the problem and a solution can be found. Those are the happy situations. Other adoptive couples may have to go even further.

As I mentioned earlier in the book, another milestone in the adoption process occurs when the adoptive couple has had the child long enough that bonding has occurred, and there is psychological evidence to prove the bonding has occurred. It could be detrimental to the child if this bonding were interrupted at this crucial stage in the child's development. This period is when the child is about five months of age or older. The court would also consider the child legally abandoned if no contact had occurred between the child and the birthmother or birthfather for six months.

Fran and Gerald found out about the legal grounds that can support adoptive parents. Gerald was a surgeon who had heard from a colleague about a child soon to be available for adoption. He and his wife, Fran, made the necessary contacts and arranged with the pregnant woman to have her give them her child two days after he was born. After the birth, they had no contact with the birth-mother for six and a half months. When she was finally contacted to sign the relinquishment papers, she and the father of the child had resumed their relationship and wanted the child.

Gerald and Fran were stunned. They'd felt the adoption was secure. They didn't know what to do. The agency said they had no choice but to comply with the wishes of the birthmother, since she had not signed the relinquishment papers. Gerald and Fran refused; they decided instead to fight the birthmother. They hired psychological experts who testified that the amount of bonding that had occurred would present significant problems to the child if he were now taken from the only home he had known. The attorney presented the case that the child, because of no contact with the birthmother for this length of time, had been legally abandoned. The birthparents appeared in court to fight the adoptive parents. The judge took time to point out the complexities of taking away the rights of birthparents but admonished them for the several times they had severed these rights and ruled against the birthparents who had changed their minds too frequently. Signing the relinquishment, while usually of critical importance, is not always the deciding factor. Bonding and abandonment are crucial legal issues after you have had the child for more than five or six months.

Another case illustrates the various means of dealing with the issues that surround the signing of relinquishment papers. Andrea and Arturo had tried for years to get pregnant. After they decided to adopt a child, the answer to their dreams came when Jody saw their ad on a bulletin board at the laundromat. She made contact with Andrea and Arturo, and they spent many hours talking together in the coming months as Jody prepared to have a baby. She genuinely loved the couple and they her. They were open with her, supportive when her boyfriend caused problems for her, helped her move, and were always willing to talk. They were wonderful to her and she felt good as she gave them a beautiful baby girl. She continued to have contact with them until she moved to another part of the state. Then the phone calls became less frequent.

After an unreasonable delay of nine months, the adoption agency met for the first time with Andrea and Arturo and the worker did *not* like them. The social worker found that Arturo could be extremely opinionated, and he openly disliked her intrusive questions. The worker objected to several things they were doing with the baby even though the baby was healthy, happy, and thriving. She ultimately submitted a negative report on their pending adoption. She asked another social worker who was to speak with Jody about the relinquishment to talk with her about this negative report.

Jody didn't know what to think when she heard the negative things the social worker had written. She couldn't understand why the adoption department was saying these people she liked so well were not good parents. She felt intimidated by the fact that these people, professionals in adoption, should know what they are doing, and she felt guilty because she wondered if she had made a mistake in placing her child with them.

Fortunately, Andrea and Arturo were not easily intimidated. They chose to make contact with Jody and explain how they felt about what was going on. They brought in a psychologist to counsel Jody and to give another opinion on the quality of their parenting. When the psychologist met with Jody, her confusion was obvious. She liked Andrea and Arturo, but she also wanted to be a good mother by choosing good adoptive parents for her daughter. The important deciding factor for Jody was the relationship that had been established between Andrea, Arturo, and Jody. Jody, after careful deliberation, decided to trust her judgment of Andrea and Arturo. She decided to sign the relinquishment papers.

Whether the social worker felt Andrea and Arturo were adequate parents or not, after nine months and a positive relationship between the birthmother and the adoptive parents, the only reasonable grounds for interrupting this adoption would have been potential harm to the child. Nowhere was there any evidence that the child was being harmed in any way. The adoption department was overruled and the adoption was finalized. To this day, Jody maintains regular contact with Andrea and Arturo and their daughter.

While there are no guarantees in adoption, there are certainly ways to minimize the risks of private adoption. Persuasion, compromise, and openness may change a birthmother's mind if she is considering asking for a child back. If that fails, legal remedies may save the adoption. How far you have to proceed in an adoption that is in jeopardy is an individual matter based on the facts and the merits of your case. Remember, most adoptions go very smoothly; your chances for an uncomplicated adoption are excellent.

What if the Adoptive Parents Change Their Minds?
In a few cases, the action of the adopting parents causes the adoption to fail. Some would argue that adoptions fail in this way because the adopting couple didn't really want to adopt. Who can be sure? There is also the possibility that adopting couples, in their zeal to adopt, overlook the ways they may sabotage the procedure. Examination of the actions of adoptive couples who might have caused adoptions to fail might prevent you from creating your own failure. No one sets out to make the adoption fail. There are not bad guys and good guys, but there are failures and disappointments.

A young couple, Kenneth and Coleen, had been working with a birthmother and a birthfather for three months. They were supporting them monthly since the birthmother was unable to work. There were several concerns they had about the birthmother and birthfather since it was very apparent that the birthmother really wanted to get married even though the birthfather did not. When Kenneth and Coleen heard about another baby that was just born, they decided they would take it. They told the birthparents they were no longer interested in their baby.

While this sounds callous, place yourself in the position of Kenneth and Coleen. They had a chance for an adoption that sounded very secure to them; the situation they were in with the young couple was very unsure. They felt they could not risk a good adoption for one that may or may not work out and one about which they had considerable doubts. They told the birthparents their reasons for choosing the other situation and let them know of an adoption counselor who would help them find another couple who would want to adopt the expected child.

The adoption counselor introduced them to Tom and Patty Gills. Tom and Patty were a very quiet, serious couple. They had a strong desire to adopt and had been interviewed by several potential birthmothers, but had never been chosen. Since they were an older couple, they knew that they had to move quickly and that they had fewer choices in adoption. The young couple chose the Gills to adopt their baby. The Gills knew of the other couple who had decided not to continue in this adoption because of the risks, but they decided they wanted to pursue this adoption anyhow. Tom and Patty were responsive to each of the demands of the birthparents. They did everything they could to make the situation positive. After supporting this young couple for three months, the birthmother decided to keep her baby just before she went into the hospital and right after she had received her support check from the Gills.

When the couple backed out of the adoption, it really didn't come as any great surprise to anyone. The counselor had expressed concern about the birthmother consistently during the process. Even knowing ahead of time that these birthparents might change their mind, Tom and Patty had decided they would take the risk. Patty was particularly distraught when she heard from the counselor that the couple had decided to marry and keep the baby. No comfort was enough to make the pain go away. The fact that they had known of the risks did not prevent the pain.

The counselor felt especially sorry for this couple and as soon as another potential birthmother came to her, she introduced the birthmother, Jane, to them. The initial meeting was strained because the pain from the previous situation lingered with both Patty and Tom. Even though it had been five months, they remained guarded. Jane chose them but only after waiting a long period of time; she felt they were very reserved, but she liked them better than anyone else she had met. In fact, Jane didn't finally decide to go ahead with the adoption until the day she went into the hospital. When Patty and Tom heard they could have Jane's baby, they had mixed feelings. All the pain of their first encounter came back. They needed to know for sure that Jane would not change her mind. They came to the hospital prepared to make certain that she would not change her mind.

They were very quiet when they came in to see the baby, who was with Jane and her sister. There were gifts that Jane had purchased for the baby and there were tears from Jane and her sister. Tom told Jane very firmly that she should be sure not to change her mind. He could have said that in a kind and loving way, but he didn't. He said it in a lecture tone that was not mistaken by Jane. She said nothing, as was her way of dealing with things, but it bothered her immensely. She thought of nothing except this lecture as she saw them walk away from the hospital. She felt she had given them the greatest gift she could give them and instead of them being forever grateful, they had chosen to give her a lecture.

All the way home from the hospital she was obsessed with what had occurred. Five hours later she couldn't take it; she went to their home and demanded the baby back. Patty and Tom were shocked. They decided they had no choice but to give the baby back. They reasoned incorrectly that she had never really intended to give them the baby in the first place or that her mother forced her to take the baby back. They were angry. They saw no fault on their side. Their anger made them blind to how they had ruined this adoption.

The sad part of this story is that Jane felt so traumatized that she felt unable to approach adoption again. She kept the baby. Even though she knew it would have been better to place the baby for adoption, she didn't have the strength to go through the process again. In many respects, adoption had failed her.

No one should blame Patty and Tom. They had been wounded before, and they were doing the best they could at this time. Adoptions are not always easy for the unwilling participants.

Sometimes adopting couples feel they have succeeded once they have made a contact with a birthmother. That is certainly not the case. In order for an adoption to succeed, the adopting couple has to continue to treat the birthmother with respect and dignity. At times this may conflict with the feelings of the adopting parents. It is very difficult for some adopting couples to understand how a birthmother could place her child for adoption. The unconscious anger of adoptive parents toward the birthmother exists to some extent in all adoptions. This may surface in how the adopting couple treats the birthmother.

The Mercers had contacted gynecologists throughout the South looking for a woman who might be interested in giving them a baby. Within a month after they had sent out their letters, they received a call from a woman who was given their letter by the receptionist at her physician's office after her pregnancy had been confirmed. The birthmother, Kirsten, felt they were the answer to her problems since she knew she could neither marry her boyfriend nor have an abortion. Being a single mother in Tennessee was more than she felt she was able to handle, so she responded to the letter.

The Mercers made arrangements for Kirsten to live with them when her pregnancy became noticeable. For the first week, things seemed not great, but OK. By the end of the second week, this bright, perceptive young woman could see major problems developing in her relationship with the Mercers. At first she tried to make the situation work because of the obligation she felt toward the Mercers. Yet, they seemed to resent her being there. She felt she was there only to deliver a baby and get out. As she grew more concerned with the situation, she decided that if she felt this way, she would never feel comfortable allowing her child to be raised by them.

Kirsten set out to find another couple. That, of course, wasn't difficult, and within a week she found another couple. She called the Mercers' lawyer and explained to him why she was not giving them her baby. He was supportive. He told her this was a decision she would live with her entire life and she needed to choose accordingly. After several lengthy phone calls, the new couple agreed to meet her the next day and see if they all liked each other. They immediately felt a rapport. They made Kirsten feel important and were concerned about her wishes as well as the baby she was carrying. They repaid the Mercers for the expenses incurred in bringing Kirsten to California, and Kirsten left with the new couple that afternoon.

The Mercers were furious. They tried to find her to get Kirsten to live up to her "obligation," but were unsuccessful. In fact, as their lawyer pointed out to them, there was no obligation. The Mercers learned that the way they treated Kirsten caused them to lose a baby that could have been theirs. They forgot the birth-mother and were only concerned about the child she would give them.

Phyllis and Rob learned a different lesson about the benefits of treating a birthmother with dignity and concern. Carolyn was a beautiful, intelligent woman who already had raised a family and who now found herself single and pregnant. She was a devout Catholic and would not consider abortion. But for her to raise an-other child at thirty-eight, after already raising four children, seemed out of the question. She was pleased when she met Phyllis and Rob; they seemed ideal, especially because they seemed eager to adopt the racially mixed child she was carrying. They were warm and open. They had lost their only child in an accident two years before and adoption was their only way to have more children. Car-olyn felt very close to them, and arrangements were made for them to adopt her baby. They grew exceptionally fond of each other as the weeks went by. Emotional support was freely given and a bond grew between them.

As the birth drew closer, however, Carolyn began to have second thoughts about placing the baby for adoption. She shared her grow-ing hesitation with them, and they encouraged her to do whatever she felt best. Finally she told them she couldn't go through with it; she could not give the baby up. Although she changed her mind, they continued to offer her their care and help. Rather than being angry and unforgiving, they continued to give her care and respect. They took her to the hospital when the baby was delivered, visited her after the baby was born, and continued to have contact.

Six months later, Carolyn, who served as a volunteer at a Cath-olic pregnancy counseling agency, heard about a single pregnant woman who needed a place to stay. Remembering her own time of need, Carolyn took this woman in and helped her when she had nowhere to go. When Carolyn realized the woman was seeking a couple to adopt her baby, she told her about Phyllis and Rob. They all met, and Phyllis and Rob adopted the baby that Carolyn helped them find. How could the birthmother help but like them after the glowing remarks that Carolyn had made about them? Although Carolyn didn't give Phyllis and Rob her baby, their genuine care for her helped them get a baby through her.

Another case where the adopting parents changed their minds

involved an absolutely ideal adoption. Shauna found out about a couple that wanted to adopt a baby from her family physician. She met the couple, liked them very much, and arranged to give them her baby. Shauna was about as close to an ideal birthmother that a couple could find. She was bright, beautiful, healthy, college educated, and absolutely sure she was doing the right thing. The plans moved ahead smoothly. They agreed to pay for weekly counseling sessions until the birth of the baby and for four sessions after the birth. Everyone wanted things to go smoothly.

Shauna entered labor early. That in itself didn't cause any significant problem, but something else did. The baby was born defective. The doctors were unable to explain what had caused the serious problem on the baby's right foot and the odd shape of the baby's head. Specialists were called in and the adopting couple waited for answers. When none came, the couple decided this was more than they had bargained for and decided, after considerable soul-searching, not to continue with the adoption. The birthmother was angry and felt hurt by the rejection.

Shauna's therapist assured her that another couple could be found who would want her baby. When she met Lillie and Frank, who were eager to have her baby, she saw the kind of love she felt her baby needed. Shauna decided to give them her baby.

Shauna's angry feelings about the first couple decreased. She was angry and puzzled about her judgment in selecting the first couple. How could she have misjudged them? she asked herself. Yet the decision facing that couple was felt by all who worked with the baby that day. Nurses argued among themselves as to what they would do under the same circumstances; some were appalled when the second couple came in and were willing to take this baby without being fully aware of the medical problems. A physician, after examining the baby and presenting the unknowns to the first couple, advised them to make a quick decision and never look back. Several other couples who really wanted a baby were asked if they wanted this baby and decided they did not. What was the right thing to do? Right or wrong is not clear in situations like these. No one can predict medical problems in an adoption like this, and they make decisions difficult when they arise.

Previously I discussed failing adoptions that were saved by counseling. This can also happen when the adopting parents are the ones who are changing their minds.

Catherine and Juan Lopez were excited about the adoption they had put together. Their Mexican background had been an asset as they searched for a birthmother whose child would be all or partly Mexican. Juan was very proud of his Mexican heritage and it was important for him to have a child with a similar background. Deciding to search in predominantly Mexican towns, they had a resumé printed in Spanish as well as English, and sent it to all of the Spanish surname physicians along the border. Ironically, they found a birthmother from a contact with their next door neighbor. The neighbor's housekeeper knew a woman named Maria who was considering adoption.

Catherine and Juan approached Maria about adopting her baby. Already the mother of a three-year-old, Maria was having great difficulties financially. Impressed that Juan was successful in his own business, Maria decided to give them her baby. She knew how difficult it was just taking care of her son; she was already unable to give him the things she felt he needed. Maria liked Catherine and Juan and knew they would be good parents for her baby.

Catherine and Juan provided a home for Maria and her son with Juan's aunt. This gave Maria a home where Spanish was spoken and added to her comfort. They also paid for her expenses and all of the medical bills. She told them she planned on saving some of this money in order to get herself a good start after the baby was born. Everyone seemed pleased with the arrangement.

Three weeks before the baby was due, Maria asked them for an additional $10,000. Catherine was angry, Juan was furious. They felt they had provided well for her and Juan was absolutely incensed that she would attempt to extort money from him. She explained that a friend had suggested that since they had so much more than she, that they might be willing to give her more money, but she was sorry it made Juan angry. He felt betrayed and told her to leave. Maria didn't know what to do.

Even in Juan's anger, he took the time to call their adoption counselor. He wanted the therapist to find another couple to take the baby. The counselor tried to discuss resolutions to the situation, but Juan said it was impossible. He indicated they would be leaving town temporarily and wanted Maria out before they returned. The counselor agreed to help.

After the counselor spoke with Maria, she felt the request for more money had been made out of Maria's ignorance and as a result of a friend's suggestion after reading an article about black market adoptions. Convinced that Maria would not change her mind and really wanting Catherine and Juan to have the baby, the counselor decided to intervene with Catherine.

It was apparent that Catherine did not want this adoption to fail. The counselor described her evaluation of the situation and how she thought they really ought to reconsider. Perhaps now that Maria knew the limits of their willingness to help, the problem would not recur. The counselor also felt that if they didn't take the baby, Maria would not even place the child, feeling she should be punished for her wickedness in asking for the money. Catherine asked the counselor to speak again with Juan. After conveying some of the same things to Juan, the counselor asked that all three talk together before making a final decision, even though the level of trust was certainly damaged between Maria and them.

Juan called the counselor back and said he would reconsider as long as Maria agreed to parameters he would set down. These included the length of time she would continue to stay with his aunt, specific guidelines about when and how much money she would be given for living expenses, her continued counseling with the therapist until after the birth of the child, and limiting the amount of contact she would have with his family. There was no question—Juan was not going to let his family get hurt a second time.

Maria readily agreed to the guidelines Juan had set forth. She felt extremely sorry for how much she had damaged the good relationship with Juan and Catherine. She and the counselor agreed the relationship could be improved in the two months while they had some contact. Maria needed to show Juan and Catherine that she could be trusted.

The relationship did improve. Perhaps it didn't get back to where it had been, but before Maria left she felt that Juan and Catherine liked her again. They helped her to get some new clothes and gave her money to fly to her home in Mexico after she signed the relinquishment papers. They continue to send things to her and her son. The birth of their beautiful daughter helped heal some of the hurt, and the signing of the relinquishment papers helped reestablish a feeling of trust. That adoption was repaired.

Adoption agreements are fragile contracts between people. Birthparents have their desires and so do adopting parents. Adoption is a process that touches all of us in many ways, not just in ways we think are related to adoption. Our strengths and weaknesses, our biases and hurts, our sense of vulnerability and judgment, our past and future—all become part of the adoption. Somehow, I feel we each get what we can handle in life.

Summary

In any adoption there are risks. But the risks are not unreasonable, considering the positive outcome of most adoptions. In order to minimize the risks, understand them. To avoid them, know them. Considering the potential problems allows you to have a dress rehearsal for your own contemplated adoption. This is not a time to pretend problems are not possible in order to protect yourself. Your greatest protection is knowledge.

The primary risk facing adoptive parents is that the birthmother may change her mind and ask for the child to be returned. This can be diminished by knowing your alternatives, listening carefully to what is being said, and carefully making the arrangements for the adoption.

Your role in the adoption process is critical. Do not view yourself as a passive participant in this process. You are not. Just as you can take control of your life and find a baby to adopt, you can also be the cause of that adoption falling apart. Pay careful attention to the role you play so that it is the role you want it to be.

Fully knowing your options minimizes your risks and increases your potential opportunities at every stage in adoption. Be knowledgeable, willing to compromise, open to new solutions, and mindful of your own participation in the process, and the chances are overwhelmingly in your favor for experiencing a healthy, happy adoption.

Faraway Babies | 6

AMERICANS HAVE ALWAYS BEEN A GROUP TO RALLY BEHIND COUN-
tries in need. Following World War II, Americans adopted many
European orphans. More recently, after the Vietnam War, plane-
loads of orphans were flown to the United States for adoption.
Adoption agencies were flooded with inquiries from people wanting to know how these children could be adopted. After earth-
quakes and other natural disasters, American couples seek ways to
bring orphans of these tragedies to this country for adoption.

The countries of the world respond differently to the generosity
of Americans. Some countries in need welcome the people who
want to provide homes for children who would otherwise be a burden. This view can change radically as the foreign country is better
able to provide for its homeless children. Then countries make
adoption by foreigners much more difficult and sometimes impossible. At times, the only children allowed to leave are handicapped
or sibling groups, while children who are easier to place are assim-
ilated into families within the foreign country.

Some countries view adoption of their children in the same way
that some black people view adoption of black children by white
families. They believe it undermines their pride and is, in effect,

an insult. Americans pursuing adoption in foreign countries need to be cautious in approaching foreigners to avoid insulting their national pride.

International Adoption: A Changing Scene

While the number of international adoptions is increasing, it still is only a small portion of the adoptions in this country. We hear of it more today because of the scarcity of available infants and because of the publicity generated from the Vietnam baby airlifts.

International adoptions are a constantly changing form of adoption. The rules and regulations continue to be changed by each of the countries involved.[1] Individual states within the United States also change their rules regarding adoption of foreign children. It is hard enough to keep up with the state laws let alone trying to keep current on the numerous countries from which one might want to adopt.

One country that well illustrates the international changes in adoption is Korea. Korea allowed a significant number of children to be adopted by Americans following the Korean conflict. These were frequently children whose birthmothers were Korean and whose birthfathers were American. These racially mixed children had great difficulty being accepted into the Korean society. The children were adopted privately by people who knew of their situation in Korea and wanted to provide homes for them. The adoption of Korean children was significantly altered by Henry Holt, who later founded Holt International Children's Services. His program significantly increased the number of children from Korea who were being placed in American homes. He publicized the plight of the children and began screening potential homes that wanted to take racially mixed children and children who had been orphaned by the war. As his group became more and more active in adoptions in this country, Korea went from allowing primarily private adoptions to adoptions involving agencies. Most of the Korean children now placed are entirely Korean and no longer racially mixed. International adoption has significantly changed over the years in this one country.

At times, countries will allow children to be adopted because they are unable to care for them. As "have-not" countries gain greater economic stability, they are better able to care for all their children and there are fewer to be adopted by foreigners. For this reason it is possible that large-scale international adoptions will eventually be a phenomenon of the past.

Changes are also occurring in the United States regarding international adoption. Up until 1978, international adoptions were frequently handled by the Department of Immigration. A private, cursory home study for those people who wanted to adopt a child from another country was often the result. A recent change in the law mandates that all international adoptions must include a home study by a state-designated agency. As a result, adoption agencies are usually taking over this function.

This change is good and it's bad. No one can fault a change based upon need. If unqualified families were adopting foreign children, extensive home studies would be indicated. However, there has been no indication that this was the case. There were criticisms of the Department of Immigration for its slowness in adoption proceedings and its lack of background for doing this type of work. If, however, the law was changed only to give additional power and control to the adoption agencies, I question the validity of the change.

Up until this law was passed, international adoptions were a viable alternative for obtaining a child if you were rejected by the adoption agencies. This new law puts prospective adoptive parents back with the adoption agencies who have already rejected them, and this means that one alternative way of getting children has been taken from them. Once again, people who cannot meet the "ideal" requirements arbitrarily established by the adoption agencies are driven out of the mainstream to seek their children elsewhere.

A Different Way for Different People

International adoptions historically have been an alternate means of adopting children. The rules and regulations, while hard to follow, have usually been fairly easy to meet. The flexibility of the couple seeking to adopt internationally was met with flexibility in the screening criteria.

The trend toward tightening this screening is evident and alarming. For the most part, agencies are looking for couples to meet the same criteria they use for screening any other couple who wishes to adopt. The only visible difference seems to be that many times the adoption agency will allow people to adopt internationally even if they already have more than two children. In general, adopting internationally follows many of the same philosophical requirements as adopting a "special needs" child. Obviously no one can fault careful screening to make certain that people will be good parents. Unfortunately, we just don't know how to do it . . . neither do the adoption agencies.

Because the institutional criteria are becoming more rigid, it is likely that an increasing number of people will seek to adopt internationally, but privately. There are two ways one can adopt internationally . . . through an agency or privately. At times, in both types of adoption, the help of an additional private agency with international contacts is used.

There are some private agencies and support groups, developed over the years, whose goal is to find people to adopt homeless children from foreign countries. They help people deal with the international complexities of the process. A few of the groups that specialize in this service are:

Holt International Children's Services
P.O. Box 2880
Eugene, Oregon 97402

OURS, Incorporated
3307 Highway 100 North
Suite 203
Minneapolis, Minnesota 55422

Latin America Parents Association
P.O. Box 72
Seaford, New York 11783

Friends for Children
445 South 68th Street
Boulder, Colorado 80303

F.A.C.E.
P.O. Box 28058
Northwood Station
Baltimore, Maryland 21239

Building Families Through Adoption
P.O. Box 550
7th and Chestnut
Dawson, Minnesota 56322

Open Arms
16429 NE 133rd Court
Redmond, Washington 98052

Covenant Children
P.O. Box 2344
Bismarck, North Dakota 58502

Bal Jagat Children's World
9311 Farralone Avenue
Chatsworth, California 91311

If you want to adopt privately, it is worth contacting these or new groups. As with many areas in adoption, these groups are regularly changing. It is difficult to know which groups will meet your needs or how reliable any specific group might be until you speak to people who have worked with them. Find out about the group you intend to work with before you give them money or sign up with them.

If you want to adopt internationally but through an adoption agency, the agency will tell you about these groups and will have you make contact with them at the same time you are working with the adoption agency. In order to work with these groups, you have to meet their criteria as well as those of the foreign country, your state, and the adoption agency if you are working with one. As you can imagine, it is a complex process.

The International Concerns Committee for Children (911 Cypress Drive, Boulder, Colorado 80303) publishes *The Report on Foreign Adoptions*, which discusses waiting periods and types of children available. Since this field changes rapidly, the nine updates a year you receive may be helpful.

Probably the best detailed source to the complexities are the step-by-step guides to international adoptions written by Jean Nelson-Erichsen and Heino Erichsen.[2] If you are seriously considering adoption from another country, it is well worth your while to acquire one of their books on the country you are most considering. You need to have a thorough understanding of the process both for an agency adoption of a child from a foreign country and for a private international adoption.

Another way to gather valuable information on international adoption is to read about others who have adopted internationally.[3] While each person's experience is different, learning how they handled the problems they had to confront can help you a great deal. Learning, too, about the cultural adjustments of the child will help you to minimize the problems the adopted child will have. Many of the books on transracial adoptions are also applicable to international adoptions.[4] Another excellent way to learn about international adoptions is to talk personally and at length with someone who has adopted from the country or source you are pursuing. You are trying to understand international adoption from a personal perspective to see where you fit.

International Adoption Through Adoption Agencies
Adopting a child from a foreign country with the help of an adoption agency is very similar to the regular agency adoption. Many of the criteria listed in Chapter 1, "The Adoption Agency Game," are applicable to couples wanting to adopt internationally. You should be aware of some differences in procedures, costs, criteria for selection, and types of children available. You also need to understand the difference between international adoptions involving an adoption agency and those that are privately or parent-initiated.

• Procedures for International Agency Adoptions
Adopting internationally isn't easy. Sometimes it's difficult even to know where to begin. If you are planning to go through an adoption agency, you first need to learn which agencies handle foreign adoptions. You can call any adoption agency in your community. It should be able to tell you who is administering all the foreign adoption homes studies. Then you make a call to find out how you begin.

Every agency will be different, of course. In general, however, in international agency-initiated adoptions, the contact with the foreign country is through the agency, not the people seeking to adopt. You are likely to have a group intake meeting, followed by a meeting between the agency worker and you and your spouse, then with each of you alone, ending with a meeting in your home. It is worthwhile to familiarize yourself with what the agency social worker is looking for in any adoption; therefore, carefully read over the "agency process" section in Chapter 1.

During each of the meetings you will have over the next several months, the social worker will be attempting to do two things: to make certain that you will be appropriate parents for a child from another country and to educate you about the adoption of a child from a foreign country. These steps complete the home study which is necessary for you to be accepted for any regular kind of international adoption.

Adopting internationally sounds very romantic. A beautiful foreign child arrives for you to save from his or her terrible fate. In reality, the children you receive are usually fearful, not grateful. Sometimes these children are not the beautiful children you have pictured in your mind but, at times, they are undernourished and unhealthy, and may possess defects that look worse than they had sounded on paper. The child you hope will love you doesn't even understand the language you speak. The social worker is trying to help you to be realistic about what your expectations are for this foreign adoption and what the potential problems are.

As the process continues, you will be encouraged to contact one of the international agencies supplying children to adoption agencies in this country. The adoption agency you are working with will tell you which agencies they have successfully worked with in the past and which agencies acquire children from which countries. Since you are going to be put on the waiting list of this international adoption agency as well as the waiting list for the adoption agency you are working with, you want to move ahead rapidly.

After you have met the criteria of both groups, you wait. In this interim, after you have been approved but have not yet received a child, some adoption agencies have monthly group meetings. This enables couples to meet others who are waiting or who have recently had children placed with them. These meetings can be a useful source of information. During this period, you are attempting to fulfill the state, federal, and immigration requirements before your application is officially accepted by a foreign-based adoption agency.

At some point, which is never as soon as you would like, the agency worker will tell you about a child who seems appropriate for you. Background information concerning the child will be given to you. You are likely to hear far less in this type of adoption than in an adoption that is with the United States. This is one of the reasons why couples are carefully screened for their flexibility.

After you have approved the child on the basis of the available information, the process can take many different turns. Some countries at this point insist that one or both of you go to the country to formally adopt the child. Other countries let an intermediary, usually a lawyer, act in your name. In other cases, the guardianship of the child is given to the adoption agency. The agency holds the guardianship during the probationary period and until the adoption is finalized in the United States.

After guardianship is established, the child must get a visa to enter this country legally. His or her status gives the child preferential treatment in this process. Even with this special status, all the steps take more time than you would like.

At last the child arrives. Undoubtedly, the child looks older than you thought because time has passed since the description of the child was made or the photograph was taken. It is hoped, at this point, that all the education the adoption agency has given you, the meetings with others who have adopted internationally, and any material you have read about international adoption will have prepared you to handle this new child. Yet nothing can completely prepare you . . . this is something only you can experience.

The procedures to adopt internationally are complex. This is a long process that no one but you seems anxious to hurry along. There are some very positive benefits to be gained in this period. The educational process is extremely valuable. The amount of red tape that the adoption agency is handling for you is significant. Ideally, too, you are using this period to make contacts with other people who have adopted internationally so that you will have resources to get help if any future problems or questions come up.

• *Criteria for Parenting International Children*
The adoption agencies are looking for specific personality characteristics in the parents they approve for international adoptions. Most of these criteria were discussed in detail in Chapter 1. Along with these traits, they want some additional characteristics. International adoptions usually fit into the category of "special needs" children (see Chapter 7). They are frequently, but not always, older children and many times they have special problems. The couples who can demonstrate a flexible and open approach are the most likely ones to be approved.

In screening parents adopting normal Caucasian children from this country, the agencies want a childless couple or a family with a maximum of only one child. In international adoptions, couples with parenting experience are considered some of the best candidates to handle the special problems of these children. In fact, adoption agencies believe the couples best suited for these children are couples whose lives revolve around their existing children. This fits in with the view that these international children are special needs children who will take a great deal of time and energy to raise properly. The optimistic view of most people adopting special needs children is another characteristic found in many of the people who successfully adopt children from foreign countries through adoption agencies.

Basically, then, you stand the best chance of passing the adoption agency screening if you know what they are looking for in the parents they choose to receive their children. Do not pretend to be something you are not, but if you do not present that which the adoption agencies believe is necessary, be prepared to look elsewhere.

• *The Costs of International Adoptions*

The costs of international adoptions vary. The home study alone, which is necessary if you are going to adopt privately from another country and find your own child, may be several thousand dollars. Agencies may charge a percentage of their regular fee for low income adoptive families. These costs may vary from state to state. Adopting internationally is not a bargain way to get a child.

• *One International Agency Adoption*

The Worth family is a good example of the kind of family that adopts internationally through an agency. The family consists of the parents, Doug and Janine, and their two children, Marni, eight, and Mike, seven. Adoption had never been an issue to them until they went to a program put on by their church one Sunday evening that discussed the plight of homeless children from different nations who needed to be adopted by American couples. This program, put on by a representative from the Holt Adoption Program, really impressed the Worth family. They felt they had ample love and money to provide for a child from another country, so they made contact with an agency in their state that took care of international adoptions.

They went to the group meeting of all the couples interested in finding out about international adoptions. Eight other couples showed up out of an expected fifteen. The woman who gave the presentation sounded extremely discouraging about adopting from another country . . . in fact, more discouraging than encouraging. She seemed to imply that any couple who proceeded in trying to get a child from another country should be prepared for the very worst. The Worths left the meeting surprised, because this wasn't quite what they had heard about international adoptions from the representative of the Holt Adoption Program.

The Worths discussed the matter thoroughly with each other and with their children. They decided to go ahead despite the presentation of the worker from the adoption agency. They regained their enthusiasm and called the agency to begin the next step.

They met with another worker who was only slightly more positive than the first worker. But by now they knew for sure that this was something they intended to pursue. The worker liked them very much. They personified just what the agency sought from the couples with whom they wanted to place children. They were loving, optimistic, and flexible. They had a stable marriage and sufficient income. They had many friends. Their religious background, while not an essential factor, was a plus. They were willing to take any child the adoption agency felt they could help. Their relatives supported the idea of an international adoption. Their neighborhood, which was primarily white, did have about a 25-percent mix of different races; it would be easy to accommodate a racially mixed child into this kind of situation. Their children were as eager about the pending adoption as Doug and Janine were. This was just about all any agency could ask for.

Because the Worths so ideally fit into the agency's criteria, it was easy for them to work together. The Worths felt everyone went out of their way to make the procedure simple for them, and it went exceptionally smoothly.

Eight months after they heard the man speak in the church, the Worth family heard about the Korean child who was to be theirs. He was six years old and an orphan. He had been crippled at birth and walked only with the aid of crutches. The orphanage where he lived believed this handicap might be correctable. In Korea, however, there was no chance for him to have this corrected. He spoke no English. Everything seemed fine to Doug and Janine and they wanted to proceed.

Two months later their new son arrived. They were delighted. The boy wasn't too sure. The first months weren't easy with him. He was quiet and seemed moody and unhappy. He didn't eat very much, but he did sneak food when he thought no one was watching him. He slowly began to open up to them, but it wasn't instant family or instant love.

Within three months he was an active playmate for Marni and Mike, who thought he was great fun. Surgery was delayed for at least a year to help him make an adequate adjustment to this country and his new home before he was put into another strange situation. The family also did not enroll him in school because they felt it would be difficult for him to adjust to too many new things at one time. However, after several months, Doug and Janine decided he was ready to try.

Doug and Janine are really glad they heard the man from Holt. They don't plan to adopt any more children, but this additional bonus to their lives was just what they wanted. To them, the adoption was a complete success. They fit perfectly into the system, so it was easy to feel comfortable.

Using an adoption agency can smooth out many of the complexities in adopting internationally. While the agency helps with the procedure, they conduct an educational program on the cultural differences your new child will experience. This helps make adoption easier for you and for your new child. At times the adoption agency's educational approach may discourage couples. People must be dedicated to the idea of adopting internationally and committed to proceeding despite the discouragement they will receive from many people, including the adoption agency. This discouragement ultimately eliminates the people who are not certain of their course of action.

Couples are eliminated also because of their inability to meet the screening criteria of the agency. Even with the relatively small number of children who are adopted internationally, the adoption agencies have far more applicants than children. Ways are sought, even in international adoptions, to eliminate potential parents who apply. You significantly increase your chances of getting a child if you know what the adoption agency wants.

Private International Adoptions

Private international adoptions are similar to private adoptions within the United States. The variety of rules and regulations found from state to state in this country is similar to the differences from country to country. If you are easily put off by confusion and ambiguity, this type of adoption is not likely to appeal to you.

As with private adoption in the United States, you must make your own contact to find an international baby. You must meet your own state's regulations and the regulations of the country from which you want to adopt. To do this you will need legal help in the other country as well as in this country. Besides legal help, you need a contact in the foreign country who will do the searching for a child to adopt. Unless you can go to the country, you will not be able to make all the necessary arrangements to find a child to adopt.

• *State Regulations*

The regulations pertaining to private international adoptions are different from state to state. Some states, in fact, do not allow private international adoptions. The only way you can be certain about your own state is to check.

Find a lawyer who knows about international adoptions. This is a very specialized area, so many lawyers will know very little about it. A good way of finding knowledgeable lawyers in the area of international adoption is to get names from other lawyers or from anyone who has adopted a child from another country.

A qualified lawyer should be a valuable source of information on all aspects of international adoption. However, a lawyer should not be considered a substitute for what *you* need to know. When you have a fair understanding of what is involved in international adoption, you will find that the input from the lawyer is much more valuable to you.

• *Understanding Private International Adoptions*

It is very simple for me to say you *should* understand as much as possible about private international adoption. To gain that knowledge isn't quite so simple. Yet there are many sources from which you can learn about adopting internationally. Even though we are discussing private international adoption, you can profit from learning about any kind of international adoption.

One of the ways to understand about the process of private international adoption is to make contact with others who have adopted in this way. The Organization for a United Response (OURS, 3307 Highway 100 North, Minneapolis, Minnesota 55422) has numerous chapters in the United States. Their major emphasis is on educating parents about adopting children from foreign countries. They also publish newsletters that are one of the best sources of current information on the rapidly changing international adoption scene. There are other international agencies that help in making contacts; each may operate in only one or two states and sometimes these groups come and go. Since many of the people working for these various groups are volunteers, there is a tremendous turnover in personnel. You need to check within your own state to see what groups are helping in the international adoption scene. The state agency that handles international adoptions can tell you of groups in the local area who will help people seeking to adopt internationally. These groups are usually made up of people who have adopted internationally and who are happy to help you in your adoption. These contacts with groups in the United States will be some of your most valuable sources of information. Explore them all!

• *Making International Contacts*
As you continue to increase your information on private international adoptions, you will learn of many ways to make contacts with people in foreign countries who might be able to help you find a child to adopt. If you already have a contact, it is much easier. Other people who have adopted internationally are also excellent sources of information about potential foreign contacts.

Your foreign contact person can be anyone who has the potential of putting you in touch with someone who has a child to adopt. Americans living abroad or working abroad sometimes become contacts for people in the United States who are hunting for children to adopt. Foreign lawyers and foreign physicians at times act as contacts, just as they do in the United States. Contacts who work in orphanages or with poor people in foreign countries also become involved in international adoptions. People involved in religious work sometimes know of children who need homes and are available for adoption.

You need to be able to trust the person who becomes your foreign contact person. It is somewhat like being able to trust your lawyer . . . you depend on the accuracy of the information this person gives you. The best basis for trust is to have someone recommend a person to you. If others have used this person before in the adopting process, you know more about how this person operates and if he or she is honest.

If the intermediary you make contact with is not someone you know about, check with the United States Bureau of Consular Affairs staff in the country with which you are working. You may be able to at least eliminate known disreputable people who prey on others trying to adopt from a country that is foreign to them. The United States consular staff is a good source to keep in close contact with throughout your adoption process.

Sometimes a couple will pick a specific country because they already have a contact there. This can greatly help in securing a child. Mel and Becky were helped in adopting their daughter by one of Mel's students. Mel taught college and became close to one of his students from Colombia. In having Juan come to their home for dinner several times, Mel and Becky were able to talk with him about one of their dreams . . . to adopt a child from another country. Juan became actively involved in their dream. His family in Colombia located a four-year-old girl at an orphanage in a small town. She was available for adoption. Juan's family helped Mel and Becky make contact with a reputable lawyer who took care of all the legal work for them. Mel and Becky went to their local adoption agency for a home study for this specific little girl. Everything went smoothly, and because of their contact through Juan's family, all they had to do was pay the legal costs and send money for the child to come to this country. They also sent part of the fare for someone to accompany their new daughter and two other Colombian children who were also being placed for adoption in this country.

Juan, Mel, and Becky met the tired little girl at the airport. Juan helped bridge the language barrier for her and allayed the fears she had in this new country with these new parents. He also was a tremendous help in giving Mel and Becky an understanding of the cultural conditions in the country where this little girl had been living. Juan's knowledge of Colombia helped Mel and Becky avoid overwhelming their new daughter with new foods, new language, and new customs. Juan and his family, in effect, took on the role that many agencies perform in international adoptions.

The importance of your contact person cannot be overstated. He or she is selecting a child for you and doing it in a country about which you probably know very little. You need to be able to trust and to depend on this important person.

• Risks of Private International Adoptions

The risks involved in adopting privately in an international adoption are greater than if you have the help of an adoption agency. The agency does a lot of work for you. They know ahead of time what to do to minimize problems. The adoption agency has lots of children they are working with and lots of couples, so they have greater flexibility in meeting any specific demands you might have. However, the adoption agency approach also takes longer, and you must take a more passive role in the entire procedure.

The risks also are greater in international private adoptions than in domestic private adoptions. Four reasons account for this increased risk. The first is the language barrier. The second factor is the meeting of international rules and regulations in addition to your own state's regulations. The lack of knowledge about your contact person also increases your risk in private international adoptions. Finally, the lack of ability to exchange information is also greater in this type of adoption.

The language barrier that must be surmounted in private international adoption is significant. All information exchanged will need to be translated. When an adoption agency is involved, they do this for you. In a private international adoption, this is up to you. Literal translations will not substitute for someone who has a working knowledge of the language and who can help you understand the intent of the messages. It is always helpful to have someone assisting you who is thoroughly familiar with the language and the country with which you are working.

Dual regulations of both state and foreign country involve risks. The risks can be minimized by using a lawyer, but these regulations add to the complexity of the adoption process. Before you begin an adoption of this kind, be sure that you are completely familiar with or advised about your own state's regulations. You will save yourself time and frustration if you do this at the outset.

Morena and David decided to save some of this red tape by approaching an international adoption in a different way. David worked frequently in Mexico and consequently knew many people who would be able to help them. They put out the word that they were looking for a baby to adopt. One of their sources helped them locate Isabella, who was eight months pregnant. The advantage of knowing the language helped them to speak personally with her and make arrangements for her to come to the United States for the delivery of her child, which she would then place with them for adoption. They felt the medical care she would receive in this country outweighed the longer delays that an adoption in this country would entail. They decided they wanted an international adoption but without certain of the risks others might take.

Unfamiliarity with your contact person is another risk in private international adoption. In private adoptions in the United States, if you don't like what is happening you can fire your contact. In private international adoptions, though, you probably won't even know what your contact person is doing. It is important that you obtain information about your contact person before you begin. In any private adoption, unscrupulous people can take advantage of those who want something very badly. Make certain you know with whom you are working.

The difficulty of exchanging information about the child you are adopting is another risk that should be taken into account. In private adoptions in the United States, you may learn a great deal about your child. You may meet birthparents or even grandparents. Agencies involved in international adoptions are likely to be able to give you some specific information about the child you are adopting. At a minimum you are likely to know about this child's medical background before you agree to the adoption. In a private international adoption, you may not know much at all about the child. Your contact might be able to get information, but it may be minimal. The child is likely to have had at least some kind of medical checkup, but it is difficult to anticipate exactly how healthy the child will actually be. You probably will not be able to learn any of the birthparents' medical history.

There are many unknowns in this type of adoption. Couples adopting internationally, but privately, have to maintain a flexible approach to the child they are going to receive.

• One Private International Adoption

In order to help you understand some of complexities of international private adoptions, it seems worthwhile to relate one couple's experience in some detail. This couple's adoption of their son is not typical—every international private adoption is different. The experience of Harold and Nina does, however, give a picture of what private international adoption is like.

Nina and Harold were a couple who inadvertently learned about private international adoptions after having been turned down by both public and private adoption agencies in their local area. They were certain they would make good parents, and they wanted a child. They decided they would try to adopt privately. They read a newspaper article about couples adopting in Mexico and contacted the woman the article mentioned, Helen, an American contact. Helen told Nina and Harold she would be glad to tell them about adopting a Mexican child and they agreed to meet. She explained how the adoptions worked, how long the wait generally was, the costs involved, and what they would need to do to proceed. Nina and Harold were excited about the possibility, and they eagerly began the process that would lead them to their son, Aaron, within six months.

They first wrote to an American woman who was the contact person in Mexico. They asked how they could get on her waiting list for a baby. She wrote back explaining that they would need to send copies of their birth certificates, a copy of their marriage license, four letters of recommendation, pictures of each of them, and a letter from them explaining why they wanted to adopt a child from Mexico. All these written documents had to be translated into Spanish; they needed to send the original English copies as well. After these papers were received, she said she would contact them and tell them how many people were ahead of them on the list.

Harold and Nina mailed everything to the woman within six weeks. Three weeks later they received a letter from her saying that their papers had arrived. Since Nina and Harold had indicated their willingness to take either a girl or a boy, the woman from Mexico said their chances of an early placement were increased. She told them that there were five couples ahead of them for a girl and only one couple ahead of them for a boy. She told them they currently had three women who were pregnant and planning to give up their children for adoption. She explained that sometimes more women came in unexpectedly, so that the number of potential babies at any time was difficult to predict. Nina and Harold were told they should prepare immediately for a trip to Mexico.

Their American contact, Helen, kept in touch with Harold and Nina throughout the entire process. They were invited to potluck dinners where many of the couples who had previously adopted children from Mexico proudly displayed their beautiful children. They discussed the problems of obtaining their babies, the waiting period, and how to get the children back into the United States. The information that was passed from one family to the next was very helpful to Harold and Nina.

In the meantime, Harold and Nina contacted the state agency that was supposed to do a home study before they brought a child in from another country. They filled out the papers and waited for the agency to begin the study. Two months passed. During this period they moved up to the number one place for a boy. One couple on the list for a girl dropped out because they received a child through someone else in the United States. Things were moving right along for Nina and Harold in Mexico, and the time for getting a child was rapidly approaching. The approach was not as rapid in the state agency that was supposed to do the home study for them. Helen reassured them they would be able to continue with the adoption even if the home study was not finished in time. That is just what happened.

Two days after their home study was finally started, the Mexican contact woman called to say that another baby boy had been born. Did Nina and Harold want him? They did. They flew to Mexico two days later to adopt their new son. They met the Mexican contact woman at the airport and she took them to their new son, Aaron, with whom they were delighted. His abundant dark hair was beautiful but disheveled. They thought he was absolutely wonderful.

They had a chance to meet many other people who were actively involved in Mexico in trying to find homes for children whose birthmothers could not keep them. They met the doctor who delivered most of the babies and the lawyer who handled the legal matters. The personal approach each of the people took in the adoption of each child was impressive.

The procedure for them to legally adopt Aaron was very different from adoption procedures in the United States. Fortunately, the Mexican contact was able to prepare them. The lawyer they had met was prepared to handle the case in court. He was also the one who was to give some extra money to the judge to make certain the adoption was expedited. This same lawyer also had the birthmother sign the relinquishment papers. At the last minute, the birthmother said she wanted something in exchange for relinquishing the baby. This was expected. The lawyer and the birthmother agreed that a sewing machine would be a fair exchange, and Nina and Harold readily agreed. The payments made to all these people may seem highly irregular to most Americans—like an illegal or black market adoption. Yet in Mexico there was nothing irregular at all. Since Nina and Harold had already heard of the differences in Mexico, they felt the entire procedure was a bargain. It cost them less, including their airfare, than if they had adopted through an American agency. Besides that, they had a wonderful vacation in Mexico. During their four-day "vacation" in Mexico, they had legally adopted their son . . . in the United States they would have waited over six months before the procedure could have been legally completed.

The primary flaw in Aaron's adoption was that, because the home study had not been completed, Nina and Harold did not have the proper papers to bring him into this country. This had happened to many other couples, so they knew what to do. Aaron's adoption was legal as far as the Mexican authorities were concerned. He had all the proper papers to leave Mexico, but it was necessary to smuggle him across the border. Nina and Harold knew that this was illegal. They felt they had no other choice, since the system was not set up to accommodate their circumstances. They were prepared.

One of the women who had previously adopted a child from Mexico met Nina and Harold at the airport in Tijuana. The woman, a dark-haired woman, bundled Aaron up and held him. The three adults simply drove up to the border with Aaron, were waved on, and drove through. Aaron slept through the entire incident.

Nina and Harold eventually completed their home study in the United States, and Aaron received the proper papers to be here. They are not lawbreakers by nature . . . they wanted Aaron to be here legally.

The story of Nina, Harold, and Aaron is an exciting account of a Mexican adoption. Their case may be different from others, but it has some of the ingredients found in many private international adoptions:

—They had tried to adopt with the local adoption agency and were rejected.
—They didn't know exactly what to do next to get the baby they so much wanted.
—They stumbled onto the possibility of adopting internationally.
—They decided to try something different since the other way hadn't worked.
—Many caring people gave them supportive help and information.
—They were adaptable to a different kind of culture.
—They flowed with the process.
—They could afford to go this route.
—They took the necessary risks and they found a baby!

Nina and Harold learned a tremendous amount about private international adoption. Since Aaron's adoption, they have helped dozens of others adopt. They didn't know when they began the process how much Aaron's adoption would change and open their lives, but their involvement in helping others adopt has had a profound and permanent effect on them. They found themselves open to experiences they never thought possible. The risks they took to adopt Aaron taught them about taking other risks also. Adopting Aaron changed their lives as much as it changed Aaron's.

Today Harold and Nina would have much greater difficulty bringing Aaron into the United States in this way. People considering Mexican adoptions need to first petition the Immigration and Naturalization Service to begin the process of immigration for the child they do not yet have.[5] The Immigration Department will not go ahead with this until a home study has been completed for the child to be adopted. Obviously, this is a "catch 22" situation that causes international adoptions to take a considerable length of time. The days of just going down to Mexico and finding a child to adopt are past. You can now be caught in a situation where you can adopt a child in Mexico or some other place and not bring your child into this country because you do not have the proper papers. In order to have the child ever become a United States citizen, he must have legal papers from the Immigration Department.

Adopting privately can be risky. Make certain your contacts are reliable. Be sure you are meeting the laws of the country from which you are adopting. Never get involved in adoptions that involve fraudulently listing yourselves as the birthparents. If you would have a problem accepting a child from a particular country don't explore adoption possibilities in that country. For example, paying high costs in Mexico for a light-skinned child may be saying something about your lack of acceptance of children from this country. Be honest from a legal standpoint, but also be honest with yourself.

Health of the Child Adopted Internationally

The health of the child you adopt is not always as clear-cut or medically sound as that in Aaron's case. He was delivered by a physician who provided some degree of prenatal and postnatal care. This is seldom the case in internationally adopted children.

Since the children being placed for adoption are frequently from poverty-level parents, many of them are malnourished. You should assume that the medical care the children have received is minimal. It may consist of an individual check when preparing them for adoption.

You may have no way of knowing exactly what has occurred in the background of a child whom you are planning to adopt. When many of these children's birthdates are not even known, how can you expect to know medical and health histories? Once again, the couple's flexibility is essential.

In an international adoption handled by an agency, you are likely to be told ahead of time about known medical problems. That health history is likely to be more complete than in a private international adoption. The entire process of private international adoption is aimed at the adoption of a specific child that you may or may not know very much about until you are committed to that adoption. For many people, maybe for you, that poses no problem at all.

Despite the fact that these children may have some health problems, most people who have adopted children internationally are amazed at the resiliency of the children. The malnourished child quickly becomes healthier, the quiet child learns to open up, the child who seemed less bright learns faster than originally anticipated. Children have a marvelous capacity to heal, to change, and to adapt.

Summary

While some people will seek out children from other countries before considering any other kind of adoption, adopting internationally is probably not the adoption of first choice for most people. Ordinarily people adopt internationally because they have been unable to adopt through the ordinary ways in the United States . . . maybe because they were not qualified to apply or maybe because they were rejected by the adoption agency. The procedure to adopt internationally is more complex than adoption in this country, yet this may be the only way a couple can obtain a child, especially a young child. The child adopted in this way, however, is just as cherished as a child adopted in any other way. The couples adopting these children are people who believe so strongly that they want a child that they will go through a great deal to get a baby from another part of the world. Maybe this is a good way for you to proceed. If it leads you to the child you want, it's worth it.

International adoption is a radically changing scene. New laws that differ from country to country constantly keep international adoption in a state of change. Recent trends indicate that more regulations and restrictions seem to be limiting international adoptions as a good alternative means for people to adopt children.

Those seeking to adopt this way must be prepared for multiple demands. They must meet their own state's demands, the immigration department's demands, the foreign country's demands, the adoption agency's demands, and the demands imposed on them by a new "special" child from a different culture. Only the hardy should apply.

The 7
Special
Kids

NO ONE HAS GAINED MORE FROM THE CURRENT BLEAK PICTURE IN adoption than previously unadoptable children. "Special needs" children had little chance of being adopted only a few years ago. Couples who adopted had a choice and wanted "normal" babies and "normal" families; that left the special needs child languishing in the foster care system indefinitely.

In a similar way, "special needs" parents (see Chapter 8) were seldom considered as potential adoptive parents. If an agency had a choice between "normal" parents and "specials," they went with the former. Now that the adoption picture has changed, special children are available. At times, special children fit best with special parents.

Does this mean that all handicapped children up for adoption are now being placed? No. Does this mean that all handicapped parents seeking children are being accepted? No. But significantly more hard-to-adopt, special needs children are being placed than ever before. All that has changed for special adopting moms and dads is that they are sometimes considered "good enough" to handle some of the special kids who need a home.

What does "special" mean? It is a euphemism for hard-to-place, unadoptable, handicapped, mentally retarded, emotionally disturbed, racially mixed, or previously unacceptable people. In the past, these children and these parents were shuffled aside so that large numbers of easy-to-handle, easy-to-place children could go through the adoption system. There was simply no time to get involved in unusual and unfamiliar kinds of adoption cases.

Today, when you go to an adoption agency and you want to adopt a child, the children most available will be "specials." If you are willing to consider one or more of the special kinds of children available in the category of special needs children, you will be kept on the active list. This is true sometimes even if you, too, are a special potential adoptive parent.

Five groups of adoptees constitute the special needs children. Handicapped children are one group; it includes physically, mentally, and emotionally handicapped children. A second group are those children who are harder to place because of their age; they are generally over three. A third group are from mixed racial backgrounds. The fourth group are siblings up for adoption—there may be difficulty in placing two or more siblings in a single home. The fifth group are children who have been unsuccessful in a previous placement for adoption. At times these groups of special needs children overlap; you may have a child who falls into more than one category.

The unique needs of some of these children may preclude private adoption. Yet couples seeking children through private adoption need to understand the issues related to special needs children. If your resumé is chosen by a birthmother who has a history of physical problems, you know ahead of time that the baby might have a handicap of some kind. You may also have to face a handicap that surfaces only some period of time after you have the child, such as discovering the child is deaf. You may be confronted with the opportunity to adopt a child who is from a mixed racial background or an older child. Private adoption today involves special needs children.

I am impressed at the responsiveness of some privately adopting parents, whose readiness to take these children has prevented some of them from going into a series of foster homes or in prolonged foster care placement. Adoption of special needs children is not always only in the domain of the adoption agencies.

But the largest group of special needs children are placed through agencies. The more severely handicapped and more psychologically disturbed the children might be, the greater the need for more careful screening and support systems than normal children. They also frequently need medical or psychological attention. The fact that most parents are not interested in adopting children in these categories means that large numbers of parents need to be available in order for the adoption agency to find the few who would be suitable for these children.

One of the major advantages with the agencies is their access to clearinghouse kinds of information on special needs children. The agencies share information about hard-to-place children and about parents seeking them. Aid to Adoption of Special Kids (AASK, 1540 Market, Suite 220, San Francisco, California 94102) helps disseminate material and publicize special needs children available for adoption. This agency is run by the DeBolts, who have done so much to publicize the adoption of special children. Another group, the North American Council on Adoptable Children, Inc. (P.O. Box 14808, Minneapolis, Minnesota 55414), provides "information, encouragement, and local contacts" for people interested in special needs children. Their reading lists and newsletters are helpful. Using these resources is rather like listing your house on a multiple listing; you significantly increase the exposure of your house by advertising, thereby multiplying the number of prospective buyers who know it's for sale. Basically, that is what happens with these hard-to-place children. The adoption agencies advertise them to other agencies in the hope of finding a prospective parent for them. This listing has been a tremendous benefit in finding homes for special needs children.

In Chapter 1, I indicated that if you are unwilling to consider having a special needs child, you might not get very far in the application process with the adoption agencies. I believe it is beneficial for you not to eliminate any of these children immediately or the agency is likely to eliminate you. On the other hand, you should not take a child you do not want! The last thing these special children need is to be placed in a home that it unprepared or reluctant to have them. Be open about what children you would consider, but you can put the stops on at anytime you feel you have reached your limits. To go beyond what you would really feel comfortable with in a child is a disservice both to you and to the child.

Agencies do a great deal of screening of prospective parents of special needs children. They are seeking parents who sincerely want special children. They are trying to weed out those potential parents who are only settling for "specials" because they can't get what they really want. They don't want families to take a special needs child as a second choice or out of pity.[1] Ideally, I concur completely. However, many times these children are taken because no "normal" ones are available and the adoptive parents don't have much choice. If you don't have much choice, does that mean these children are not then second-choice children? Isn't adoption itself a second choice for most people? In actuality, many who adopt them are taking these children somewhat out of pity. These are people who feel this would be a worthwhile thing to do, to take a child no one else wants. Others, labeled liberal or radical, take a hard-to-place child because they believe this will strengthen and improve our world.[2] These "do-gooders" can make good parents. Altruism has a place in parents too.

The primary intent in agency screening of potential adoptive parents should focus less on motivation for adoption of a special needs child and more on making certain that parents understand the potential problems as well as the potential joys of these children. Although it would be ideal for all parents of special needs children to be outstanding parents (this is true for all adopted children and children by birth as well), this is probably less critical than the parents' willingness to be parents under special circumstances. Certainly the same motivation is not always present in the parents who biologically produce a special needs child. Screening out is inappropriate but screening in is critical.

Some of the writings suggested by North American Council on Adopted Children, Inc., are helpful sources to read before considering adopting a special needs child. The vignettes, information, poetry, and personal insight of a mother of fifteen is conveyed in a new book, *Commitment: The Reality of Adoption*[3], which deals with the many different kinds of special needs children available. Many times potential adoptive parents have little understanding of the kinds of children who are considered special needs. Perhaps reading about different situations might help you to consider the rewards of adopting a different kind of child.

The concept of adopting the special child who is different because of his or her mental or physical condition runs counter to the perfect family that some people are looking to achieve. In fact, it runs counter to the concept of aborting the child who has any problems in utero or the idea that children of one race should be placed only in homes of the same race. Life needn't be consistent.

While some people would categorically reject the idea of knowingly having a defective child, others would feel that this was meant to be for them. Some people would say to adopt a child of a race different from their own would be detrimental to the child, and others would say they could offer a child a home who otherwise might not be adopted. Neither group is right or wrong; their views are merely different. Surely we have room for differing views in our society on a subject as basic as the right each child has for a home and loving parents.

Special needs children need homes . . . they need parents, they need families, they need houses, they need activities, they need stability, and they need love. They need to be adopted. The potential is there for these children to be adopted. The potential is there for these children to have a chance to lead a more normal life. Every effort needs to be made by the adoption agencies to secure homes for these special kids.[4]

Handicapped Children as Adoptees

Usually when people think of special needs children, handicapped children—especially physically handicapped children—come to mind. Perhaps this is because we imagine things visually, and a physical handicap is something we can most easily picture. We can imagine a child who is in a wheelchair or who is blind or who is in leg braces. Yet many kinds of handicaps are not handicaps we can see.

The decision to adopt a handicapped child needs to be seriously considered before beginning the adoption process. The variety of handicaps possible are far too vast for most people to grasp. In the past, the standard question of the adoption worker was, "Would you consider taking a child with a correctable physical handicap?" Adoptive parents had a choice; in fact, they had one of three choices as a way to answer the query:

1. No, I want a child who has no known physical problem.
2. Yes, I will take a child with a physical problem as long as it is correctable.
3. Yes, I will take a child with a minor physical problem.

The fourth choice, which was not even mentioned to the adoptive couple of the past, was a child with a major problem that was not correctable. The only times these children were placed for adoption was when a couple sought a severely handicapped child. As you can imagine, this was not frequent. Children with handicaps, especially severe ones, were placed in foster home care indefinitely. Today, many of these children have a chance to be adopted.

• *Physically Handicapped Children*

What constitutes a physical handicap is not always clear. What appears to be severe to one person may not be considered a serious physical problem to someone else. Some couples would be overwhelmed to have a child who is epileptic; this same physical limitation in another home situation might be considered only as a minor inconvenience.

Before you begin to pursue adopting a child with a physical handicap, find out what kinds of physically handicapped children are available. Learn what these different handicaps might mean to your life. Most people have only heard of cerebral palsy; few people could describe what a child with cerebral palsy actually faces. Do you know? What about a child with spina bifida? What about a child who is deaf? What about a child without arms? The list could go on.

While you probably cannot know all the physical handicaps a prospective adoptee might have, you can know some things in general about how you would raise a physically handicapped child. Is it important to you to have a child who appears normal? Is it important to have a child who can be treated in a rural facility if your current home is not in the city? Is it important to have a child who can travel because travel is an important part of your life? Is it important to have a child who is not confined to a wheelchair because you have all the bedrooms upstairs and no extra money to move or to change this? Is it important to have financial help if the child has significant medical bills that your family could not afford? Is it important that the child have the capabilities to live alone as an adult? You need to think about what kinds of physical handicaps could be integrated into your life without disrupting it. Not every child with a handicap will fit with the same ease.

Fortunately you don't have to know exactly how every different handicap might affect you and the child. You will learn gradually from the adoption agency worker about different kinds of problems. The worker will not tell you to hastily pick up this specifically handicapped child without giving you a great deal of time to consider how the child would fit in your family. You will have plenty of time to consider, to read about, and to plan how a specific physically handicapped child would fit into your home.

Adopting a child with a physical handicap is a major commitment that exceeds the commitment to raise a normal child. Not all people can do this. The DeBolt family most vividly demonstrates the commitment it takes to make adoption truly successful with a physically handicapped child.[5] Their story, depicted on television, probably did more to advertise the joy of adopting a child with a physical handicap than any adoption agency promotion ever did. Their thirteen adopted children, many with severe physical handicaps, cause most of us to look on with sheer admiration for the life they have chosen.

One of the significant advances in recent years in helping parents adopt physically handicapped children has been that some states now subsidize adoption of handicapped children. These subsidies allow people of moderate or low incomes, who would otherwise be unable to afford the expensive medical cost of caring for these children, to adopt children who are physically handicapped. It also opens the way for the foster parents who have cared for these children for long periods of time to adopt a child without losing the financial support that they needed in order to maintain these children on a foster care basis.

The situation with Kathy is a good example of subsidized adoption for physically handicapped children. Kathy was placed in a foster home when she was just two years of age. After another year of hesitancy, her divorced mother finally decided to relinquish her for adoption. She had been with her mother until her mother found she was unable to meet the demands of having a child with cerebral palsy. Kathy's foster parents had become very attached to her in the fifteen months they had her in their home. They had struggled with her as she learned to walk. Her limited use of both hands had prompted her foster parents to help her strive for independence rather than to overprotect her and cause her to become unnecessarily dependent. In all ways, these foster parents were ideal for Kathy. They had even considered adoption, but hesitated because they felt unable to meet her medical costs, which from time to time were very high. The need for surgery in her third year would have been completely impossible for them if she had been their own child. The adoption worker, recognizing their financial situation and the difficulty of placing Kathy in another home, approached her foster parents about adopting Kathy with a subsidy to help with medical costs. The foster parents and Kathy were delighted with the prospect. The procedure in this case was relatively simple because it met everyone's needs.

In other cases, assistance for the high medical costs of raising a physically handicapped child is given by Crippled Children's Services. This was the case of Gary, who had been crippled with arthritis from birth. His adoptive parents felt able to handle the problems Gary's handicap might present. He needed considerable attention given to his exercises to prevent extreme pain, but at the same time these exercises could also be somewhat painful. These time-consuming and emotionally draining activities presented no problem to the people who wanted to adopt Gary. As Gary grew older, the loving support of his adoptive parents helped him with the taunts and jeers he received from his not-too-understanding peers. His arthritis was not only painful, but it was also visible. At times, his medical bills were exceedingly high. While his normal medical costs could be handled by his adoptive family most of the time, at times they needed some extra help, which they were able to get from Crippled Children's Services.

The adoption of a baby born defective discussed in Chapter 5 was an excellent example of a private adoption that met the needs of a child with a physical handicap. Privately, the couple who adopted that child will have to be more resourceful to find out what programs are available to their child. Had this child been adopted through an agency, that information might have been made available to the couple who adopted him. This couple will have to face the handicap in much the way most couples do when confronted with the birth of a child who is handicapped.

Sara and Joel Miller were confronted with a handicap, but not at the beginning of their adoption. Everything had gone smoothly on their adoption of Micah. They had met the birthmother, knew of her mental and physical background, saw no problems developing, and proceeded uneventfully on their adoption. It wasn't until the child was four months old that Sara felt something was wrong with Micah. She discussed with her pediatrician her concerns that Micah was not responding to sounds. Micah, after extensive testing, was found to be almost totally deaf. The adoption wasn't final. They could refuse to go ahead. Deafness wasn't in their plans. Sara and Joel felt this could have been the situation in a child that had been born to them. Nothing was different. While they attempted to find out from the birthmother if there was anything they should know about Micah's background that might pertain to his deafness, they handled Micah's deafness as any normal parent would have. Micah's birthmother apologized to Sara and Joel, but they reassured her of their love for Micah and that they were prepared to do what was necessary to make his life proceed as normally as they could. Micah was their child and they were doing what was expected as parents.

Adopting a child with a known physical handicap should be carefully thought out by families or individuals who are considering this possibility. Undoubtedly, the assimilation of a child with these specific needs into a new family is far more difficult than when a "normal" child is adopted. But none of us know at what point our child might be a handicapped child. More important than being a special child is being merely a child.

• Mentally Handicapped Children

As with physically handicapped children, it is not always easy to define who is a mentally handicapped child. For couples who want only a quick-learning and bright child, a child of average ability could appear mentally handicapped. In general, when we speak of mentally handicapped children, we mean children whose level of intellectual functioning is below normal. These are children who may need some special help to function in society because of the degree of impairment they experience. The severely mentally handicapped child may never be able to function independently in society.

The dilemma of choosing one of these children is similar to that of choosing a physically handicapped child. You need to fully understand what this means to you and to your life situation. If you enter this process with a clear understanding of what adopting a mentally handicapped child would mean, you are likely to find the experience rewarding. If you enter this process unsure of what you are undertaking, you can end up feeling overwhelmed and disappointed.

Few people have a chance to experience the problems encountered by those who work with or raise children who are mentally limited. If you might consider adopting one of these children and have not been with children who are mentally retarded, make the opportunity. Visit schools for mentally retarded youngsters. Learn the difference between a slightly retarded child, a moderately retarded child, and a severely retarded child. See if you have limits and see if you have specific choices. These schools can tell you about parent groups in your local area. Go to the group meetings and learn about the problems and the delights of raising a child who is first a child and second, a child with a unique and special need.

Some advantages accrue to the family that adopts a child who is mentally handicapped that do not exist if the child is born to them. While our society believes a physically handicapped child can result through no fault of the parents, less understanding is given the family that produces the mentally or emotionally handicapped child. In some ways the family stigma of these handicaps is removed from families where the child is adopted. The family does not have to bear the burden of guilt that they believe occurs with the birth of the child. This is true even though mental retardation knows no limits any more than physical handicaps do. Any family is at some risk of having a child who is mentally retarded.

Closely associated with the idea of fault in producing a mentally handicapped child is the role that environment plays in changing this particular child's level of functioning. Most researchers would agree that environment plays a significant role. If a child is extremely limited in his or her level of mental functioning, a positive, healthy environment can improve this situation, but it does not make a bright child out of a child who is considerably below average. Modifying, enhancing, and influencing are all things the environment can do . . . even perhaps bringing the child closer to his or her potential is possible in a stimulating, loving, attention-providing environment. The change seen in *Flowers for Algernon*, where a mentally retarded man becomes a brilliant person, is simply not possible today.[6] Adopting parents need to understand the limits of environment.

You may not always be aware of your child being mentally retarded until the child grows older. This is one of the ways that adoption is like having a child by birth. Many children with no known family history that would indicate the child might be retarded may have or develop problems in learning. No one can guarantee you that your child will be bright when you have a child or when you adopt a child. Fortunately, adopting parents are like most parents and they adapt to the problem in the same way. They provide the help needed and do the best they can. You may not set out to adopt this type of special needs child, but it is possible for anyone to end up with a special needs child.

People planning to adopt a mentally retarded child need to be prepared for the response of others. Friends, relatives, neighbors, and even professionals frequently discourage adoption of these youngsters or other special needs youngsters.

Elizabeth and Roger had spent a long time considering adoption to increase the size of their family. Their two boys were nine and eleven and Elizabeth felt she had the time, patience, and energy to consider raising another child . . . a special one. Elizabeth and Roger wanted a girl. But they also wanted to adopt a child who might have difficulty finding a home. After spending many hours with their caseworker from the adoption agency, discussing different kinds of special needs children, they finally decided that a mentally retarded girl was what they wanted most. As they sought to share their enthusiasm in this new venture, they found neither of the child's future grandparents very eager for this new family addition. In fact, both sets of parents repeatedly suggested they not do this "radical" thing. They told Elizabeth and Roger that a mentally retarded child would be a burden on them and would not fit into the family. Elizabeth and Roger were upset with their parents' response but they were determined to proceed. The social worker from the agency urged them to give the future grandparents time to digest the thought as both Elizabeth and Roger had. Eventually their parents came to accept the new baby granddaughter Elizabeth and Roger brought them, but their reluctance made the process much more difficult. Their sureness of what they were doing gave Elizabeth and Roger the strength to pursue their goal despite the discouragement.

In some ways it is easier to prepare yourself to adopt a child with a mental handicap, as opposed to a physical handicap, because a mental handicap is more limited, more specific. You can focus your attention on one area and learn about it. With physically handicapped children, you have great difficulty anticipating what physical problems your potential child might have. On the other hand, people are generally more accepting and less cruel to children and adults who have physical limitations than to those who have mental limitations. No matter which type of handicap your adopted child has, it is obvious that a loving, supportive home can best provide these youngsters with the stability they need to face a world that sometimes stares at and frequently whispers about them.

• *Emotionally Handicapped Children*

Emotionally handicapped children are probably closer to mentally handicapped than physically handicapped children in the problems they experience. Again, the problems are less visible and harder to understand for many people than those which accompany a physical handicap. Emotionally handicapped children are probably less understood and, consequently, shunned even more than mentally handicapped children. Usually emotionally handicapped children are also older or we would not be aware of the problem.

Emotionally handicapped children include children with a number of different kinds of problems. Children with compulsive personalities who need order to maintain their aggressive feelings when their behavior becomes extreme would fit into this category. Frequently children who have been shifted from home to home can develop mistrustful personalities; they become suspicious and paranoid. At times, children experiencing emotional problems become isolated; they retreat into a fantasy life. Other children react to their life situation with emotional problems that they act out; they become aggressive and difficult.[7]

These are only some of the kinds of behaviors that can confront the parents who consider adopting an emotionally handicapped child. Without knowing what particular disorder your child might have, it is difficult to prepare yourself for the unique problems your child might bring with him or her. Your social worker from the adoption agency will explore with you the different kinds of children available who are exhibiting symptoms of emotional disturbance. However, in order for you to evaluate how a potential adoptee could fit into your life, you need to understand the specific problems that confront the specific child you might adopt.

The way to determine how impaired a child might be and how likely you might be to help a child with this problem is to find out as much as possible about the birthparents and child's history. You want to understand the potential genetic basis of the disorder this particular child has. Then, either consult someone who specializes in helping emotionally disturbed children or read about this particular kind of emotional disturbance so that you clearly understand what this specific child might mean in your life. These children are called high-risk adoptions. It is estimated that one in eight of these children is returned to an agency before the adoption is finalized.[8] Your chances of success in adopting a child with an emotional handicap are less than in adoptions involving normal children.

The belief that love will conquer all the problems leaves families in a weaker position to solve problems than if they had adequately prepared for them. Find out before you move ahead how you need to respond to help a specific child. Find out what the chances of success are in a given set of circumstances. Find out if this disorder is caused by the child's life situation or if it is a hereditary problem that you are unlikely to be able to solve.[9] Find out the information you need so that you can evaluate your fitness to handle the situation in the best possible way.

Rusty and Dana had met in college when they were both training to teach classes for handicapped children. Their obvious similar interests drew them together immediately and they married a year later. Soon thereafter, Dana had their first child. They had always wanted to adopt because they felt overpopulation was the most significant problem facing the world, so they decided that they would enlarge their family through adoption for their second child. They also decided they had special skills they could bring to parenting a special needs child because of their background. Dana especially wanted this opportunity because she had never had a chance to use her experience and training in teaching.

An adoption agency in Chicago gave Rusty and Dana their chance. After a lot of scrutiny about their motives, the social worker from the adoption agency began to speak with them about Tina. Tina was four and had recently been relinquished by her birthmother after a long legal battle. Tina's mother had routinely abused her. Perhaps her mother's divorce at the time of Tina's birth had caused the mother to focus all her negative feelings on Tina. Perhaps it was because Tina was premature and had spent her first month in a hospital, so the bonding process was not established as it should have been. No matter what the cause, Tina was a frightened, withdrawn child who had asthma, nightmares, and little trust for anyone. The adoption worker felt Tina might be just who Rusty and Dana wanted and Rusty and Dana might be just what Tina needed.

The process of establishing trust with Tina was extremely slow. Even now, after two years, the problems she had in her first four years have reemerged. Dana's patience has been critical. Her ability to reach out to Tina but to not overwhelm her have helped Tina in her struggle with her many fears. Both Rusty and Dana have learned a great deal about child abuse and the effects it has on the child. They are also trying to understand Tina's first mother in order to help Tina understand as she grows older what might have been happening in her early years. Obviously their college training has helped them understand special children, but even more important to their success has been their willingness to be open, to seek help when needed, to learn, to read, and to listen.

Frequently children are emotionally handicapped because of the home situations in which they have been raised, as in the case of Tina. These children have many times been in other adoptive placements that have failed. Emotionally handicapped children, because of the high-risk factor and the multiple home backgrounds they come from, frequently are the older children placed for adoption. These children have many strikes against them. Patience and understanding of the adoptive parents are critical ingredients in the success of these adoptions. Most adoptions of emotionally disturbed children are very successful. Most people who have adopted a child with these kinds of problems strongly believe it has been worth all the efforts involved in making the adoption work.

Older Children as Adoptees
No one buys a cat; they buy a kitten. No one wants to bring home a dog; they want to bring home a puppy. The same is true in adoption . . . everyone wants an infant; few people would choose an older child.

Everything we learn about child development says the child is formed in the very early stages. The impact we as parents make on the lives of our children is most significant before the age of five. Some child psychologists would say our most significant impact is made by the age of three. Psychologists recognize the need for bonding between parent and child to begin as early as possible in the child's life in order for the child to achieve maximum emotional development. Some psychologists maintain that a person who has never been able to feel love as a child will have great difficulty forming loving relationships later in life.

Given the fact that all this might very well be true, then what do we do with the older children who need homes . . . throw them away? We won't do the same things with children that we do with dogs and cats. Therefore, our usual technique is to shunt them aside, mostly into foster homes, and to try to forget about them. The older, hard-to-place children seem to share the plight of the elderly in our society . . . we simply don't know what we should do with them!

Older children are considered hard-to-place and also are special needs children because they are not as much in demand for adoption as infants. What constitutes "older" children is not always clear. It used to be that children over six months were considered older children. Then children over three were the new breaking point. Now, older children are those over six or maybe even over eight years of age.

The reasons these children are older at the time of placement varies. Some children are available for adoption late in life through a death or deaths of the only existing relatives they have. In other words, they entered the system at a late age. Other children have only recently been released for adoption. Their parents may not have been willing to relinquish them, in the hope that maybe they could reestablish family stability and take the children back. These children may have been in and out of foster homes for several years. Other children are older because of compounding problems that have previously prevented their adoption, such as emotional disturbance or medical problems or being part of a sibling placement. It is estimated that between 100,000 and maybe as high as 250,000 older children are currently waiting for families to adopt them.[10]

The amount of trauma the child has received as a result of the delay in adoption depends on the child's life history. It is possible to adopt an eight-year-old child who has been in only one home. The primary problem here would be to deal with the separation from the one known family. This child may have experienced in his eight years great stability and love. Another four-year-old may have been in seven or eight homes by the age of four. She may have lived with a parent, then relatives, back to parents, then into multiple foster homes. Age alone will not tell you the extent of the rejection the child has experienced. Ideally, the history will. Be sure to get as many details on the child's history as possible from the adoption agency.

Renee and Jay were in their late thirties when they married. They knew Renee could not have children because she had a hysterectomy three years before they married. Adoption was the only way they were going to have a family. Renee wanted to raise a child but was not intent upon having an infant. When their adoption worker recognized this openness, she directed their home study toward considering an older child. Both Renee and Jay felt this would offer them many advantages. They began reading about the problems of adopting an older child and felt they could handle the situation. Their worker agreed and introduced them through pictures to a nine-year-old boy. Danny was a nice-looking, attention-seeking young man. He was being removed from his current foster home because his foster parents were divorcing. He had been in two previous foster homes. He was extremely reluctant to leave his current foster home because he had established strong ties with his foster sister and brother. Unfortunately, he had no choice. He met Renee and Jay on a picnic. He thought they were OK, but he still didn't like the situation. He finally was willing to "give it a try" even though he was hardly overjoyed. He moved in but didn't want them to try to get him to change his name. Renee and Jay took their time. They anticipated some of the problems and had not planned on "instant love," so they were not disappointed. Knowing of Danny's background, his previous attachments and rejections, helped them handle the situation with realistic expectations.

Adopting an older child, as in all adoptions of special needs children, has some unique problems. You are adopting a child who has a past. In order to have the adoption be successful you cannot pretend that the past does not exist.[11] Rather, it is of utmost importance that you help the child become comfortable not just with who he is now, but also with who he has been before you adopted him. The use of photo albums from previous homes to help the child integrate his life have become a very common part of adoption of older children.

A new use of this idea has been to have the potential adoptive parents prepare a photo album for the child they are considering adopting. In this way, the older child gets to learn about her potential adoptive family in a more controlled and cautious way for her. The pictures show the child the people who are interested in adopting her, any other existing family members, the house, the kinds of things this family likes to do, any pets, the room the child would be in, and anything else that would help the child learn about this potential family. The child finds out quite a bit about the family through a medium that communicates fully with the child . . . pictures.

In adopting older children, especially in private adoptions, there may be a need for continuing contact with significant relatives of the child. Gerald was seven when his mother decided that the demands of raising this energetic, impulsive, and at times, rebellious young boy were overwhelming. She saw his leadership potential being used in destructive ways and felt without a radical change, he would become a street gang leader rather than a student government leader. She decided she needed to have him have a chance for a structured, stable, and supervised life in a normal family. She decided to place him for adoption.

Her decision to place this child for adoption shattered her mother, who had spent considerable time with him in his growing years. Gerald's mother was sure of what she was doing and proceeded without the blessing of her mother. Gerald's mother knew that she would need to find a home for him where she could hear how he was doing and knew that precluded agency involvement. She also learned that if she went through an agency, they would place him in foster care and would not guarantee how long that placement would last.

She decided to find a couple on her own that would take her son and she did. She felt they were just what she was looking for and they were excited about Gerald. Gerald also felt his new home with other brothers and sisters would be a good place for him. The home change was made and the adoption papers to adopt Gerald were filed.

When Gerald's grandmother found out that he had new parents, she made contact with them. She wanted to maintain contact with her oldest grandson. She showed her obvious unhappiness with the situation by continuing to refer to him by his name before the adoption. The adopting mother wrote to her to clarify their willingness to maintain contact with her as long as she could be accepting of the fact that Gerald had a new home, new parents, and a new name. This has not been easy for Gerald's grandmother, but she is slowly being won over as she sees the many achievements of a positive nature her grandson has now begun to experience. Gerald maintains contact with his grandmother and even with his birthmother, whom he now refers to by her first name.

Gerald came with a history and with existing relatives. Adoption cannot change that nor should the attempt be made to weed out people in his life that might help to make the transition smoother for him. Everyone is satisfied with the situation as it is working.

In order for the adoption of an older child to work, the child is usually involved in approving the prospective parents. This is the reason that these adoptions are frequently referred to as being more of a marriage than an adoption. These adoptions work because, not only do the adoptive parents want it, but the older child also makes a conscious decision to accept these parents. In addition to needing both adoptive parents and the adopted child to make the situation work, integrating the child with children already in the home is also crucial to the success of adoptions of older children.[12] Perhaps one of the reasons these adoptions work at all, despite all the potential problems that might complicate them, is this very involvement of the older child who really wants to be adopted.

One of the ways to learn about adopting older children is to talk with others who have done so. You have to talk with them for a period of time because many times people just quickly tell you all the good things and fail to mention the difficulties. Your social worker from the adoption agency can give you names of people or groups who work as support systems to people adopting older children. Read books on adopting the older child.[13] Also read books designed for older adopted children in order to understand their perspective.[14]

Since adopting older children usually involves both parents and child agreeing to the adoption, the process is handled somewhat differently from regular adoptions. You may have several meetings with the child before the child goes home with you. You may also take the child home for a temporary visit before the actual placement occurs. Placements of older children for adoption are usually handled very slowly in order to assure their success.

It is becoming more common to have postadoption group sessions for parents who adopt older children.[15] These kinds of support systems help these adoptive parents deal with the problems instead of just responding with fear. People who anticipate the stages of adjustment that the older child experiences in an adoptive home are prepared to handle them effectively.

As with other special needs children, sometimes the problem is more complex than it appears on the surface. Sometimes these children are placed at an older age because they have other problems as well. Perhaps they have been in other adoptive placements which did not work out. It is never possible to completely piece together the history of an older child placed for adoption. As a result, current behavior or responses of the child are at times difficult to understand. Yet understanding is the critical ingredient in making these kinds of adoptions work.

Adopting an older child is different from adopting an infant. It has its own special advantages and its own problems. It is not for everyone, but those who do overcome the problems are delighted with the success. As with all adoptions, most adoptions of older children are great successes.

Siblings as Adoptees

The idea of instant family sounds good on television and in the movies. It is even a romantic concept, when we think how cute twins or triplets are. Few people, however, really want to start families this way. Yet this is just what occurs in sibling adoptions. Because this idea sounds best from a distance, few ultimately choose to adopt more than one child at a time.

Sibling adoptions become hard-to-place adoptions not only because of the number of children involved, but also because of the ages of the children. In all hard-to-place adoptions, the time lag works to the disadvantage of the children being placed. The longer they are not adopted, the more unadoptable they become.

The placement of siblings together should be a prime consideration in the adoption of these children. When these children have been together for years, they frequently become the only stable factor in each other's lives. Siblings, as any parent can attest, usually cling together when other factors are working against them. Brothers and sisters can present a strong defense when united. This response on the part of siblings being placed for adoption gives them an added sense of security in their new home. To lose parents through rejection is one thing or to lose foster parents through multiple moves is another, but to then lose the brother or sister who has been a source of united strength and stability is almost always too much of a hardship. Every possible effort should be made, and usually is made, to keep siblings together.

In the case of siblings, as in the case of all special needs children, the families willing to adopt these children have significantly increased since fewer infants are available for adoption. Families who do not find their first choice open to them when they seek to adopt are more willing to consider the alternatives available to them. As you expand your openness to adopt someone other than the white infant, you increase your chances of adopting.

For some people, adopting siblings can be an especially good solution to their childlessness. The older, childless couple who really want a family can get a quick solution to their problem and can provide a home for more than one child at a time. Meredith and Jeremy had been married for three years, both for the second time. Since they were forty and forty-two, the adoption agencies would not consider giving them an infant but would consider only an older child. That was fine with them. Never, however, had they ever considered more than one child at a single time. Then they heard about two brothers from Mexico who needed a home. These brothers, four and six, had been without any family contacts for three years. They lived in a loosely run orphanage in a border town. No one had ever relinquished them. After consulting a Mexican attorney, Meredith and Jeremy found out how they could adopt these "abandoned" boys. The adoption itself went rather quickly as Mexican adoptions frequently do (see Chapter 6). The shock of the two additions to their family was handled with relative ease once the language problems began to dissolve. The sibling relationship cushioned the impact for each of the boys in this rapid and radical life change. Meredith and Jeremy didn't set out to adopt two children, they set out to begin a family. When confronted with the possibility, it sounded great to them. They strongly advocate adopting this way.

It is difficult to find many people who have adopted more than one child at a time; this is less common than most types of special needs adoptions. There are not the same parent groups to act as support systems to adoptive parents of siblings. These parents must forge ahead on their own. However, the problems they confront are often only a matter of multiplication of the problems faced by the parents who adopt a single child.

In the past, adopting anyone other than the white infant was viewed as altruistic behavior on the part of the adoptive parents . . . they were do-gooders and, as such, were highly suspect. Their "save the world" philosophy did not fit the mold the agencies were looking for in their adoptive parents. Even the adoption agencies wondered about the motives of people who would seek children that were not like ordinary children. As a result, many times these children were not even offered for adoption. Even further down the line were sibling groups; siblings were seldom suggested because the agency *knew* people didn't want them. Today, siblings are adoptable as a unit. It is merely a matter of finding a couple who wants this situation, because certainly some people do.

Racially Mixed Children as Adoptees
No area of adoption of special needs children has received as much publicity, or is as controversial, as adoption of children from racial backgrounds that are different from their adoptive parents. The professional reaction from the National Association of Black Social Workers has been loud.[16] The legal reaction from the courts has been strongly felt. The emotional reaction from minority groups

and from white neighbors of some adoptive families has been mixed.[17] Very few remain quiet, except the adoption agencies who make many of these placements.

The primary controversy centers around white parents who adopt racially different children. Some of these children have been brought to the United States in the Vietnam baby airlifts or from other countries where poverty is significant. Usually these children are from Asian or Latin American backgrounds (see Chapter 6). The primary interracial adoption that has aroused controversy in this country has been the black child or the partially black child who is adopted by white parents. The adoption of Indian children has also caused alarm from the Indian community. The cry from the minority groups whose children are being adopted by white families is that the child loses his or her racial identity. Charges of racial genocide are hurled into the battle.

For years white adoption agencies catered primarily to the white community. Little effort was made to recruit minority homes for the minority children who were relinquished for adoption. Many of these minority children spent the majority of their growing years in foster care. Now the trend has been reversed. At the same time that there is greater demand for children of different racial backgrounds, the social workers are reluctant to put these children in white homes.

Lou Ann and Jim knew it would not be easy to adopt a child from a mixed racial background. They wanted to adopt a second child and felt they would need to expand their views of what kind of child they would accept. After considerable thought, they decided they wanted a child who was partly black. They told the social worker at the adoption agency, and she was reluctant. They told their relatives they were going to adopt a black child, and Lou Ann's mother was furious. They told their friends they were going to adopt a black child, and they were surprised. They scrutinized birth announcements looking for just the right one to proclaim to the world they had adopted a black child. They examined their living situation, the potential schools, and all areas that they felt might be affected by having this black child. After an uphill battle, the agency worker agreed that they would get their partly black child. Their four-month-old black child, whose birthfather was black and whose birthmother was white, arrived. He really didn't look black but they assumed he would get blacker looking as time went on. He grew older but remained not very black. Their total preparation of their lives to accommodate a black child appeared to be in vain. The family conflict was unnecessary.

If Lou Ann and Jim tried to adopt their son today, rather than twelve years ago as they did, they would meet with much more difficulty. The first approach most adoption agencies use today is to try to place black children in black homes. Agencies have become much more active in recruiting in the black community. Individual adoption agencies, in response to criticism by black social workers, have attempted to recruit black social workers and administrators for their staffs and for their boards. Stories of black children available for adoption have been stressed on radio and television. Pamphlets and lecturers have sought to inform the black community about adoption through agencies. The black parents who wanted to adopt but who previously were eliminated because they did not fit the typical agency model of parenting are now being recruited.

One of the reasons many minority children were not adopted was the financial burden it placed on minority parents whose incomes were significantly lower than that of white parents. Blacks complained they could not outbid their white counterparts for the black infants who were available for adoption. As subsidized adoption becomes available for lower-income families, especially foster care families, these families find themselves able to adopt a child when previously this was not possible for financial reasons. As blacks have learned about the availability of children for adoption, as they have learned they will be accepted by the adoption agencies, and as they have learned about potential financial assistance, they have significantly increased their adoptions of black children.[18]

Despite the increased recruiting of minority parents, the effort still lags behind the demand. This lag is also apparent in countries such as Canada and Great Britain.[19] Minority children are frequently special needs children for reasons other than race alone. Because they are harder to place, they frequently become older children. Their lack of stable homes increases their emotional difficulties. Their problems compound because the system does not fit their needs.

Adoption agencies are only beginning to understand the parents who seek to adopt a child of a race different from their own. As a result, agency workers frequently are skeptical of those seeking "different" children. The outcry of black social workers against placing blacks or partially black children in white homes has alarmed adoption workers, who are not usually questioned on agency policies or decisions. Agencies have significantly decreased the number of interracial adoptions, yet they deny any wrongdoing on their part. Because the agencies remain in a position of tremendous power in the adoption scene, they seldom directly respond to criticism other than to change directions from time to time.

Many mixed racial adoptions take place in the private adoption realm. While private adoption is primarily a white institution, as is adoption in general, more and more black couples are considering adoption privately and more and more women pregnant with black or mixed racial children look to adoption as a means to provide a good home for their babies. Private adoption is establishing a major foothold in this previously agency dominated group. The reasons black women or women carrying racially mixed children are beginning to look at private adoption are the same as for other birthmothers. They know they can get some financial help with the pregnancy, they can have some say in the home their baby will be placed, they know their child will not be in foster care, and they can maintain some contact with the adopting family to see how the child is developing.

Amelya was nineteen when she discovered she was pregnant. She was going into her junior year in college and felt like her only possibility to move ahead in life was to complete her education. She had volunteered time with an agency that was part of the Head Start program, and she was keenly aware of the problems faced by the many single mothers she encountered. She was not willing to put her child into that situation. She contacted the adoption agencies and learned of the foster care situation that her child would be in after his or her birth. She was appalled that they would be unable to tell her how long that "temporary" status would continue. She called an attorney to discuss private adoption. At first she was told that it might be difficult to find a home for her black child, but then was given the name of a therapist who was more actively involved in the black community and who helped her. After meeting several couples, Amelya found just what she was looking for. She decided on a mixed racial couple who were eager for her baby. They supported her for the remainder of her pregnancy. She went on welfare to have the baby, which was essential to the couple she had chosen; they had limited resources since he was a minister of a small church. Money wasn't the issue in finding the right parents for her baby, but the love the minister and his wife had for people was. Amelya maintains contact with them about once a year. She feels fortunate.

Couples who adopt across racial boundaries may or may not be asked questions about their readiness to adopt this child if the child is found through a private adoption. This in no way lessens their need to understand the problems they might encounter in an adoption of this sort. However, this is true in any adoption that has special circumstances.

I frequently ask couples considering adoption how they would feel about adopting a child of another race or a racially mixed child. Their responses vary a great deal. One of the responses I frequently hear is that it wouldn't be fair to the child. I don't usually pursue this with them because that generally tells me they are not ready to adopt that specific kind of child and that is fine. In all fairness to the child, we know the child is better off in some home rather than no home. The first choice may be a home that is just like his natural parenting family. However, many times that home isn't available. Then we must look to other solutions to finding a home for that child. The second response I frequently hear is that these children have problems when raised in a family that isn't the same race they are. Studies have shown the contrary. A recent British study underscores the lack of problems for adoption across racial boundaries while emphasizing the need to continue to recruit black homes to meet the needs for homes for black children.[20]

Potential parents who seek a child of another race would do well to know of the support systems in their community. The Open Door Society, which exists throughout the United States and Canada (5 Weredale Park, Westmount, Quebec), offers valuable information in its newsletter and meetings. It is worthwhile to get on the mailing list of OURS, Inc. (3307 Highway 100 North, Suite 203, Minneapolis, Minnesota 55422), as an additional source of information on adoptions of racially mixed children; this group also exists throughout the United States. The chapters of these groups vary from area to area but you can certainly find out about the one closest to you by contacting any of these agencies. These groups have meetings at which you can learn about the problems and peculiarities involved in interracial adoptions. The individuals involved in these organizations are also a great source of information about the response you might receive from the local adoption agency when you seek a child of a different race. Adoptive parents who have worked through the system can give you valuable information on how the system works.

Several books have been published on the subject of interracial adoption.[21] They are worth reading to get a perspective on the difficulties you are likely to encounter. There are also some excellent books for children in mixed racial families that are worth reading to understand the child's perspective on his unusual family.[22] Anyone who considers adopting a child of another race should read the story of *Edgar Allan*[23], which vividly tells of an adoption that failed.

Another way to understand interracial adoptions is by speaking with people who have been adopted. Simply talking with children who have been adopted can teach all of us a great deal about many kinds of special needs adoptions. Anthony, our son who was adopted when he was seven, added a new dimension to my knowledge of adopting an older, racially mixed child. He teaches all of us daily. One particularly poignant lesson occurred the second week we had him. He, his two sisters, and I sat comfortably in the yogurt shop one day after school. He asked nonchalantly if I thought it was strange that he was the only black person in our family. I defensively reminded him that he was not all black but then asked him what he thought about it. He replied, "I think we owe it all to Martin Luther King." I think he is quite right.

Adopting a minority child is like adopting any special needs child. It has some unique problems and some unique rewards. This kind of adoption is best entered into if you fully understand the process before you begin.

Summary

Children with special needs who are placed for adoption present problems for everyone. They simply don't fit into the mainstream of our picture of adoption. They seem to make people work harder to figure out where to put them, and they seem to create more problems in making the fit between parent and child work.

Sometimes the placement of these special children does not work. Sometimes a similar misfit occurs between biological children and their parents. There is certainly no question that more of these "disruptions," as they are called in the adoption field, occur in this group than in "normal" adoptions. Yet the amazing thing is that the great majority work. Adoption of special needs children works even though everything seems to be working against it. Agency social workers say the reason they work so well is because of the effective screening of parents. Maybe. But then again maybe the success rate exists *despite* all the ways we interfere and separate these children from others. Perhaps our belief that these children are hard to place does in fact make them even harder to place. Our view that these are the last-chosen children may cause us to suggest them only as a last resort.

Special needs children have a great deal in common, partly because the specific groups of special needs children overlap and merge. The demands on the families who adopt these children, while different in specific ways, are common in many others. The happiness that these children bring to the families who share their lives is another characteristic they share.

So many of the demands, problems, and joys these special needs children share is because they are children first and "special" second. They are grouped under "special needs" so that we can discuss them separately, but in reality their specialness is not primary in their lives. Their specialness is a label for our convenience in considering them. On a personal basis this label is not of value. You deal with Johnny or Suzie or Tim . . . they are specific people with unique sets of needs, desires, hopes, and dreams. So while you cannot separate the children from the "special needs" they have, that is not who they are . . . they are much more . . . they are really just like everyone . . . they are unique individuals. Ultimately, no one has such a handle on life that in some way he or she could not be labeled a "special needs person."

The Special Moms and Dads | 8

CHILDREN WITH SPECIAL NEEDS HAVE DIFFICULTY BEING PLACED FOR adoption; parents with special needs who want to adopt have difficulty being accepted. The main problem both of these groups have is that they are different. Because they are different, it is hard to accept their appropriateness for being part of our stereotyped American family. They do not fit our Walt Disney model of daddy coming home to mommy in a house with a white picket fence and the boy, the girl, and the dog running out to greet him. The fact that the Disney-like model of the American family seldom exists does not seem to improve the acceptance of "different" kinds of families.

The "special" moms and dads in our society include single parents, handicapped parents, parents with medical problems, parents of larger families, older parents, foster parents, and homosexual parents. Each of these groups of people runs into special problems when they seek to adopt a child; however, each group has demonstrated successful parenting skills when children have been born to them. We do not try to take their children away from them because they do not completely fit our picture of the ideal parents.

We question their capacity to parent only when they seek to adopt a child.

Single Parents as Adopters

Single people have adopted children ever since adoption has been part of our society. At times these arrangements were informally made between the new parent and a friend or relative. Many times arrangements were made through private adoption. Not until 1965 did the adoption agencies put their official stamp of approval on large-scale, single-parent adoptions by their active entrance into this type of "special" adoption.[1] Then, just as this area of adoption began to open up, the baby shortage occurred. Babies were not available and the priority for the regular families pushed single-parent adoptions into the bottom drawer of the agency's files.

Single parenting is not a new idea. Many families with two parents are, in reality, examples of single parenting. The rise in divorce rates in recent years has made single parenting a common phenomenon. In many cases of divorced parents raising children or of single parents adopting, we are talking more about temporary singleness rather than single parenting. Most single parents are single only for a time.

Even children placed in adoptive homes with couples must contend with the possibility that they too will be raised by single parents for a period of time. Adopting a child is no marital guarantee. Divorce, or even death, is a possibility in homes that adopt children. The adoption agencies' emphasis on two-parent homes can be an exercise in futility.

Studies of single parents who adopt, compared with couples who adopt, find that the children from single-parent homes do better emotionally.[2] Fewer failed adoptions occur in single-parent adoptions. When other factors are controlled, such as the age of the child at placement, the researchers find that little difference exists between the children's adjustment to single-parent adoptions and to the adjustment children make in adoptions by couples. The studies find differences in characteristics such as the age of adoptive parents, level of education, amount of income, and other demographic details, but not on success of adoption or on adjustment of the child to adoption. Single adoptive parents seem to be doing a good job if they can get through the system to get a child.

That isn't a very easy task. Adoption agencies view single parents who seek to adopt as parents of last choice. And ironically, the adoption agencies give the least desirable, hardest-to-raise children to the parents they view as least desirable and least equipped to be good parents.

Adoption agencies carefully scrutinize the motives of the single person seeking a child. Be prepared with the appropriate answers for their questions. They will also want to know of the support systems in your family. Single parents who have support from and strong relationships with friends and relatives are viewed much more favorably by the adoption agencies. Show the social worker that the child will have people of both sexes in his or her life. This factor, coupled with all the ordinary traits adoption agencies hunt for in prospective parents, is essential in order to be considered. Yet, even when you clearly demonstrate that you meet all of the agency's specific criteria, you still have a minimal chance against a couple who wants the same child. You, as a single parent, are in a difficult place to compete in the adoption game if you are going through an adoption agency to find a child.

In some special situations, agencies welcome the single parent. Alicia was thirty-two, single, and black. Her singleness was not to her advantage when she went to adopt, but her race was. The fact that she wanted a child who was at least five was also a distinct advantage. The adoption agency welcomed her with open arms. They had far more black children than they had black homes. If they could not place a black child with a couple, their second choice would certainly be a black single woman. Even though white couples actively seek black children, this is a last alternative for the adoption agencies.

While most couples who are white would wait for a long period of time to have a child placed with them, Alicia was rapidly processed and approved. Within six months of her initial inquiry, the agency invited her to hear about Alexandra. Alexandra was six years old. She had been relinquished about ten months previously because the birthmother felt unable to care for her child. Before her relinquishment, Alexandra had a series of baby-sitters who had been her primary caretakers. Alexandra seemed exceptionally mature in her ability to handle most situations but exceptionally immature in dealing with people. She carefully evaluated and tested people before allowing anyone to get close to her. She was used to temporary relationships and consequently believed all relationships to be the same. With this in mind, the adoption agency worker felt the home Alicia could provide would be a good one for Alexandra.

Alexandra would not be as overwhelmed as she might be in a two-parent home.

Alicia and Alexandra met and slowly got to know each other. The placement of Alexandra did not occur until Alicia had a vacation from her job as a schoolteacher, so that they could spend time together before school began. The first day of Christmas vacation, Alexandra and one small suitcase came to stay permanently in her new home. Even Alexandra is beginning to believe this is a permanent home for her now that her adoption has been finalized and she has been with Alicia for over a year. She had never been with any one person before for that long a period of time.

A few situations compel the adoption agencies to seek single-parent homes for children they place, as with Alicia. A child may have some specific problems that preclude his or her adjustment to two parents at the same time. For example, a child may have been the recipient of sexual abuse in a previous home, which may prevent his or her adjustment in a couple adoption. Another child might simply not find an adoptive placement with a couple; most agencies would believe that a permanent placement with a single parent is far better than no placement at all.

As a single parent who seeks to adopt, help teach the agencies about the role single parents can have in remedying problems of certain special children. Convince the agency of your ability to help with the special needs child; however, as a single parent, your chance of convincing them that you are the better parent for the "normal" infant is almost zero.

Harriet was an exceptionally bright, independent woman who had completed medical school and was in private practice in a small community. She had never been married and did not consider this a possibility in the near future, but she did want to have a child. She felt she had a great deal to offer a child. She felt very strongly about the effect of early childhood experiences and therefore she wanted an infant. She approached the adoption agency in a nearby city and told them what she wanted. Everyone at the agency who met her was impressed with her friendly, intelligent manner. Her financial independence was obviously in her favor also. She was thirty-one, which was well within the age limits the agency sought for parents of infants. Yet her single status worked against her. At any other time when babies were more available, the adoption agency would probably have accepted an applicant of Harriet's caliber. But in today's adoption scene, Harriet's application was denied. The

adoption agency would not consider giving her an infant. The social worker from the agency talked with her about older children
or children with other special needs but Harriet really felt she wanted
an infant and was not ready to compromise. She left the agency
with little encouragement. Alone, she simply could not compete
with a couple in the adoption agency's view of what was needed to
be a good parent.

Jake was twenty-nine and single. He had been active in Big
Brothers for five years, and he decided he wanted to do even more
with children. He decided he wanted a son to share his life. He
knew he had little chance with an adoption agency. He knew it
was even harder for a single male to be accepted than for a single
female. He had almost given up hope when he met Jason. Jason
was five and one of eight children. Jason's parents both worked,
and the children were pretty much left on their own. Jason spent
more and more time with his neighbor and new friend, Jake. Every
day Jason came to Jake's house, or the fire station where Jake worked,
so that he could spend time with his friend. Because of Jake's work
schedule, he was able to spend a lot of time with the boy. Jason
and Jake traveled together during summer vacation. Jake had Jason over to dinner most nights of the week. It wasn't long until
Jason was hardly ever at his "real" home. Jason was outspoken about
wanting to come and live with Jake. He asked Jake if he could stay
permanently. Jake agreed that he, too, would like this but he didn't
know how Jason's parents would accept the idea. Finally, Jake made
arrangements to meet with Jason's mother and father. The parents
felt Jason was happier with Jake than when he was home, and they
felt unable to make things any better for him, so they agreed to
have Jake legally adopt Jason. This was a rare way for anyone to
find a son, but it worked. It's possible that Jake's strong desire for
a son led him into a situation where he could find one. Jason still
has contact with his birthparents and his brothers and sisters, but
he calls Jake "Dad."

The easiest way for single people to get a baby is to find a child
privately. This is probably the only way a single person will get a
normal infant. If you, as a single parent, expect to get a child through
an adoption agency, be prepared for a long, arduous process. Be prepared to prove your parenting skills and motives. Be prepared to be
put far down on the waiting list for a child to adopt. Be prepared
to accept a special needs child. The singles who are most likely to
get a child are those who really go after one. The person who is

not content with waiting to hear from an adoption agency goes out to find a child. Pursue all the agencies, but also pursue a child privately. If you really want a child, go after one . . . even if you are single.

Find out about the problems of both obtaining and of raising a child as a single person. All the literature on single parenting is equally appropriate to adoptive parents as it is to other single parents. Write to the Committee for Single Adoptive Parents (Post Office Box 15084, Chevy Chase, Maryland 20815) for additional information. Attend group meetings of parents who have special needs children, because if you can adopt a child through an adoption agency, that is probably the kind of child you will have placed with you.

Adopting a child is an uphill struggle for a single parent. People will question your motives and react with disbelief that you, a single person, would willingly choose to raise a child alone. You must be highly motivated; the more work, the more effort, and the more approaches you pursue, the greater the likelihood of finding a child.

Physically Handicapped Parents as Adopters

The chance of an adoption agency placing a child with a parent who has a major physical handicap is slight except in unusual circumstances. Adoption agencies seldom publicize this because they would have lawsuits immediately charging discrimination. The discrimination is not on the books but rather in the attitude.

If there were many babies and few applicants, physically handicapped people would have less difficulty adopting through an adoption agency. Since just the reverse is true, physically handicapped people are placed in an extremely difficult position. They simply are too far down the list of acceptable applicants to have a chance for a child.

In certain situations, the adoption agencies believe that a child with a physical handicap might be best placed in a home where one of the parents has a physical handicap. For instance, the special needs of a child permanently confined to a wheelchair mandate that the home be able to accommodate the wheelchair. A parent with a similar physical handicap may provide a home already equipped for the child. To convert a home to accommodate a wheelchair can be quite costly. Another instance would be when a child's adjustment to his or her handicap is not going well. The emotional support of a parent who also has a handicap might help the child adjust.

Lauren was a case of a child who did not adjust well to her handicap. She was twelve years old and had cerebral palsy. She had spent most of her life in a wheelchair because of her medical problems. She was withdrawn and depressed. She had made two suicide attempts that ultimately caused her to be made a ward of the court, because her mother felt unable to cope with her depression and her rages. At the time, much negative publicity concerning long-term foster care caused Lauren's social worker to approach the birthmother about relinquishing Lauren for adoption rather than having her remain in her current foster home. Lauren's mother felt that any possibility would be worth it if Lauren would be happier. Lauren had been in psychotherapy for several years; her therapist felt her depression was related to seeing herself as different from everyone else and recommended that, if possible, she be placed with a person who had a similar handicap. The adoption agency's psychological evaluation found similar evidence that Lauren would be best placed in a home with someone who had a similar problem.

These recommendations gave Ted and Marie the only chance they had to adopt a child. Marie had been confined to a wheelchair since she was paralyzed in an automobile accident at the age of nine. Since that time, she had learned to be relatively self-sufficient. She could drive a car that was specially equipped for her wheelchair. Ted and she had made all the necessary changes in their house to accommodate her wheelchair. The halls were wider than usual, there was a ramp to the front door, the shower was specially designed, and the doors were all extra-wide. Ted's help and understanding and Marie's fortitude and perseverance had enabled Marie to function rather independently. The adoption agency felt Marie's example and Ted's help could be extremely beneficial to Lauren.

Lauren met Ted and Marie. She told her social worker she didn't like them. The social worker encouraged Lauren to give it some time. Lauren stayed overnight with them and began to watch Marie as she maneuvered about the house so expertly in her wheelchair. The young girl could see Marie doing things she had never considered doing for herself. Each new visit brought Lauren closer to Marie and Ted. She finally admitted to the social worker that she wanted to stay. Lauren's change has been dramatic in her new home; it doesn't usually happen that quickly. Lauren found a new way of life because she found some "special" parents who wanted to adopt a child.

These circumstances mentioned above are rare. Most handicapped people would not be willing to wait for these occasional occurrences. As a result, these special parents generally seek a child elsewhere. Fortunately, most handicapped people are able to have children biologically without anyone's permission. Many times, if the wife is able to have children but the husband is unable to impregnate her, their problem of childlessness may be helped through artificial insemination. Others, who want to parent and who have not succeeded, probably seek a child privately rather than through an adoption agency. Generally, these special people would prefer to adopt through an adoption agency, but they recognize that such a choice is seldom available to them.

I received a letter from one woman who describes beautifully the plight of the physically handicapped person seeking to adopt. I hesitate to include a "fan" letter but I believe this woman tells the story better than I possibly could. I have never met her but her letter tells a great deal about her:

Dear Cynthia:

There are no words to adequately describe what you have done to my life. As I write this, my three-month-old son is squealing with delight at the antics of his father. He fills my heart with a joy I would never have known without you and your work. Your book gave my husband and me the courage to try to adopt once again.

Even though I have cerebral palsy and have been in a wheelchair for twelve years, my husband and I were devastated by our rejection by the state Adoption Exchange nine years ago. After allowing us to go through the interviews and screening process for a year we were turned down on the basis of my disability. It was a shock to us as we felt we had much to offer a child and felt that the agency would see that through the process. Unfortunately they couldn't see anything past my wheelchair.

During the years since we have filled our lives with careers and each other. We have always been happy, yet we were truly incomplete. We resolved to forget about a family but never could. Nothing filled the void of what might have been.

One of the ways I tried to compensate for the lack of a child was my involvement in the disability movement. It was this involvement which made me aware of the new laws that prohibit discrimination. Our hope that things had changed was the foundation of our decision last July to try once again to adopt.

The very first step we took was buying your book. I went in to find information on adoption and I found you. I read it (I should say devoured) in two days. My husband took the next two and within the week we had appointments with agencies and gynecologists, and had the name of a good lawyer. We followed your instructions to a "T," however we didn't get very far with the agencies. On the second Tuesday of our "project," I made contact with a woman who worked as a clerk in a shop we went into. We told her (as we decided we would tell as many people as possible) that we wanted to adopt and if she heard of any pregnant women who might be interested in adoption to please let us know. She called four days later, we referred her to the attorney whom we had contacted in the meantime, and four months later our son was born.

Our attorney was wonderful. The woman in the shop was wonderful and will keep the information about the birth and adoptive parents confidential at the request of all concerned. At this point, the state where we were adopting him was not discriminatory in any way.

The next step is the final one in court. We hope to get a court date within the next two weeks.

Dearest Cynthia, the next time you get burnt out by the injustices in the world, or the frustrations that befall each of us, know that 2,000 miles away is a family that is complete because you cared enough to share your heart and soul with the world. If I could wrap you in a rainbow, it wouldn't be enough.

Her letter speaks for the problems many handicapped people are forced to face.

Handicapped people are not very well understood in our society. We look at them from afar and generally our response is pity for them and gratitude that we are not in their place. We debate philosophically at what point we would no longer want to survive as a disabled person. This is easy to debate when it isn't reality. Few people understand the richness and the value of living that is open to the handicapped person. Unless you have personal knowledge of someone who is handicapped, it is difficult to comprehend that life. Very few of these handicapped people would evaluate their lives as worthless or unproductive. They anticipate and enjoy life in many ways that are similar to "normal," and in some ways that are not open to "normals."[3]

In the past, handicapped people were not expected to live long or productive lives. With technical and medical advances, the life span and the capabilities of people who are the most seriously handicapped have been significantly improved. Emotionally, our responses to them are still antiquated. Our primary concessions to the physically handicapped population are parking places and special restroom facilities. We are not yet able to view them as people with similar needs and dreams. We are not able to view them as meeting our criteria for becoming adequate parents.

Physically handicapped parents have a hard battle to fight to get children from adoption agencies. They have to overcome the ignorance of society in terms of their limitations and capacities. At the same time they fight society's prejudices, they must also confront the biases of the adoption agency's social worker. They have to prove themselves adequate to undertake an endeavor that is basic to most people . . . parenting.

Older Parents as Adopters

People who are older than most parents fall into the category of "special parents"—they do not fit into the fixed categories that adoption agencies have set as the normal ages for parenting. Therefore, when older couples approach adoption agencies, the only children the adoption agencies will consider giving to them are special children. Usually these are handicapped or older children.

Nature has set a biological limit on women who want to have children. Once a woman has reached menopause, usually in her late forties, she can no longer conceive. In our society, women generally have children in their twenties, but this age is increasing because many women are delaying their first pregnancy. The adoption agencies are looking for parents of what they would consider "normal" childbearing age. In general, this means someone who is between twenty-two and thirty years older than the child they wish to adopt. The forty-year-old woman's choice to have an infant is denied since the agency deems her choice not within the normal range.

The greater the number of children available, the greater the age range considered appropriate for an adoptive parent of an infant. So, in this time of scarcity, older parents become "specials" who must be willing to accept special children or they will not be considered by most adoption agencies.

Millie and Lester had led an interesting life since their marriage twelve years earlier. They had both served in the Peace Corps in their early twenties and had met at the time of their training. They both loved to travel and so when they met again years later, they married and set off to see the world. They collaborated on articles that supported their expenses as they lived in one country after another. When they finally decided they were ready to settle down in one place and raise a family, Millie was thirty-nine and Lester was forty-two. They found no reason that would explain their infertility. After trying for a year, they approached the local adoption agency. They wanted a baby. The social worker spoke with them about the scarcity of babies and about older children who would be available sooner. But Millie and Lester felt they wanted to experience a baby first, so the adoption agency turned them down. Fortunately, Lester and Millie in their world travels had met many people in different foreign countries. These connections eventually led them to an infant born in Colombia. They flew to Colombia, filled out the necessary papers, received their baby, and came home. Their adventure in baby hunting gave them not only a darling baby daughter, Lina, but also an article that they subsequently sold.

Obviously, Millie and Lester don't fit into the regular categories of parenting. At the same time, it certainly seems that the interesting backgrounds of their lives would be a great addition to the life of any child they would adopt. From the adoption agency's standpoint, they could have enriched an older child's life just as much. But it's hardly as if Millie or Lester were ready for a geriatric ghetto at their ages. Many parents have successfully raised children they have had late in life.

Sandy and Al wanted a child even though they were in their early forties. When they approached the adoption agencies, they were told of the situation. As they heard about adopting an older child, this concept seemed extremely appealing to them. They wanted a child; a baby wasn't the issue for them. They were able to work within the adoption agency system. This doesn't make them any better parents than Millie or Lester, who couldn't fit into the adoption agency system.

Older parents definitely fit into the category of "special" moms and dads. If these special parents want special children, they may be able to get one through an adoption agency. The quality of parenting from older parents is not the issue, because there is no reason to believe older people make better or worse parents than others. The issue is more that older parents aren't "normal," and the adoption agency system is currently designed primarily for "normal" moms and dads.

Parents with Medical Problems as Adopters

People who have medical problems but wish to adopt children through adoption agencies are in an extremely difficult position. Adoption agencies routinely seek a medical checkup before they will consider placing a child with a couple. If this checkup indicates there are any serious medical problems, the adoption agency will undoubtedly place this home on the ineligible list.

Although people who are not in the best of health get pregnant and people who have children may discover at any point that they have a serious medical problem, this same "luxury" is denied the infertile couple. Excellent health is a prerequisite for parenting . . . at least if you are adopting.

John and Susan sought to adopt a child through an adoption agency ten years ago and were turned down. John is a diabetic who must use insulin to control his disease. The adoption agency denied their application because of his medical problem. The couple felt they had no other choice but to adopt independently.

Sarah and Allan wanted to adopt a child through an adoption agency. Sarah had a heart problem, and the adoption agency would not consider their application. Sarah and Allan know that she may not live to an old age, but they do believe she is is likely to be able to live at least until a child reaches adulthood. No matter how unable they are to foresee their future, they know they want a child in it. Their search took slightly longer than a normal couple, but they found a child. They spoke honestly with the birthmother about Sarah's condition. The birthmother is satisfied with the home she has chosen for her son.

Margo and Brian had been married for four years and had been unable to have a child. The doctors finally decided Margo will be very unlikely to ever have a child because of severely scarred tubes. Margo and Brian went to the local adoption agency but felt they received a very cold response. Their application for a child was never accepted. No one told them why they were rejected but they both believe it was because of Margo's weight. Margo weighs two hundred and twenty-five pounds. She does not believe her weight affects her ability to adequately mother a child. The fact that they have subsequently adopted two children who are happy and healthy verifies Margo's belief in herself as a mother. It would have been easier for Margo and Brian to adopt through the adoption agency. The question for them was not will we adopt but how will we adopt.

Kelly and Frank presented a different problem. They knew the agency would not consider them because Kelly had cancer. For four years the cancer had been in remission and they felt they didn't want to wait any longer to begin experiencing the joys of parenting. They decided to pursue private adoption. The question for Kelly was what to say about her cancer. She agonized over this because she was an honest person who knew she could not personally hide the problem from the birthmother. However, to talk "cancer" in her resumé seemed too much a red flag. She finally decided to not mention this in her letter but knew she would tell the birthmother after she met her. This honesty she felt she owed the birthmother was repaid when Kelly and Frank met Beverly. Beverly really liked Kelly and she appreciated Kelly's honesty. Kelly's period of remission convinced her that Kelly was cancer free. Beverly's strong positive feelings toward Frank and the kind of father he would be was the backup she needed to convince her these were the people for her child. The guarantees of the quality of parenting were the most important factors to Beverly. She gave them Michael, seven pounds and two ounces.

All these couples wanted a child and their first choice would have been to go through the adoption agencies. But agencies, seeking the "best" parents, have set standards none of these couples can meet. This is certainly an understandable problem in today's adoption scene, but it does not make it fair to the many applicants that it eliminates. Surely there are ways the adoption agency system can accommodate these people, too . . . especially since these people want and ultimately can get children for adoption anyhow.

Parents of Large Families as Adopters

Couples wishing to adopt but who already have two or more children have very little chance of adopting through an agency. This may be because of the lack of adoptable children, but the other cause could be that, once again, these adopters fit into the category of "different." According to agencies, couples with more than two children are termed large families.

The adoption agencies' belief that a large family system could not meet the special needs of an adopted child, especially one who may have some difficulties, usually prevents the placement of children in homes with large numbers of children. While the successes of large adoptive families such as the DeBolts, with their thirteen adopted children, are well known, it is clear that they cannot get their children through the regular adoption agencies. Probably most agencies would have rejected the DeBolts before they adopted any children, on the basis that they already had children. Through lack of understanding, large families are not considered appropriate.

A large family, rather than being detrimental or a family of second choice, to some children would be the best home available. Margaret Ward, a Canadian writer, speaks of the kinds of children who might be better placed in a large family adoptive home:

1. Children who cannot relate easily to adults or parental figures.

2. Children who are emotionally detached, who need to move slowly in forming new relationships.

3. Children who become stifled by the demands of adoptive parents for intense parent-child relationships.

4. Children who need to experience social contact in a small close situation before being able to handle the demands of society for social contact.

5. Children who are withdrawn, who may need stimulation.

6. Children who have language problems because they have not learned to verbalize adequately.

7. Children who need structure, but structure with flexibility.

8. Children at high risk.

9. Children in need of nurturing.

10. Children lacking a firm sense of identity.[4]

The involvement of not only adoptive parents but multiple siblings provides diverse role models and sources of contact. At the same time, the contacts are not as concentrated or as intense. Large families are generally verbal, which enhances communication. Siblings take on more important roles in large families, which may be especially beneficial to certain adopted children. Having many members in a family gives many sources of love and affection and offers a miniature society in which children can experiment with

different behaviors. Large families, while generally imposing structure and demands on each member in order to function, are seldom
rigid. They simply don't have the time to be rigid. This allows the
flexibility that certain children need.

Molly came from a family of nine children, Tim from a family
of five children. When they married, they knew they would like to
have a large family. They had three children by birth and then,
unexpectedly, Molly had to have a hysterectomy to correct a medical problem. Undaunted, they went to the local adoption agency,
intent upon enlarging their family in a different way. They were
good parents, acceptable to the adoption agency in every way except that they already had three children. Despite all their pleas,
they were told that their application would not be accepted because there were simply not enough children to go around to all
the people who wanted them. Molly and Tim didn't know where
else to go. Two months after their rejection, the social worker from
the adoption agency called them and asked them to come in for
another interview. They learned of a birthmother who insisted that
her child be placed in a home with at least three or four children.
The adoption agency now wanted Molly and Tim to complete their
home study so that this child could be placed with them if things
worked out. They had a fourth child in their family within two
months.

Molly and Tim are not a good example of a family whose child's
needs would best be met in a large family, but they are a good
example of the adopting agency bending rules to meet people's needs.
They are also a good example of the control the birthmother can
have in the placement of her child through an adoption agency if
she insists on certain requirements. The need exists for greater
pressure on adoption agencies to modify their procedures. Adoption agencies routinely turn down requests from parents with large
existing families. Parents who wish to adopt and who are in this
position need to take more aggressive roles in educating the adoption agencies about the quality of life in large families.

The concept of the large family as a desirable choice for some
children being placed for adoption has not been studied thoroughly.
It is difficult to study something that happens so rarely in adoption. Before categorically eliminating this choice, perhaps it should
be proved inappropriate first. The obvious and usual successes of
large families by birth would point to the appropriateness of children being placed in this type of family situation. Adoption agen-

cies, however, do not have to defend their choices. But remember, they are not the only game in town!

Large families offer a special milieu that may be beneficial to some children. Many large families will continue to adopt children, but most will do this through independent adoption . . . they have no other choice.

Foster Parents as Adopters

Foster parents are not like any other kinds of parents. They have children but they don't really. They are supposed to love them and commit to them but also to easily give them up when the "temporary" placement is ended. They are supposed to be available to, but not demanding of, the social workers with whom they work. They are supposed to be knowledgeable about raising children, but they cannot be involved with the decisions about the child's welfare. If children in foster care are called "children in limbo," many foster parents could well be called "parents in limbo."

Many children are currently in foster homes; estimates range as high as 500,000.[5] Basically, children who are in foster homes are children whose birthparents for some reason do not choose to care for them or who are unable to care for them. Parents who are unable to cope with their children, for one reason or another, find someone to become a substitute parent. People who have little money have their children put in foster homes. People who have enough money to hire a substitute parent use baby-sitters, boarding schools, nannies, or relatives to help. If we could add up the large numbers of children who are being raised by people other than birthparents but who are not actually in foster care, the figures become alarmingly high.

Children in foster homes fall into one of several categories. The first group are children waiting for adoption. These are children who have been relinquished and for whom no home has yet been found. Most of these children will have no difficulty being placed for adoption.

The second group of children are those whose birthparents are committed to them but due to temporary problems are unable to care for them. These are children who have contacts with their families but live in temporary foster homes.

The third group, and currently the group being given considerable publicity, are children who have not been released for adoption but whose original families do not remain committed to them.

Nothing is being done to change the circumstances for the child, nor is anything being done to change the circumstances of the parents. These children stay and stay and stay in foster homes.

The foster parents of these different groups of children have different feelings about their parenting. The first two groups see their role as temporary, as indeed it usually is. The third group of parents find themselves providing homes for these children on a more permanent basis. These foster parents at times want to adopt the child for whom they have become primary parents. The permanency of the situation has created strong family ties in these foster homes. Previously, adoption agency workers who saw this closeness developing between foster parents and foster children immediately removed the child.[6] These parents were approved to be foster parents, not adoptive parents. To allow these foster parents to adopt would drain a valuable source of good foster care homes. The rules for becoming adoptive parents were also more stringent than for becoming foster parents; many of the foster parents as a group were older, less educated, and less financially stable than the pool of parents seeking to adopt. Since many times the most difficult-to-raise children are kept in foster homes, it would seem that the foster parent is the parent who should be most carefully screened.

Foster parents, resenting the contradictions of their role and the unfairness in past practices regarding their eligibility to adopt these children, have become more organized. Groups like the National Foster Parent Association (NFPA, Post Office Box 16523, Clayton, Missouri 63105) offer help to foster parents in gaining greater control over the children they raise. These groups also provide information to foster parents who want to adopt the children they have been raising, and they disseminate information to foster parents on subsidized adoption programs.

Some states now have laws on their books saying that in long-term foster home placements, the foster parents must be the home first considered for the child if the foster parents want the child. Even in states where this is the case, the rights of the foster parents at times are ignored. Lois was Deek's foster mother for three years. Lois and her husband, Walter, had grown more attached to Deek than to any of the other twelve foster children they had previously had in their home. They indicated to the supervisor that they were interested in adopting Deek when they heard that he was to be placed for adoption after finally obtaining the approval of the courts. His birthmother was in a mental institution and unable to sign the relinquishment papers. The supervisor made it clear to Lois and Walter that they were not considered an appropriate home because of their ages and that a more suitable home would be found. Lois was crushed. She sought help and found out that age could not be used as a factor against her in the adoption process.

She approached the supervisor again but the reason for rejection was now different. Now she was told that with Deek's birthmother's problems he would need to be in a home that could accommodate Deek's having potential significant psychological problems. Lois told the worker that they were totally familiar with his background and felt sure they could handle the situation. The worker insisted that they read books on mental problems to be sure they knew what they were doing and continued to try to discourage the placement.

Lois and Walter were consistent; they read the books and said they still wanted Deek. The worker still said they were not qualified to be the adoptive parents. She indicated there were more qualified people to raise Deek. Lois and Walter decided to hire an attorney, who approached the social worker in charge of the case. One appointment to clarify the rights of Lois and Walter with the social worker seemed to convince the worker that this couple would indeed be an appropriate couple. The irony is that this child with multiple problems would even be considered for placement in another home before first trying to have him remain where he was secure and loved. To disrupt his life after over three years would be to significantly increase his chances of having severe mental problems. Deek's best chance of growing up normally would be in the home he had known since he was two days old. Deek's adoption has taken three years to complete; Lois and Walter's determination has been the key to their son.

Foster parents are slowly gaining greater control in decisions involving the children who are in their care. At times, their opinions are solicited before adoption proceedings are formalized or adoption placements are made. They are seeking greater control over the length of time a child will stay with them and why the child will be removed. Most important, they are receiving consideration as adoptive parents of the children who have been in their care for long periods of time. Foster parenthood used to prevent people from being chosen as adoptive parents. In some cases, the reverse now can be true; foster parenting can be a way to become an adoptive parent.

Arlene and Howard had been foster parents ever since their biological children entered school. It was a means to earn a little money for Arlene while she stayed home, but her primary motivation was her real love for children. They had two foster children when two-year-old Jody came to live with them. It was supposed to be a temporary placement but the birthmother repeatedly hesitated to sign the relinquishment papers that would have allowed Jody to be adopted. Her visits became shorter and less frequent, but nothing could be done to persuade the birthmother to move ahead more rapidly. Arlene and Howard became "Mommy" and "Daddy" to Jody, who heard her foster brother and sister refer to them as such. Jody had one additional problem . . . she had only one arm. Arlene and Howard helped her in her adjustment to her handicap, enjoyed her, loved her, and saw her through two additional years of her life. This was the first foster child they had nurtured for a long period of time and they understandably became very attached to her and she to them. When Arlene and Howard learned that Jody's birthmother had finally signed the relinquishment papers, they asked the social worker for consideration as Jody's adoptive parents. The social worker was hesitant. Even though Jody was considered a special needs child, she would be easier to place than many others because she was still under five and she was a girl. Arlene and Howard persisted in their requests. After a lot of investigation, they were finally approved as a potential adoptive home. They had to go through the same process as people who were completely unknown to the system. Finally, Arlene and Howard were approved and six months later, Jody became their legal daughter.

Arlene and Howard were fortunate that they had no strikes against them. Anything that could possibly have been used to deny their petition to adopt Jody would have been. Foster parents are not first-choice adoptive applicants. The term "psychological parent," which entered the adoption scene with the publication of the book *Beyond the Best Interests of the Child*, did more to change the status of foster parents than any other single factor. This same book has also made a tremendous impact on the overall view of long-term foster care in general. The amount of time considered tolerable for a child to be apart from his or her parents before the child experiences feelings of abandonment has been reconsidered. Psychological abandonment varies on the basis of the child's age. The authors of this book would maintain that the younger the child the sooner this takes place. As a result, long-term foster care is being given careful consideration. At times, a more active and aggressive stance is being taken by agencies to have foster children declared legally aban-doned so they can be placed in a permanent adoptive home sooner.

The biggest difficulty for children who have been caught in the foster care system is not being able to establish a feeling of per-manence or rootedness. Children who come to feel that all homes are temporary learn to withhold love. When these children are fi-nally released for adoption, the task for the adoptive parents is a difficult one. This is the reason why the current push toward short-ening the stay of children in foster homes has occurred; it is also the reason that, in some cases, adoption of children by their foster parents is now being allowed. At least the beginning stage of estab-lishing roots has been started in the foster home.

A different approach to foster parenting is being taken by some adoption agencies. In order to facilitate the early placement of chil-dren into permanent homes, children are sometimes being placed in the home that will eventually adopt them; they are placed prior to the birthmother's signing the relinquishment. The approach, termed "fost-adopt," is somewhat riskier, but it does help facilitate the child to develop a sense of permanence as early as possible. This "fost-adopt" program is a direct result of the increasing ben-efit seen by social agencies in trying to make temporary place-ments into permanent placements. The adoption agencies who are seeing successful adoptions coming from foster home placements have taken the practice a little further by instituting programs de-signed for foster care to ultimately become adoption.

As the role of the foster parent changes, foster parenting is being seen for the first time as an avenue toward adoption. Some agen-cies recommend that this approach be used regularly in cases in-volving special needs children. While foster parents are now being accepted as adoptive parents, this does not mean that it is cur-rently a good way to adopt a child. Foster parents are not adoptive parents of first choice; they are treated as "special" moms and dads who are finally being at least considered in adoption cases.

Homosexuals as Adopters

The emotional response to the entire issue of homosexuality is ev-ident in many areas of our lives. The avowed homosexual has only recently felt any degree of confidence in proclaiming his or her sex-ual preference. With the proclamations have come condemnation. Homosexuals have been fired, harassed, and ridiculed. Homosex-uality has won many legal battles under the banner of discrimination but it has only begun to win slight approval or tolerance in our society. One area where this is most certainly evident is in the adoption of children.

Homosexual parents are like just about any parents. They are as good or as bad as any other group of parents one could evaluate. There has been nothing that would substantiate fears that children raised by homosexuals become homosexuals. Yet the sexual orientation of gay people frequently affects court decisions about their parenting rights and significantly affects how adoption agencies view them as potential parents.[7]

Despite the data that indicate homosexuals are like any other parents, adoption agencies do not knowingly place children for adoption in homes of homosexuals. Recently one noteworthy exception to this discrimination gained publicity when David Frater, an acknowledged homosexual, legally forced the California Department of Social Services to allow him to adopt a seventeen-year-old boy who had been placed with him before the adoption agency learned that David was gay.[8] The agency's position is understandable because of the potential criticism from nongays who are seeking a child. However, the negative publicity this issue generated runs counter to the low profile that adoption agencies strive to maintain. The adoption agencies have no written policy about placing children with homosexuals because to do so would be overt discrimination.

Discrimination is not a new concept for adoption agencies. When any group discriminates against another, they usually do it against a small group that is not vocal. Adoption agencies discriminated against blacks until blacks gained more power and became vocal. Then the outcry of the blacks forced changes by the adoption agencies. Adoption agency discrimination against gays has the same potential to change as gay rights are more vocally asserted.

Lori and Sally knew of discrimination against lesbians. They had lived together in a lesbian relationship for over six years. They were happy, productive, and in many respects living a normal life. Lori went to work daily as a social worker. Sally reluctantly worked as a grocery store clerk, but her real desire was to have a child. She approached a physician to perform artificial insemination but it did not work for her. After six months of trying, she gave up on the idea of becoming pregnant. Because Lori's experience as a social worker with the Department of Welfare kept her abreast of adoption agency procedures, she recognized that she and Sally were not going to be given a child by the adoption agency. Sally nevertheless tried an adoption agency in an attempt to adopt as a single mother, but they told her there were no children available for single women. Then Lori heard of a woman on welfare who was unhappily pregnant and too far along for an abortion. Lori talked to her about giving the child to her and Sally. She was open about the relationship she had with Sally. She emphasized the stability of the relationship and how loving a person Sally was. The pregnant woman met Sally and liked her. She already liked Lori so she decided she would give them her child when it was born. Sally adopted the child legally as a single mother. The agency investigating the home never learned about her relationship with Lori. Sally and Lori were lucky . . . the odds were really against them ever getting a child to adopt. Most homosexual couples would not have these contacts or this good fortune.

In order to effectively prove that homosexuals are unfit for parenting, studies will have to substantiate this claim. So far none has. In fact, the subject is seldom studied at all. One recent study reported in the *Lesbian Tide* found that children of lesbians are different from children raised by nonlesbians.[9] The researcher found that the sons of lesbians were more gentle and concerned with other people's feelings than were other boys. She also found the daughters of lesbians had stronger qualities of leadership and outgoingness than other girls. Other studies of lesbian mothers are finding that they raise their children in highly traditional ways and the children show no increase in gender-related problems, sex-role confusion, or in general development.[10] The impact of these studies has certainly not been felt by most lesbians wishing to adopt.

Some recent changes have occurred in the area of adoptions by lesbians. A case in Denver, Colorado, was won by a lesbian who was the lover of a woman who had died, leaving her custody of a seven-year-old daughter.[11] The lesbian sought and won custody of the child despite the objections of the deceased woman's family. Recently several other states have sought gay foster parents for gay teenagers with behavioral problems. These are substantial gains into previously excluded areas for people who are openly gay. However, the changes are as yet isolated pieces of progression. Some legal battles are still fought emotionally and not from the research evidence. A Missouri court as recently as 1982 concluded that "contact with their mother's lesbian lover would impair the children's emotional development" and therefore awarded custody of the children to the father in a divorce hearing.[12]

The homosexual person seeking a child through an adoption agency is fighting a losing battle at this point. That does not mean the battle should not be fought . . . in fact, someone always has to pave the way for change to occur. On the other hand, the greatest chance for homosexuals to have children is to have them biologically (as most do), to become pregnant by artificial insemination, or to adopt independently.

Am I advocating placing children with avowed homosexuals? I would advocate placing children with anyone who wants them unless it can be shown that it would be harmful to the child. If it can be proven that there would be harm in placing a child with a homosexual, then a child should not be placed in a homosexual home. If it cannot be proven, then why not place children in homosexual homes?

Summary

For some "specials" the current picture of adoption is a blessing and for others it is a curse. The "special" child has a better chance of being adopted now than ever before, but the "special" parents have less chance of finding a child to adopt than ever before.

At the same time, the "specials" in our population, when closely examined, become less "special." About one of every ten children is labeled handicapped and one out of every five adults is labeled handicapped; this constitutes a significant number in our society who are mentally retarded, emotionally disturbed, physically handicapped; have learning disabilities, or impairments of speech, vision, or hearing. Despite these large numbers of people labeled handicapped, adoption remains a difficult, and at times, impossible process for the person labeled handicapped or "special."

It is hard enough in the United States today for anyone to adopt, but for "special" parents, adoption through the normal adoption agency channels is nearly impossible. The few who will succeed are those who really push to prove their parenting ability and those who are just plain lucky. No matter what your chances, fight the system if you want a child, but be prepared to lose. Get on the adoption agencies' waiting lists but be prepared to wait indefi-

nitely. If you are "special" and want to be a parent, look around
. . . look everywhere. Your options are more limited, so you must
be even more creative and diligent in your approach than most people who want to find a child to adopt.

Deep Dark Secrets | 9

SECRETS ARE POWERFUL. THEY ARE POWERFUL PRODUCERS OF CURI-
osity, action, guilt, rumor, and panic. They cause people to feel
worthless. They demean and shame people. They haunt people
and they obsess people. The impact of secrets is jolting and far-
reaching.

Despite the tremendous power, mostly negative, that secrets hold,
no single institution is as riddled with secrecy as adoption. Adoption secrecy supersedes the amount of secrecy surrounding mental
health. It ranks above the secrecy that shrouds physical illness. It
surpasses the secrecy of issues such as cheating, abortion, drugs,
premarital sexual activity, or illicit affairs. Secrecy permeates the
adoption scene from the moment adoptive parents learn of their
infertility, from the discovery of the pregnancy by the birthmother,
from the careful choice of words to describe in nonidentifying ways
the "other" parents, from the surreptitious transfer of the child from
one home to another, from the fearful sealing of adoption records,
and from the reluctance of the adoption agencies to support needed
change.

Why, in our society today, is this secrecy in adoption necessary?
What are we supposed to be trying to protect? Is it healthy for the

people involved in adoption to have this much to hide? Are the reasons for the secrecy as valid today as they were a generation ago? What's wrong with being open about adoption?

The primary area of secrecy currently coming under attack is the sealed record. This single issue has caught the imagination of the media and the attention of legislators. The sealed record issue has also caused the adoption agencies to cringe and protect, the adoptive parents to shout and fear, the adoptees to unite and fight, and birthparents to fantasize and anticipate.

The sealed birth record is not the only secret part of adoption, it is merely the issue of today. The changes in this area will predict the potential opening of other secret areas in the adoption process. It is impossible to tamper with one area of adoption without causing reverberations throughout the whole system. No matter whether we are opening Pandora's box with the aim of unsealing the sealed birth record or not, the militants (who must exist for any significant change to occur) say they will not rest until birth records are open.

Current Laws on Adoptee's Birth Record

The laws giving adoptees access to their original birth certificate vary from state to state and certainly from country to country. Few laws on this subject are specific, and therefore, they are open to the individual judge's interpretation. Even if the birth records are opened, exactly what information will be disclosed to the adoptee is not clear. Unless the laws are clarified, the end result is likely to be many individual and frequently contradictory rulings.

The laws from state to state vary from year to year also. Since 1976, Minnesota, Connecticut, and North Dakota have opened birth records for controlled access by adoptees. Ohio mandated the disclosure to future adoptees of nonidentifying medical and social histories, but Virginia and Louisiana have passed measures to curtail access to their records.[1] Many bills introduced but dropped in recent legislative sessions will undoubtedly be reconsidered.

The current Minnesota law is being given the most attention and is frequently referred to as the model legislation for other proposed laws. This law provides that adoptees over twenty-one can have their original birth certificates unsealed as long as the birthparents consent. This consent can be given at any time. If an adoptee seeks the opening of these records, the Department of Public Welfare has six months to contact the birthparents. If either parent listed on the original birth certificate refuses, is no longer living, or cannot be located, the birth certificate can be unsealed only by obtaining a court order.

States vary a great deal in their specific laws; some say the adoptee must be eighteen, not twenty-one; some have review boards if the adoptee does not like the decision; others give out information but not identities. In order to know what is happening in each specific state, you need to check with that state at the time you want to have access to the records.

While other countries have fewer adoptions than in the United States, they seem to view opening of the records for adult adoptees in a much more liberal way. Scotland made provision for adult adoptees to have access to their original birth records at the time they established a basis for adoption. In Canada, nonidentifying information is relatively easy to obtain, but there is a need to show "cause" for records to be opened with identifying information, and variability is shown on this interpretation from one province to another. Great Britain in 1975 recognized the need for adult adoptees' legal right to have birth information made available to them.[2] While this opening of the record occurs only with some type of meeting with a counselor for all adoptees seeking birth records, the records have been opened rather quickly from the time adoptions became significant in Great Britain. Other countries obviously are more flexible on this issue than the United States. One Canadian writer suggests the explanation for the difference in legislative action on opening the birth records for adult adoptees may be because of the weakening of the kinship found within the family structure:

> Adoptive kinships, having been grafted onto the mainstream family system and intended to simulate it in all ways, became thus a kind of symbolic bulwark against the progressive weakening of the family as institution . . . Perhaps the adoptive family and the legislation that brought it into being represents the last possibility on this continent for an assertion of institutional authority and control in family matters.[3]

No matter what the cause of the intercountry differences in the records being opened for adult adoptees, it is essential to learn from the lessons of those countries that are currently experiencing the effects of these opened records. We can all learn from one another and save making the same mistakes.

Definition of Terms

The terms used in discussing the sealed birth records are not always clear. In order to discuss this topic with clarity, it is important that the terms used are familiar.

Sealed birth record refers to the original birth certificate that is replaced by an amended one at the time the child is legally adopted. The original birth certificate with the name of at least the birth-mother is then sealed and may not be opened unless the specific requirements of the state are met.

Adoption records are the records kept by the adoption agency about the individual adoption; they include the names of birthparents and much additional information. Medical and background information on birthparents, adoptive parents, and the adopted child are found in these records.

Good cause is a legal term used in cases where sufficient grounds to open birth records to the adoptee are determined. An example of good cause would be suspicion of a genetic life-threatening medical history that might be verified by contacting the birthparent. Good cause is interpreted differently from state to state and from court to court.

Searchers are adoptees who seek information on their birth history. They may want general information, they may want specific identifying data, and/or they may want to have contact with the birthparents. Most people agree that the adoptee should be an adult before receiving help in his or her birth search.

Reunions are the personal contacts of the adoptee with the birthparent.

Changes in Adoption

When adoption procedures were first instituted, the needs of the child were considered far less important than they are today. The adoptive parents were the primary clients being served; they were the ones who had saved this orphan from a terrible fate. At times, the motivation for adoption was more to provide help to the adoptive parents than to find a home for an unwanted child. These adoptions were conducted on a rather informal basis.

As time went by, the procedures and motivations for adoption changed. Children became slightly more valued. Bloodlines were considered less important, at least intellectually, in the United States, where it was believed that anyone could be successful if he or she tried. This same factor is probably why adoption was a slower process to evolve in Great Britain. In the early 1930s, formal adoption emerged; it was a white institution founded to place white infants in white families. Concurrently, the field of social welfare developed. Adoption became a formal process handled by the formal institution called the adoption agency. Emphasis was on screening children to find the right child for the couple. The child was not yet the central ingredient; the adopting parents were.

As adoptive parents formalized this process legally, they also sought privacy to build their future around this new family that they wanted to be "normal." In order to maintain privacy, the birth records were officially sealed. In other words, no one could find out who the birthparents of an adopted child were without going through the courts. The adoptee, or anyone else, could have access only to the amended birth certificate which identified the child only with his or her adoptive parents. The only way the birth certificate was identified as that of an adopted child was the fact that it said "amended" on it.

The next change in the adoption scene was the development of the "in the best interest of the child" concept. The new emphasis on the child came about as babies, especially white ones, were more in demand. There were more people who wanted babies than there were babies. So now we began to put the emphasis on what would be best for the child. This is a relatively new concept in adoption.

Clamor for More Change

Until fairly recently, no one seemed upset about the fact that birth records were sealed. This should be no surprise. In the first place, despite the fact that there are at least five million adoptees in the United States,[4] they constitute a small minority. This minority group is fragmented into other special groups such as white adoptees, black adoptees, and older adoptees. It is hard to get these diverse segments to identify strongly enough with each other to make their impact felt, but that is changing.

The second factor in the recent emphasis on opening the sealed record is the age of the adoptees. Since birth records were not sealed until around the 1940s, the demand to open these records has been fairly recent. Many of the adoptees affected by sealed records are only currently reaching the age of majority.

The third fact which has underscored the sealed record controversy has been the advent of militancy as a means of causing changes in our society. The sixties showed the United States the impact of vocal minorities when they shouted in unison. Groups previously quiet rose up as they saw other minority groups succeed by making continued, loud demands.

The fourth factor influencing the demands to unseal the birth records of adoptees has been the recent emphasis on genealogical and historical heritage. The popularity of Alex Haley's *Roots* strongly emphasized people's heritage and links with the past.[5] We are part of a long chain of history that needs to be understood if we are to understand ourselves. For the adult adoptee, that part of this chain of identity is missing.

The fifth factor emphasizing the need to open the birth records of adoptees was the cry of discrimination. Discrimination in most forms is viewed negatively in our society. There is no doubt that in adoption, discrimination is rampant.

The clamor for change was not voiced by all the people involved in adoption. In fact, the clamor came primarily from one group. Perhaps the advent of the concept that adoption should be in "the best interest of the child" made adoptees feel they had a central place in adoption and they sensed the power this gave them. Now they wanted to exercise their power. They sought to have the laws changed. They wanted their birth records opened.

The adoptive parents, the birthparents, and the adoption agencies responded differently to demands of adoptees that their birth records be opened. All involved, however, including some of the adoptees, have responded defensively.

The Emotional Issue of Opening the Birth Record

Adoption itself, as we have discussed, is an emotional issue. The opening of the sealed record seems to be symbolic of the entire adoption issue. The pain for each of the participants is real, yet none of the antagonists seems to understand the opponent's pain. The pain seems shared but different . . . separate but equal . . . to all the people involved in adoption.

Each of the participants must deal with the stigma of shame and guilt attached to adoption and currently embodied in the issue of opening the sealed record. The adoptive couple must once again confront their feelings of failure in not conceiving. The artificiality of adoption brings this home for them as they recognize that their children are not children born to them. Our society believes that adoption is a secondary means of achieving parenthood, and so do most adoptive parents. The potential opening of the sealed birth record of their adopted child further enforces in their minds that these are different children and they are different parents. If they had not failed to conceive in the first place, they would not be experiencing this problem. They feel guilty and ashamed that they are not *real* parents.

The adoptee must deal with the likely stigma of his or her past. The specter of illegitimacy is not as great today as in previous years, but it still exists. If the birth record is opened, the adoptee would no longer be shielded from knowledge of potential inherited weaknesses. Yet, the unknown stigma for the adoptee may seem worse than the reality of the known, no matter how bad. The stigma of rejection is never fully erased for the adoptee, even with the continual reassurance of having been "chosen." The adoptee feels guilt for his rejection.

The stigma of guilt and shame falls also on the birthparents when the entire foundation of adoption is being scrutinized. The birthmother especially must look again at an issue that involved great pain for her at another time in her life. Her problem may be compounded by how she has incorporated the relinquished child into her new life. A hidden secret, the relinquished child, may cause the feelings of guilt and shame to be exacerbated. Her unresolved feelings about having "given away her child" may cause her guilt to reemerge with great intensity.

The stigma of guilt and shame is also raised by the role of the adoption agencies. Beliefs of the past are no longer held as truth. The agencies, viewing their past roles in convincing the pregnant woman what was best for her, are now not quite so sure. The secrets of the past may now be opened, and the role of the adoption agencies may not look quite so humanitarian under careful scrutiny. The adoption agencies are being asked to account for their roles in past practices in which they no longer believe and in which they may even regret their participation.

Along with all this guilt and shame, fear emerges. Adult adoptees fear they won't like what they find out about themselves or they fear the second rejection from the birthparent. The birthparents fear the blame their son or daughter will have for them for what they have done. The adoptive parents fear the loss of their child to another set of parents. The adoption agencies fear criticism for what they have done and for what they have tried to do.

The fear, the stigma, the defensiveness all come with each of the participants as they seek to solve the sealed record problem. No one listens, everyone seeks to prove his or her point. Research studies, seldom conclusive, are quoted to support the side each person chooses to defend. Everyone shifts the blame to someone else. Communication becomes nonexistent. The wheels of compromise and understanding grind to a halt.

A Suggested Approach

So what is the answer to the problems posed by opening the sealed records of adoptees? How do we overcome the issues each side presents? Where do we find the meeting ground of compromise?

Of all the chapters in this book, this one has been by far the hardest for me to write. As with everyone else involved, the issues here are personal for me, too. It is so easy to take a stand to support my role as an adoptive mother. Yet, that is too frequently the case for all of us who are so close to the issues being debated. It is time to stop taking stands and approach the problem differently.

As I read and speak with the people on all sides of the issue, I am struck by several things:

Each person I speak with or read about really believes in what he or she is saying about opening the sealed adoption records.

I essentially believe what each person tells me . . . they convince me of the rightness of their stand.

If everyone is right, then this must be an individual issue.

Individual issues must be handled individually, even in adoption.

I am struck by these points because of the philosophical point I begin with as I examine this emotional issue. The only way to solve the problem of the conflicting views on opening the sealed records must be to have a philosophical stand on the issue; mine is based on being a birthmother, an adoptive mother, a wife, a daughter, a psychologist, and a teacher.

I believe in the individual adult's ability to decide for himself or herself. For me to tell others what is best for them is to imply that *they* are not competent to run their own lives. For me to decide the direction of another person's life is to be arrogant and pompous. For me to prevent people from making mistakes says mistakes are wrong, but they aren't. I can help people see other ways of approaching an issue but I cannot make decisions concerning anyone's life but my own. If I allow people to make only the decisions with which I agree, it means I have not really believed in people at all.

This is a time to seek to understand the views of others, not to find fault with their views. To seek to assess blame is futile and divisive. Right or wrong is not necessary to establish in order to find direction. One person is not made right by another's wrongness. On personal issues, right is a personal matter.

The most critical ingredient in solving problems is open communication. If we try to communicate our specific view and our opponents try to communicate their specific view, this is not communication. Communication is possible only with listening. Talking isn't the key . . . *listening is.* You already know where you are on this issue; now *really* seek to hear where the other people are. Try to figure out what possible reasons they have for taking the position they do, rather than looking for the fallacies in their argument.

The ability to be open to change is an essential ingredient in life because we live in a changing world. The absolutes of yesterday are the outdated concepts of today. New situations demand new solutions. New needs of people demand different policies. If there is no room to change or modify our positions, there is no need to try to communicate.

In order to evaluate the importance of any disagreement, you must evaluate the potential loss if the other side wins. What is the worst thing that can happen if you lose this battle? If winning the battle becomes the most important goal, then the issues are no longer of importance. We are then arguing simply out of pride. Seeking vindication prevents seeking solutions. Ultimately, even if a "wrong" solution is imposed, people will survive. The resiliency of children involved with adoption exists in adults also.

Different Views on Opening the Sealed Record
In order to better understand the issues involved in opening the birth record of the adoptee, it is essential to look at some of the

ways each person is or might be affected by this change. What is the stand of adoptees and why? What does opening the sealed record mean to adoptive parents? What happens to the birthparents in this process? What is the role of the adoption agencies and what could this role be? There is no way to consider this issue without trying to look at it from the perspective of each of the people involved.

• *The Adoptee and the Sealed Record*

When the sealed record issue is brought up, it is the adoptees who are first considered. They are the ones who want information on their history. Some want general information and others want specific facts and names. Virtually all adoptees believe the information given out about birthparents and adoptees' history should be provided only after the adoptee reaches adulthood.

The studies of adoptees so far are limited. We do know generally some things about adoptees who search for additional information and reunions with their birthparents. We know several things, for example, from the research reported in *The Adoption Triangle*:[6]

1. Most adoptees who search are female.

2. More reunions seem to be sought by adoptees who are told fairly late in life of their adoptions.

3. Most adoptees were satisfied with their reunions.

4. About half the adoptees developed a meaningful relationship with the birthparents.

5. Searches for birthparents were usually triggered by some significant event like the birth of a child or the death of the adoptive parent.

6. The adoptive family relationship was rarely permanently damaged as a result of the reunion.

This research is not based on a truly random sampling of adoptee and birthparent reunions because the subjects voluntarily came forward to be studied. However, it is the best research reported so far.

We don't know how many adoptees would really search for their birthparents if the records were in actuality open. In Scotland, where birth records of adoptees are open, approximately one percent of the adoptees seek this information.[7] One adoption agency in Texas reported that less than one percent of the 14,000 adoptees they have placed have initiated attempts to locate or identify their birthparents.[8] It is difficult to predict from these figures how many adoptees would indeed search. The dilemma now is that even if the adoptee wants to search, he or she cannot in most states in this country.

We have only sketchy background material on this subject, because studies are necessarily new and quite limited. Therefore, it is important to read primarily personal views on this subject. That's great . . . those are the best kinds. Remember, this is a personal issue. We are trying to understand all the views of each of the people involved in the adoption picture, and personal accounts can tell us their stories in a context within which we can identify.

The Search for Anna Fisher[9] is one woman's account of the trauma of her search. This book was one impetus behind the quest of adoptees to have their birth records opened. Florence Fisher, who wrote the book, has been an outspoken voice for opening the birth records of adoptees. Her story is a moving, emotional appeal to open the birth record for any adoptee who wants this information.

An even earlier voice was that of Jean Paton from a group called Orphan Voyage. Her work in this area forms a steady plea for change. Reading the literature from her group is helpful in understanding the needs of adoptees.[10]

The single book most representative of the research being done on the effects of adoption reunions is *The Adoption Triangle*, mentioned earlier. This book, written by a team of social workers from Vista Del Mar, a former adoption agency, is "must" reading by all who choose to debate the subject of opening the sealed birth record. Other helpful books and articles have been written by adoptees telling their side of this issue.[11] Just about any of these will help people understand the specific point of view of each of these individual authors.

The book *Faint Trails*[12] is designed to help adult adoptees and birth parents in reunification searches. This book, written by someone who himself was adopted and who became a searcher, describes many potential means of searching.

Another source of help in understanding the adoptee's point of view is to attend meetings of some of their organizations. These support groups help other adoptees in their searches. They usually welcome people from other sides of the adoption picture, such as birthparents and adoptive parents. Groups such as the Adoptees' Liberation Movement Association (ALMA, Post Office Box 154, Washington Bridge Station, New York, New York 10033), Orphan Voyage (2141 Road 2300, Cedaredge, Colorado 81413), International Soundex Reunion Registry (Post Office Box 2312, Carson City,

Nevada 89702), or Adoptees in Search (Post Office Box 41016, Bethesda, Maryland 20014) are all adoptee organizations. Remember, these groups are as varied as adoption agencies. Some will seem extremely harsh in their approach. Others will seem more moderate. The approach of each group changes as its membership changes.

Carey found the help of one group in California extremely important in her search for her birthparents. Carey was twenty-five and had just gotten divorced when she read in a local newspaper about the possibility of adoptees finding their birthparents and the impacts of the reunions. The more she thought about this concept, the more it appealed to her. It wasn't because she was unhappy with her adoptive parents; she wasn't. In fact, as she told them of her thoughts, they told her they would be glad to help her. She sought information about her birthparents from the private adoption agency in Texas from which she was adopted, but she was turned down immediately. A letter from her adoptive parents indicating their support in her search didn't help.

Prior to Carey's divorce, she had learned she was having difficulty becoming pregnant. Her physician asked for information about her mother and her birth history. Carey realized she had none of the requested information. Because of her need for medical information, because of her adoptive parents' support in her search, and because of the help from a group of adoptees who told her what to do at each step, she contacted a lawyer in Texas who indicated his willingness to legally seek to have her records opened. The judge in the case was in complete agreement with the cause Carey had shown for opening her record. And, with this judgment in her favor, she received the name of her birthmother. But then what? Again, the adoptee support group told her of ways to seek her birthmother now that she had a name . . . ways that had worked for other adoptees. Carey was able to find out that her mother had lived in a small town near the agency when she had relinquished her child. Relatives in the town, after hearing of an "old friend" who was hunting for her, gave Carey the information that would allow her to make contact with her birthmother.

Even with this information, Carey was not sure how to proceed. At this point, she even went into limited psychotherapy to examine her motives for searching. Fortunately, her therapist encouraged her to go on in her search. The therapist also urged her to be mindful of the others involved, because Carey's birthmother had remarried. Finally, a friend of Carey's contacted Carey's birthmother on the phone. The friend asked if this was a good time to talk; she had information about the woman's daughter whom she had placed for adoption twenty-five years ago. The woman said the caller was wrong, but she didn't hang up. The friend asked if there would be a better time to talk and Carey's birthmother said yes. They arranged to talk the next day. Carey, listening to the call, was elated, fearful, anxious, and apprehensive. She called the next day and identified herself to her birthmother. Her birthmother acknowledged to Carey that she was her mother but that was over now . . . she had a new family who knew nothing about Carey. Carey's birthmother said her husband had just had heart surgery and he could not learn about this now.

She knew that somehow she would meet her birthmother and her half brothers and half sister. But for now, she was willing to wait. Carey talked to her birthmother three times that year. They exchanged pictures and some information. She is hoping to ease her birthmother into the relationship, but she says adamantly that she will not wait forever. She knows that at some point she will show up on the doorstep and announce her arrival, with or without an invitation.

Carey says she is not seeking a new family; she is seeking a missing link. This attitude is frequently conveyed by those adoptees who search for their roots. Reunions, or sometimes simply just additional information given to the adoptee, will complete this missing link. Without it, the adoptee's identity is not complete.

Some argue that searchers will not like what they find. There are histories of incest, child abuse, and mental disease. The adoptees respond that truth is better than fantasy. Truth helps the adoptee know what he or she is up against even if the reality is harsh.

Jill was my first introduction to an adoptee's fantasies and search. I was in my first year of teaching in high school and she was a member of my ninth-grade English class. I was twenty-four and she was fifteen. She began to send me anonymous letters saying she thought I was her mother. Then she began to call me, and I told her we should talk about this in person. She finally agreed and came forward. We talked for a long time about her adoption. She felt her parents knew of her birthparents but wouldn't tell her. She had searched through everything in the house trying to find out the identities of her birthparents. She had no reason to think I was her birthmother, but she wanted one so much that she fantasized that women she liked were her "real" mother.

It is difficult for anyone who is not adopted to fully understand what being adopted means. At times, the militancy of the searchers catches others off guard. Their anger seems so out of proportion. They feel an intense sense of frustration in their attempts to piece together their genetic medical history or even just their social history. Not all adoptees will experience this intense need to search for their birthparents. For those who do search, however, the barriers they encounter seem to them to be senseless walls dividing them from themselves . . . they seem like roadblocks to wholeness.

• *The Adoptive Parents and the Sealed Record*
Adoptive parents look at the current upheaval in adoption and feel their own fate is once again out of their hands. To be dependent on others through their infertility struggle and through their efforts to adopt a child had been bad enough. But now the threat of having their children taken from them again by another set of parents gives them a lack of control over the destiny of their own lives. Many adoptive parents are alarmed. Their illusions of their "normal" family are shattered.

Not all adoptive parents respond with fear. In fact, because searches are such a personal matter, it is hard for many adoptive parents to even understand what precipitates an adoptee's search. Dana and Jim had given little thought to searches by adoptees except to be curious about the current articles they were seeing. But it was not really relevant to them because their adopted children, Mark and Amy, were only thirteen and ten. Perhaps they would cross that bridge sometime but they hoped not. Amy had many more questions about her birthmother than Mark, but they felt that they had handled her questions without much trouble. So when Mark stated one evening that he needed to find out about his birthparents, Dana and Jim were shocked. Mark knew the hospital in California where he was born. He further and quite accurately reasoned, "There could not be that many baby boys born at 7:08 in the morning in that hospital on that day." He wanted to call right then and get his birthmother's name. Dana and Jim felt awful. All the thoughts of failure rushed through their minds. Trying to remain calm, Dana told Mark she didn't think the hospital would give him this information although he was welcome to try, but why did he want to know? Mark responded with great seriousness,

"I really want to find out if I'm related to George Washington." Searches are very personal.

Adoptive parents who learn more about searches become less threatened by the prospect. Knowledge, especially personal knowledge, seems to make searches or reunions less potentially harmful to the adoptive relationship. The amount of literature from the adoptive parents' perspective on the issue of the sealed birth record is limited. However, as accounts of reunions and searches are read, adoptive parents learn how others have responded.[13]

The support groups that adoptive parents have established have been a helpful system for them. Yet these groups have been one of the primary reasons why much of the legislation on opening the sealed records has been stopped. With the tide continuing to flow toward opening the records anyhow, reunions and searches become more common to the members of these groups. Adoptive parents will know better how to react when this threat is posed to them.

As an adoptive parent, no matter how hard you wish, you cannot wish away the existence of another set of parents for your child. Your love for the child is a commitment to raise the child, not to cut him off from anyone in his life. In fact, the child may need your love and commitment even more if he chooses to search for his birthparents. People who argue that searches bring grief or pain do not consider the potential help of the adoptive parents who are supportive of the child they have raised to adulthood. The marriage of a child does not lessen the bond of those people who have raised her; it is simply a different kind of relationship . . . a noncompetitive relationship because there is no need to compete. Adoptive parents have already done that which they sought to do . . . to raise a child. This is the same case in reunions. Birthparents are just different people who do not compete with what adoptive parents have done because, again, the adoptive parents have already done it.

One of the reasons birthparents are threatening to adoptive parents is a fantasy. Adoptive parents, frequently older than birthparents, have difficulty viewing birthparents as growing older. Because of the secrecy in adoption, we seem to freeze these people as beautiful, youthful people . . . they aren't. Marta was adopted independently when she was six days old. Her adoptive parents, Sue and Rod, met the birthparents. They maintained contact through the years by letter, but it wasn't until Marta was eight that the birthfather asked to see her. The meeting was arranged to be held at a park where the birthfather could watch Marta play but not have direct contact with her. Sue took Marta. The meeting at the park may have helped the birthfather but nothing like it helped Sue. Sue's last contact with him had been eight years before when the father was young and handsome. She and Rod were ten years older than either of the birthparents. To now see the birthfather eight years older was a revelation to Sue. The concrete image helped her to dispel the fantasy she had established about Marta's birthparents. As with adoptees, the fantasy we have may create more problems than the reality we might experience.

Adoption is a different way of parenting, yet there are many ways that it is like any other kind of parenting. We are all seeking to make our children happy, self-sufficient human beings. We are trying to meet their needs without forgetting that we, too, have needs. But it is possible that both can be met in similar ways. One adoptive mother whose background in raising special children speaks poignantly of good parenting:

On first reflection there is something threatening to a parent about a child wanting to go off and find his or her "real parents." It feels like rejection, as if the adoptive parents were not all they should have been or did not do their job well. But when examined from the perspective of the child's needs, it is apparent that good parenting involves encouraging or even becoming a partner in the search. In a sense, the true function of parents is to make themselves obsolete; that is, to prepare their children for the time when they will no longer be dependent on the parent.[14]

Allow your children to grow and to become. No one can take them from you because you do not own them. For a significant part of their lives, you were a significant person. After you have been that in another person's life, it can never be taken away. If searching is an important thing to your children, then help them to search. There is nothing you can save them from, nor anything you can do for them. Your help and support, and maybe your permission, is what they want and need from you. If pain is the result of their search, help them with their pain. If joy is a part of their search, then experience this joy with them by your participation in and permission for their endeavor.

• The Birthparents and the Sealed Record

Birthparents have been the primary sufferers in adoption, the ones who may have felt only the pain and anguish. For some, the pain has lingered ever since the relinquishment of the child, despite the reassurances of "You are doing the right thing," or "You will put this behind you and build a new life." Like everyone else in adoption, each birthparent has responded to the opening of the birth records in a very personal way.

Some birthparents have welcomed the opening of the sealed records as a possible second chance to tell their story to the child they gave away. Others wait in dread for the phone call or knock on the door which may bring back their past. Some birthparents search for their children placed for adoption, and some hide for fear they will be found. Most birthparents seem to feel positively about the potential contact they might have with the children they placed for adoption.[15]

Previously, birthparents have sat quietly at the sidelines as others in the adoption scene wrestled over what to call them. "Biological parents" was the chosen term for a time, despite the mechanical ring. "Natural parents" was found objectionable to adoptive parents, who already felt unnatural enough. "Real parents" met the same objection. Other choices that have been used from time to time have been "genetic parents," "original parents," or "first parents." Birthparents seems to be the term of choice for today.

Perhaps our choice of terms to describe women who have placed their children for adoption is somewhat based on our acceptance of them. The changing view about pregnancies of unmarried women and their greater acceptance today undoubtedly help the birthparents of the majority of children now placed for adoption. As birthparents have become more vocal, we better understand their position. Books such as *Birthmark* help us to understand the plight of the woman who chooses to place her child for adoption.[16] This story of one woman's hopes to do otherwise and her continual involvement with her daughter helps others on the adoption scene to more realistically view the birthparent.

Organizations of birthparents like Concerned United Birthparents, Inc. (CUB, 2000 Walker Street, Des Moines, Iowa 50317) help birthparents find support that further encourages them to come out of hiding. These organizations help birthparents feel less stigma than previously. They also help the birthparents who seek reunions with their adopted children to know how to search for them.

The role of the birthparents in the opening of the birth record is a controversial one. The question exists as to what rights the birthmother has in this area. If she placed a child for adoption in the belief that the record was forever sealed, what now happens to this implied contract? Some of the more militant proponents for opening the birth record say she has no rights . . . she abdicated her rights at the time of her relinquishment. Others say that her rights must be protected because she was told that her secret would never be revealed. Still others would say that most birthmothers want to meet or know of their child. A small group would go even further and advocate that the birthparent's right to have contact with the child she placed for adoption should be resumed even before the child reaches the age of eighteen.[17] And the remainder say, "Let's ask her first." Let's set up the means to update information and also to update feelings about the necessity of confidentiality. Today is not the same as yesterday.

In *The Adoption Triangle,* subjects, including birthparents, voluntarily came forward to discuss their adoption experience.[18] While this sample is necessarily biased, it is the only study of people who placed children for adoption. Of the group of thirty-eight birthparents, half of them continued to feel the loss and pain of the relinquishment; this was despite the fact that they had relinquished their children between ten to thirty-three years before the interviews. Of the group, eighty-two percent said they would be interested in a reunion, but eight percent said they did not want reunions because of their present families. A small percentage of birthparents were actively searching for their children. Not wanting to hurt or upset the adoptive parents was mentioned by the great majority of the birthparents who were interviewed. While these figures are helpful, the personal letters quoted by the authors show with more impact the views of the birthparents.

Birthparents' abilities to incorporate their past child into their lives vary. Eleanor just turned fifty-three. She has been married for thirty-five years to a man who, until this past year, did not know she had a child when she was eighteen. In fact, neither did Eleanor's son nor any of her other relatives know of her daughter's birth. Eleanor's secret was always safe because so few people knew. Then the publicity started coming out on adoptees searching for their birthparents. Eleanor read the stories with mixed feelings. On the one hand she felt it would be wonderful to hear from her daughter, to know what she looked like and how she was doing in life. On the other hand, she felt fearful of how others in her life would respond to the news of a daughter. Then the day for which Eleanor could never be quite prepared came when her daughter called. A reunion was set up that allowed time for Eleanor to break the news to Frank, her husband. The reunion was strained but satisfactory. The life of Eleanor's daughter had gone in a direction completely different than Eleanor's, and they found they had little in common except a birth history. They exchanged short letters after their meeting but little other contact was ever made. That seems to be satisfactory to each of them. At the same time, each of them discusses the reunion with positive feelings. It met a need for each of them and they are happy they met.

The role of the birthfather is more obscure than even that of the birthmother. Some reunions are between adoptees and their birthfathers. Alex wanted to meet both of his birthparents. The meeting with his birthfather was even more critical after he found that his birthmother was mentally retarded and in an institution. Fortunately, his birthmother's relatives were able to provide him with the information he needed to find his father. He made contact with his birthfather and found they had phenomenal areas of similarity. They both were avid fishermen, they both liked wildly colored shirts, and they had jobs in similar fields of work. Alex maintains contact with him on a regular basis. He even introduced his birthfather to his adoptive parents, who supported his desire to search for his birthparents.

Birthparents are frequently viewed as they were at the time they relinquished the child. The adoptive parents of the child often view them as young and mixed-up. The adoption agencies continue to view them as young people who were immature, sexually permissive, and confused. Our image of the birthparents is frozen because they are finished with the adoption process after they fulfill their function of providing a child. There is no continuing contact with the birthparents, and so we know very little about them. The birthparent is not allowed to mature, to grow older, to get straightened out, or to change his or her mind.

In order to understand the position of birthparents in adoption, we must speak with them and listen to them. We must try to understand their place today, because viewing them from an outdated, twenty- or thirty-year-old perspective distorts who they are and prevents us from understanding their place in adoption today.

• *The Adoption Agencies and the Sealed Record*

The adoption agencies approach the sealed record from a perspective slightly different from that of the adoptee, the adoptive parent, or the birthparent. However, as with each of these other groups, the adoption agencies also have a personal perspective. Adoption agencies have policies, but it is the worker who personally experiences the joy, the rejection, the fear, or the hurt . . . not the adoption agency.

The adoption agencies have rules about how their social workers are to respond to requests for birth information. Each agency has its own general framework and each worker interprets the rules of the agency somewhat differently. While each worker feels some obligation to support the system within which he or she works, many workers are actively seeking changes within the system. Other social workers are incensed with the potential opening of birth records to adoptees and are actively seeking to maintain the past system.

The adoption agencies and their workers feel trapped by the cries for change in opening the records. They find themselves the scapegoats for everyone's anger. At times, the criticisms are justified, and at times the criticisms are unfair. Birthmothers who look back on their time of relinquishment feel that they were unduly influenced by the social workers who told them that it was the best thing to do. They forget their confusion and desperation when they came to the agency for help. Adoptive parents are angered with the adoption agencies who guaranteed they would be the permanent parents for their adopted child. They also now feel they were not given accurate and complete information on their child's background. They, too, forget their feelings of expectation and gratitude toward the agency as they received their greatly desired child. The adoptees, feeling like pawns in the system, vent hostility on agencies who have the information they want about who they are. They, too, forget the adoption agencies were acting in the way the times dictated. Times have changed rapidly, and agencies have not always changed with equal speed.

In the past, the adoption agencies have been very much in control of the adoption process. Laws that have been passed seem to put adoption agencies more and more in control. While minor setbacks have occurred—such as when they were mandated to provide accurate, truthful, and complete information to adoptive parents on the child's medical and social history—the power of the adoption agencies has increased over the years. The greatest threat that the adoption agencies have ever experienced is the opening of the sealed birth record. Some agencies believe that opening the birth record will signal the end of adoption as we know it in the United States. Other agencies are already accommodating the proposed changes.

The approach of some agencies is to do nothing . . . to wait until the courts mandate an opening of the records. This approach says that to set up the current system so that records could be updated would take too many people and would be contrary to the temporary role adoption agencies have traditionally maintained.[19] Many agencies, feeling pressure, are advising all the principals involved in adoption of the potential changes occurring in the law. Some agencies will go no further than that. Others are far more creative and forward-looking.

Already, some agencies, when contacted by the birthparents, the adoptee, or the adoptive parents, are seeking to do what these people request. One private adoption agency was contacted by a birthparent who wanted to know about the child she had placed twelve years ago. She wanted to know if the adoptive parents would be willing to give her some additional information about the child. The adoption agency contacted the adoptive parents, who willingly consented, and asked that the birthmother also update her medical file with the adoption agency. The same agency is actively passing information back and forth between people involved in adoption. Sometimes this merely consists of information but not identities. At other times, identities may be given. This adoption agency does not feel it is its choice to decide how much information will be passed on. They believe that the people involved are the ones who should decide.

Obviously, approaching adoption in this way is time-consuming, but it is also a humane way to serve the people the adoption agencies say they want to help. This humanitarian approach to adoption is exemplified by Linda Burgess, an adoption agency social worker, who maintains that to force an adoptee to show "good cause" for opening his or her own birth record perpetuates the dependency the adoptee has on the judgment of others. She maintains that the changes needed to bring about the opening of the birth records will cause concern for some of the people in adoption in order for other people in adoption to grow:

The agencies, the courts, the doctors, and the adoptive parents, faced with the eventuality that facts formerly hidden will be revealed, will have to substitute candor for concealment and honesty for distortion. The effects will ripple backwards to free adoptees still in childhood from adult pretense. Adoptive parents will more readily face the fact that their adopted children are not their possessions, that they are born in one heritage, raised in another and will emerge as adults into the larger world which belongs equally to everyone.[20]

Adoption agencies are approaching the opening of the sealed records in widely divergent ways. Perhaps this is a necessary time so that many alternative ways to opening the record can be considered. One of the reasons adoption has failed to meet the current needs of many people in our society is because adoption has been approached from a single, rigid standpoint. Maybe we can profit from previous mistakes and provide multiple ways to meet people's varied needs.

Preparing for Opening the Birth Records

Adoption agencies need to prepare themselves and their clients for the potential opening of the birth record. So, too, do the individuals involved in adoption need to prepare themselves. Birth records are likely to be opened on a gradual basis and everyone has a part.

Agencies need to keep the letters that come from people who are seeking contact. Even though birth records are not opened now, when the records are opened, current statements from people stating their wishes will be important. Agencies should encourage their past clients to make their wishes known. At times the auxiliary groups of some of the adoption agencies are very active. Suggesting through these auxiliary groups and their publications that adoptive parents communicate their wishes to the agencies might help agencies to be more timely in their arguments. The use of the news media to help agencies encourage the updating of addresses and information would be a helpful preparatory approach. Even if the birth records were never opened, this procedure would enable people to have medical updating of the records that might be extremely helpful.

Each of the adoption participants should inform the adoption agency of how they feel about the possible opening of the sealed birth record of adoptees and make certain their file is updated.

Adoptive parents who believe it would be fine for their children to have additional information and/or to have reunions with their birthparents could inform the adoption agency. Just updating information on the child you have adopted may help the birthparent who wants information about the child she has relinquished. As an adoptive parent, you may inadvertently prevent the agency from releasing records that may be of help to your child if the agency feels it needs your permission before they will give out even general information to your child. It may be the formal permission that gives the adopted child the psychological permission to search.

The birthparent could make contact with the adoption agency also. The birthparents certainly should keep their file updated with significant medical information. At the same time a birthparent could update the file with personal information and file his or her wishes about contact with the adoptee. The adopted child who is having some problems with his or her adoption may be satisfied just to know a bit more about the birthparent as he or she is now. This may be especially helpful if the birthparent chooses not to have contact with the child but is willing to provide information about himself or herself. While information and reunions involve more birthmothers than birthfathers, it is helpful to have accurate and timely information on both birthparents. If either birthparent is willing to have contact with the adoptee when the child becomes an adult, this is important information for the adoption agency to have.

The adoptees, of course, need to take responsibility to let the adoption agencies know of their feelings about opening the sealed record. Before an adoptee seeks legal recourse to obtain the birth record, he or she should first see what the attitude of the adoption agency is. The adoption agency may be able and willing to provide all the help the adoptee needs. It certainly is the place to start. When adoption agencies testify about the limited numbers of adoptees who want records opened, it might be because adoptees have not first tried asking the adoption agencies. Also, if the adoptee would like to have contact with the birthparent, he or she should be certain that the adoption agency knows this.

Adoption agencies are supposed to be experts in the adoption process. They are supposed to know what everyone wants in respect to the opening of the sealed record. Their views are sought by lawmakers who scrutinize pending legislation. Currently, adoption agencies are not in a position to represent any of the parts of the adoption triangle with any degree of accuracy. The only way the views of all the adoption participants will be known to adoption agencies is if many people tell them. We must not depend on the adoption agencies for our welfare as in the past . . . we must educate the adoption agencies about where we are on this important issue.

While it is important for the adoption agency to know each individual's desires about opening the birth record, it is also important that these personal thoughts be conveyed to legislators. Legislators look to the adoption agencies to be experts and to represent all the parties in adoption. That may be inappropriate. It may also be that a certain bias prevents adoption agencies from representing all the individuals involved in adoption. In order to be certain your views are conveyed to the lawmakers, contact individual legislators and tell them how you feel. No one else represents you as well as you do.

Summary

Previously, the potential that an adoptee would try to make contact with the birthparents was frightening. The stigma attached to having a child out of wedlock was too great. Our society had too strong an emotional response to sex outside of marriage and to illegitimate children. Everyone needed to be protected from finding out about the "sinful" details that surrounded adoption.

Despite phenomenal changes in our attitudes toward sexual behavior, including sex outside of marriage, illegitimate pregnancy, and single parents, these changes are slow to be felt in the adoption scene. Adoption is still viewed in a maternalistic manner . . . everyone needs to be protected. The adoption agencies believe they know what is right for the child, for the adoptive parents, and for the birthparents. Even when all the parties involved would like to try new, innovative approaches, the adoption agencies frequently resist. Traditional adoption is maintained with great resistance to change.

The same secrecy safeguarding the identity of each person in agency adoptions is maintained in the court system by the sealing of the birth certificate of the adopted child. Perseverance, luck, and occasional help by an individual adoption agency or court may unlock these records for some adult adoptees. But many adult adoptees who search for information on their past will be denied access to the information that primarily concerns them.

Adoption agencies have an opportunity, with the potential opening of the birth records, to review previous policies and practices. Perhaps the changes brought about by opening these records will provide the impetus to review the whole secrecy issue that has pervaded adoption in the past. When adoption can shed its dependence on secrecy, it has the potential to become a healthier, viable alternative method of parenting.

Letting In Some Light | 10

SECRECY IMPLIES SHAME. THERE IS NEITHER NEED NOR JUSTIFICATION for the amount of secrecy that currently exists in adoption. The sealed birth record discussed in the last chapter is only the tip of the secrecy iceberg in adoption. The adoption process can survive and thrive with openness and honesty. It is time to let in some light on adoption.

Some of the ways to become more open and honest about adoption are quite simple. They involve changes that can easily be adapted into the adoption scene now. Other changes involve the more basic ways in which adoptions operate. Some changes involve individuals, and some changes involve the institution. The question is not whether there is a need for change in adoption; the question is which things should be changed first.

Individual Honesty in Adoption
Such a simple statement . . . put honesty into adoption . . . and yet it is so complex. The "differentness" of adopting causes new problems for families and compounds the regular family problems. To say we should be honest in order to avoid additional conflicts

is readily agreed upon by most people. To put this concept into practice is the real test.

David Kirk, an adoptive parent, speaks to the need of incorporating empathy and understanding in adoptive families. The mutualism of their shared adoptive situation is the very ingredient that helps each child accept his or her adoption:

> Sentiments of belongingness are strengthened when members are engaged in mutual aid arising from mutual needs. The condition of mutual needs in the adoptive parent-child relationship is the condition of mutual need of all parent-child relations, enlarged and emphasized by the discrepancies and losses both parents and children have suffered. As a method of integrating the child into the family, mutualism always begins with the parents. They must institute it and make it work. It is for them to set up the channels within which they can identify themselves with the child's situation, so that he, in his turn, can reach out to them and recognize them as the people to whom he unqualifiedly belongs. To be able to do this, the parents must have come to accept naturally, with comfort, their position in family and society.[1]

The adoptive parents must be honest with themselves about their infertility and their substitute method of parenting. Without this personal honesty that precedes sureness and confidence, the adoptive parents cannot empathize with or understand fully their adopted child and his or her pain. Love is a critical ingredient in all families, but the adoptive family also needs understanding and empathy.

The adoptive family is built on pain. We gloss over this as we talk of "chosen babies" and "how lucky we are to have found you" and how "your first mother gave you away because she loved you." But in truth, that is not what happened. These phrases pretend that pain was not there . . . they describe specialness by omission. Adopted families are special, I have no doubt about it. The specialness comes out mostly with honesty, not with omissions, illusions, fantasies, and pretenses. These give a false foundation to all the participants. There is no substitute for honesty in adoption.

Honesty begins first with the parents, the adoptive parents. Early in this book, the importance of coming to grips with your infertility was discussed. If you have pretended that it was *not* important that you failed to become pregnant and it *was* important, this stays with you for a long time . . . forever. If, rather than pretend, you can tell your spouse or someone else significant to you how truly important this was, you are laying the foundation of honesty with yourself. In order to be honest with your child, you must learn to first be honest with yourself.

Another means of pretending to yourself is making believe that your adopted family is like a "regular" family. It isn't. It is different. If you try to live with the illusions, then comments about "other" parents or "real" parents become especially painful. These comments plunge you back into reality. You leave yourself open to hurt when you fool yourself about yourself. If you know your family is different, you don't have to have your defenses up when someone tells you your family is different. You have a foundation that is based on reality.

If you are clear in your own mind about adoption and how you fit in society, the questions from your child about his or her adoption are easy to answer at any time. Feeling secure yourself about adoption lets your child feel secure also. If you hide aspects of and feelings about the adoption, this implies that something must be bad about adoption to make it necessary to hide.

When your three-year-old adopted daughter asks about her birth, tell her the truth . . . never lie to her. You are beginning a long process that tests your trustworthiness and your self-confidence. Even if it is easy to handle the three-year-old's questions with fibs or fabrications, the three-year-old will soon be a thirteen-year-old.

The messages and questions of the child who is older are more subtle. The eight-year-old adopted boy whose friend's parents have divorced and each remarried can talk about how hard it is for his friend to have two sets of parents. What is he really saying? Is he talking about himself? Why not ask? Why not draw the unspoken parallel for him? Why not use this as an opportunity for openness and honesty about his adoption?

The same problems you confronted with insensitive people about your childlessness now confront your child about his or her adoption. The seven-year-old girl's friends' questions about her adoption force her to deal with her differentness. She is just not like her friends at a time when she wants to be *just like* her friends. If you have set the foundation of honesty and openness with her as a child, she can afford to bring her concerns to you. If you have implied you are uncomfortable with the topic of adoption, or if you seemed threatened by her previous questions, she learns early that these questions are too painful to bring to you. If you present adoption as only beautiful and rosy, she feels there must be something wrong with her when she feels hurt and different.

The later problems and questions the adolescent has concerning his or her adoption are a whole different matter. This is a time for coasting if you have been honest and open in the past. You have already answered the difficult questions. If the foundation was never built, it's tough to do it now. The possibility of another opportunity to be open and honest about adoption is slight. Nevertheless, no matter what the odds are, try it.

Adolescence is a time when most of the concerns and questions about adoption are answered by peers. Your primary task is to make certain that the child has learned to be strong enough as a toddler and as a preadolescent to ask questions. As the child grows older, the adoptive parents need to convey to him or her that questions about birthparents are not threatening . . . questions are okay to have and to ask. Many times adolescents are very concerned that they not hurt their adoptive parents. The fearful adolescent, or the adolescent with no apparent questions, can be encouraged by the adoptive parents to bring up questions.

When Melinda was twelve, her best friend Jessie began to mature physically much faster than Melinda. Melinda's astute adoptive mother used the developing difference between them to help Melinda talk about her feelings about being adopted. Her mother brought up that she imagined that Jessie's mother had matured early physically also and probably Melinda's birthmother hadn't. This gave them a chance to talk about ways that adopted children can't look to their adoptive parents to get clues as to how they are likely to develop. It was a chance to say that even though many children don't look like or develop like their birthparents, it is a bit easier when you know what your birthparents look like. Mainly this was a time to open up the subject of adoption with Melinda.

There are many times like this. If the child has an eye problem and no one else in the family has one, or if the seventeen-year-old boy begins to show signs that he may bald early, or if the adolescent has a strong interest in something no one else in her adoptive family is interested in . . . all these situations are opportunities to deal openly about adoption. You are helping the adopted child feel comfortable with his birthparents, which ultimately helps him accept himself.

Movies, books, television, and newspapers are other sources of conversation-openers. General questions are usually more readily answered than questions such as "How do *you* feel about being adopted?" If you read an article on illegitimacy increasing in teenagers, ask your child if she read it and what she thinks about it. If you have a book that relates to adoption, ask your son if he has read it. Some excellent movies have appeared on television about teenagers relinquishing their children for adoption . . . these are usually easy to discuss even with young people. Ask what each character should have done or who had the hardest time. Give your opinions also. You certainly don't want this to sound like an inquisition. Maybe after a while you will have each opened up enough to say, "What would you do under these circumstances?" Make opportunities for openness.

One school of thought on adoption says not to tell the child that he or she is adopted or to wait until the child is of school age. The psychological issues that are involved here are clear. In all theories of child development, the importance of a trusting relationship with parents is stressed. The child uses the parent as a sounding board to the larger world. The child who feels betrayed because his parents lied to him has great difficulty developing the ability to trust others. The child thinks, "If these people who love me lie to me, then, of course, other people who don't love me will lie to me, too." The need to lie about adoption is simply not there.

To tell a child her first mommy gave her away because she loved her tells her that if she is loved she may be given away. Instead tell the truth in a way that is appropriate to the child's age, the previous questions she has asked, her level of maturity, and what she has already learned from others. Even a young child can be told that her mother was very young and in school when she became pregnant. She had no money and felt the child would be better with people who were married and who could give her a home and love, too. To say "I don't know" when you don't know is also appropriate. To say "I'll tell you about that when you are older" is also appropriate if you will tell later. Whatever your approach, however, let it be based upon honesty.

Does this mean that when your adopted six-year-old son asks you to tell him about his birthmother that you tell him everything you know? Not at all. You wouldn't say, "Your birthmother was a drug pusher who slept with every guy in town" even if she was and did. You might say, "Your birthmother was a young woman who was having a great deal of difficulty in her life and who couldn't keep you because of the problems she was having." Answer questions honestly but appropriately.

If you have learned to be honest with yourself and honest with your children about adoption, you can also be honest with relatives and friends. You would think that, after you had fielded all the questions about why you couldn't have children, you would be an expert on callous, unthinking questions about adoption. The experience helps but it doesn't prevent this whole new group of questions from being asked.

When your relatives ask about your adopted child's background, it is important to be honest with them. There is no necessity to reveal all to them if you don't want to, but whatever you do choose to tell them should be true. Your stories to these people will ultimately be stories to your adopted children. You want the stories they hear from Auntie and Grandma to be the same ones they hear from you.

Honesty carries over to areas that you don't like . . . for example, how relatives respond to your child's adoption. One adopted child's grandmother consistently introduced her grandson as her adopted grandson. She was proud of him . . . she even liked his specialness because of his adoption. The adoptive mother finally said to her mother that she didn't like her son being introduced this way. They discussed together that this was not intended to be negative and that the grandmother was indeed proud of this little boy and loved him deeply. The discussion held openly and honestly enabled them each to deal with their feelings about adoption and how being special sometimes doesn't feel good. It hurt a little bit because most people don't like to be criticized. It helped a lot because it openly solved a problem and it was truthful.

Sometimes it is okay to hurt when you are being honest also. A newly adoptive mother had a neighbor who continually pried into the background of their new child. It started out fairly innocuously . . . how old was the mother, was she from this area? Then the questions became too specific. The adoptive mother finally said to the woman, "I am uncomfortable with your questions about Tony's background. We feel this is a very personal thing and we don't want to talk about it." The neighbor was indignant. She said she didn't want to pry. A rift developed between the neighbor and this family. That's sad. It didn't need to be that way, but the neighbor chose to handle it in that manner. Being honest isn't always pleasant, but neither were the prying questions from this nosy woman.

The adoptive parent has an additional chore in this process in order to fully help the child resolve his or her own feelings about the adoption. The adoptive parent is the primary provider of information and of understanding of the birthparents' side of adoption. The adoptive parent, who wants to help his or her child feel positive about being adopted, must seek to feel positively about the birthparents who relinquished the child. Only the adoptive parents who can identify with the birthparents' pain can present these people lovingly to the adopted child. Sometimes adoptive parents who have not adequately resolved their feelings about the birthparents pass their unsettled and perhaps competitive feelings about them on to their adopted child. Adoptive parents who know or who have met the birthparents generally have the easiest time conveying positive feelings about the birthparents to the adopted child. Some adopting parents have sought this level of understanding of birthparents by attending meetings of birthparent groups.

These are individual ways to be honest and open about adoption. It's hard to do this if you are not sure of yourself and your views about adoption. It is also hard to do this when the whole system of adoption you have been involved with has encouraged secretiveness and pretends everything is "normal."

Honesty and Openness in the Adoption System

Many simple ways exist within the current system that would allow for increasing the openness and the honesty in adoption. Making every effort to be forthright encourages the people who use adoption to view the process more positively. In a system that deals with people who have experienced so much hurt and pain, it is essential that the process resolving this pain be built on positive, not negative, solutions.

The adoption agency system today is designed to be in the best interest of the child. In the initial stages of adoption proceedings, except in some "special needs" adoptions, the child is the one who has the least pain over the process. In some ways we need to be less concerned about the child and more concerned with all the other adoption participants who are in greater need of help. Birthparents, adoptive parents, and foster parents could be dealt with differently than they now are, which could significantly improve the mental health of the people involved.

Many of the changes in openness and honesty in adoption could be easily incorporated into the adoption agency system that now exists. I believe that the system needs a basic philosophical overhaul, but I am also a realist. Since many of the adoption agencies will never go as far as I suggest in the next section on open adoptions, it seems important to suggest interim means of changing to a less secretive and consequently healthier approach to adoption.

• *Adoption Agencies and Birthparents*

People are naturally far more perceptive than we think. You frequently know how people view you without anyone saying a word to you. You also know when you dislike someone and you convey this to them. The same is true when you like them. Adoption agency workers are likely to show in some way their feelings toward the clients they serve. The negative view that adoption workers at times have of birthparents is difficult, if not impossible, to hide.

The attitude of adoption workers toward the birthparents comes out in many ways. The small group meeting in one class on adoption brought this point out vividly. The head of an adoption agency who had worked with pregnant women giving up their babies for adoption for twenty years spoke to the group. She was discussing not adoption, but sex. She felt premarital sex was *absolutely immoral.* There were no circumstances that she could think of that would condone this type of behavior. All sex outside of marriage indicated promiscuous behavior. It would have been impossible for this woman not to convey her feelings to the hundreds of birthmothers and, at times, birthfathers, with whom she had been working for over twenty years. It would be difficult for these birthparents to gain positive feelings about themselves in this stressful time when their own social worker felt so negatively toward them.

If the social worker from the adoption agency is shocked by the behavior of the birthparents, this negative view is likely to be conveyed. If the social worker does not like the birthparent, she will probably show this in some subtle way. If the worker is disapproving of the woman because she sees her as sexually permissive or loose, these feelings will be difficult to hide from the birthmother. The social worker who wants to be effective with her birthparent client must be able to genuinely care for this person. To try to provide help for someone you do not respect, like, or approve of is impossible and dishonest.

It seems reasonable to suggest that social workers should have some degree of respect and genuine concern for the people they say they are counseling and helping. In order to sell someone a car, concern and caring aren't necessary. In order to provide information to someone, this type of therapeutic relationship isn't necessary. But to counsel someone, to help them therapeutically, is impossible if the counselor disapproves, dislikes, or distrusts them.

Does this mean social workers have to like every client? *Yes.* If they want to help the client, it's imperative. When workers find that they do not have positive regard for the client they are working with in a therapeutic relationship, they should be honest with themselves and with the clients and turn the cases over to other social workers. Either the clients are sent to workers who can like them and feel positively toward them or they should be told that they will be given information only. When a social worker feels the client is so incompetent that he or she cannot make decisions, there should be no pretense that the client is being counseled. The client may be told what to do, but he or she should not be manipulated under the guise of counseling.

The client who is truly being helped will be given thorough consideration of where he or she is in this adoption process. The social worker should find out the best way for the individual client to relinquish the child and should work to make the relinquishment as healthy and growth-producing as possible for the client. To do this may entail modifying agency procedures. If this is impossible within an adoption agency, the adoption agency is wrong. If adoption agencies are not really providing counseling to the people they say they serve, then they are merely providing babies. It is just another form of selling babies.

Birthparents at times resist going through adoption agencies because they know that they will want updates on how their child is doing from time to time. This, too, should present no problems to an adaptable adoption agency. As long as adoptive parents know this is to be part of the adoption, what is the problem with periodic updates for the birthparents?

Birthparents at times resist using adoption agencies because they want to know the adoptive parents. These cases should not be too difficult to comply with, and many adoptive parents would readily agree. It doesn't mean the identities are necessarily exchanged, it just means people meet and talk together. If the parties involved aren't against this idea, why should the adoption agency prevent this small degree of openness to the people who wish it?

Birthparents at times resist adoption agencies because they receive little or no financial support while they are producing the baby. This should be an issue addressed by each adoption agency. Financial help does not mean a baby is being sold. Financial help allows a woman to maintain her dignity and the health of her unborn child, despite the fact that the child will be placed for adoption.

In serving any client therapeutically, the social worker must first find out that person's feelings about and wishes for the relationship. *The role of a social worker in an adoption agency is not to provide solutions for people, but rather to help people find the best solutions for themselves.* The social worker is a facilitator in the client's growth, not the leader. The social worker is a helper toward the client's goal, not the decider of his or her fate.

A great need exists to counsel people who are considering relinquishment of their children for adoption. This is one of the main reasons for going to an adoption agency in the first place. When adoption agencies begin to view the needs of all the people who come to them in adoption as equally important, then counseling, real counseling, will be provided.

• *Adoption Agencies and Adoptive Parents*
The fact that adoption agencies are threatening to most people who apply with them for a child should be viewed by these agencies as a failure on their part. Certainly the adoption agencies are in a position of power in the adoption process, but the goal for adoption agencies should be service, not power.

If the adoption agencies viewed potential adoptive parents as clients to be served, how much more effective and honest everyone could be with each other. If you as an adoptive parent felt the agency worker were there to help you rather than eliminate you, how much more beneficial this time would be for you. The emphasis in adoption studies should be on preparing people for parenting.

Adoption agencies are not currently preventing parents they reject from adopting babies (although maybe more than they should be). The agency may say you are not good enough for us, but that doesn't stop you from going elsewhere to get a baby. Recognizing this, it seems that the agencies should examine why they feel a couple is not ready for a child and help them get ready, rather than to merely eliminate them from the system or to force them to find a child somewhere else. This is the only place in our entire society where people are screened for parenting. Why not use this vehicle as a place to improve parenting skills rather than simply say no?

The adoption agencies, of course, reply that because there are too many parents and not enough chlidren to adopt, they must eliminate people. Why? Why instead don't they seek to improve their services to all the people involved? Maybe then adoption could be more positive and appealing to more women and the scarcity of infants could be alleviated.

The adoption agencies tell their prospective parents to be honest with the agency. The reward for their honesty many times is elimination. *The "winners" of babies are selectively truthful.* They know that to be totally honest is likely to cause their elimination. They have learned how critical it is to be secretive in adoption.

The time the potential parents spend with the social worker from the adoption agency should be real counseling time. All their feelings of deficiency and inadequacy about infertility should come out here. Their fears about adopting a child should be discussed here. Their disappointments about this kind of parenting should be dealt with here. These are not insurmountable problems . . . these are not problems that indicate a couple *should not* adopt a child. This is the place where counseling of this nature should occur. This is the place where adoption agencies say that it does occur. But how can it occur when the adoption agency is trying to judge your fitness to parent? Judging and counseling are not compatible goals. Counseling adoptive parents can be effective only if the system's goal is to help the adoptive parents become the best parents possible to their newly adopted child. Some people may become better parents than others, but that is not the question. The goal of the adoption agency needs to be changed from the judging of to the helping of people who want to adopt children.

• *Adoption Agencies and Foster Parents*
The role that adoption agencies take with foster parents fails to utilize the foster parents to the best advantage. Foster homes become a place to tuck away children while the social worker at the adoption agency decides the child's fate. Isolation of the foster parents results, and they become little involved with either the child's

past or future. This makes it harder for foster parents to be involved in the child's present situation.

As adoption is currently set up, the child who is adopted by some chosen couple is placed with foster parents until that placement is determined. In actuality, the foster placement in most adoptions should be eliminated. When foster placement is necessary, the stay should be as brief as possible. When there are complications with the child or with the birthparents, the child's stay may be longer. It seldom needs to be as long as most foster home placements are. While I strongly believe these stays should be as brief as possible, I also believe that the foster home needs to be more integrated into the adoption process. The increased involvement of foster parents as important participants in the adoption scene can improve the process for the child, the birthparent, the adoptive parents, and the foster parents.

The foster parents who believe their opinion is valued could become more involved with the child's care. The adoption agency should want to know how the foster parents evaluate this particular child. What things does this child respond to? Is this a demanding child? Is the child socially responsive? The foster parents can make a valuable contribution to the evaluation of a child because they know the child; therefore, they should be involved in the future placement of the child. Especially in long-term foster care, who knows more about the child than the foster parents? Even in short-term foster care of one or two months with an infant, there is seldom anyone else who knows as much about the child or who has spent as long a period of time with the child as the foster parents have. As you increase the importance of the position of the foster parents in adoption, you are also likely to attract more and more qualified people to this position.

When foster parents see their role as being important, they are more likely to do a good job. Foster parents who view themselves as only temporarily useful, but never very important, have less involvement with the child than those who see their role as more critical to the child's future placement.

The birthparent who turns the child over to an agency should also turn the child over to the foster parents. What information the birthmother has about her child will be most valuable to the next people who will be caring for the child. This makes the transition healthier for all of these people. The birthmother has a chance to view herself as caring enough about her child that she wants this transition to be smooth. If she has spent any time at all with her child, she should have a chance to discuss the child with the next people who will care for him or her. It makes the birthmother's role more important, and it makes the transition of the child easier.

The foster parents should also be involved in the transition of the child from their home to the new adoptive home. There should be an opportunity for these two sets of parents to talk about the child's habits and behavior patterns. Depending on how long this child has been in a foster home, the role of these people takes on increasing significance. To have the foster parents merely write down the child's schedule and a few items about him or her minimizes the role these parents have had with the child. Meeting the foster parents, like meeting the birthparents, makes them more real to the adoptive parents. The adoptive parents can see how the child has been cared for . . . how the diapers are put on, how the bottle is held, how the bath is given. The child, even as an infant, is a creature of habit. Changes in his or her routine are not easily tolerated. The fewer changes made during major transitions, the better for the child.

The role of the foster parents in adoption is varied. The part the foster parents might have as potentially adoptive parents is discussed elsewhere in this book (see Chapter 8). The primary area of discussion at this point is the need for foster parents *not* to become invisible parents in this transition period of the child's life. The importance of foster parents' role should be increased. Opening of contacts between each of these sets of parents should strengthen the continuity the child feels in this difficult period. The child who is experiencing this upheaval in his or her primary parenting figures needs as much consistency as possible in the move. Eliminating the separateness between each of his or her homes should help in giving greater consistency and increasing a sense of stability.

Many of the things adoption agencies can do to increase honesty and openness in adoption are simple. The changes don't necessitate the system being shaken to the core. The changes do require adoption agencies' commitment to the elimination of secrecy and separation and to the addition of honesty and openness in their place.

Open Adoption
Open adoption has been a concept studiously avoided by adoption agencies. Their entire being is based upon the role of intermediary . . . the adoption agency is the go-between, the decision-maker, the chooser, the eliminator, the secret-keeper. They keep people apart . . . open adoption brings people together.

Open adoption is a difficult concept to define, mostly because it is multifaceted. Open adoption is basically where there is some degree of contact between the principals involved. The amount of contact is variable. All private adoptions are to some extent open adoptions. The adoption agencies, until recently, have avoided contact between birthparents and adoptive parents. Some degree of openness is beginning to emerge in many of the agencies seeking to compete with the advantages offered by private adoptions. Few, however, go to the extent of exchanging identifying information.[2] Controversy within the ranks of the social workers over the long-term effects of open adoptions is causing change to be painful.

• Different Kinds of Open Adoption
To illustrate the tremendous variety of options possible in open adoption, it is worthwhile to show some examples. Minimal, moderate, and maximum contact in adoptions are the terms used to describe the varying degrees possible. As a means of hanging material together, even though it seldom fits this neatly, I have chosen to define minimal openness as contact between birthparents and adoptive parents only at birth of the child and no more. Moderate openness in adoption is used to describe adoptions where there is some continuing, but not personal, contact between birthparents and adoptive parents. The maximum degree of openness would be where visitations continue between the birthparents and the adoptive parents while the adopted child lives with the adoptive parents.

Minimal Contact in Open Adoption
Probably most private adoptions would fit into this category. At a minimum, names of birthparents and adoptive parents are exchanged. At times, a contact is made in the hospital when the adoptive couple comes to pick up the baby.

Many times this minimal contact between birthparents and adoptive parents is a feared part of private adoptions. In open adoptions it would be an accepted part of the process. It would be viewed as a planning and exchange session between two sets of caring parents.

Hank and Teresa had a chance to participate in an open adoption even though it occurred twenty years ago. They didn't realize how far ahead of their time they were. Hank and Teresa could not make babies, even though they had tried every fertility specialist around their area. They were planning to apply for adoption with an agency when they heard from a neighbor about her sixteen-year-old niece, Mary Beth, who was pregnant and wanted to place the child for adoption. The neighbor arranged for Hank and Teresa to meet Mary Beth. It just seemed the right thing to do at the time. The three people agreed that Hank and Teresa would raise Mary Beth's baby after it was born. Hank and Teresa paid for Mary Beth's prenatal care. Just before the baby was born, Mary Beth's parents wanted to meet Hank and Teresa also. This time the five of them sat down together and talked about the baby. This would be the first grandchild for Mary Beth's parents, and they were concerned about the welfare of the child. The meeting lasted three hours and included a friendly dinner together. Everyone wanted what was best for the child, but they also wanted to feel good about their role in the adoption. As Mary Beth and her parents talked to Hank and Teresa, they found out a great deal about the home in which this child would be raised. In turn, they felt they had a chance to let Hank and Teresa know about each of them and their beliefs and interest. When the meeting was over, everyone left with an extremely positive feeling.

Three weeks later a baby girl was born to Mary Beth. Hank and Teresa visited Mary Beth in the hospital. They wanted to bring their new daughter home immediately, but it was also important to them to see Mary Beth, who had become a very special person to them. Mary Beth said she didn't want to maintain contact with them. She said the contact would be too painful for her and would prevent her from moving ahead with her life. She also told them she didn't need to have contact because she knew how Hank and Teresa would raise her baby. Mary Beth never again made contact with Hank and Teresa. However, the couple felt they could always talk positively to their daughter about the caring, involved people who were part of her life before they adopted her.

This example of a minimum contact went especially well for all the people involved. There certainly is no reason why this same type of contact could not have been made in an adoption agency setting. It is just that it is not . . . the limitations are the agencies' limitations. These people didn't see anything particularly unusual in their open adoption. What they did seemed natural to them, and they saw no reason to impose any limitations on the process.

Moderate Contact in Open Adoption

Moderate contact in open adoptions involves longer contact between the people involved but not personal contact. It is easy to identify with the examples that involve no hesitation between the people involved, but sometimes there are problems.

The case involving Gloria and Don's adoption of a baby boy was filled with problems. Gloria and Don heard about a baby boy who had been left with a neighbor by a young woman, Julie. The neighbor knew Julie's sister. Julie had been involved in drugs and sex since she was twelve. She was a high school dropout at the age of fourteen. Her parents had no control over her. She was slightly retarded from an injury at birth that had also caused her to develop epilepsy. She had been in and out of foster homes and juvenile hall. At eighteen, she had gotten pregnant by a man she barely knew. His past history of violent behavior and a short term in jail for armed robbery didn't deter Julie from having her baby. After she delivered the baby, the father said he didn't want it but she could come with him if she left the baby. Julie left the baby with Gloria and Don's neighbor and took off.

It was obvious that the baby boy had not been well cared for before she left him with the neighbor. When Don and Gloria heard about the child, they were very interested in adopting him. They wanted to know more about him. They contacted the physician who delivered him, who blatantly said to them that this child was a "mess." He warned them about the mother's lack of prenatal care and the potential for long-term physical and mental damage. He advised them to pass this one up.

They met the grandmother of the boy. It was reassuring to see that she seemed normal and there was no evidence of mental retardation.

Then the father of the boy heard that Don and Gloria were interested in the baby. He talked to them on the phone and they became alarmed. He sounded so rough and coarse. They became concerned that he would try to get money for the child because of threats to them and threats to take the child away. They became fearful and said they didn't want the child. They were willing to pass on any information to anyone else who was interested in adopting the baby.

The next couple, Susan and Joel, learned all of the details from Don and Gloria. Susan and Joel made some additional contacts with the family members, had some testing done on the boy, who was now seven weeks old, and consulted a lawyer. Everything seemed acceptable to them . . . not good, but acceptable. Their lawyer said he would handle the case as long as the couple did not go along with any of the birthfather's demands. They agreed.

The other provision the family stipulated as a condition for Susan and Joel adopting the boy was that they maintain contact with the child's biological grandparents. Joel and Susan felt this was a reasonable request. They agreed to write to the grandparents regularly and to send pictures of the boy as he grew.

Joel and Susan hoped to get the birthmother and the birthfather to sign relinquishment papers. Since the birthparents' whereabouts were unknown, this possibility was uncertain. If they were not found, the plan was to begin abandonment procedures. The biological family of the boy completely supported Joel and Susan's adoption of the child. They knew that if this boy, with all the negative factors in his background, entered into the adoption agency system, he would be viewed as a "special" child. His adoption could be delayed by months, maybe years. They knew they needed to find an open couple who would be able to handle the negative as well as the positive information about this boy. They did.

The exceptional part of this story is that nothing was hidden. Everything was out in the open, and the adoptive parents felt the information could be handled. Most moderate contact adoptions are not as complex as this one. In fact, the case of the Kennersons is probably much more typical.

The Kennersons found their child by sending a letter to a physician in Missouri. He passed on the information to Merideth when she said she could not keep the baby she had just learned she was carrying. Merideth was a bright twenty-one-year-old woman who knew that she was not ready to raise a child, but was also not willing to lose total contact with a child she would give up for adoption. When she heard about the Kennersons, they sounded like warm, open people who might consider having contact with her throughout her child's growing years. She was right. They discussed what Merideth expected from the Kennersons and what they in turn expected from her. Everyone seemed satisfied, so when

Merideth delivered an eight-pound baby girl, the Kennersons became the delighted parents. Merideth's desire to keep in contact with them has always been honored. In the seven years since the birth, letters and pictures have gone back and forth between the two households. No one's position is threatened because they all trust each other and everyone knows they want what is best for the daughter they share.

Adoptions sometimes are very simple and other times they are very complex. The desire to adopt a child is strong enough for most people to weather the complexities that may face them. Adults, like children, are resilient. The protective screening of information, even negative information, implies people are not able to handle it or work the situation through. This simply is not the case. You merely need to find the right people to handle it.

Maximum Contact in Open Adoption

The third type of open adoption entails the greatest amount of contact between the birthparents and the adoptive parents. Because adoption agencies do not encourage contact between any of the groups involved in adoption, the example must once again come from private adoption.

Kent and Adrianne never considered adoption. They had two children and were quite content with their family. They were shocked when their very good friend, Tricia, called in a state of panic to tell them she was pregnant. Adrianne encouraged her to come over and talk about the situation.

Adrianne and Tricia had been roommates before Adrianne had married Kent five years ago. Tricia had never married; she remained a close friend to Adrianne and Kent and their children.

Tricia was extremely agitated as she told Adrianne about her pregnancy. She had never dreamed she was pregnant. She had been sexually involved with a man with whom she had broken up two months ago. When her periods seemed a bit irregular, she thought little about it until this last month when she didn't have one at all. Thinking it was related to stress over being out of work, she did nothing. As she didn't feel quite like herself, she decided to go to her doctor for a checkup. She was amazed to learn that she was pregnant and very pregnant at that . . . she was over three months along. There was no way Tricia, who was Roman Catholic, would consider having an abortion . . . especially being this far along in her pregnancy.

As Tricia talked more and more with Adrianne about the situation, she calmed down considerably. She discussed adoption and how hard it would be to give her baby away to strangers. She discussed keeping the child, which she felt was impossible in her circumstances. She kept coming back to adoption but felt it would simply be too much for her to handle. Then she surprised Adrianne by suggesting that Adrianne and Kent adopt her baby. Adrianne didn't know what to say.

Adrianne and Kent discussed the situation. They finally decided that if certain areas could be agreed upon with Tricia, they would seriously consider the possibility. The three of them talked about the situation numerous times in the next five months. They all agreed that Kent and Adrianne would be parents . . . totally. Tricia could not interfere in the way they chose to raise the baby. Tricia completely agreed. They felt it was difficult enough for two people to agree on raising children without adding a third point of view. Tricia was also very approving of Kent and Adrianne's approach to their one-year-old and three-year-old . . . her knowledge of how they were as parents made her confident about how they would raise her child. They all agreed that they would not tell the child that Tricia was the birthmother unless the child asked if she was. They were determined to be honest with the child. They felt that if the child discovered Tricia was his or her mother, that would not destroy Kent and Adrianne's relationship with the child. At the same time, they all agreed that it was easiest for the child to relate to Kent and Adrianne in the growing-up years as his or her only parents.

These arrangements took place six years ago. Adrianne and Kent are delighted with their three children. Their youngest daughter, Carrie, is a joy. Tricia is a regular visitor to the home and enjoys seeing Carrie and the other children grow. She would never dream of interfering. She is grateful to Kent and Adrianne, who agreed to this unusual open adoption. Kent and Adrianne are also grateful.

This type of adoption would not appeal to everyone, but as of now, few people ever get a chance to consider it as a possibility. The world is full of many types of people . . . there should be room for many types of adoptions.

• Adoption Agencies and Open Adoption

Few adoption agencies advocate a need for open adoptions beyond letting the birthmother have a chance to read background information or personal letters written by people seeking to adopt. Most adoption agencies seem more interested in controlling all adoptions than in enlarging the scope of the adoption process. There are, however, some noticeable cracks in the usual unified front of adoption agencies.

One of the first voices to break rank with the traditional stance of no contact between adoptive parents and birthparents came from the adoption agency that began the research on opening the sealed birth record, Vista Del Mar, in California. This group maintains that there is a need for a new, different approach to adoption that would appeal to the pregnant woman who is uncomfortable with traditional adoption approaches:

> The young, single mothers who have an emotional attachment— whether positive or negative—to their children desperately need a new kind of adoptive placement in which they can actively participate. They want the security of knowing that they have helped provide their children with a loving, secure existence and yet have not denied themselves the possibility of knowing them in the future.[3]

These glimmers of new creative approaches to adoption within the adoption agency system hold out hope for seeing the changes necessary to make adoption a healthier, more positive alternative for the unhappily pregnant woman.

A second, more recent shift comes from an adoption agency in Washington, D.C., which will give both sets of parents the option to exchange names, visitation rights, and personal histories. The social workers require all the people involved to at least keep the adoption agency up-to-date so that the birthparents can know about the child they have placed for adoption.[4]

One of the reasons for this more open approach is Linda Burgess, a progressive social worker who believes that open adoptions will make "more children available for adoption while making adoption healthier for the child and all other parties involved."[5] Burgess, who has written about other progressive adoption methods, believes that more mothers would willingly give up their children if adoption were approached differently, with new options as to how the adoption is handled.[6] She feels that the traditional adoption process can't compete with adoption and keeping the baby. She advocates open adoption as a way to decrease the adopted child's sense of rejection. Being able to tell the child of the birthparents who wanted to be involved in the child's future will ease the feelings of being rejected. The meeting between the birthparents and the adoptive parents will help lessen the birthparents' sense of guilt over leaving the child. A chance to sit down and talk together should benefit both sets of parents and ultimately the child, too. As part of this new approach, the adoption records will be opened to the child when she or he becomes an adult.

Another agency, Lutheran Social Services of Texas in San Antonio, is encouraging more open adoption.[7] This progressive agency actively encourages the exchange of letters between the adoptive parents and the birthmother. Common myths about adoption are dispelled in this manner. This agency believes, and I certainly agree, that some myths about adoption have hindered the healthy direction in which adoption needs to progress. The myths they discuss in their book, *Dear Birthmother*, are the following:

1. "The birthmother obviously doesn't care about the child or she wouldn't have given him away."

2. "Secrecy in every phase of the adoption process is necessary to protect all parties."

3. "Both the birthmother and birthfather will forget about their unwanted child."

4. "If the adoptee really loved his adoptive family, he would not have to search for his birthparents."[8]

This book is a very helpful source of information for people considering open adoption because it is likely to open up your own ideas on adoption.

Obviously these agencies' approach to open adoption will be closely watched by other adoption agencies. The courage to be different in this field deserves applause and support.

• Open Adoption Historically

Open adoption has probably played a more significant part in adoption in our society in earlier times. Especially in rural areas where adoption agency services were less expansive, the informal contact between adoptive parents and birthparents was more common in the 1920s and 1930s. As the adoption agency system expanded and became more powerful, these open adoptions decreased. But in this area, as in many other areas of our lives, some of the lessons from the past have valuable application to today.

The experience of people who have been adopted through open

adoptions is valuable to us. At times, contacts that have been maintained have even included the full knowledge of the adopted child that this other woman is his or her birthmother. Open adoptions have even included temporary visits with the birthmother, which appear to have been beneficial to each of the people involved. There is no evidence to prove any damage has resulted from these open adoptions.

In some parts of the world, adoption has remained open despite changes within the system. In the Hawaiian and the Eskimo cultures, forms of open adoption have been successfully practiced for years. The problems in these cultures seem to arise not with the openness of adoption, but more when the modern American form of secret adoption is imposed. Before effective birth control, poor people used informal adoption within their extended family. While this is used far less today, some minorities, who do not use agencies in response to their problems or who do not trust agencies to work on their behalf, still resort to more informal adoption procedures within their own family network.

• *Risks in Open Adoption*
Of course there are risks in open adoption. Traditional adoption is not without risks either. The ultimate risk in open adoption is "Can I lose my adopted child?" Yes, you can. But you can lose any child. Remember, no one owns his or her children, adopted or biological. The risk of losing a child to the birthparent in an open adoption is no greater than the risk of losing your child in a traditional adoption. The risk is more apparent because you know and can identify the threat . . . the other parent. This is true in divorce cases also. In divorce cases, however, there is generally more competition for the child. In open adoption, the basic underlying agreement is that there will be no competition for the child. It seems you have far less risk of losing your child in an open adoption than you might have of losing your child in a divorce.

In many ways it is far easier in any kind of competition to know who your competition is. To compete with a child's fantasy of his or her birthparent is probably much more difficult than to have this clearly out in the open.

Summary
A significant number of women are rejecting adoption as an alternative to their unwanted pregnancy. It is not an appealing prospect

to them. For them, adoption fails to meet a need. We need to understand this failure and to make the necessary changes within the system to make adoption appeal to more of these women. The adoption process must change.

In our individualistic society it is important to be adaptable. Many kinds of women become pregnant. The healthiest way to deal with each woman's pregnancy is with a custom-made solution. There is room in our society for many kinds of pregnancy solutions and many kinds of adoptions.

It is difficult to sell things that are hidden. Adoption is facing a public relations problem. It simply does not appeal to as many people as it needs to . . . that's why we have a shortage of babies available for adoption. One of the best ways to remedy this problem is to develop a new image . . . an image based on openness.

Changes in adoption involve changes not just in the attitudes of adoption agencies but also in the attitudes of individuals. Honesty is ultimately an individual issue. If you believe strongly enough in it, your influence will eventually be felt by the institutions who serve you and others in adoption. If enough people who go to the adoption agencies seek new approaches, more open approaches, adoption will change. In order to help the most people toward a more healthy outcome from adoption, we need these changes toward open, honest adoptions, and we need them now.

Cleaning Up The Game | 11

NO BOOK HAS ALL THE FINAL ANSWERS ON ADOPTION. ADOPTION NEEDS to fluctuate and change with the changes in our society. Constant shifting requires an underlying attitude of adaptability. I, too, want that adaptability. The questions, answers, and recommendations I have put forth in this book are not the only ones for adoption. As adoption changes, newer and better approaches should be suggested and tried.

Certain factors could radically alter adoption as we know it today. New advances in curing infertility could drastically change the numbers of people who need to adopt children. Changes in society's attitude toward abortion could end the scarcity of babies available for adoption. The adoption field should be designed to accommodate changes rather than to perpetuate past practices.

It is apparent that most adoption agencies have not accepted the challenge to change. When an institution fails to keep in touch with the people it serves, it loses its perspective. The institution of adoption has not remained vital . . . it has lost touch with the people that justify its existence. Most adoption agencies are *not* responsive to the needs of their clients.

Lawmakers, looking to the adoption agencies for information about adoption, pass laws that reflect the adoption agencies' view. As a consequence, the laws governing adoption are not any more responsive to the need for change than the adoption agencies are. The most adaptable people in adoption seem to be the ones who seek to fight the adoption system. The birthparents and the adoptive parents who find their own ways to make adoption work show creativity and hope in an exemplary way.

I have made numerous suggestions that I believe would significantly improve what is being done in this area today. These suggestions are not the only possible solutions, but I believe they would improve adoption for all the people involved. Both adoption agencies and adoption laws should be based upon a system adaptable to the changing needs of society. My first two sets of recommendations are specifically directed to the adoption agencies and the state legislators.

Finally, I have recommendations for you people who want to adopt a child. The recommendations for you as potential adoptive parents are somewhat different. They are based not on a need for change, but rather on the ingredients you need for a successful baby search. After all, helping you succeed in your search for a child is what this book is all about.

Adoption Agency Recommendations

Although this book is intended primarily to help people find the child they want, the need to communicate with the adoption agencies is also apparent. Adoption agencies need to carefully scrutinize their procedures, rules, and goals. The recommendations that follow are suggestions for changes urgently needed within the adoption agency system. They also demonstrate to the adoptive applicants the obstacles which confront them.

RECOMMENDATION I: ADOPTION AGENCIES SHOULD BECOME ACTIVELY INVOLVED IN RECRUITING BABIES FOR ADOPTION.

Adoption agencies have stayed in their sequestered agency settings long enough. The time has come for these groups to go into the community and promote adoption. More than a million women a year are obtaining abortions. Few of these women even know about or consider adoption as an alternative. The adoption agencies need to present the adoption alternative to these women. It's not enough for adoption agencies to wait for women to show up on their doorstep between nine and five, Monday through Friday. Pregnancy decisions can't wait for the convenience of the adoption agency; the agency needs to reach out to the women who are pregnant when the women need the help.

"Pregnancy counseling" is being done by lay counselors in the local communities. Few of the groups doing this "counseling" understand the current state of adoption and the scarcity of babies for adoption, nor the techniques of counseling necessary to help a woman make the best pregnancy decision for her. Reliance on these "pregnancy counselors" to present adoption as a good alternative to an unwanted pregnancy is naive and obviously not working.

The adoption agencies should become activists in promoting adoption in the pregnancy counseling clinics where pregnant women go to make their decisions. If the scarcity of adoptable infants is to be alleviated, the adoption agencies must talk to the woman before she decides what to do about her unwanted pregnancy. As the current system operates, the only women who go to the adoption agencies are those who have been unable to find a better way out of their dilemma. Adoption should be designed to be viewed as a good alternative to their pregnancy problem.

Adoption can be a healthy alternative to abortion or to keeping an unwanted child. Adoption agencies need to believe this enough to convince many of the women who chose abortion or who chose to keep a child they aren't certain they want. Whatever stops women from considering adoption as an alternative to an unwanted pregnancy should be carefully examined to see if it can be changed.

Adoption agencies need to hire professional public relations firms in order to effectively "sell" adoption through television, radio, newspapers, and magazines. Free public service advertisements should regularly be used by adoption agencies to promote adoption as an alternative to an unwanted pregnancy. Booths should be established at local shopping centers and public events to tell about adoption. Schools should have presentations by enthusiastic, young social workers telling about adoption and the large demand for babies. Newspapers are always seeking interesting stories; adoptions are interesting stories. Counterculture newspapers especially should be used. The attempt should be made to move out into the community to appeal to pregnant women instead of sitting back and *hoping* they will come to the established adoption agencies. Many women would elect to place children for adoption if it were effectively sold to the public.

Adoption agencies need to be advocates for adoption. If adoption agencies aren't, who will be? Who is now an advocate for adoption?

RECOMMENDATION 2: ADOPTION AGENCIES SHOULD SERVE ALL THE PARTIES IN ADOPTION EQUALLY.

There is no logical reason to believe that only one primary client's interests need to be served more than any others in agency adoptions. The agencies should be committed to meeting the needs and serving the interests *equally* of all the people involved in adoption . . . the child, the birthparents, and the adoptive parents.

This philosophical change from serving only the interests of the child to equally serving the interests of all the people will be a radical change. This change alone should modify and improve the approach the adoption agencies take with birthparents and with adoptive parents. It also will change the approach the adoption agencies take with adult adoptees.

One of the primary differences a change of this nature makes is that the clients being served are adults as well as children. When adults are served by the adoption agencies, their thoughts and their wishes must be given a high priority. Adoption agencies cannot speak for them as they have been able to for the young child. The implications are clear. The change would mean that adoption agencies would work with their clients to help them. Adoption should be a shared venture, with the agencies and their clients working toward a common goal. The agencies should commit themselves to helping each and every person who comes for help. No one should be sent away as a reject. The adoption agencies need to commit to a new mission . . . equality in adoption for every man, woman, and child.

RECOMMENDATION 3: ADOPTION AGENCIES SHOULD MAKE ADOPTION THROUGH ADOPTION AGENCIES MORE APPEALING TO THE BIRTH-MOTHER.

A pregnant woman who is considering adoption should be able to go through her pregnancy with dignity and self-respect. This is not easy to do with the adoption agency system operating the way it currently is. The adoption agencies need to change to make adoption through them more attractive to the pregnant woman.

If a woman is pregnant, she can obtain an abortion for a small cost. If she chooses to carry this child to term and place the child for adoption privately, some eager couple will gladly pay her expenses. If she chooses to carry the child to term and place it for adoption with an adoption agency, the pregnancy expenses must be borne by her. She may be forced to go on welfare, borrow money from family or friends, or barely subsist. No financial help is given her if she plans to place her child with an adoption agency. This is wrong. There is no reason adoption agencies could not change policies or even laws that prevent them from providing the woman with the financial help she needs. A woman should receive financial help with her medical and personal expenses when she plans to give up the child for adoption.

In order for the pregnant woman to end up in a better place after this experience, she needs to feel good about herself during her pregnancy. A regular financial allowance to help her with expenses other than medical expenses is just and reasonable. The adoption agencies have the ability to help change the laws related to the expenses a birthmother may receive. This allowance should be enough to make her not feel demeaned or punished by her decision to place her child for adoption. Would it be wrong if some women even chose to become pregnant for pay?

Medical and nonmedical costs could be passed on to the adoptive couple in most cases. If the same couple adopts privately, they will usually incur these expenses for the birthmother. If they get involved in black market adoptions, they will assuredly pay far more. If the additional financial assistance would help more women to place children for adoption, it certainly should be considered.

The pregnant woman should have the right to be involved in when and where the adoption agency places her child. Pregnant women should be able to have a say about the type of family the child will be placed with, the amount of contact or specific information she wants to have with the adoptive parents, and the potential of an immediate placement of the child in a new home. The adoption agencies should promote this to women as an incentive for them to use an agency. The decisions about the adoption should be made by birthmothers and the adoption agencies as *equal* partners.

RECOMMENDATION 4: ADOPTION AGENCIES SHOULD LIBERALIZE ACCEPTANCE OF ADOPTIVE PARENTS.

Every effort needs to be made by adoption agencies to accept the people who apply to them to adopt a child. Only in the most extreme cases should people be turned away. With proper help and support, most people's parenting skills can improve. The effort of the adoption agency should be to improve the parenting skills of potential adoptive parents, not to send them someplace else to find a baby. When these parents obtain a baby somewhere else, it will be without the improvement that could have been made in their parenting skills.

Adoption agencies that become more flexible in meeting the wishes of birthparents also can become more flexible in accepting different kinds of people as adoptive parents. The adoption agency should ultimately decrease its power to accept and reject applicants and allow the birthmother to become more active in the decision about who will be the adoptive parent of her child.

RECOMMENDATION 5: ADOPTION AGENCIES SHOULD PROVIDE COUNSELING TO THEIR CLIENTS.

Adoption agencies should be set up to offer counseling to the birthparents, the adoptive parents, and the adoptee. At a very minimum, a pregnant woman who elects to relinquish her child to an adoption agency should be assured that she will receive adequate counseling. Certainly, an adoptive couple should be assured that they will receive counseling on how to find a child and the potential areas of difficulty they might have with adopting. The adoptee having difficulty with his or her adoption should be able to receive counseling from the adoption agency.

Most adoption agencies are not providing counseling services to their clients. To truly counsel means to accept the client and be nonjudgmental. In order to counsel with a client, you must believe there are choices; the person who needs to make the choices is the client.

The pregnant woman should be accorded greater respect from adoption agencies. Only social workers who genuinely like and respect the woman should counsel her. Anyone who disapproves of what the birthmother has done will pass their disapproval on and do more harm than good in the name of counseling her. The relationship between client and counselor should be based on mutual positive regard.

Counseling should be ongoing if the client wishes. The staff of the adoption agency should be open to contacts anytime after a placement is made, even when the adopted child becomes an adult.

Counseling feels good if it is done correctly. When it is nonjudgmental and accepting, counseling is very appealing to most people . . . a chance to talk about themselves with an objective person who helps them view things from many sides. The adoption agencies are ideal places for counseling all their clients involved in adoption; this would benefit them and society.

RECOMMENDATION 6: ADOPTION AGENCIES SHOULD ENCOURAGE OPENNESS AND HONESTY IN ADOPTION.

Adoption is ready to come out of the closet. The secrets in adoption are no longer necessary. The hiding and the separateness should be forced out of the adoption agency system and be replaced by openness and honesty.

Adoption's entire image needs to personify openness and honesty. The setting should be part of this changed image. Today, visiting the typical adoption agency is like visiting a medical clinic. The receptionist acts as a guard to all of the closed doors that line the long, dim corridors. Each cubicle holds hidden secrets. Amazingly, children are rarely seen at the adoption agency. The surroundings are professionally foreboding at best. The setting needs to be opened, the people need to be opened, and the adoption process needs to be opened.

One means of achieving this physical openness is to go out more into the community. The agencies should become part of the community by having small centers that are open to talk about adoption in shopping areas. The free clinics and the pregnancy counseling agencies need to have friendly, equal interaction with the adoption agency social workers. Adoption agencies need to have their social workers on staff at the community agencies and their literature on site. Both staff and literature should be carefully chosen to appeal to young women. Visits to the schools can be made outside of the ordinary adoption agency setting. Take the message about adoption to the community in an open, outgoing manner.

Use the people who have adopted or who are adopted to openly sell adoption. Have art displays from adopted children. Have open houses where people involved with adoption can tell the public how rewarding it is.

Encourage the sharing of information in adoption from one person to the next. Instead of hiding one person from another, go the opposite direction. Let some social life into the social agency. Encourage the free sharing of information that brings people together rather than separates them.

Conditions that make it impossible for one person to adopt a certain child can be completely acceptable to another person. As adoption agencies accept many different kinds of adoptive applicants, it will be easier to adopt with openness and honesty. There is nothing to hide in adoption. The absolute worst imaginable things in adoption are acceptable to someone.

Openness and honesty can also mean to become actively involved in helping bring about reunions between birthparents and adult adoptees when requested. Reunions can be held in many different forms. The adoption agencies have a beautiful opportunity to help with reunions in the way the involved people wish. Reunions can be held with or without identities. Information can be relayed that meets some people's needs without going any further. Reunions can be made to order; let people have reunions in their own way. This is their game.

RECOMMENDATION 7: ADOPTION AGENCIES SHOULD FACILITATE AND ENCOURAGE IMMEDIATE ADOPTIVE PLACEMENTS WITH NO TEMPORARY FOSTER HOME CARE.

Foster homes are an inadequate substitute for permanent adoptive home placements. The child who is being shifted from one mother to the next should have as few switches as possible. In most infant placements, the child should be placed in the adoptive home immediately after the birthmother surrenders the child. Foster care between the two homes, while it provides absolute security and certainty about the birthmother's position, is detrimental to the child and to the adoptive parents.

Bonding is necessary in order for the child and the parents to feel secure in the new relationship. The earlier this is done, the better. The positive benefits of early bonding far outweigh the risks that the recommendation for immediate placement might entail.

There will be errors with this change. Some birthmothers may change their minds after the placement, but before the legal relinquishment is made. Those will be difficult cases. The adoptive parents need to understand the potential for this happening. If properly presented, most adoptive parents will still choose this alternative over the "security" of having a foster mother raise their child for the first month or more.

RECOMMENDATION 8: ADOPTION AGENCIES SHOULD BECOME INFOR-
MATION CENTERS ON ADOPTION.

Adoption agencies should become the creative, dynamic hub of
a healthy, vital adoption system. They should be the place to find
out about all forms of adoption. They should be the place to which
all information on adoption is channeled. Rather than trying to choke
off all other ways to adopt, the adoption agencies should become
centers to help all kinds of people find babies from everywhere.

The person trying to adopt a child today needs to search for huge
amounts of information before beginning the process. The pregnant
woman needs to know the right place to go before she seeks help
in making her pregnancy decision. No single source of help and
information is available to people to help them find the best direction. Adoption agencies could be this expansive, helping source.

Adoption agencies should know which lawyers in town are best
qualified to assist in the adoption of a child from a foreign country;
which doctors are best for low-cost abortions; which parent groups
provide support systems for private adoption in Mexico; which
physicians in town provide the most creative help to increase fertility. Adoption agencies that accept the alternative forms of adoption and all of the different kinds of people can afford to be creative
and expansive.

Legal Recommendations

Some of the areas in need of change in adoption are the responsibility of neither the adoption agencies nor the adoptive parents.
Changes involving the institution of adoption, at times, primarily
concern the legal framework that has developed around adoption.
Laws, customs, and precedence determine how adoption operates.
The following recommendations are based on the belief that some
of the laws in adoption need to be changed.

RECOMMENDATION I: ALL ADOPTIVE PARENTS, WHETHER WAITING FOR
PRIVATE PLACEMENTS, INTERNATIONAL PLACEMENTS, OR PLACEMENTS
THROUGH AN ADOPTION AGENCY, SHOULD BE EASILY LICENSED BEFORE
THE PLACEMENT.

In effect, this recommendation means that adoptive parents receive a license to be a parent. This license should be good anywhere in the United States. It would mean that you have met the
requirements necessary to adopt a child.

The standards for receiving your license should be the minimal standards deemed necessary to be a parent. It should be like the test to obtain a driver's license . . . not so difficult that most people can't pass, but not so easy that if you are unfit you will be allowed to drive. If there are deficiencies in your parenting skills, remedies should be sought that will correct the problem and allow you to be licensed to receive a child for adoption at a later point.

There are several reasons for this recommendation. First, there is no evidence that being eliminated by an adoption agency stops people from adopting children. Second, adoption agencies, with all their careful screening techniques, show no better results than private adoptions, where little screening takes place. The third reason for this recommendation is that if there were any obvious parenting problems, this would allow people to remedy them. The fourth reason is that if people are licensed ahead of time, any child that becomes available for placement could then be placed more quickly with anyone who is already licensed.

Licensing should be acceptable in all agencies. Adoptive parenting licensure should have provisions for periodic updating.

RECOMMENDATION 2: THE POST-PLACEMENT WAITING PERIOD IN ADOPTION SHOULD BE REDUCED OR ELIMINATED ENTIRELY.

The post-placement waiting period before adoptions are legalized is an unnecessary intrusion in adoptive families' lives. This time period should be significantly reduced or eliminated. It does little good and great harm.

If home studies prior to placement can't identify significant problems, why would additional home studies after the couple has the child be any more effective? In a very few cases, a family incompatibility might be detected. The same incompatibilities are found at times in biological homes.

This unnecessary and repetitive study of the adoptive home prevents bonding from occurring between the adopted child and the adopting parents. For this period of time, the adoptive parents are merely foster parents because the agency can remove the child from the home at any time. The child and the parents must fully feel the permanency of the relationship if the necessary parent-child bond is to be firmly established. This is a time for total, not partial, commitment.

RECOMMENDATION 3: FOSTER CARE SHOULD BE FORCED TO BE TEMPORARY.

Foster care becomes a way for people to avoid making decisions about the child. It prevents birthparents from deciding to keep or to relinquish a child. It prevents adoption agencies from moving ahead rapidly in placing children for adoption. It prevents birthparents from making the necessary changes in their lives in order to reclaim the child they have placed in foster care.

Except in rare circumstances, every child is adoptable. There is no reason a child needs to remain in foster care for lack of an adoptive home. When agencies find no home for a specific child, it means they have not gone far enough, been open enough, or been creative enough in their approach.

Foster care serves a useful temporary care approach for families having difficulty coping with day-to-day living problems. If the situation is not remedied in a brief period time, the child deserves to have a permanent solution anyhow. Either the family is helped to reinvolve the child in their lives or the child should be given another chance with another family.

Foster care is expensive in terms of the child's mental health and in terms of the taxpayers' money. To allow children to remain permanently in temporary foster care is a disservice that can be remedied by mandating the length of time any child can be left in this state of limbo.

RECOMMENDATION 4: PREGNANCY COUNSELING AGENCIES SHOULD BE INVESTIGATED.

To advertise that a pregnant woman will receive counseling about her pregnancy is a very serious commitment. Counselors in most states are licensed by the state to make certain that they are qualified to perform the services they advertise. Yet, in the area of "pregnancy counseling" the same standards are not upheld. Anyone is allowed to counsel the pregnant woman.

Whenever pregnancy counseling is offered, the counselors should be qualified. The pregnant woman who seeks help with the decision about her unborn child believes the "counselor" she speaks with has the necessary qualifications and skills to help her; she should be assured that her counselor is qualified.

In some agencies that offer pregnancy counseling, their livelihood is based on which decision the woman chooses for the resolution of her pregnancy. Kickbacks, whether for sending the woman for an abortion or sending her to someone who deals in selling babies, prevent objective counseling.

Obviously, pregnancy counseling clinics are meeting a need or they would not exist. In fact, many of their reasons for success should be lessons to the usual, traditional health care systems. It is time now to improve the operation of the pregnancy counseling groups. At the very least, the groups should be called pregnancy information centers, not pregnancy counseling centers. Then the woman will know she received *information* about her pregnancy, not *counseling*. However, each agency should have some trained counselors to help women who are trying to decide what to do about their pregnancy. These trained counselors should fully understand the implications of each of the alternatives to an unplanned pregnancy.

The pregnancy counseling a woman receives can significantly affect her long-term medical health. It is unfair for women to receive counseling that may create problems for them in years to come. Having had an abortion is not a requirement necessary to a "pregnancy counselor." Women need an opportunity to make well-thought-out decisions for themselves on how to handle their unwanted pregnancy. As in most areas of counseling, the choice must be the clients'; their manner of making the choice can be greatly aided with the help of a trained counselor.

RECOMMENDATION 5: LEGAL PROVISIONS SHOULD BE MADE TO CHANGE THE ADVERSARY ROLE IN ADOPTION.

The legal fee for most "normal" adoption proceedings is significant. The fee includes a minimum amount of work by an attorney and a brief visit to court the day the adoption is legalized. In most routine adoptions, the work of the attorney can be done by a secretary or by the parties involved in the adoption; the routine court appearance is a procedure with little value. Adoption in most cases should be a routine civil procedure that needs neither an attorney nor an appearance in court.

This possibility should be considered as a means to reduce costs to the adoptive parents. Certainly there should be room for many kinds of adoption proceedings just as the public has insisted on making the same provision in divorce proceedings. Some divorces are such that the couple is able to do the legal work without the help of a lawyer; others are far more complex and necessitate extensive legal help. Adoption is ready for a similar distinction.

RECOMMENDATION 6: LEGAL PROVISIONS SHOULD BE MADE TO OPEN BIRTH RECORDS OF ADOPTEES.

The legal provisions to open birth records of adult adoptees should be enacted. Rather than have the issue forced, the records should be opened in an orderly fashion. Preparation should be made now for this ultimate eventuality. All current adoptions should include preparation for the opening of the birth records when the child becomes an adult. Adoption agencies should become involved with updating past adoption cases.

RECOMMENDATION 7: MANY DIFFERENT KINDS OF ADOPTION SHOULD BE ENCOURAGED.

In this time of scarcity of adoptable children, many kinds of adoption should be encouraged. Now is the time to be creative in attempting to make adoption an appealing alternative to unhappily pregnant women. With the many kinds of people there is ample room for many kinds of adoption. Open adoption is appropriate for some people; traditional agency adoption is appropriate for others. Some people's needs will be best met in private adoptions, others in agency adoptions. There is room for many kinds of adoption.

Adoption monopolies must be vigorously resisted before adoption agencies gain absolute control over all adoptions. No one group, no matter how well meaning, should be allowed to dominate adoption or to set rules and regulations for everyone. To meet the problem of the lack of adoptable children by giving all the power and control to the adoption agencies is merely to develop a monopoly and is not a solution. No one group has all the answers for all the people in adoption. The law should reflect this.

Recommendations for Adoptive Parents

Many suggestions for finding your child have been given throughout this book. In all the suggestions made, there is a great deal of overlap. Ultimately, searches for a child are based upon a philosophical approach to adoption. Specific suggestions fall into a general feeling about searching for a child. The following recommendations are basically the philosophy of a search for a child.

RECOMMENDATION 1: BE THOROUGHLY INFORMED ABOUT EACH STEP YOU TAKE.

Throughout this book, the theme—knowledge of what you are doing—has been repeated. It is a critical ingredient in achieving success in pursuing a child or in getting the most out of many areas of life. You can save yourself time and frustration by knowing what you are doing ahead of time. The knowledge you have enables you to ask the right questions and to give the correct answers.

You need to be knowledgeable in pursuing alternative ways to have a child if you are infertile. Know the doctors to go to, read the right books, ask the important questions. Know how far you need to go, for you.

You need to be knowledgeable in your visits with the adoption agency. Learn about the agency you are going to, read about adopting through an agency, find out what they are looking for in adoption applicants. Know how these fit you.

You need to be knowledgeable about private adoption as well as agency adoption. Know the differences, the similarities, the risks, and the advantages. Figure out what sounds best to you, but don't eliminate other options.

Knowledge can be gained from many sources—individuals, parent groups, adoption agencies, lawyers, physicians, and books. Hear all sides because one source won't inform you of all options.

The knowledge with which you pursue adoption will help you assess where to go, when to stop, where to go next, and how best to proceed. Knowing yourself and the adoption system gives you the ability to most effectively move toward your goal.

RECOMMENDATION 2: BE ASSERTIVE AND A LITTLE BIT MORE.

The people who really want to find a baby are willing to push the issue. They actively pursue their goal rather than passively waiting for something to happen. They are able to be assertive in their baby search.

At times, it is necessary to take an approach that is a little bit more than assertive. This is not necessarily a combative approach, but it is more than just taking no for an answer. If the adoption agency turns you down, go back and seek the reasons why. Don't just take no and leave. After all, what do you have to lose? Find out if you can remedy your potential parenting "faults," whatever they are. What recourse do you have available to you to get the agency to change its position?

There are times when additional letters of reference may prove your fitness. Evaluation of your mental health by a psychologist or psychiatrist may prove to the adoption agency your serious intent to pursue the attainment of a child to the limits. Let the adoption agency know you intend to find a child.

Sometimes a letter from an attorney discussing discrimination might be in order. At times, the reasons for a person's rejection are discriminatory.

Take control and go after what you want. In many ways your willingness to seek your goal vigorously is the most overt sign of the strength of your desire to have a child. Fight the system if you can; certainly fight the system if it might get you your baby.

RECOMMENDATION 3: BE ADAPTABLE.

Adoption is a time of testing . . . testing your limits, testing your openness and flexibility, testing your patience and perseverance. Pursuing a child will cause you to stretch your limits in all these areas; this requires adaptability. Be open to the many different ways to find a child. Be flexible in what kind of child you might consider adopting. Be creative in how you approach adoption with the child you ultimately find. Basically, be adaptable to today.

Think carefully before you say "no" to any of the suggestions that might be put before you. Is there a way for your "no" to possibly be a "yes"?

Your openness to different ways to look for a child, things to read, places to go, people to meet, all significantly increase your chances of getting a child. It is easy to sit at home and think about how it would be best to simply become pregnant or how it would be great to have the agency hand you a darling new baby. The daydreams are nice, but you have to deal realistically with the world as it is. Determine what the critical ingredients in your dreams are. See if many situations might meet your criteria and if other parts of your dreams aren't quite as critical as you thought. Adapt your dreams to the reality of adoption today.

RECOMMENDATION 4: PURSUE FINDING A CHILD FROM MANY APPROACHES SIMULTANEOUSLY.

Adoption should be pursued from more than one direction at a time. Before you can be sure you need to adopt, you may need to be certain you are infertile. At times this final diagnosis is difficult to make. However, you may want to begin to look for a child even before you are absolutely positive you cannot become pregnant.

Time is ticking by as you proceed on each course to find a child; you must use your time wisely. If you wait until you are certain that this course will not give you a child before you go on to a subsequent course, you might be too old to pursue all of the many possibilities open to you. Pursue alternatives concurrently. After it seems you are unlikely to become pregnant, begin to pursue adoption even before you have a definite answer about your fertility. Pursue a child privately at the same time you are trying to adopt through the adoption agency. You will increase your chances of success significantly.

If all of a sudden you simultaneously find yourself accepted by the adoption agency, pregnant, and a lawyer is calling to say he has a baby for you—that's great. There are plenty of people around who want the children you are not able to accommodate . . . no one will be left out. The dilemma this poses is certainly better than pursuing one alternative at a time. Just knowing that you have some other possibilities makes failure at any juncture easier to handle.

RECOMMENDATION 5: BE PREPARED BEFORE YOU BEGIN.

Opportunities come up in adoption that you need to be prepared to act on quickly and decisively. I have seen people deliberate for several days about a particular situation only to find the baby has been taken by someone else. Know ahead of time what you will consider in adoption so that good opportunities do not pass you by. The time to consider how you will respond to opportunities is before they come up.

Knowing yourself and your spouse will help you be prepared. Preparation for adoption is an exciting time that allows you to learn more about you and your partner.

RECOMMENDATION 6: TRY TO BE COMFORTABLE WITH FAILURE.

Failure is the primary result you will have as you search for a child. All you need is one success, so expect some failure before your one success. You may fail in your fertility attempts, you may be rejected when you apply to adopt, you may find most people unable to help you find a baby. It is important to view the search for a child as a series of failures until your one success . . . a baby.

I always like the lesson I learned from one of my students years ago. He tried to explain how he had failed at his task. He said he didn't really fail, it was actually a "near success." Perhaps adoption searches are not filled with many failures but merely a lot of "near successes."

RECOMMENDATION 7: ONCE YOU HAVE YOUR CHILD, ENJOY HIM FULLY WHILE YOU HAVE A CHANCE TO PARTICIPATE IN HIS LIFE.

I hope your journey to find a child has taught you to be risk-taking, flexible, persevering, open, assertive, and eager to participate in raising your child. The adoption search will probably have improved your parenting ability, so the search itself has not been a waste of time.

Some studies have indicated that adoptive families seek psychological help for problems in greater numbers than non-adoptive families. Researchers imply that this is because the people who have worked with adoption agencies come to rely on agencies to solve their problems. Ideally, today's adoptive parents will have learned far more than their adoptive parent predecessors.

Let the lessons you have learned carry over into your concepts of parenting. Enjoy your child so that he can learn to enjoy life. Be honest with him about life and about his origins so he can learn that honesty is not only tolerable, but also desirable. Teach him to pursue the things in life that are valuable to him, as you have done. Help him view the problems he confronts from many directions so that he sees many solutions to life's dilemmas. Encourage him to become comfortable with his failures, not so that he becomes defeated by them, but so that instead he becomes resilient and ready to try new approaches. Show him the value of new ideas that open up new choices for him when he feels the rest of the alternatives have been exhausted. Let him experience the rewards of being in charge of his life rather than being buffeted by others.

Adoption searches have value beyond the goal that is pursued. The quest for a child teaches us many of life's lessons. Share your learning with your child in order that he, too, may gain from your finding him.

And Finally

The adoption game isn't an easy game to play, but it can be an exciting one. Illogical rules and undocumented, unspecified criteria

for success make the game suitable only for the most skillful players. Still, it is no wonder that people willingly participate . . . the
winners get such a fantastic prize.

There is a strong need to change the adoption game—in fact, to
eliminate adoption from being viewed as a game at all. But the
unnecessary barriers and the artificial roadblocks in adoption create a gamelike quality to the adoption process. Adoption will no
longer be a game when it becomes a healthy system designed to
thoroughly serve all the people who participate.

While adoption remains a game, it is incumbent on you, who
seek to use the adoption system, to make it as positive an experience as possible. It is hoped that the experience you have in the
adoption game will cause you to become motivated to change the
system to a healthier, more vital means of finding a child to raise.
Your adoption involvement does not end with finding a child . . .
that is merely a point along the way. In one way or another, adoption holds you forever once you begin.

Adoption can be a negative or a positive in your life. Infertility
can be viewed as a deficiency and a punishment, or it can be viewed
as an exciting opportunity to pursue a different kind of family. Your
search for a child can be viewed as an opportunity for growth and
new experiences. Your ultimate success in finding a child can be
viewed as a culmination of your search to have a family like everyone else, or it can be viewed as a beautiful chance to borrow a child
to enrich both your life and the life of the child. While feelings of
rejection, deficiency, and isolation will undoubtedly be a part of
your baby search, do all that you can to feel positively about the
time of your life you are experiencing. You *can* make a positive
out of a negative.

Believe you will get a child and you are most likely to find one.
While you maintain hope you have a chance—a good chance—to
find a child. When you become discouraged, talk about it, think
about it, find out why you are discouraged, and then begin again.
Discouragement means not defeat; rather it signals a time to approach the search in a different way.

The problem is not whether there is a child for you, but how you
can get to your child. If you truly believe there is a child out there
for you somewhere, your goal is to be creative, adaptable, and innovative in how you reach that union. Believing in yourself creates
miracles—miracles like children.

Appendix A

Prospective Parent Resumés

We need your help, and any assistance you can lend will be greatly appreciated.

Our names are Kathy and Phil Smith, and we are hoping to adopt a second child. We can offer a warm, loving, financially secure home to a new baby, and we are most anxious to talk with anyone who can help.

Phil and I had our first date ten years ago, fell in love, and married within three months. We have a wonderful young son and a wonderful life together . . . and we want to share it with another baby.

We own a charming natural wood ranch-style house with two large yards and a beautiful lake view. While we are very "family" oriented, we love to see new places and do new things together. Our hobbies center on activities we can do together—picnics, movies, trips and other family outings, as well as just popping popcorn by the fireplace.

We are both college educated (Phil has a master's degree), and we have traveled extensively. Phil owns a small computer business , and I do freelance screenplay writing. We were both reared in and maintain a Christian household. Phil was born in Ohio and is six feet tall, and I was born in Alabama and am a little more than five feet. Many of our family and relatives live locally, and we see grandparents to cousins frequently. We have two small dogs (mutts) and two parakeets.

We love our lives, our child, our home, our jobs, and our community. And we want another baby to share our love. Can you help us?

Kathy and Phil Smith
P. O. Box XXXX
New City, California XXXXX
(XXX) XXX-XXXX (collect)

We want to be a family.

We are a couple with a tremendous capacity to love. We offer a child an opportunity to grow up in a warm, nurturing environment. We offer understanding, patience, laughter, and Christian values. We offer time filled with music, books, and sharing.

We are able to look inward and recognize our strengths. We have an ability to give of ourselves; to love each other without reservations; to appreciate the synergy of a relationship where two together are greater than the sum of two apart.

We bring a variety of experience to our family. Having both worked as teachers and in business, we are not only experienced care-givers, but are practical as well. We balance our capabilities for love and support with knowledge of how to maintain a stable environment for a family. We have traveled and seen much of the world. We have learned about other cultures and appreciate the differences and similarities.

We are stable in our careers and earn enough money to give a child a sense of security. We own our own house. It's older (built in 1919) and had been neglected by recent owners. We've painted, cleaned, and landscaped for two years. We're not yet finished but are on our way to having a very special home.

We live in a middle-class neighborhood bustling with kids of all ages. Bicycles, hopscotch, and wonderful childish giggles fill our block after school and on weekends. Our home is filled with kids wanting to help cook, paint, garden, and (most frequently) play with us and the dogs.

We are well-educated, having both earned degrees from the University of Michigan, where we met. We are continually learning, whether through formal schooling or informal reading. We believe in higher education and, even though we put ourselves through college, are committed to providing an education for our children.

We love music. The stereo is on much more frequently than the television. We are active in the symphony support group, "Friends of the Symphony." We spend evenings reading or occasionally watching television. We keep in shape by running two to three miles each morning before work. We are actively involved in our jobs and in the community, yet find much time to spend together.

We ask your help in completing our family. Please call collect if you know of a baby available for adoption or a mother who would like to give her baby a good home.

Kathy and Phil Smith
3333 Good Street
Rolling Hills, Pennsylvania 91111
(XXX) XXX-XXXX

We are Kathy, Phil, and Christopher. We need your help in finding a baby to adopt.

We embraced our first child, Christopher, three hours after his birth in January 19XX. Christopher joined our family through an independent adoption. Our family plans always included more than one child, and we are anxious to add another son or daughter to our hearts. With your help, we can become parents again through a private adoption.

Phil and I are a couple bound to each other by our love, friendship, and mutual respect. We have an established, well-tested marriage. We are financially secure and emotionally mature. We have a strong commitment to our relationship and to providing a loving, healthy, and wholesome environment for our children. We feel we have the love, patience, experience, flexibility, sense of humor, and endurance to be excellent parents.

We own a warm, three-bedroom home in New City, Oregon that we share with our two golden retrievers. We are within walking distance to parks, schools, and churches. We are accomplished do-it-yourselfers and take pride in the creative projects we have completed. We are a good crew together and share in all indoor and outdoor activities. Cooking, biking, hiking, fishing, water sports, and browsing are among these activities. We are amazed at how easy it has been to include Christopher into this time and we delight in the surprises it brings. We take full advantage of our free time together and want to share this time with a second child.

Christopher has a pleasant disposition and a healthy body. He delights in playing with his dogs and eagerly shares his toys and food with them. He enjoys social gatherings with other children, and we feel he would warmly welcome a brother or sister. When he matures he will have full knowledge of his biological roots and the positive perceptions we gained from our meetings with his birthmother and birthfather.

Kathy is from South Dakota. She was raised Roman Catholic. She is an educational psychologist who specializes in learning disabilities and eventually, after the children are in school, plans on returning to work. Her transition to motherhood has been smooth and comfortable. She has a creative touch she hopes to instill in her children.

Phil is from Nebraska. He has a degree in math and chemistry. He is a manager with a large computer corporation where he directs communication design projects. He has a variety of interests and enjoys mechanical and construction projects at home. He's been very busy lately trying to master toy-making. He is an eager participant in Christopher's caretaking and nurturing.

We have miles of experience in life and mountains of love to share. Do you know of another baby for our mountain? Call us collect at (XXX) XXX-XXXX. Our attorney is also available to advise you on this matter.

Kathy and Phil

My husband and I have reached a crossroads. We are happily married, having fallen in love with one another during our school days, and are eager to raise a family.

Despite many hours with numerous doctors and infertility specialists coast to coast, undergoing extensive testing, trying therapies and enduring surgery over the years, we are unable to have a child. This is why we seek your help in our pursuit of a private adoption.

Our life together has been rich in love and shared experiences. We earned advanced degrees and established careers that have brought us financial security. Phil founded a sports medicine center in Cleveland that has become very successful. I am a buyer for a major department store chain; my specialty is the women's fashion department.

We want a family like the families we had growing up. We have all those fond memories and the deep love for one another. To share these feelings and our love with children is our greatest dream.

Our family roots and interests assure a child a rare opportunity to grow to his or her fullest potential. Phil and I enjoy a large modern home in the city with a lovely view and grassy grounds ideal for safe, carefree child's play. We have three fun cats and two dogs. We ski, run, swim, hike, and play tennis. Our travels have taught us about many cultures, values, and ways of life.

We know that many times financial help is necessary for a woman who is pregnant. In a private adoption, the adopting parents can legally help with maternity-related expenses. Private adoptions also enable the child to be placed directly with the adopting couple and avoid long delays and foster home placements. We think this is desirable for everyone involved in adoption.

If you know of an opportunity where the child would benefit from the love we offer, PLEASE CONTACT US IMMEDIATELY. You can call us collect at one of the following numbers: (XXX) XXX-XXXX during weekdays or (XXX) XXX-XXXX weeknights and weekends. If you prefer, contact our attorney, Michael Jones, collect at his office (XXX) XXX-XXXX.

Sincerely,

Kathy and Phil

P.S. We are enthusiastic about sharing our love and life with a son or daughter—please help us.

What do you do after seven years of trying to have a baby and you have met nothing but frustration and disappointment? You reach out for help, and that is exactly what we are doing. We are looking for someone to help us find a baby to love through private adoption.

Our names are Kathy and Phil Smith, ages thirty-five and thirty-two. We have been married for fourteen years. Our infertility problem is medically categorized as "unexplained." After many years of tests, surgery, and mis-carriages, we want to move on and try to fulfill our dream. Just being with our families' and friends' children, we have no doubt of our capacity to love and cherish any child.

Phil grew up in a large city in California. He decided after school to set up business in a small town where the pressures of life are less and to really enjoy his life. He loves the outdoors and also is a terrific handyman. Skiing, sailing, and golf are sports he enjoys; he even takes the seven-year-old boy next door, Christopher, to play golf each week. He hopes to be teaching our own son or daughter very soon.

My childhood was spent in a small town in California, Auburn. That is where Phil and I met. I am the eldest of four and have always had children as a major part of my life. I majored in elementary education and now teach school in a delightful small school in our area. My real desire is to spend my time at home with our child.

Together we enjoy experiencing new places, watching and participating in sports, and especially being with our families and friends. Since we both come from close-knit families, the baby we adopt will have loving grand-parents, aunts, uncles, and cousins.

We have a lot of love to share and a good home to offer. If you can help us in any way, please call us collect. Our home number is (XXX) XXX-XXXX. You may prefer to call our attorney, Michael Jones. His office number is (XXX) XXX-XXXX. Also feel free to call our adoption counselor, Shirley Green, at (XXX) XXX-XXXX. We are two caring people who really want to find a baby to help make our life complete. Thank you for any help you can give us in having our dream come true.

Kathy and Phil

We are Kathy and Phil Smith and we need your help. We are unable to have children and want very much to adopt a baby.

We met ten years ago in Phoenix, Arizona. We fell in love and married two months later. Our lives have remained filled with love. We live on a quiet street four blocks from a park, in a comfortable home with a room just waiting to be a nursery. (We already have a crib.)

Phil is thirty-five years old, very active and energetic. He enjoys playing softball weekly in a league; golfing, fishing, working on cars, and gardening. Since 1980 he has worked as a manager of a company that rents equipment to the construction industry. Phil's immediate family, originally from Pennsylvania, now lives in Oregon but visits us regularly.

Kathy, who is twenty-seven, is a part-time secretary for an architect a few blocks from home. She enjoys antique collecting and using her gourmet cooking skills in classes and to entertain friends. Having attended college as a journalism major, she takes pleasure in writing and reads avidly. Kathy was born and raised in Phoenix, where most of her family lives now.

Together we lead a very active life—going to professional sports events, walking our dog, Bear (a golden retriever who loves children), decorating our home, and spending time with our friends, many of whom have children. We are close to our families and visit them often. We are godparents of a four-year-old daughter of a dear friend. She visits several times a year and we enjoy playing an important role in her upbringing.

Won't you please help us start our family? If you are pregnant and considering giving your baby to a loving adoptive couple, or if you know someone who is, please contact us.

Thank you,

Phil and Kathy Smith

(XXX) XXX-XXXX—Home phone—(collect)
(XXX) XXX-XXXX—Michael Jones—Attorney—(collect)
(XXX) XXX-XXXX—Maggie White—Friend—(collect)

Appendix B

April XX, XXXX

Dear Mary:

When Kathy and I heard through our doctor that there might be a baby available for adoption, we were like two kids at Christmas. We've been married for five years and have not been able to have a child. Kathy has been through dozens of diagnostic tests and procedures, a laparotomy, and two rounds of in vitro fertilization—so far without success. Recently we applied to an adoption agency, but as you may know, it's a process that can take two to three years, so the possibility that a baby might be available within the next few months seemed like a real gift from heaven.

We know that this must be a difficult time for you. Obviously you love your baby very much, as you've chosen to give it life; we're sure you want that life to be a good one. You probably have many questions about us. I'll do my best to give you a "picture" of Kathy and me—what we're like as people, what we believe in and care about. If, after reading this letter, you think we are the kind of family you would like your baby to become a part of and you would like to meet us, we would be more than happy to meet with you.

Kathy was born in Minneapolis, Minnesota. When she was ten they moved to Spencerville, a small town in Pennsylvania. She graduated from the University of Pennsylvania in 1966 with a B.S. in physical therapy. She worked for two years for a company specializing in internationally distributed equipment to be used in physical therapy; this gave her an opportunity to visit Japan, Italy, Thailand, Hong Kong, and India. At present, she works part-time at College Park Hospital in the pediatric ward. She also does volunteer work for a pediatric clinic that specializes in children with physical handicaps. As you can see, she is a very caring person who generously gives her time to others. If a neighbor or friend is sick or needs help or moral support, she is "always there." Kathy has one brother, who lives in Connecticut. Her parents are retired and continue to live in Spencerville, but we expect that they will be moving into our area within the next eighteen months. As they have no other grandchildren, they are understandably very excited about the possibility of our adopting a child.

I was born and raised in Pittsburgh. I graduated from Amherst in Massachusetts in 1969 and went on to get my medical degree from the University of Chicago. I came here in 1976 to finish my training in internal medicine. I am now a partner in a large medical group. Being a doctor is a very big part of my life. It's what I wanted to do, even as a small boy. Although there are times when the work and stress become oppressive, it still holds a great magic for me. When I come home from work at night, I enjoy playing the piano (which I do for at least a half hour), reading, and sharing the day's events with Kathy. My family still lives in Pittsburgh. My sister, Carol, is married and they have a twelve-year-old son. She works as a school psychologist. My mother and stepfather are nearing retirement but both continue to work full-time. They too look forward to moving closer to us within a few years.

Kathy and I met in 1978 when we were both involved at the local university hospital. We were married at a ski resort a year later. We have a very close and loving relationship. Although we each hold strong opinions that sometimes differ, we've never had any trouble resolving conflicts. Disagreements are generally worked out within a half hour, and we *never* go to bed with hard or hurt feelings. I think that one of our great strengths is that we're responsive to each other. If I come home from work in bad humor, Kathy makes an effort to make me feel better, and I make myself respond to her by giving up rather than clinging to my "mood." We share a strong belief that God's purpose for us, while not always clear, surely involves helping others and, in our own small way, making the world a better and more peaceful place. Raising children seems to us to be an essential part of our purpose.

We think that our home would be a good one for children. We own a comfortable house in Raleigh with a small backyard. We have two dogs, an Australian shepherd (Rolf) and a fox terrier (Alphie). In the living room is a large grand piano and a fireplace. Off the living room is a small study/computer room. The houses in our neighborhood are about thirty years old, and the families range from young people with small children to retired couples. On weekends Kathy and I play golf, sail, or cycle. Our home is close to the water, so it's easy to be out on the water within just a few minutes. A club near us has a sailing program for kids age five and up. Our closest neighbors, the Mitchells, are active in their support of the sailing program, and each of their boys (age eight to fifteen) is already a good sailor.

Most of our friends, like us, are in their thirties; all have young children. Sally and Ken have a ten-month-old girl named Kelly; Joe and Janice a five-month-old named Kristy; and Margie and Howard have a three-year-old, Joshua, with another one "in the oven." While we adore these children and our roles as Aunt Kathy and Uncle Phil, their presence has really intensified our own desire for a family. We look forward to having birthday parties, picnics, and bike rides with our own child in a kiddie seat on the back. We want to watch our own child grow up along with Kelly, Kristy, and Joshua. As we've watched our friends raise their children, we've naturally developed our own ideas about how we would raise a child. First off, we believe that a child needs a great deal of time from both parents— time for cuddling, storytelling, playing, and just being silly. Kathy would probably stop working at least until the child was old enough to begin preschool. We would try to provide a rich educational environment so that the child could find his or her love, whether it be in music, art, sports, or scholastics. We feel that a child needs discipline and order in his or her life, but in a loving and mutually respectful environment where punishment is rarely necessary.

Kathy and I don't know much about you or your needs. Certainly we would be willing to assist you in any way we can, recognizing that in your last months of pregnancy it may be difficult for you to work. If you would like we would be happy to be with you during your labor and delivery. We would be happy to communicate with you from time to time, sending pictures and progress reports. We know that many if not most adopted children develop a keen interest in knowing something about their birthparents. We would not interfere with that process if it were your desire for your child to know you.

If you wish to know more about us but do not wish to meet with us, our adoption counselor has offered to meet with you on our behalf. We're sure that whatever decision you make will be one that you believe is best for you and your baby. Whatever you decide we wish you the best.

Sincerely,

Kathy and Phil Smith

Appendix C

Infertility

To want a child and not be able to have one is one of life's ironies. People throughout the world desperately seek to prevent unwanted births, while others with equal desperation seek to conceive. Millions of dollars are spent to find the "new" method of contraception; few but the infertile wish for the same amount of money to be spent to help couples conceive. Infertility is not an easy cross to bear in a society that seems to be going in absolutely the opposite direction.

Medical advances in solving the problems of infertility could provide solutions for about half the people who would otherwise be unable to have a child.[1] Advances in our knowledge about conception, in corrective reproductive surgery, and in the correction of hormone deficiency, have significantly decreased the number of infertile couples. Some of these advances have been a direct result of the increased interest in infertility due to the lack of children available for adoption.

Infertility is not just a medical problem, it is also an emotional problem. In the past, the emotional side was frequently blamed for infertility. Evidence does not support this belief. All the friendly advice about "relax" or "forget about it and you will get pregnant," while well-meaning, does not usually help a woman become pregnant. Rather, the physiological problems causing infertility can cause serious emotional problems.

Following some of the advice given by fertility specialists may solve the problem with no further medical intervention. Suggestions frequently given to couples who are having difficulty getting pregnant are:

1. Just because you haven't gotten pregnant doesn't mean you are sterile. It simply means you have not yet become pregnant. About eighty percent of couples get pregnant within the first year they try to have a baby. The odds are that you will also. Unless you are sure there is some reason you have a fertility problem, give nature a chance.

2. Regular sexual intercourse is necessary to get pregnant. Regular means every two or three days. To have sexual relations

more frequently may, in fact, decrease your chances of getting pregnant because it decreases the quantity of sperm available to fertilize the egg.

3. Be mindful of keeping yourself in good shape. This will increase your chances of getting pregnant and of being healthy while you are pregnant. Maintain a balanced diet, exercise regularly, and get the right amount of rest for you.

4. No specific coital position is necessary to achieve a pregnancy. As long as there is full penile penetration and the man ejaculates inside the woman's vagina, he is doing everything just the way he should.

5. Both of you, but especially the man, should avoid excessive use of alcohol, tobacco, caffeine, and other drugs. Research shows that the number of sperm and their consequent ability to travel effectively are significantly altered with the use of drugs, chemicals, and tobacco.

6. The man should also be aware of his local environment so he isn't exposed to excessive or prolonged heat. Heat—as in hot baths, hot tubs, or saunas—just before intercourse decreases sperm production and interferes with the correct environment to store the sperm. This decrease lessens the likelihood of pregnancy. Loose-fitting underwear is generally a good idea, since the male body will keep the sperm at the right temperature if clothing does not interfere.

7. Learn about the woman's menstrual cycle so you know when you are most likely to achieve a pregnancy. For the woman to become pregnant, she must have intercourse shortly before or after the time she ovulates. This is usually between ten and seventeen days after she starts her period. In order to know about your individual cycle, you need to learn when you ovulate. Thinner vaginal mucous discharge generally indicates you have ovulated and are most fertile. You can also get a basal thermometer, which measures small changes in oral temperature. Just before you ovulate, a slight drop in your temperature will occur. Knowing the right time to try to achieve a pregnancy significantly increases your chances of conception.

8. If you have an obvious problem that might be interfering with your ability to conceive a child, correct it. If you are overweight, try to reduce. If you are under considerable stress at work, see if you can change that situation. If you have been sick a great deal, try to discover what is creating your susceptibility. Make

any necessary corrections you can, to increase your chances of getting pregnant.

These hints will solve the infertility problem of most couples. They really didn't have a problem with infertility at all; they merely were waiting the normal period of time to get pregnant. They really didn't belong to the ten or fifteen percent of the population that is infertile. If you have tried the above suggestions and still have not become pregnant, if you have consulted a physician or physicians who specialize in infertility, if you have undergone the ordinary tests and the regular treatments to try to remedy the apparent problems, the following choices are open to you.

Infertility Help

As you become aware that a baby is not going to "happen" to you, get ready to find help. This is a difficult step for many people because it, more than anything up to this point, admits openly that you have a problem. This is the point at which you are forced to confront the reality of sterility. "Infertile" is harsh enough, but "sterile" sounds so much worse. Yet someone in your relationship is sterile at this time; you need to figure out what you are going to do about it.

• Finding a Physician

As the tears increase with each new menstrual period, it becomes more apparent that other steps need to be taken. The first step you are likely to take is to talk with the physician you know the best. From this departure point, you are on your way.

Your physician is likely to recommend another who knows more about infertility. When your physician makes a referral, find out on what grounds he or she is suggesting this new person. This is also a good time to consult other people; it is important to find a physician who has expertise in the field of infertility and additionally is the kind of person with whom you want to work.

This is a time to shop around and ask questions. Call your local infertility association or write to the American Fertility Society (2131 Magnolia Avenue, Suite 201, Birmingham, Alabama 35256), for general information on doctors working on infertility in your area. Contact a RESOLVE group near you or write RESOLVE, Inc. (5 Water Street, Arlington, Massachusetts, 02174) to find the group nearest to you. This is a support group for people experiencing infertility problems, and they are an excellent source of information on physicians working in the area of infertility. Go to the nearest university medical school and ask for suggestions. You may be involved with this physician for the next year or more. Even though the initial stages of an infertility study are relatively simple, your infertility work may become more involved; your physician may require a lot of your time and money over the months ahead. Spend some extra time now and find the physician who is right for you.

After you have gathered names of the people you have heard are the best, contact them. By this time you will have formed some opinions on what kind of person you are seeking. Interview your potential doctor to make certain this is the person you want. Find out the background he or she has in infertility work. Ask for his or her opinion on the kinds of problems you have and what the possibilities are for you. Know enough about what is happening so that you can try to assess your potential physician's knowledge in infertility. Not all physicians, in fact not even all infertility specialists, know equal amounts. By talking about his or her background and your problem, you should be able to choose your physician wisely.

If you find one physician isn't all you hoped for, consult another one. There are some outstanding physicians in this field, and they are the kind you want.

If a physician suggests major surgery for your infertility problem (or for any other problem as well), consult another physician for a second opinion. Most times this will verify the previous recommendation. The time to make certain of your decision is before surgery.

In the past, physicians have held a position of unquestioned authority with most people. Don't be intimidated by your physician; you are trying to find someone to hire to do a service for you. More and more we are learning that physicians can help most if we, the patients, are actively involved in the treatment plan. No one knows more about you than you!

• *Learning About Infertility*
How can you, a layperson, ask intelligent questions of a physician, the expert, if you don't know much about the subject? You can't. This is why it is important to learn about infertility. You will end up learning about infertility somewhere along the way whether you want to or not. You may as well find out about the subject right at the beginning and have your information work for you.

Many sources of information are available on infertility. Some of these may be too technical, in the beginning stages especially, but others are aimed at people without medical backgrounds. The more you find out about the subject, the more difficult and technical information you will understand.

One of the best sources of information on infertility is a local infertility society. If you don't know about the one closest to you, check with the American Fertility Society (2131 Magnolia Avenue, Suite 201, Birmingham, Alabama 35256) to see where your local chapter is located. These groups frequently have meetings with people who are experiencing infertility problems. They discuss the general procedures used with infertility studies, innovative techniques in reproductive medicine, the psychological consequences of infertility, the best physicians, and other areas of concern to people who are having difficulties getting pregnant. They frequently have guest lecturers who are experts in this field. The informal knowledge passed from individual to individual is priceless. You will also have found a support system that is exceedingly valuable in many ways.

Another source of information is available through reading. Information on infertility is published in many different forms. Become familiar with all of them.

Books on infertility are available.[2] Some are written for physicians, but some are written in less technical language. Read current books because this is a rapidly changing field. Your neighborhood library or a college library may have some appropriate books for you on this subject.

Articles in popular magazines regularly discuss infertility. Some of these are excellent sources of material since they are frequently more timely than books can be. If nothing else, they will help you understand enough about the subject of infertility to talk with and ask questions of your physician.

As you become more knowledgeable about the subject, you may wish to go to the medical libraries and read current articles on infertility that are written for physicians. These are not as difficult to read as you might think, especially after you begin to acquire a greater background in this field.

Newspapers also have articles on recent advances in reproductive medicine. They may not provide a lot of details, but they may help you talking with your physician. They may also give you another source to contact.

In all of your sources of information, don't hesitate to write to the experts about whom you are reading. They can answer questions and be a valuable source of additional information to you.

You can understand why it is so important to have a cooperative working relationship with your physician as you begin this process. If he or she can't answer your questions or doesn't like you "meddling" in the treatment, you will be restricted in how much you can be involved. You may also find out some ideas that will help your physician in your treatment. Be willing to help educate your physician; patients are a primary source of learning for physicians.

If you are infertile, it is one of the most important issues you are likely to face in your life. Face it intelligently, openly, frankly, and thoroughly. Seek the help of experts, but trust yourself to be involved in this important life experience.

Experimental Methods of Reproduction

Experimental ways of having a child are never first choices for the people who try them. In fact, they are generally third or fourth choices. Ask the couple attempting to have a child by artificial insemination why they are doing this. You are likely to hear that first they tried to get pregnant and failed, so they sought the usual medical remedies for their infertility. When these failed, they tried to adopt a child and failed, and now they are at this point. You get to this point only by a process of elimination . . . you have no other choices left or this choice seems better to you than the remaining ones.

What then are these newer ways to make babies? What hope is open to the couple who does not respond to the usual medical remedies for infertility?

• Artificial Insemination

Of all the more unusual methods of conceiving a child, artificial insemination is probably the oldest, the most secretive, the least studied, and the most used. It is estimated that in this country alone, between 10,000 and 20,000 children per year are produced by this method. Some estimates on the potential use of artificial insemination indicate that this process "may be responsible for the births of 1.5 million Americans by the year 2000."[3] Yet we keep few records on the outcome of artificial insemination, we know little about the psychological consequences for the people involved, and we offer little help and support to those considering this procedure.

Artificial insemination takes many forms. Basically, it means fertilization of the egg by artificial, not "regular," means. This technique is used when a husband has a low sperm count—under 100 to 150 million sperm—which would prevent his sperm from impregnating his wife. Some people would say that the artificial part of artificial insemination means using some other man's sperm . . . it's not from the real father. Other people would say the artificiality is when sperm is put into the woman's vagina by means other than intercourse.

When a husband has a low sperm count, one technique is the accumulation of the father's sperm. Once a sufficient number of sperm is acquired, the physician identifies the most ideal time of the woman's cycle to insert the accumulated and concentrated dosage of her husband's sperm. This form of artificial insemination sometimes produces a child.

Some women seek artificial insemination because they are single and wish to become mothers. Approximately ten percent of artificial insemination is performed on single women. A new answer, designed especially for single women seeking artificial insemination, is the newly forming feminists' sperm banks. Undoubtedly, most single women who wish to have a child simply go out and get pregnant. Others have moral objections to having sexual relations without being married, so they seek the help of a physician.

The most common form of artificial insemination currently practiced by physicians is artificial insemination by donor (AID). The woman who is fertile, and whose partner is sterile, is artificially inseminated by a physician who uses sperm from a donor. The donor is generally unknown to the couple.

At times, sperm of several donors are mixed so that it is impossible to know which donor's sperm impregnated the egg. This is an additional safeguard to protect the donor's anonymity. Sometimes the sperm of the husband, even if it is quite low in numbers, is mixed with a donor's sperm so that there is a possibility that the sperm of the husband may have actually been the one to impregnate the wife's egg. Many times this mixing of the husband's sperm with the donor's sperm makes artificial insemination acceptable to a couple who would otherwise have refused it.

With the rapidly expanding use of artificial insemination and with the nonmedical expansion of this procedure, the controversial nature of the procedure is underscored. In response to the rise in sperm banks—and especially sperm banks such as the Repository of Germinal Choice, a controversial selective sperm bank—legislation is being proposed to require state licensing of sperm banks and to require specific information be given to prospective parents. Both sides of this controversial issue clamor to be heard.[4]

In the more usual type of artificial insemination currently being done, records are seldom kept on whose sperm is used to inseminate which woman. Although this assures anonymity for the donor, it also presents some problems. The sperm of a single donor may be used to impregnate many women in a given geographical area. The possibility of the resulting children meeting and marrying at a later time obviously exists. This possibility is far greater with children who are the products of artificial insemination than it is with adopted children who might ultimately marry siblings unknown to them as brothers or sisters.

Another problem comes from the lack of medical history of the genetic father. The valid cry from adoptees who seek their medical history can also exist for the child produced by artificial insemination. Half their parental medical history is lost to them forever.

Anonymity for the donor, on the other hand, is critical. If the identity of the donor was known, he could be sued for the support of his child. Few men would be willing to donate sperm if there existed the possibility of being identified. The donor's response to fathering multiple children has never been studied.

The need for research in this area is strongly apparent. A team of researchers at Vista Del Mar is attempting to research this subject and other factors related to artificial insemination by donors. Publication of their findings is due in the near future. Their research focuses on the consequences of artificial insemination on the individuals who have been donors, the parents through artificial insemination, and the children from artificial insemination.[5]

Certain legal consequences exist for the people involved in artificial insemination by donors. Not only can there be risks of legal problems for an identified donor, but in divorce cases, a father by artificial insemination might try to deny support for the child who was produced by this procedure. One father supported his wife while she became pregnant through artificial insemination, but later changed his mind. The reality of his wife carrying another man's child proved overwhelming. As this procedure is performed more frequently, partially because of the lack of children to adopt, the potential for problems also increases. Some states have ruled that artificial insemination is illegal.

Religious implications also exist for couples using artificial insemination; some churches object to it. As in other areas where people ignore the doctrine of their church, the problems they may experience are increased because of their religious guilt.

A new issue related to artificial insemination has recently come up with the rising number of cases of AIDS.[6] If professionals were worried before about controversy surrounding this method of contraception, the problem has now worsened. It is possible to transmit AIDS through artificial insemination, and now extra precautions need to be taken to decrease the likelihood of that happening.

The secrecy surrounding artificial insemination is designed to protect everyone involved. Yet it is known that secrecy can compound psychological problems. How does one lead a healthy life when secrecy is such a critical underlying ingredient? Couples electing this process must develop a healthy communication between themselves to offset the effects of this lifetime secret they share. People trying to hide adoption from the adopted child seldom succeed in their attempt. Their failure is usually because others know and tell the adoptee. At times they fail because they get angry and use the secret as a weapon to hurt their spouse or their child. The secret of the child conceived through artificial insemination is usually considered far more important to guard than the adoption secret.

• *Test-Tube Babies*

Of all the new ways of producing a child that an infertile couple can try, the "test-tube" baby method, formerly called the in vitro fertilization method, has been given the most recent publicity. The concept of a child being conceived outside the mother is at once exciting, futuristic, awesome, interesting, and frightening. With all these emotional responses, the world heralded the arrival of baby Louise, the first "test-tube" baby.

Baby Louise was born in England in 1978, amid publicity that rivaled the birth of the Dionne quintuplets two generations before. Her birth brought hope for thousands of infertile couples, and fear of the tremendous power of science. Her family was paid handsomely for her story, which was sought for broadcast throughout the world. The mother of Louise had blocked Fallopian tubes that prevented her from conceiving a child. Her physicians, after several attempts, successfully removed one of the mother's eggs, fertilized it in the laboratory with the father's sperm, and then implanted that fertilized egg, and two others that did not stay implanted, into the mother's womb. Louise was the result.

Another similarly produced child was delivered by the same doctors. The attending physicians, Dr. Patrick Steptoe and Dr. Robert Edwards, recently discussed a number of failures that have resulted from this same procedure. They had 156 failures before attaining success. They also have discussed two fetuses that were grossly distorted and that aborted spontaneously, one after ten weeks and one after twenty weeks.

The work of Dr. Steptoe and Dr. Edwards has met with mixed response. The majority of Americans (ninety-three percent) knew of the birth of baby Louise soon after the story hit the newspapers. Of those who knew of her birth, the response was two to one in favor of the use of this new technique of conception.[7] Prior to the birth of Louise, the public outcry in the United States temporarily halted research on this technique. The original clinic in the United States, in Virginia, met serious opposition from the community.

Now, partly because of Louise and how healthy she is, and partly because of pressure from infertile couples seeking a child, new clinics are emerging throughout the United States. Opposition to this procedure seems destined to be overcome because of the great demand for the services these clinics offer. In order to avoid any additional negative publicity, many of the clinics are quite restrictive about who they will accept for the procedure. As the procedure becomes more available, the high costs and the discriminating restrictions will be lowered.

Although this technique has enjoyed tremendous publicity since the birth of baby Louise, it is not the best technique to correct sterility in women whose tubes are blocked through scarring. The technique of microsurgery has been found to be far more effective for the majority of women with this problem.[8]

Some of the unfavorable response to this new conception technique is centered on the research that has been done to develop the procedure. Right to Life groups have been critical of the procedure based upon the number of fetuses that have been destroyed while trying to perfect this method.[9]

Other criticisms of this method of conception question the impact science is having on the family. No longer is a child necessarily the result of a shared, loving moment between a husband and a wife. No doubt this is true. Neither, however, are conceptions that result from rape or forced sexual contact, or from scheduled sexual contact for infertile couples, or from artificial insemination that is clinically performed in the stirrups of the gynecologist's treatment table. This is simply another technique that opens the way for a couple to have a child. Couples merely learn to make the best of a situation that is not their ideal, but a reasonable substitute.

• *Embryo Substitutions*

Another new way to make a baby involves the use of a surrogate (substitute) mother's embryo. Embryo substitutions are similar to artificial insemination, but use the embryo of a donor rather than the sperm of a donor. Two methods are currently used: fertilization outside of the surrogate mother and then implantation into the infertile mother's womb, or fertilization inside the mother and then washing the fertile ovum from the donor's womb and transplantation into the infertile mother's womb. This technique falls slightly more into the questionable area for some people because it uses another woman and not just the mother and father.

Embryo implantation has occurred in the cattle industry for years. Embryos of cows are frozen until needed. Then they are artificially inseminated and implanted in the mother-to-be cow. The increase in the number of calves the individual cow can produce has been dramatic, and the cattle industry and consumer have profited.

Using animal research as a basis for their experimentation, physicians in India experimented on infertile women in a similar manner. As a result, in 1978, a baby was born that was fertilized using a frozen embryo from a surrogate mother. The physicians responsible for the birth of this child had over one hundred failures before they achieved success. Predictably, the response from people was mixed. The government of India became embroiled in this experimental event, which was lauded and condemned simultaneously.

Researchers experimenting with this technique look toward the near future, when embryo banks will be available for infertile couples.[10] Infertile couples will be able to purchase the frozen embryos, catalogued by types. The chosen embryo will then be fertilized by the sperm of the father and implanted in the uterus of the mother-to-be.

The same difficulties discussed under artificial insemination by donors exist in this procedure. Details are lacking because this procedure is so new, but it is likely that the same privacy concerns for the donor will exist. At some point in the future, it will be necessary to do research to learn how women feel about having their children born and raised by someone else, just as we need to understand how this affects sperm donors.

• *Surrogate Mothers*

Surrogate mothers are not new. They probably have existed long before adoption became a legally formalized process. Basically, an infertile couple, because of the wife's sterility, has the father impregnate another woman either directly or through artificial insemination. The surrogate mother agrees to carry the child to term and give it to the couple to adopt after it is born.

Legally this is permissible. Most states will allow this to occur as long as the woman receives no money for her services. The reason that the woman cannot be paid is that no laws relate directly to surrogate parenting; instead, the surrogate mother comes under the adoption laws, which forbid payment for a child. Medical and pregnancy-related expenses can be paid, but nothing can be paid to the surrogate mother for her time or effort to produce this child.

Surrogate mothers still attract headlines in news media.[11] When the controversy over who was responsible for a defective child born to a surrogate mother was taken up on the Phil Donahue television show, the issue and all its potential problems attracted national attention.[12] Yet despite all the problems, the emotions, the lack of laws, and the assault on the traditions of the family, surrogate mothers are having more babies each year for infertile mothers. Surrogate parent centers are emerging throughout the country to meet the demands for this service.

The motivation for becoming a surrogate mother can be complex. Money is frequently, but not always, the primary factor. Surrogate mothers are usually paid about $10,000. With the expansion of surrogate parent centers the cost may decrease. Money is the primary legal issue involved, since paying a woman for her child violates the laws of most states.

In some states surrogate mother services are not legal. A judge in Michigan ruled that it was illegal for a couple to pay a woman for bearing and relinquishing to them a child conceived through artificial insemination with the father's sperm. The judges ruled that it would violate Michigan's adoption laws. The prosecutor maintained that to allow them to pay the woman would lead to a commercial market for babies and would affect a woman's decision to place a child for adoption. The attorney for the infertile couple said the suit would do just the opposite, since it would clearly establish a legal precedent for couples seeking surrogate mothers.

Recent publicity given the Baby M. case has brought considerable attention to the surrogate mother issue. Lawyers would say that the outcome of that case has strengthened the contractual basis for surrogate mothers. The fact that so few surrogate situations have ever been brought to court probably argues for the safety of this method of reproduction.

Many emotional issues surround surrogate motherhood, with little research to back up the strongly held beliefs.[13] Once again we are faced with the disparity between the impact on the society and on the individual. Far-out? Yes, but it seems so only if you can have a baby the "easy" way. If you don't have one and you want one, it sounds so much more reasonable.

Summary

Despite the far-out reproductive concepts that are being developed, the goal is quite simple . . . a baby. Genetic manipulations, highly selective donor insemination, and embryo implants are all techniques that have far-reaching implications for society, but the implication for the infertile couple is less complex: having a baby may now be possible.

Choices—again we are involved with choices! What do we do with the knowledge of reproduction we have available to us? Do we ignore it because it sounds too far-out? Do we ignore it because it sounds too futuristic? Do we ignore it because it sounds too elite or too cruel? Do we ignore it because this is tampering with nature or with God? Or do we use the information we have to allow people to choose the direction they believe best suits them?

Notes

A FEW WORDS BEFORE YOU BEGIN.

1 R. B. Hampson, and J. B. Tavormina, "Feedback from the Experts: A Study of Foster Mothers," *Social Work*, vol. 25, 1980, pp. 108−112.

2 N. E. Finkelstein, "Children in Limbo," *Social Work*, vol. 25, 1980, pp. 100−105.

3 B. Kantrowitz, "Three's a Crowd," *Newsweek*, Sept. 1, 1986, pp. 68+.

4 K. Laverty, "Psychological Well-Being in Parents and Non-Parents Beyond the Age of Child Rearing: A Comparative and Descriptive Study," Doctoral dissertation, California School of Professional Psychology, San Diego, California, 1979.

CHAPTER 1: THE ADOPTION AGENCY GAME

1 "Pros, Cons of Adopting During Infertility Treatment," *Adopted Child*, vol. 5, 1986.

2 H. Bruch, *Eating Disorders: Obesity, Anorexia Nervosa, and Person Within*, Basic Books, New York, 1973.

3 "They Said We Were Too Fat to Adopt a Baby," *Good Housekeeping*, vol. 189, 1979, pp. 98+.

4 "The End of the Legal Road for Timmy—And a Beginning in New Mexico," *Behavior Today*, July 3, 1978.

5 C. H. Zastrow, *Outcome of Black Children−White Parents Transracial Adoptions*, R. & R. Research Associates, San Francisco, California, 1977.

CHAPTER 2: YOUR OWN GAME

1 W. Meezan, et al., *Adoptions Without Agencies: A Study of Independent Adoptions*, Child Welfare League of America, Inc., New York, 1978.

2 J. Seglow, et al., *Growing Up Adopted*, National Foundation for Educational Research in England and Wales, Great Britain, 1972, p. 177.

3 "Doctors, Lawyers Disappoint Parents," *Adopted Child*, vol. 1, 1982, p. 4.

4 J. Goldstein, et al., *Beyond the Best Interests of the Child*, Free Press, New York, 1973.

5 T. Kornheiser, *The Baby Chase*, Atheneum, New York, 1983.

6 S. Arms, *To Love and Let Go*, Knopf, New York, 1983.

7 B. Gradstein, et al., "Private Adoption," *Fertility and Sterility*, vol. 37, 1982, pp. 548.

8 P. J. Boyer, "South Carolina's One-Stop Adoptions," *Los Angeles Times*, Feb. 21, 1984.

9 L. McTaggart, *The Baby Brokers: The Marketing of White Babies in America*, Dial, New York, 1980.

10 R. S. Lasnik, *A Parent's Guide to Adoption*, Sterling, New York, 1979.

CHAPTER 3: LOOKING ELSEWHERE AND EVERYWHERE

1 "Doctors, Lawyers Disappoint Parents," *Adopted Child*, vol. 1, 1982, p. 4.

2 "Adoptive Parents Rated as Resources," *Adopted Child*, vol. 1, 1982, p. 4.

3 M. W. Yogman, et al., "Perinatal Characteristics of Newborns, Relinquished at Birth," *American Journal of Public Health*, vol. 73, 1983, pp. 1194–1196.

4 H. R. Boer, "On Religious Affiliation of Mothers Relinquishing Their Newborns," *American Journal of Public Health*, vol. 74, 1984, p. 623.

5 "Facts at a Glance," *TAPP-WREC Newsletter*, Nov., 1984, p. 2.

CHAPTER 5: PROBLEM SOLVING (AND SOME PROBLEMS THAT CAN'T BE SOLVED)

1 J. H. Plumez, *Successful Adoption*, Harmony Books, New York, 1982, pp. xii–xiv.

CHAPTER 6: FARAWAY BABIES

1 J. Nelson-Erichsen and H. R. Erichsen, *How to Adopt Internationally: Africa, Asia, Europe and Latin America*, St. Mary's College, Winona, Minnesota, 1980; American Public Welfare Association, *Intercountry Adoption Guidelines*, U.S. Government Printing Office, Washington, D.C., 1980; American Public Welfare Association, *National Directory of Intercountry Adoption Service Resources*, U.S. Government Printing Office, Washington, D.C., 1980; J. Nelson-Erichsen and H. R. Erichsen, *Gamines: How to Adopt from Latin America*, Dillon, Minneapolis, 1981.

2 J. Nelson-Erichsen and H. R. Erichsen, 1980 and 1981.

3 D. C. Anderson, *Children of Special Value: Interracial Adoption in America*, St. Martin's, New York, 1971; J. B. Blank, *19 Steps Up the Mountain: The Story of the DeBolt Family*, Lippincott, Philadelphia, 1976; J. deHartog, *The Children: A Personal Record for the Use of Adoptive Parents*, Atheneum, New York, 1969; J. Rigert, *All Together: An Unusual American Family*, Harper & Row, New York, 1973.

4 R. Caudill, *Somebody Go and Bang a Drum*, Dutton, New York, 1974; L. J. Grow and D. Shapiro, *Transracial Adoption Today: Views of Adoptive Parents and Social Workers*, Child Welfare League of America, Inc., New York, 1976; J. A. Ladner, *Mixed Families: Adopting Across Racial Boundaries*, Anchor Books, New York, 1977.

5 A. Geyer, "How to Adopt a Child in Mexico," *Los Angeles Times*, Mar. 4, 1984.

CHAPTER 7: THE SPECIAL KIDS

1 J. McNamara, *The Adoption Adviser*, Hawthorne, Inc., New York, 1975.

2 A. R. Silverman and W. Feigelman, "Some Factors Affecting the Adoption of Minority Children," *Social Casework*, vol. 58, 1977, pp. 554–561.

3 G. Sandness, *Commitment: The Reality of Adoption*, Mini-World, Maple Grove, Minnesota, 1984.

4 P. J. Kravik, *Adopting Children with Special Needs*, North American Council on Adoptable Children, Riverside, California, 1976.

5 J. P. Blank, *19 Steps Up the Mountain: The Story of the DeBolt Family*, Lippincott, Philadelphia, 1976.

6 D. Keyes, *Flowers for Algernon*, Harcourt Brace Jovanovich, New York, 1966.

7 P. D. Steinhauer and Q. Rae-Grant, *Psychological Problems of the Child and His Family*, Macmillan, Toronto, Canada, 1977.

8 F. Green, "The High-Risk Adoption and the Highroad to Heartache," *San Diego Union*, Feb. 4, 1980.

9 S. Kety, et al., "Mental Illness in the Biological and Adoptive Families of Adopted Individuals Who Have Become Schizophrenic," *Behavior Genetics*, vol. 6, 1976, pp. 219–225.

10 D. C. Manuel, "Plight of the Older Adoptees," *Los Angeles Times*, Dec. 4, 1981.

11 R. Tod (ed.), *Social Work in Adoption*, Longman Group Limited, London, 1971, p. 78.

12 "Siblings Need Help When Older Child Arrives," *Adopted Child*, vol. 2, 1983, p. 1.

13 C. L. Jewett, *Adopting the Older Child*, Harvard Common Press, Harvard, Massachusetts, 1978; A. Carney, *No More Here and There*, University of North Carolina Press, Chapel Hill, N.C., 1976; A. Kadushin, *Adopting Older Children*, Columbia, New York, 1970; J. Rigert, *All Together: An Unusual American Family*, Harper & Row, New York, 1973; F. R. Rondell and A. M. Murray, *New Dimensions in Adoption*, Crown, New York, 1974.

14 P. Beaty, *That's One Ornery Orphan*, Morrow, New York, 1980; G. Connors, *Don't Disturb Daddy!*, Brandon Press, Boston, 1965; E. Enright, *Then There Were Five*, Holt, New York, 1944; M. Miles, *Aaron's Door*, Atlantic Monthly, Boston, 1977; F. S. Murphy, *Ready-Made Family*, Scholastic Book Service, New York, 1972; P. Windsor, *Mad Martin*, Harper & Row, New York, 1978.

15 M. M. Gill, "Adoption of Older Children: The Problems Faced," *Social Casework*, vol. 59, 1978, pp. 272–278.

16 J. A. Ladner, *Mixed Families: Adopting Across Racial Boundaries*, Anchor Books, New York, 1977.

17 A. Howard, et al., "Transracial Adoption: The Black Community Perspective," *Social Work*, vol. 22, 1977, pp. 184–189.

18 R. J. Simon, "Black Attitudes Toward Transracial Adoption," *Phylon*, vol. 39, 1978, pp. 135–142.

19 O. Gill and B. Jackson, *Adoption and Race*, Batsford Academic and Educational Ltd., London, 1983.

20 *Ibid.*

21 J. A. Ladner, *Mixed Families*; V. Salkmann, *There Is a Child for You: A Family's Encounter with Modern Adoption*, Simon & Schuster, New York, 1972; R. J. Simon and H. Altstein, *Transracial Adoption*, Wiley, San Francisco, 1977; C. H. Zastrow, *Outcome of Black Children–White Parents Transracial Adoptions*, R. & R. Research Associates, San Francisco, California, 1977.

22 C. Bunin and S. Bunin, *Is That Your Sister?*, Pantheon, New York, 1976; S. B. Stein, *The Adopted One: An Open Family Book for Parents and Children Together*, Walker, New York, 1979; H. L. Sobol, *We Don't Look Like Our Mom and Dad*, Coward-McCann, New York, 1984.

23 J. Neufeld, *Edgar Allan*, New American Library, New York, 1968.

CHAPTER 8: THE SPECIAL MOMS AND DADS

1 E. Branham, "One Parent Adoptions," *Children*, vol. 17, 1970, pp. 103–107.

2 J. J. Curto, *How to Become a Single Parent: A Guide for Single People Considering Adoption or Natural Parenthood Alone*, Prentice Hall, Englewood Cliffs, N.J., 1983.

3 M. Vieni, "Why Should Physically Handicapped People Want to Adopt?" *Adopting Children with Special Needs*, North American Council on Adoptable Children, Riverside, California, 1976, pp. 43–44.

4 M. Ward, "Large Adoptive Families: A Special Resource," *Social Casework*, vol. 59, 1978, pp. 411–418.

5 R. B. Hampson and J. B. Tavormina, "Feedback for the Experts: A Study of Foster Mothers," *Social Work*, vol. 25, 1980, pp. 108–112.

6 W. Meezan and J. F. Shireman, *Care and Commitment: Foster Parent Adoption Decisions*, State University of New York Press, Albany, New York, 1985.

7 G. E. Hanscombe and J. Forster, *Rocking the Cradle—Lesbian Mothers: A Challenge in Family Living*, Alyson Publications, Boston, 1982; E. Mehren, "Lesbian Mothers: Two New Studies Shatter Stereotypes," *Los Angeles Times*, June 1, 1983.

8 J. Cummings, "Gay 'Father' Opens Legal Door," *San Diego Union*, Jan. 11, 1983.

9 "Kids Get Home with Gays," *Lesbian Tide*, vol. 9, 1980, p. 12.

10 Mehren, *Los Angeles Times*.

11 R. A. Lasnik, *A Parent's Guide to Adoption*, Sterling, New York, 1979.

12 Mehren, *Los Angeles Times*.

CHAPTER 9: DEEP DARK SECRETS

1 J. D. Harrington, "Legislative Reform Moves Slowly," *Public Welfare*, vol. 37, 1979, pp. 49–57.

2 H. D. Kirk, *Adoptive Kinship: A Modern Institution in Need of Reform*, Ben-Simon Publications, British Columbia, Canada, 1981.

3 *Ibid.* p. 141.

4 J. W. Small, "Discrimination Against the Adoptee," *Public Welfare*, vol. 37, 1979, pp. 38–43; J. Hanania, "Secrecy Practice Is Eliminated," *Los Angeles Times*, Feb. 26, 1982.

5 A. Haley, *Roots*, Doubleday, Garden City, N.Y., 1974.

6 A. D. Sorosky, et al., *The Adoption Triangle: The Effects of the Sealed Record on Adoptees, Birth Parents, and Adoptive Parents*, Anchor Books, New York, 1978.

7 J. Triseliotis, *In Search of Origins: The Experience of Adopted People*, Routledge & Kegan Paul, London, 1973, p. 2.

8 A. Foster, "Who Has the 'Right' to Know?" *Public Welfare*, vol. 37, 1979, pp. 34–37.

9 F. Fisher, *The Search for Anna Fisher*, Arthur Fields Books, Inc., New York, 1973.

10 J. M. Paton, *The Adopted Break Silence*, Life History Study Center, Philadelphia, 1955.

11 H. Ehrlich, *A Time to Search: The Moving and Dramatic Stories of Adoptees in Search of Their Natural Parents*, Paddington Press, Ltd., New York, 1977; M. Howard, "I Take After Somebody: I Have Real Relatives: I Possess a Real Name," *Psychology Today*, vol. 9. 1975, pp. 33+; B. J. Lifton, *Lost and Found: The Adoption Experience*, Dial, New York, 1979; J. Krementz, *How It Feels To Be Adopted*, Knopf, New York, 1982; K. Maxtone-Graham, *An Adopted Woman*, Remi Books, Inc., New York, 1983.

12 H. Aigner, *Faint Trails*, Paradigm Press, Greenbrae, California, 1980.

13 L. Lowry, *Find a Stranger, Say Good-Bye*, Pocket Books, New York, 1978; L. Dusky, *Birthmark*, M. Evans, New York, 1979.

14 L. Flynn, "A Parent's Perspective," *Public Welfare*, vol. 37, 1979, pp. 28–33.

15 Sorosky, et al., *The Adoption Triangle*.

16 Dusky, *Birthmark*.

17 U. Vils, "When Birth Parents Seek Their Children," *Los Angeles Times*, Apr. 23, 1981.

18 Sorosky, et al., *The Adoption Triangle*.

19 R. Zeilinger, "The Need vs. the Right to Know," *Public Welfare*, vol. 37, 1979, pp. 44–47.

20. L. C. Burgess, *The Art of Adoption*, Acropolis, Washington, D.C., 1976, pp. 153–154.

CHAPTER 10: LETTING IN SOME LIGHT

1 H. D. Kirk, *Shared Fate: A Theory and Method of Adoptive Relationships*, Ben-Simon Publications, British Columbia, Canada, 1984.

2 "Open Adoptions: What Effect on Families?," *NASW News*, May, 1986, pp. 3+.

3 Sorosky, et al., *The Adoption Triangle*, p. 210.

4 R. Conniff, "Adapting to Open Adoptions," *Next*, vol. 1, 1980, p. 88.

5 *Ibid.*

6 Burgess, *The Art of Adoption.*

7 K. Silber and P. Speedlin, *Dear Birthmother*, Corona Publishing Company, San Antonio, Texas, 1983.

8. *Ibid.*

APPENDIX C: INFERTILITY

1 M. Culverwell, "The Odds on Overcoming Infertility," *Los Angeles Times*, March 13, 1983.

2 S. L. Corson, *Conquering Infertility*, Appleton-Century-Crofts, Norwalk, Connecticut, 1982; S. Borg and J. Lasker, *When Pregnancy Fails: Families Coping with Miscarriage, Stillbirth and Infant Death*, Beacon Press, Boston, 1981; R. Friedman and B. Gradstein, *Surviving Pregnancy Loss*, Little, Brown and Company, Boston, 1982; M. Blais, *They Say You Can't Have a Baby: The Dilemma of Infertility*, W. W. Norton and Company, New York, 1979; A. Decker and S. Loebl, *Why Can't We Have a Baby?*, Warner Books, New York, 1978; J. T. Howard and D. Schultz, *We Want to Have a Baby: The Couple's Complete Guide to Overcoming Infertility*, E. P. Dutton, New York, 1979; B. E. Menning, *Infertility: A Guide for the Childless Couple*, Prentice Hall, Inc., Englewood Cliffs, New Jersey, 1977.

3 P. Bagne, "Brave New World of High-Tech Begetting," *San Diego Union*, Oct. 12, 1983.

4 R. C. Paddock, "Bill Would Curb 'Master Race' Sperm Banks," *Los Angeles Times*, Mar. 1, 1983.

5 D. Smith, "Artificial Birth and Its Effects," *Los Angeles Times*, Mar. 1, 1983.

6 "Fresh Sperm for Insemination Criticized," *San Diego Union*, May 22, 1986.

7 G. Gallup, "Most Favor Funding of 'Test Tube' Births," *San Diego Union*, Dec. 14, 1978.

8 B. Varro, "Scientific Advances in Fertility," *Los Angeles Times*, Aug. 28, 1979.

9 "Test Tube Babies," *Living*, vol. 10, 1979, p. 4.

10 H. Nelson, "Human Ova Will Be Transplanted," *Los Angeles Times*, June 16, 1982.

11 B. Kantrowitz, "After the Baby M Case," *Newsweek*, April 13, 1987.

12 E. Goodman, "Wombs for Rent: New Era on the Reproduction Line," *Los Angeles Times*, Feb. 8, 1983.

13 L. Denton, "Surrogate Parenting," *The APA Monitor*, vol. 18, 1987, pp. 6–10.

Bibliography

(*Asterisks indicate books for children related to adoption.)

*Adams, B.: *Like It Is: Facts and Feelings About Handicaps from Kids Who Know*, Walker and Company, New York, 1979.

"A Daughter's Search for 'Lost' Mother," *U.S. News & World Report*, June 25, 1984, p. 63.

Adcock, G. B.: *Intercountry Adoptions: Where Do They Go from Here?*, Bouldin-Haigh-Irwin, Washington, D.C., 1979.

*Adoff, A.: *All the Colors of the Race*, Lothrop, Lee & Shepard Books, New York, 1982.

"Adolescence Not the Best Time for a Reunion," *Adopted Child*, vol. 3, 1984, p. 4.

"Adopted Children: May Have More Problems But Majority Are Still Normal," *Adopted Child*, vol. 3, 1984, pp. 1+.

"Adopted Foreign Kids May Face Woe," *San Diego Union*, Oct. 10, 1981.

"Adoptees' Lesser Achievements," *Psychology Today*, February, 1984.

"Adoptees Unite," *Newsweek*, April 28, 1975, p. 86.

Adoption Factbook: United States Data, Issues, Regulations and Resources, National Committee for Adoption, Washington, D.C., 1985

"Adoptive Parents Rated as Resources," *Adopted Child*, vol. 1, 1982, p. 4.

Aigner, H.: *Faint Trails: An Introduction to the Fundamentals of Adult Adoptee–Birth Parent Reunification Searches*, Paradigm Press, Greenbrae, California, 1980.

"Almost 3 in 10 Pregnancies Found to End in Abortions," *Los Angeles Times*, Jan. 6, 1980.

Altman, L.: "Researchers Report Genetic Test Detects Huntington Disease," *New York Times*, Nov. 9, 1983.

American Public Welfare Association, *Intercountry Adoption Guidelines*, U.S. Government Printing Office, Washington, D.C., 1980.

———, *National Directory of Intercountry Adoption Service Resources*, U.S. Government Printing Office, Washington, D.C., 1980.

*Ames, M.: *Without Hats, Who Can Tell the Good Guys?*, E. P. Dutton & Co., Inc., New York, 1976.

Anderson, D. C.: *Children of Special Value: Interracial Adoption in America*, St. Martin's Press, New York, 1971.

*Anderson, H. C. (retold by L. B. Cauley): *The Ugly Duckling*, Harcourt Brace Jovanovich, New York, 1979.

Andrews, L. B.: "Yours, Mine and Theirs," *Psychology Today*, vol. 18, 1984, pp. 20+.

Andrews, R. G.: "A Clinical Appraisal of Searching," *Public Welfare*, vol. 37, 1979, pp. 15–21.

*Angell, J.: *Tina Gogo*, Laurel-Leaf, New York, 1977.

Annarelli, J. M.: "We Were Lucky to Get Our Baby," *USA Today*, Mar. 9, 1984.

Annest, J. L., C. F. Sing, P. Biron, and J. G. Mongeau: "Familial Aggregation of Height, Weight and Body Mass," *American Journal of Epidemiology*, vol. 117, 1983, pp. 492–506.

Anonymous: "Because I Loved You, Jennifer," *American Journal of Nursing*, vol. 74, 1974, p. 471.

Anselm, R.: "A Natural Mother's Wish: 'I Would Like to Hold My Son,' " *Los Angeles Times*, June 8, 1980.

Arens, L., W. Robertson, and C. Molteno: "The Adoption of the 'At Risk' Baby," *South African Medical Journal*, vol. 56, 1979, pp. 311–314.

Arms, S.: *To Love and Let Go*, Alfred A. Knopf, Inc., New York, 1983.

Arnold, R.: "Sperm Banks: Parents Are Proud . . . But Not Talking," *Los Angeles Times*, Sept. 16, 1980.

"Artificial Insemination," *Accent on Living*, vol. 25, 1980, pp. 22–29.

"As Adoptions Get More Difficult," *U.S. News & World Report*, June 25, 1984, p. 82.

Askin, J., and B. Oskam: *Search: A Handbook for Adoptees and Birthparents*, Harper & Row, Publishers, New York, 1982.

"Australians Have First Test-Tube Quads, All Boys," *Los Angeles Times*, Jan. 7, 1984.

Babikian, H., and A. Holdman: "A Study in Teenage Pregnancy," *American Journal of Psychiatry*, vol. 128, 1971, pp. 755–760.

"Baby Boomlet: Its Impact on the 80's," *U.S. News & World Report*, June 15, 1981, pp. 51–52.

"Baby-Selling Wrong; It Should Be Illegal," *USA Today*, Mar. 9, 1984.

Badinter, E.: *Mother Love: Myth and Reality*, The Macmillan Company, New York, 1981.

Bagne, P.: "Brave New World of High-Tech Begetting," *San Diego Union*, Oct. 12, 1983.

———: "Storing Seed of the Future: Sperm Banks Put Choice into Natural Selection," *San Diego Union*, Oct. 11, 1983.

Baran, A., A. Sorosky, and R. Pannor: "The Dilemma of Our Adoptees," *Psychology Today*, vol. 9, 1975, pp. 38+.

Barglow, P., M. Bernstein, D. Exum, M. Wright, and H. Visotsky: "Some Psychiatric Aspects of Illegitimate Pregnancy in Early Adolescence," *American Journal of Orthopsychiatry*, vol. 38, 1968, pp. 672–687.

*Bates, B.: *It Must've Been the Fish Sticks*, Archway, New York, 1982.

* ———: *Bugs in Your Ears*, Holiday House, New York, 1977.

Baudry, F., and A. Winer: "A Woman's Choice: Pregnancy or Abortion," *Mademoiselle*, April, 1984, pp. 34+.

*Bauer, M. D.: *Foster Child*, Laurel-Leaf, New York, 1977.

*Beatty, P.: *That's One Ornery Orphan*, William Morrow & Company, Inc., New York, 1980.

Behrens, D.: "The Pill: 20 Years Later, No Magic," *Los Angeles Times*, Jan. 1, 1981.

Benning, B. E.: "The Infertile Couple: A Plea for Advocacy," *Child Welfare*, vol. 54, 1975, pp. 454–460.

Berkow, R., and J. H. Talbott: *The Merck Manual of Diagnosis and Therapy*, 13th ed., Merck Sharp & Dohme Research Laboratories, Rahway, N.J., 1977.

Berman, C.: *We Take This Child: A Candid Look at Modern Adoption*, Doubleday & Company, Inc., New York, 1974.

Bernard, J.: *The Children You Gave Us*, Jewish Child Care Association of New York, New York, 1973.

Bernstein, G. S.: "Conventional Methods of Contraception: Condom, Diaphragm, and Vaginal Foam," *Clinical Obstetrics and Gynecology*, vol. 17, 1974, pp. 21–33.

Bernstein, L.: "Birth Parents Strive for Contact in Adoptions," *Los Angeles Times*, May 17, 1987.

Bigelow, R. E.: "One Father's Dissent," *Los Angeles Times*, June 8, 1980.

Billiter, B.: "Quest for Identity Hinges on Finding Her Real Father," *Los Angeles Times*, Dec. 5, 1982.

———: "State May Set Rules on Motherhood," *Los Angeles Times*, June 20, 1982.

Bing, E., and L. Colman: *Having a Baby After 30*, Bantam Books, Inc., New York, 1980.

Bird, C.: *The Two-Paycheck Marriage: How Women at Work Are Changing Life in America*, Rawson, Wade Publishers, Inc., New York, 1979.

"Black Children Are Adopted Less Often," *Behavior Today*, Nov. 21, 1983.

Black, S., and M. Sykes: "Promiscuity and Oral Contraception: The Relationship Examined," *Social Science and Medicine*, vol. 5, 1971, pp. 637–643.

Blais, M.: *They Say You Can't Have a Baby: The Dilemma of Infertility*, W. W. Norton & Company, Inc., New York, 1979.

Blake, J.: "The Teenage Birth Control Dilemma and Public Opinion," *Science*, vol. 180, 1973, pp. 708–812.

Blank, J. B.: *19 Steps Up the Mountain: The Story of the DeBolt Family*, J. B. Lippincott Company, Philadelphia, 1976.

*Blue, R.: *Me and Einstein*, Human Sciences Press, New York, 1979.

Bluford, R., and R. E. Petres: *Unwanted Pregnancy: The Medical and Ethical Implications*, Harper & Row, Publishers, New York, 1973.

Blum, H. P. "Adoptive Parents: Generative Conflict and Generational Continuity," *Psychoanalytical Study of Child*, vol. 38, 1983, pp. 141–163.

Blumberg, B. D., M. S. Colbus, and K. H. Hanson: "The Psychological Sequelae of Abortion Performed for a Genetic Indication," *American Journal of Obstetrics and Gynecology*, vol. 122, 1975, pp. 799–808.

Boer, H. R.: "On Religious Affiliation of Mothers Relinquishing Their Newborns," *American Journal of Public Health*, vol. 74, 1984, p. 623.

Bohman, M.: "The Interaction of Heredity and Childhood Environment: Some Adoption Studies," *Journal of Child Psychology and Psychiatry*, vol. 22, 1981, pp. 195–200.

Bolles, E. B.: *The Penguin Adoption Handbook*, Penguin Books, New York, 1984.

*Bond, M.: *A Bear Called Paddington*, Houghton Mifflin Company, Boston, 1958.

Borg, S., and J. Lasker: *When Pregnancy Fails: Families Coping with Miscarriage, Stillbirth and Infant Death*, Beacon Press, Boston, 1981.

Borgman, R.: "The Consequences of Open and Closed Adoption for Older Children," *Child Welfare*, vol. 61, 1982, pp. 217–226.

Boyer, P. J.: "South Carolina's One-Stop Adoptions," *Los Angeles Times*, Feb. 21, 1984.

Bracken, M. B., M. Hachamovitch, and C. Grossman: "Correlates of Repeat Abortions," *Obstetrics and Gynecology*, vol. 40, 1972, pp. 816–825.

Bracken, M. B., L. V. Klerman, and M. Bracken: "Coping with Pregnancy Resolution Among Never-married Women," *American Journal of Obstetrics and Gynecology*, vol. 130, 1978, pp. 251–262.

Braden, J. A.: "Adoption in a Changing World," *Social Casework*, vol. 51, 1970, pp. 486–490.

Bragonier, J. R., R. G. Smith, C. V. Ford, N. M. Simon, and J. R. Cavanaugh: "Why Do Unmarried Women Fail to Use Contraception?" *Medical Aspects of Human Sexuality*, vol. 7, 1973, pp. 154–168.

Branham, E.: "One Parent Adoptions," *Children*, vol. 17, 1970, pp. 103–107.

Brazelton, T. B.: *On Becoming a Family: The Growth of Attachment*, Dell Publishing Co., Inc., New York, 1981.

"Brighter Days for 'Unadoptable' Children," *U.S. News & World Report*, vol. 85, 1978, p. 80.

*Brightman, A.: *Like Me*, Little, Brown and Company, Boston, 1976.

Broadhurst, D. D., and E. J. Schwartz: "The Right to Know," *Public Welfare*, vol. 37, 1979, pp. 5–8.

Brockhaus, J., and R. Brockhaus: "Adopting an Older Child: The Emotional Process," *American Journal of Nursing*, vol. 82, 1982, pp. 288–294.

Brody, J.: "Avoiding Unwanted Pregnancy," *San Diego Union*, Oct. 16, 1983.

———: "The Sponge: What's Good About the New Contraceptive," *San Diego Union*, May 8, 1983.

Brody, S., and S. Axelrad: *Mothers, Fathers, and Children: Exploration in the Formation of Character in the First Seven Years*, International Universities Press, Inc., New York, 1978.

*Brodzinsky, A. B.: *The Mulberry Bird: Story of an Adoption*, Perspectives Press, Fort Wayne, Indiana, 1981.

Brown, D.: "Independent Adoptions Are on Increase," *Los Angeles Times*, Aug. 9, 1984.

Bruch, H.: *Eating Disorders: Obesity, Anorexia Nervosa, and the Person Within*, Basic Books, Inc., New York, 1973.

Bryan-Logan, B. N. and B. L. Dancy: "Unwed Pregnant Adolescents: Their Mother's Dilemma," *Nursing Clinics of North America*, vol. 9, 1974, pp. 57–68.

Buck, P. S.: *Children for Adoption*, Random House, Inc., New York, 1964.

*———: *Matthew, Mark, Luke and John*, The John Day Company, New York, 1966.

*———: *Welcome Child*, Random House, Inc., New York, 1964.

*Budbill, D.: *Bones on Black Spruce Mountain*, Dial Press, New York, 1978.

Bumpass, L., and C. Westoff: "The 'Perfect Contraceptive' Population," *Science*, vol. 169, 1970, pp. 1177–1182.

*Bunin, C., and S. Bunin: *Is That Your Sister?*, Pantheon Books, Inc., New York, 1976.

Bunin, S.: "Black, White, & Tan Family," *Parents*, April, 1984, pp. 88+.

Burgen, M.: "Should Whites Adopt Black Children?" *Ebony*, December, 1977. pp. 63+.

Burgess, L. C.: *The Art of Adoption*, Acropolis Books, Washington, D.C., 1976.

*Byars, B.: *The Pinballs*, Harper & Row, New York, 1977.

*———: *The Summer of the Swans*, Avon Camelot, New York, 1970.

Cadoret, R., L. Cunningham, R. Loftus, and J. Edwards: "Studies of Adoptees from Psychiatrically Disturbed Biological Parents: Medical Symptoms and Illnesses in Childhood and Adolescence," *American Journal of Psychiatry*, vol. 133, 1976, pp. 1316–1318.

Cain, A. C., M. E. Erickson, I. Fast, and R. A. Vaughan: "Children's Disturbed Reactions to Their Mother's Miscarriage," *Psychosomatic Medicine*, vol. 26, 1964, pp. 58–66.

*Caines, J.: *Abby*, Harper & Row, Publishers, New York, 1973.

Callahan, D.: *Abortion: Law, Choice and Morality*, The Macmillan Company, New York, 1970.

*Campbell, H.: *Home to Hawaii*, W. W. Norton & Company, Inc., New York, 1967.

Campbell, L. H.: "The Birthparent's Right to Know," *Public Welfare*, vol. 37, pp. 22–27.

Canape, C.: *Adoption: Parenthood Without Pregnancy*, Holt, Rinehart, and Winston, New York, 1986.

*Carlson, N. S.: *A Brother for the Orphelines*, Yearling Books, New York, 1959.

*———: *The Happy Orphelines*, Dell Publishing Co., Inc., New York, 1957.

Carney, A.: *No More Here and There: Adopting the Older Child*, The University of North Carolina Press, Chapel Hill, N.C., 1976.

*Carr, J.: *Felix the Cat*, Scholastic, Inc., New York, 1986.

Carsola, A. T. and S. D. Lewis: "Independent Adoptions: The Preferred Adoption," *Family Law News*, vol. 4, 1981, pp. 1–3.

Carson, D.: "Legislative Role Asked on Sperm Banks," *San Diego Union*, May 2, 1983.

*Caudill, R.: *Somebody Go and Bang a Drum*, E. P. Dutton & Co., Inc., New York, 1974.

Cawley, P. B.: "Natural Parents Seeking Changes in Adoption Laws," *Daily Californian*, Nov. 1, 1978.

Chandler, R.: "Medical Promise, Ethical Peril," *Los Angeles Times*, Apr. 21, 1984.

"Charlie Finally Finds a Home—and Love," *U.S. News & World Report*, May 7, 1984, p. 52.

Chavira, R.: "Baby-Selling Probe Finds Only Distress," *San Diego Union*, Apr. 6, 1981.

———: "Smugglers Find New Commodity: Babies," *San Diego Union*, Apr. 5, 1981.

Cheetham, J.: *Unwanted Pregnancy and Counseling*, Routledge & Kegan Paul, Ltd., London, 1977.

Chemerinsky, E.: "Defining the 'Best Interests': Constitutional Protection in Involuntary Adoptions," *Journal of Family Law*, vol. 18, 1979–1980, pp. 79–113.

Chen, E.: "Sperm Bank Donors All Nobel Winners," *Los Angeles Times*, Feb. 29, 1980.

"Children Now Running Behind Automobiles as a 'Consumer Preference,' " *Behavior Today*, June 4, 1979.

Chilman, C. S.: "Teenage Pregnancy: A Research Review," *Social Work*, vol. 24, 1979, pp. 492–498.

*Chinnock, F.: *Kim: A Gift from Vietnam*, World Publishers, New York, 1969.

Choney, S.: "Motherhood: Choice for Single Women," *San Diego Union*, June 24, 1983.

Churchill, S. R., B. Carlson, and L. Nybell: *No Child Is Unadoptable*, Sage Publications, Beverly Hills, California, 1979.

Claeys, W., and P. DeBoeck: "The Influence of Some Parental Characteristics on Children's Primary Abilities and Field Indpendence: A Study of Adopted Children," *Child Development*, 1976, pp. 842–845.

Clarke, A. M., and A. D. B. Clarke (eds.): *Early Experience: Myth and Evidence,* The Free Press, New York, 1976.

*Cleaver, V., and Cleaver, B.: *Trial Valley,* Bantam Books, New York, 1978.

*Clewes, D.: *Adopted Daughter,* Cowand-Mc Cann, Inc. New York, 1968.

Cohen, D.: "Adoption," *Psychology Today,* November, 1977, pp. 128+.

Colen, B. D.: "Use of Pill in Sharp Decline," *Los Angeles Times,* Nov. 18, 1979.

Comfort, A., and J. Comfort: *The Facts of Love: Living, Loving, Growing Up,* Crown Publishers, Inc., New York, 1979.

Committee on Adoption and Dependent Care: "Adoption of the Hard-to-Place Child," *Pediatrics,* vol. 68, 1981, pp. 598–599.

Conniff, R.: "Adapting to Open Adoptions," *Next,* vol. 1, 1980, p. 88.

*Connors, G.: *Don't Disturb Daddy!,* Brandon Press, Boston, 1965.

Corson, S. L.: *Conquering Infertility,* Appleton-Century-Crofts, Norwalk, Connecticut, 1982.

Culverwell, M.: "The Odds on Overcoming Infertility," *Los Angeles Times,* Mar. 13, 1983.

Cummings, J.: "Gay 'Father' Opens Legal Door," *San Diego Union,* Jan. 11, 1983.

Cuniberti, B.: "For the Test-Tube Doctors, It Was a Triumph of Will," *Los Angeles Times,* Jan. 5, 1982.

Cunningham, L., R. J. Cadoret, R. Loftus, and J. E. Edwards: "Studies of Adoptees from Psychiatrically Disturbed Biological Parents: Psychiatric Conditions in Childhood and Adolescence," *British Journal of Psychiatry,* vol. 126, 1975, pp. 534–549.

Curie-Cohen, M., L. Luttrell, and S. Shapiro: "Current Practice of Artificial Insemination by Donor in the United States," *New England Journal of Medicine,* vol. 300, 1979, pp. 585–590.

Curto, J.: *How to Become a Single Parent: A Guide for Single People Considering Adoption or Natural Parenthood Alone,* Prentice Hall, Inc., Englewood Cliffs, N.J., 1983.

"Cutting the Risks of Childbirth After 35: The Reassurance Amniocentesis Can Provide," *Consumer Reports,* vol. 44, 1979, pp. 302–306.

*Daringer, H. F.: *Adopted Jane,* Harcourt Brace, New York, 1973.

Dart, J.: "Ethicist Examines Social Issues of Surrogate Motherhood," *Los Angeles Times,* Jan. 2, 1982.

Davids, L.: "Foster Fatherhood: The Untapped Resource," *Family Coordinator,* vol. 20, 1971, pp. 49–54.

Decker, A., and S. Loebl: *Why Can't We Have a Baby?,* Warner Books, New York, 1978.

deElejalde, F.: "Inadequate Mothering," *Bulletin of the Menninger Clinic,* vol. 35, 1971, pp. 182–198.

deHartog, J.: *The Children: A Personal Record for the Use of Adoptive Parents,* Atheneum Publishers, New York, 1969.

Dell, P. F., and A. S. Applebaum: "Trigenerational Enmeshment: Unresolved Ties of Single-Parents to Family of Origin," *American Journal of Nursing*, vol. 47, 1977, pp. 52–59.

Denes, M.: *In Necessity and Sorrow: Life and Death in an Abortion Hospital*, Basic Books, Inc., New York, 1976.

Denton, L.: "Surrogate Parenting," *The APA Monitor*, vol. 18, 1987, pp. 6–10.

Depp, C. H.: "After Reunion: Perceptions of Adult Adoptees, Adoptive Parents, and Birth Parents," *Child Welfare*, vol. 61, 1982, pp. 115–119.

Depp, C. H.: "Placing Siblings Together," *Children Today*, vol. 12, March–April, 1983, pp. 14–19.

Deutsch, H.: *The Psychology of Women: A Psychoanalytic Interpretation*, 17th ed., Grune & Stratton, Inc., New York, 1944, 2 vols.

Deykin, E. Y., Campbell, E., and Patti, P.: "The Postadoption Experience of Surrendering Parents," *America Journal of Orthopsychiatry*, vol. 54, 1984, pp. 271–280.

"Diaphragm Risk Reported," *San Diego Union*, Oct. 15, 1982.

Diddle, A. W.: "Rights Affecting Human Reproduction," *Obstetrics and Gynecology*, vol. 41, 1973, pp. 789–794.

Djerassi, C.: "Birth Control After 1984," *Science*, vol. 169, 1970, pp. 941–951.

*Doane, P.: *Understanding Kim*, J. B. Lippincott Company, Philadelphia, 1962.

"Doctors, Lawyers Disappoint Parents," *Adopted Child*, vol. 1, 1982, p. 4.

"Doctors Make Progress in Treating Infertility, but Costs Are High," *Wall Street Journal*, Oct. 12, 1984.

Doheny, K.: "Contraceptive Research Has Entered the Planting Stages," *Los Angeles Times*, Mar. 20, 1984.

*Doss, H.: *The Family Nobody Wanted*, Little, Brown and Company, Boston, 1954.

*———: *The Really Real Family*, Little, Brown and Company, Boston, 1959.

Dougherty, S. A.: "Single Adoptive Mothers and Their Children," *Social Work*, vol. 23, 1978, pp. 311–314.

Douglas, W.: *The One Parent Family*, Graded Press, Nashville, Tennessee, 1971.

Drehsler, A.: "Waitress Wages Long Battle for Child," *San Diego Union*, Oct. 12, 1978.

Dukette, R.: "Perspectives for Agency Response to the Adoption-Record Controversy," *Child Welfare*, vol. 54, 1975, pp. 545–555.

Dukette, R., and N. Stenson: "The Legal Rights of Unmarried Fathers: The Impact of Recent Court Decisions," *Social Service Review*, vol. 47, 1973, pp. 1–15.

*DuPrau, J.: *Adoption: The Facts, Feelings & Issues of a Double Heritage*, Julian Messner, Publishers, Inc., New York, 1981.

Dusky, L.: *Birthmark*, M. Evans and Company, Inc., New York, 1979.

Duty, J.: "Church Offers Promise of Adoption for Black Child," *Los Angeles Times*, Apr. 18, 1982.

Dywasuk, C. T.: *Adoption—Is It For You?*, Harper & Row, Publishers, New York, 1973.

Easson, W. M.: "Special Sexual Problems of the Adopted Adolescent," *Medical Aspects of Human Sexuality*, vol. 7, 1973, pp. 96–105.

Ehrlich, H.: *A Time to Search: The Moving and Dramatic Stories of Adoptees in Search of Their Natural Parents*, Paddington Press, Ltd., New York, 1977.

*Eisenberg, E.: *The Pretty House That Found Happiness*, Steck-Vaughn Co., Austin, Texas, 1964.

Eldred, C. A., D. Rosenthal, P. H. Wender, S. S. Kety, F. Shulsinger, J. Welner, and B. Jacobsen: "Some Aspects of Adoption in Selected Samples of Adult Adoptees," *American Journal of Orthopsychiatry*, vol. 46, 1976, pp. 279–290.

Elonen, A. S., and E. M. Schwartz: "A Longitudinal Study of Emotional, Social, and Academic Functioning of Adopted Children," *Child Welfare*, vol. 48, 1969, pp. 72–78.

"Embryo Transfer Process Produces 'Beautiful Little Girl,' " *San Diego Union*, Mar. 25, 1984.

"The End of the Legal Road for Timmy—And a Beginning in New Mexico," *Behavior Today*, July 3, 1978.

Engs, R. C.: "The Characteristics of Volunteers in Crisis Intervention Centers," *Public Health Reports*, vol. 89, 1974, pp. 459–464.

*Enright, E.: *Then There Were Five*, Holt, Rinehart and Winston, Inc., New York, 1944.

Erichsen, J., H. Erichsen, and G. Gallber: *How to Adopt from Asia, Europe, and the South Pacific*, International Adoption Center, Austin, Texas, 1983.

Erikson, E. H.: *Identity: Youth and Crisis*, W. W. Norton & Company, Inc., New York, 1968.

"Facts at a Glance," *TAPP-WREC Newsletter*, November, 1984, p. 2.

"Family Law: Father's Rights Clarified for Custody Determination," *The Los Angeles Daily Journal*, Oct. 26, 1984.

Fanshel, D.: *Far from the Reservation: The Transracial Adoption of American Indian Children*, Scarecrow Press, Inc., Metuchen, N. J., 1972.

Fanshel, D., and E. B. Shinn: *Children in Foster Care*, Columbia University Press, New York, 1978.

*Fassler, J.: *One Little Girl*, Behavioral Publications, New York, 1971.

*———: *The Boy with a Problem*, Behavioral Publications, New York, 1971.

*———: *Don't Worry Dear*, Behavioral Publications, New York, 1971.

"Federal Help for Test-Tube Births Urged," *Los Angeles Times*, Jan. 4, 1982.

Feigelman, W., and A. R. Silverman: *Chosen Children: New Patterns of Adoptive Relationships,* Praeger, New York, 1983.

Feigelman, W., and A. R. Silverman: "Single Parent Adoptions," *Social Casework,* vol. 58, 1977, pp. 418–425.

Fein, E., L. J. Davies, and G. Knight: "Placement Stability in Foster Care," *Social Work,* vol. 24, 1979, pp. 156–157.

Feinstein, S. C., and P. L. Giovacchini (eds.): *Adolescent Psychiatry,* vol. 5, Jason Aronson, Inc., New York, 1977.

"Feminists Have Own Sperm Banks," *Los Angeles Times,* Nov. 18, 1982.

Fenly, L.: "Adopting a Baby: Most Must Enter the 'Gray Market,' " *San Diego Union,* July 16, 1981.

————: "But She Believed in Miracles," *San Diego Union,* Sept 26, 1982.

————: "Pregnancies by Proxy," *San Diego Union,* Aug. 1, 1982.

Festinger, T. *Necessary Risk: A Study of Adoptions and Disrupted Adoptive Placements,* Child Welfare League of America, Inc., Washington, D.C., 1986.

————: *No One Ever Asked Us: A Postscript to Foster Care,* Columbia University Press, New York, 1983.

Finkelstein, N. E.: "Children in Limbo," *Social Work,* vol. 25, 1980, pp. 100–105.

"First Donated Embryo Birth to Be in California," *Los Angeles Times,* Jan. 21, 1984.

*First, J.: *I, Rebekah, Take You, the Lawrences,* Franklin Watts, New York, 1981.

Fisch, R. O., M. Bilek, A. Deinard, and D. Chang: "Growth, Behavioral, and Psychologic Measurements of Adopted Children: The Influences of Genetic and Socioeconomic Factors in a Prospective Study," *Journal of Pediatrics,* vol. 89, 1976, pp. 494–500.

Fisher, F.: *The Search for Anna Fisher,* Arthur Fields Books, Inc., New York, 1973.

*Fitzgerald, J.: *Me and My Little Brain,* The Dial Press, Inc., New York, 1971.

Fitzgerald, J., and B. Murcer: *Building New Families Through Adoption and Fostering,* Basil Blackwell & Mott, Ltd., Oxford, England, 1982.

Fletcher, C.: "A Baby Boom in the Making? The New Phenomenon of Older Motherhood," *Los Angeles Times,* Sept. 9, 1981.

————: "Childbirth in the 80's: It's a Whole New Dimension," *Los Angeles Times,* Sept. 9, 1981.

Flores, E.: "New Surgical Sterilization Methods Told," *San Diego Union,* Oct. 28, 1978.

Flynn, L.: "A Parent's Perspective," *Public Welfare,* vol. 37, 1979, pp. 28–33.

Flynn, L. M., and W. Hamm: "TEAM: Parent-Agency Partnership in Adoption Services," *Children Today,* vol. 12, March–April, 1983, pp. 2–5.

Foster, A.: "Who Has the 'Right' to Know?," *Public Welfare*, vol. 37, 1979, pp. 34–37.

"Foster Care Big Business," *Marriage and Divorce Today*, Sept. 14, 1981, pp. 3–4.

"Foster Parents Win Fight to Adopt 2-Year-Old," *Los Angeles Times*, Dec. 23, 1978.

Frank, J. K., and L. M. Flynn: "Group Therapy for Adopted Adolescents and Their Families," *Children Today*, vol. 12, March–April, 1983.

Frankfort, E.: *Vaginal Politics*, Quadrangle Books, Inc., New York, 1972.

Franklin, B.: *The Fun and Hassles of Adoption*, Vantage Press, New York, 1983.

Freed, D.: "Judge's Policy Throws Certain S.D. Adoption Cases into Limbo," *Los Angeles Times*, Nov. 25, 1984.

———: "San Diego Gets Artificial Insemination Service," *Los Angeles Times*, Mar. 1, 1983.

"Fresh Sperm for Insemination Criticized," *San Diego Union*, May 22, 1986.

*Freudber, J., and Geiss, T.: *Susan and Gordon Adopt a Baby*, Random House, New York, 1986.

Friedman, R., and Gradstein, B.: *Surviving Pregnancy Loss*, Little Brown and Company, Boston, 1982.

Froelich, W.: "It's Possible Now to Choose Offspring's Sex," *San Diego Union*, Nov. 14, 1982.

———: "Synthetic Hormone Helps Infertile Women Give Birth," *San Diego Union*, Dec. 2, 1983.

"Future 'Rewards' No Reason to Become a Parent," *Behavior Today*, Aug. 17, 1981.

Gadpaille, W. J.: "Adolescent Sexuality and the Struggle Over Authority," *Journal of School Health*, vol. 40, 1970, pp. 379–393.

Gallagher, U. M.: "What's Happening in Adoption?" *Children Today*, vol. 4, 1975, pp. 11+.

Gallup, G.: "Most Favor Funding of 'Test Tube' Births," *San Diego Union*, Dec. 14, 1978.

Garn, S. M., S. M. Bailey, and P. E. Cole: "Similarities Between Parents and Their Adopted Children," *American Journal of Physical Anthropology*, vol. 15, 1976, pp. 539–543.

"Genetic Counseling Given New Impetus," *Los Angeles Times*, July 13, 1979.

Geyer, A.: "How to Adopt a Child in Mexico," *Los Angeles Times*, Mar. 4, 1984.

Gill, M. M.: "Adoption of Older Children: The Problems Faced," *Social Casework*, vol. 59, 1979, pp. 272–278.

Gill, O. and B. Jackson: *Adoption and Race: Black, Asian and Mixed Race Children in White Families*, Batsford Academic and Educational Ltd., London, 1983.

Gillette, P. J.: *Vasectomy: The Male Sterilization Operation*, Paperback Library, New York, 1972.

Gilman, L.: *The Adoption Resource Book*, Harper & Row, Publishers, New York, 1984.

Gillmon, R.: "Priest's Goal: More Black Adoptions," *San Diego Union*, Jan. 9, 1982.

"Girls in Greater Demand for Adoption," *Adopted Child*, vol. 3, 1984, p. 2.

Golden, A.: "Couple Held at Border with Illegal Alien—6-Day-Old Girl," *San Diego Union*, Oct. 28, 1981.

Goldstein, J., A. Freud, and A. J. Solnit: *Beyond the Best Interests of the Child*, The Free Press, New York, 1973.

Goodman, E.: "Babies and Jobs—Biological Clock Ticks On," *Los Angeles Times*, Sept. 16, 1982.

———: "Wombs for Rent: New Era on the Reproduction Line." *Los Angeles Times*, Feb. 8, 1983.

*Gordon, S.: *The Boy Who Wanted a Family*, Harper & Row, Publishers, New York, 1979.

Gorman, T.: "Unwed Pregnant Women Find Home," *Los Angeles Times*, Dec. 26, 1983.

Gormley, M. V.: "Adoptee Faces Formidable Barriers," *Los Angeles Times*, May 10, 1984.

Gorney, C.: "For Love and Money," *California*, vol. 8, 1983, pp. 88+.

Gradstein, B., M. Gradstein, and R. Glass: "Private Adoption," *Fertility and Sterility*, vol. 37, 1982, pp. 548–551.

Grayson, J.: "Shouldn't Adoptees Know About Their Heritage?" *Seventeen*, March, 1975, p. 72.

Green, F.: "The High-Risk Adoption and the Highroad to Heartache," *San Diego Union*, Feb. 4, 1980.

Green, H.: "Risks and Attitudes Associated with Extra-Cultrual Placement of American Indian Children," *Journal of American Academy of Child Psychiatry*, vol. 22, 1982, pp. 63–67.

*Gregg, D.: *The Story of Megan*, Social Science Education Consortium, Inc., Boulder, Colorado, n.d.

Grotevant, H., S. Scarr, and R. Winberg: "Are Career Interests Inheritable?" *Psychology Today*, March, 1978, pp. 88+.

Group for the Advancement of Psychiatry: *The Joys and Sorrows of Parenthood*, Charles Scribner's Sons, New York, 1973.

Grow, L. J., and D. Shapiro: *Transracial Adoption Today: Views of Adoptive Parents and Social Workers*, Child Welfare League of America, Inc., New York, 1976.

Haimes, E. and N. Timms: *Adoption, Identity and Social Policy: The Search for Distant Relatives*, Studies in Social Policy and Welfare, London, 1985.

Haley, A.: *Roots*, Doubleday & Company, Inc., Garden City, New York, 1974.

Hallenbeck, C. A.: *Our Child: Preparation for Parenting in Adoption—Instructor's Guide*, Our Child Press, Wayne, Pennsylvania, 1984.

Halsema, J.: "The Long, Hard Road to Adoption," *San Diego Union*, May 29, 1984.

Hamm, W., T. Morton, and L. M. Flynn: *Self-Awareness, Self-Selection and Success: A Parent Preparation Guidebook for Special Needs Adoptions,* North American Council on Adoptable Children, Washington, D. C., 1985.

Hampson, R. B., and J. B. Tavormina: "Feedback from the Experts: A Study of Foster Mothers," *Social Work*, vol. 25, 1980, pp. 108–112.

Hanania, J.: "Secrecy Practice Is Eliminated," *Los Angeles Times*, Feb. 26, 1982.

Hanscombe, G., and J. Forster: *Rocking the Cradle—Lesbian Mothers: A Challenge in Family Living*, Alyson Publications, Boston, 1982.

Hansen, K., and G. Omenn: "Genetic Counseling: The Search for the Adopted Child," *Journal of Legal Medicine*, vol. 4, 1976, pp. 8AA+.

Haring, B.: "Adoption Trends, 1971–1974, *Child Welfare*, vol. 54, 1975, pp. 524–525.

Harrington, J. D.: "Legislative Reform Moves Slowly," *Public Welfare*, vol. 37, 1979, pp. 49–57.

Harrison, S. I., and J. F. McDermott: *Childhood Psychopathology: An Anthology of Basic Readings*, International Universities Press, Inc., New York, 1972.

Hartman, A.: *Finding Families: An Ecological Approach to Family Assessment in Adoption*, Sage Publications, Beverly Hills, California, 1979.

Hass, A.: *Teenage Sexuality: A Survey of Teenage Sexual Behavior*, The Macmillan Co., New York, 1979.

Havemann, J.: "Women Having Babies Less Often But Births Out of Wedlock Rise," *Los Angeles Times*, Apr. 26, 1984.

*Haywood, C.: *Here's a Penny*, Harcourt Brace Jovanovich, New York, 1944.

Heim, A.: *Thicker Than Water? Adoption*, David and Charles, North Pomfret, Vermont, 1983.

Helfer, R. E., and C. H. Kempe (eds.): *The Battered Child*, The University of Chicago Press, Chicago, 1974.

Hendin, D., and J. Marks: *The Genetic Connection*, New American Library, Inc., New York, 1978.

Herst, J.: "Adoption: Parents Provide Insights to Experience," *Denver Post*, May 27, 1984.

Hoffman, L. W.: "The Employment of Women, Education and Fertility," *Merrill-Palmer Quarterly*, vol. 20, 1974, pp. 99–119.

Holtan, B., and L. Strassberger (eds.): *They Became Part of Us: The Expe-*

rience of Families Adopting Children Everywhere, Mini-World Publications, Maple Grove, Minnesota, 1985.

Horn, J.: "The Texas Adoption Project: Adopted Children and Their Intellectual Resemblance to Biological and Adoptive Parents," *Child Development*, vol. 54, 1983, pp. 268–275.

Horn, J., J. Lochlin, and L. Willerman: "Intellectual Resemblance Among Adoptive and Biological Relatives: The Texas Adoption Project," *Behavior Genetics*, vol. 9, 1979, pp. 177–201.

Howard, A., D. D. Royse, and J. A. Skerl: "Transracial Adoption: The Black Community Perspective," *Social Work*, vol. 22, 1977, pp. 184–189.

Howard, J. T., and D. Schultz: *We Want to Have a Baby: The Couple's Complete Guide to Overcoming Infertility*, E. P. Dutton & Co., Inc., New York, 1979.

Howard, M.: "I Take After Somebody: I Have Real Relatives: I Possess a Real Name," *Psychology Today*, vol. 9, 1975, pp. 33+.

*Hulse, J.: *Jody*, McGraw-Hill Book Company, New York, 1976.

Humphrey, M.: "Childless Marriage as a Basis for Adoption," *Mental Health*, vol. 25, 1966, pp. 17–18.

Hunter, N., and N. Polinoff: "Lesbian Mothers Fight Back," *Quest*, vol. 5, 1979, pp. 55–58.

Hyde, M. O.: *Foster Care and Adoption*, Franklin Watts, Inc., New York, 1982.

Hynum, C.: "The Rights of Adult Adoptees," *Western Journal of Medicine*, vol. 136, 1982, p. 166.

Inglis, K.: *Living Mistakes: Mothers Who Consented to Adoption*, Allen and Unwin, Inc., Winchester, Massachusetts, 1984.

"Italy Bars Adoption—Parents Over 40," *Los Angeles Times*, Aug. 25, 1983.

Jackson, L.: "Unsuccessful Adoptions: A Study of 40 Cases Who Attended a Child Guidance Clinic," *British Journal of Medical Psychology*, vol. 41, 1968, pp. 389–398.

Jennings, K. P.: "Practice Is an Insult to Human Dignity," *USA Today*, Mar. 9, 1984.

Jewett, C. L.: *Adopting the Older Child*, Harvard Common Press, Cambridge, Massachusetts, 1978.

*Johnson, D.: *Su An*, Follett Publishing Company, Chicago, 1968.

Johnson, J. M.: *Thought on Adoption*, Children's Home Society of North Carolina, Greensboro, N. C., 1978.

Jones, I. S.: "Private Agency in Detroit Eliminates Adoption Obstacles," *Ebony*, June 1976, p. 53+.

Juhasz, A. M.: "To Have or Not to Have—Children? That Is the Question," *Journal of School Health*, vol. 43, 1973, pp. 632–635.

Kadushin, A.: *Adopting Older Children*, Columbia University Press, New York, 1970.

Kane, F. J., and P. A. Lachenbruch: "Adolescent Pregnancy: A Study of

Aborters and Non-Aborters," *American Journal of Orthopsychiatry*, vol. 43, 1973, pp. 796–803.

Kane, F. J., P. A. Lachenbruch, L. Lockey, R. Auman, L. Pocuis, and M. Lipton: "Motivational Factors Affecting Contraceptive Use," *American Journal of Obstetrics and Gynecology*, vol. 110, 1971, pp. 1050–1054.

Kantrowitz, B.: "After the Baby M Case," *Newsweek*, April 13, 1987.

————: "Three's a Crowd," *Newsweek*, Sept. 1, 1986.

Kaplan, S., and M. J. Rillera: *Cooperative Adoption: A Handbook*, Tri-adoption Library, Inc., Westminster, California, 1984.

*Karl, J. E.: *Beloved Benjamin Is Waiting*, Laurel-Leaf, New York, 1980.

Katchadourian, H. A., and D. T. Lunde: *Fundamentals of Human Sexuality*, Holt, Rinehart and Winston, Inc., New York, 1972.

Katz, L.: "Adoption Counseling as a Preventive Mental Health Speciality," *Child Welfare*, vol. 59, 1980, pp. 161–167.

Kaufman, J.: "Midlife Maternity," *Wall Street Journal*, May 19, 1981.

Kenyon, K.: "The Littlest Immigrants," *Star News*, Nov. 8, 1979.

Kety, S.: "Mental Illness in the Biological and Adoptive Relatives of Schizophrenic Adoptees," *American Journal of Psychiatry*, Vol. 140, 1983, pp. 720–27.

Kety, S., D. Rosenthal, P. Wender, F. Schulsinger, and B. Jacobsen: "Mental Illness in the Biological and Adoptive Families of Adopted Individuals Who Have Become Schizophrenic," *Behavior Genetics*, vol. 6, 1976, pp. 219–225.

Keyes, D.: *Flowers for Algernon*, Harcourt Brace Jovanovich, New York, 1966.

"Kids Get Home with Gays," *Lesbian Tide*, vol. 9, 1980, p. 12.

Kiester, E.: "Should We Unlock the Adoption Files?" *Today's Health*, August, 1974, pp. 54–60.

Kim, D. S.: "Issues in Transracial and Transcultural Adoption," *Social Casework*, vol. 59, 1978, pp. 477–486.

Kirk, H. D.: *Adoptive Kinship: A Modern Institution in Need of Reform*, Ben-Simon Publications, British Columbia, Canada, 1981.

————: *Shared Fate: A Theory and Method of Adoptive Relationships*, Ben-Simon Publications, British Columbia, Canada, 1984.

————: *Shared Fate: A Theory of Adoption and Mental Health*, Free Press, New York, 1964.

Kittson, R. H.: *Orphan Voyage*, Vantage Press, New York, 1968.

Klein, C.: *The Single Parent Experience*, Walker and Company, New York, 1973.

*Klein, N.: *What It's All About*, The Dial Press, Inc., New York, 1975.

Klibanoff, S., and E. Klibanoff: *Let's Talk About Adoption*, Little, Brown and Company, Boston, 1973.

Kline, D.: "He's Ours . . . He's Really Ours!," *McCall's*, March, 1984, pp. 56+.

Kline, D. and H. M. F. Overstreet: *Foster Care of Children: Nurture and Treatment*, Columbia University Press, New York, 1972.

*Koch, J.: *Our Adopted Baby: How You Came Into Our World*, Parkway, Roslyn Heights, N. Y., 1983.

————: *Our Baby: A Birth and Adoption Story*, Perspectives Press, Fort Wayne, Indiana, 1986.

Koh, F.: *Oriental Children in American Homes: How Do They Adjust?*, East-West Publications, Minneapolis, 1981.

Kornheiser, T.: *The Baby Chase*, Atheneum Publishers, New York, 1983.

Krames, L. A.: *Contraception? Facts on Birth Control.* Price/Stern/Sloan Publishers, Inc., Los Angeles, 1979.

*Kraus, R.: *Another Mouse to Feed*, Windmill Wanderer Books, New York, 1980.

Kravik, P. J.: "Adopting a Retarded Child: One Family's Experience," *Children Today*, vol. 4, 1975, pp. 17–21.

Kravik, P. J. (ed.): *Adopting Children with Special Needs*, North American Council on Adoptable Children, Riverside, California, 1976.

Krementz, J.: *How It Feels To Be Adopted*, Alfred A. Knopf, Inc., New York, 1982.

Krier, B.: "Surrogate Motherhood: Looking at It as Business Proposition," *Los Angeles Times*, Mar. 30, 1981.

Ladner, J. A.: *Mixed Families: Adopting Across Racial Boundaries*, Anchor Books, New York, 1977.

————: "Mixed Families: White Parents and Black Children," *Society*, vol. 14, 1977, pp. 70–78.

*Lapsley, S.: *I Am Adopted*, Bradbury Press, New York, 1974.

Larson, A.: "San Diego Program Places Children with Prospective Parents," *Los Angeles Times*, Sept. 5, 1984.

*Lasker, J.: *He's My Brother*, Albert Whitman & Company, Chicago, 1974.

Lasnik, R. S.: *A Parent's Guide to Adoption*, Sterling Publishing Co., Inc., New York, 1979.

Laverty, K. H.: "Psychological Well-Being in Parents and Non-Parents Beyond the Age of Child Rearing: A Comparative and Descriptive Study, Doctoral dissertation, California School of Professional Psychology, San Diego, California, 1979.

Lawton, J. J., and S. Z. Gross: "Review of Psychiatric Literature on Adopted Children," *Archives of General Psychiatry*, vol. 11, 1964, pp. 635–644.

Leavitt, D. K.: *Counseling Clients in Independent Adoptions*, California Continuing Education of the Bar, Berkeley, California, 1980.

Leishman, K.: "Teenage Mothers Are Keeping Their Babies—With the Help of Their Own Mothers," *Ms.*, vol. 8, 1980, pp. 61+.

Leynes, C.: "Keep or Adopt: A Study of Factors Influencing Pregnant Adolescents' Plans for Their Babies," *Child Psychiatry and Human Development*, vol. 11, 1980, pp. 105–112.

Liddick, B.: "The Agony of Infertility—One Woman's Story," *Los Angeles Times*, Sept. 18, 1977.

*Lifton, B. J.: *I'm Still Me*, Alfred A. Knopf, New York, 1981.

———: *Lost and Found: The Adoption Experience*, The Dial Press, Inc., New York, 1979.

———: *Twice Born: Memoirs of an Adopted Daughter*, McGraw-Hill Book Company, New York, 1975.

*Lindgren, A.: *Pippi Longstocking*, Viking Press, New York, 1950.

Lindley, M.: "Adoptive Parents Argue for Keeping Records Closed," *Los Angeles Times*, June 8, 1980.

Lindsay, J. W.: *Open Adoption: A Caring Option*, Morning Glory Press, Buena Park, California, 1987.

———: *Pregnant Too Soon: Adoption Is an Option*, EMC Publishing, St. Paul, Minnesota, 1980.

*Livingston, C.: *Why Was I Adopted?* Lyle Stuart, Inc., N. J., 1978.

Loehlin, J., J. Horn, and L. Willerman: "Personality Resemblance in Adoptive Families," *Behavior Genetics*, vol. 11, 1981, pp. 309–330.

Lowry, K.: "The Designer Babies Are Growing Up," *Los Angeles Times Magazine*, November 1, 1987.

*Lowry, L.: *Find a Stranger, Say Good-bye*, Pocket Books, Inc., New York, 1978.

Lynn, D. B.: *The Father: His Role in Child Development*, Brooks/Cole Publishing Company, Monterey, California, 1974.

Macaskill, C.: "Post-adoption Support: Is It Essential?" *Adoption and Fostering*, vol. 9, 1985, pp. 45–49.

Macmanus, S.: *The Adoption Book*, Paulist Press, Ramsey, New Jersey, 1984.

Maddux, R.: *The Orchard Children*, Harper & Row, Publishers, New York, 1977.

Mady, T.: "Surrogate Mothers: The Legal Issues," *American Journal of Law and Medicine*, vol. 7, 1981, pp. 323–352.

Mamanus, S.: *Adoption: A Viable Alternative*, Paulist Press, Ramsey, N. Y., 1984.

Manuel, D.: "Plight of the Older Adoptees," *Los Angeles Times*, Dec. 4, 1981.

Marion, T. S.: "Psychoeducational Groups for Adoptive Parents," *Infertility*, Human Sciences Press, New York, 1984.

Margolies, M.: "Adopting a Child If You're Single," *Mademoiselle*, December, 1972, pp. 136+.

Marindin, H.: *Handbook for Prospective Single Parents*, Committee for Single Adoptive Parents, Washington, D.C., n.d.

Marks, J.: "Children of Crisis: True Tales of High-risk Adoptions," *New York*, vol. 12, 1979, pp. 31+.

Martin, C.: "If All Are Happy, Who's The Victim?," *USA Today*, Mar. 9, 1984.

Martin, C. D.: "Psychological Problems of Abortion for the Unwed Teen-age Girl," *Genetic Psychology Monographs*, vol. 88, 1973, pp. 23–110.

Matejcek, Z., Z. Dytrych, and V. Schuller: "Children from Unwanted Pregnancies," *Acta Psychiatrica Scandanavia*, vol. 57, 1978, pp. 67–90.

Maxtone-Graham, K.: *An Adopted Woman*, Remi Books, Inc., New York, 1983.

————: *Pregnant by Mistake: The Stories of Seventeen Women*, Liveright Publishing Corporation, New York, 1973.

Mayfield, M.: "New Birth Control Devices Described," *Los Angeles Times*, Oct. 7, 1982.

Maynard, J.: *Baby Love*, Alfred A. Knopf, Inc., New York, 1981.

McCormack, P.: "Much Skepticism on Natural Birth Control," *Los Angeles Times*, June 27, 1980.

McEwan, M. T.: "Readoption with a Minimum of Pain," *Social Casework*, vol. 54, 1973, pp. 350–353.

McGuire, P.: *It Won't Happen to Me: Teenagers Talk About Pregnancy*, Delacorte Press, New York, 1983.

McNamara, J.: *The Adoption Adviser*, Hawthorne Books, Inc., New York, 1975.

McRoy, R. G., and L. A. Zurcher: *Transracial and Intracial Adoptees: The Adolescent Years*, Charles C. Thomas, Publishers, Springfield, Illinois, 1983.

McTaggart, L.: "Babies for Sale: The Booming Adoption Racket," *Saturday Review*, Nov. 10, 1979, pp. 15+.

McTaggart, L.: "Choosing A Child's Sex by 'Weeding Out' Father's Sperm," *Los Angeles Times*, Nov. 30, 1980.

McTaggart, L.: *The Baby Brokers: The Marketing of White Babies in America*, The Dial Press, Inc., New York, 1980.

Mead, M.: "In the Best Interests of the Child," *Redbook*, October, 1978, pp. 100+.

————:"What's Right and Wrong About Adoption Today," *Redbook*, September, 1978, pp. 39+.

Meezan, W.: "Foster Parent Adoption: A Literature Review," *Child Welfare*, vol. 61, 1982, pp. 525–535.

Meezan, W., S. Katz, and E. M. Russo: *Adoption Without Agencies: A Study of Independent Adoptions*, Child Welfare League of America, Inc., New York, 1978.

Meezan, W. and J. F. Shireman: *Care and Commitment: Foster Parent Adoption Decisions*, State University of New York Press, Albany, New York, 1985.

Mehren, E.: "A Capital Site for a Surrogate Parent Center," *Los Angeles Times*, Apr. 19, 1983.

———: "Lesbian Mothers: Two New Studies Shatter Stereotypes," *Los Angeles Times*, June 1, 1983.

———: "She's a Dedicated Single Working Mother," *Los Angeles Times*, July 11, 1983.

Melina, C. M. and L. Melina: The Family Physician and Adoption, *American Family Physician*, vol. 31, 1985, pp. 109–118.

Melina, L. R.: *Raising Adopted Children: A Manual for Adoptive Parents*, Harper & Row, Publishers, New York, 1986.

Menning, B. E.: *Infertility: A Guide for the Childless Couple*, Prentice Hall, Inc., Englewood Cliffs, N. J., 1977.

*Meredith, J. C.: *And Now We Are A Family*, Beacon Press, Boston, 1971.

Merritt, S., and L. Steiner: *And Baby Makes Two: Motherhood Without Marriage*, Franklin Watts, New York, 1984.

*Miles, M.: *Aaron's Door*, Atlantic Monthly Press, Boston, 1977.

*Milgram, M.: *Brothers Are All the Same*, E. P. Dutton & Co., Inc., New York, 1978.

*Milowitz, G. D.: *Unwed Mother*, Tempo Books, New York, 1977.

Mohr, B.: "The Search for Natural Parents: A Difficult Refocusing on Visions Long Faded," *San Diego Union*, July 16, 1981.

"Monkeys Without Ovaries Give Birth: Hope for Infertile Women," *San Diego Union*, Oct. 28, 1983.

*Montgomery, L. M.: *Anne of Green Gables*, Bantam Books, New York, 1979.

Morain, D.: " 'Casual' Fathers Win More Control in Adoption Case," *Los Angeles Times*, Oct. 23, 1984.

———: "Parents of Adopted Child Fighting Bid for Custody by Teen-age Father," *Los Angeles Times*, Dec. 15, 1984.

Moran, B.: "Ann's Search: Her Life May Depend On It," *Los Angeles Times*, Apr. 1, 1983.

"Motherhood Rated on Happiness Scale," *Los Angeles Times*, May 9, 1980.

*Murphy, F. S.: *Ready-Made Family*, Scholastic Book Service, New York, 1972.

Nash, A. L.: "Reflections on Interstate Adoptions," *Children Today*, vol. 3, 1974, pp. 7–11.

Nelson, H.: "Human Ova Will Be Transplanted," *Los Angeles Times*, June 16, 1982.

Nelson, H. and E. Chen: " 'Orphan' Embryos Raise Legal, Ethical Questions," *Los Angeles Times*, June 19, 1984.

Nelson-Erichsen, J., and H. R. Erichsen: *Gamines: How to Adopt from Latin America*, Dillon, Minneapolis, 1981.

———: *How to Adopt Internationally: Africa, Asia, Europe and Latin America*, Graduate research project in human development, Saint Mary's College, Winona, Minnesota, 1980.

*Nerlove, E.: *Who is David? The Story of an Adopted Adolescent and His Friends*, Child Welfare League of America, Washington, D.C., 1985.

*Neufeld, J.: *Edgar Allan*, New American Library, Inc., New York, 1968.

"New Birth Control Techniques," *San Diego Union*, Oct. 1, 1982.

"Newborn Fever," *Time Magazine*, Mar. 12, 1984.

"New Contraceptives for Both Sexes Seen," *Los Angeles Times*, Oct. 24, 1978.

Nickman S.: *The Adoption Experience*, Julian Messner, New York, 1985.

Norvell, M., and R. F. Guy: "A Comparison of Self-concept in Adopted and Non-adopted Adolescents," *Adolescence*, vol. 12, 1977, pp. 443–448.

"Numerically, the Handicapped Are Far from 'Exceptional,' " *Behavior Today*, Mar. 10, 1980.

Okie, S. "The Pill: Major Study Adds Fuel to the Controversy," *Los Angeles Times*, May 3, 1981.

"Open Adoptions: What Effect on Families?" *NASW News*, May, 1986.

*Oppenheimer, J. L.: *Which Mother Is Mine?*, Bantam Books, New York, 1980.

Osborn, E.: "Adopting an Infant: 'Gestation Period' Drags on for Years," *The Register*, May 21, 1981.

Osment, N.: "Bringing Children Again . . . Into a Sterile Marriage," *San Diego Union*, Sept. 12, 1982.

———: "For This Couple, A Happy Picture," *San Diego Union*, Feb. 1, 1981.

Otten, A. L. "Medical Efforts to Help Childless Couples Pose Host of Difficult Issues," *Wall Street Journal*, Aug. 7, 1984.

Paddock, R.: "Bill Would Curb 'Master Race' Sperm Banks," *Los Angeles Times*, Mar. 1, 1983.

*Palmer, F.: *And Four To Grow On*, Rinehart & Company, Inc., New York, 1960.

Palmer, S. E.: "Predicting Outcome in Long-term Foster Care," *Journal of Social Service Research*, vol. 3, 1979, pp. 201–14.

Pannor, R., and E. A. Nerlove: "Fostering Understanding between Adolescents and Adoptive Parents through Group Experience," *Child Welfare*, vol. 56, 1977, pp. 537–545.

Parachini, A.: "Decline in Fertility Confirmed: Age Diminishes Woman's Chance to Conceive," *Los Angeles Times*, Feb. 19, 1982.

———: "The Quest for an Acceptable Male Contraceptive," *Los Angeles Times*, Feb. 17, 1984.

Parker, P. "Surrogate Motherhood: The Interaction of Litigation, Legislation and Psychiatry," *International Journal of Law and Psychiatry*, vol. 5, 1983, pp. 341–354.

*Parsell, M. S.: *A Look at Adoption*, Lerner Publications, Co., Minneapolis, 1978.

Paton, J. M.: *The Adopted Break Silence,* Life History Study Center, Philadelphia, Pennsylvania, 1955.

*Paterson, K.: *The Great Gilly Hopkins,* Thems Y. Crowell Co., New York, 1978.

Phillips, K.: "Mother & Son: Before the Adoption Came the Adaption," *The San Diego Reader,* Dec. 2, 1982, pp. 1+.

Pierce, R. I.: *Single and Pregnant,* Beacon Press, Boston, 1970.

Pines, M.: "How Old Is Too Old to Have a Baby?" *McCall's,* vol. 107, 1980, pp. 91+.

Plomin, R.: "The Colorado Adoption Project," *Child Development,* vol. 54, 1983, pp. 176–189.

Plumez, J. H.: "Families: The Adoption Option," *Working Woman,* May, 1983, pp. 148+.

———: *Successful Adoption,* Harmony Books, New York, 1982.

Powell, J. Y.: *Whose Child Am I? Adults: Recollections of Being Adopted,* Teresias Press, Inc., New York, 1985.

Powledge, F.: *The New Adoption Maze and How to Get Through It,* C. V. Mosby Co., St. Louis, 1985.

———: *So You're Adopted,* Charles Scribner's Sons, New York, 1982.

"Pregnancy Failures Linked to Chemicals," *Daily Breeze,* Jan. 2, 1981.

"Pregnancy Risk Factors Are Reviewed," *San Diego Union,* Dec. 14, 1984.

Pringle, M.L.K.: *Adoption Facts and Fallacies,* Longmans, Green & Co. Ltd., London, 1967.

"Pros, Cons of Adopting During Infertility Treatment," *Adopted Child,* vol. 5, 1986.

Pufki, P. M.: "Silly Questions and Straight Answers about Adoption," *Children Today,* vol. 12, 1983, pp. 11–14.

Putterman, R.: *To Find My Son,* Avon, New York, 1981.

Rains, P. M.: *Becoming an Unwed Mother,* Aldine Atherton, Inc., Chicago, 1971.

Rao, L. M.: "A Comparative Study of Childlessness and Never-Pregnant Status," *Journal of Marriage and the Family,* vol. 36, 1974, pp. 149–157.

Rauh, J. L., R. L. Burket, and R. R. Brookman: "Contraception for the Teenager," *Medical Clinics of North America,* vol. 59, 1975, pp. 1407–1418.

Raymond, L.: *Adoption and After,* Harper & Row, Publishers, New York, 1955.

*Read, E.: *Brothers by Choice,* Farrar, Straus & Giroux, New York, 1974.

"Research: Many More Lesbians Choosing Parenthood," *Behavior Today,* July 20, 1984.

"Researchers Protest Fertility Study," *Los Angeles Times,* Sept. 16, 1981.

Reza, H.: "Mother Seeks Children She Last Saw in 1967," *Los Angeles Times,* Jan. 9, 1984.

Richards, M. P. M. (ed.): *The Integration of a Child into a Social World,* Cambridge University Press, London, 1974.

Rigert, J.: *All Together: An Unusual American Family,* Harper & Row, Publishers, New York, 1973.

Rillera, M. J.: *The Adoption Searchbook: Techniques for Tracing People,* Triadoption Library, Huntington Beach, California, 1981.

Rillera, M. J., and S. Kaplan: *Cooperative Adoption: A Handbook,* Triadoption Publications, Westminster, California, 1985.

Rivers, L. M.: "There Is No Wrong In Paying for a Baby," *USA Today,* Mar. 9, 1984.

Roberts, J., and D. C. Robie: *Open Adoption and Open Placements,* Adoption Press, Minneapolis, 1981.

*Rodowsky, C. F.: *P.S. Write Soon,* Laurel-Leaf, New York, 1978.

Roles, P.: *Facing Teenage Pregnancy,* Eterna Press, Oak Brook, Illinois, 1984.

*Rondell, F., and R. Michaels: *The Adopted Family: Book I, You and Your Child,* Crown Publishers, Inc., New York, 1951.

*————: *The Family That Grew,* Crown Publishers, Inc., New York, 1951.

Rondell, F., and A. Murray: *New Dimensions in Adoption,* Crown Publishers, Inc., New York, 1974.

*Rosenberg, M. B.: *Being Adopted,* Lothrop, Lee & Shepard Books, New York, 1984.

*————: *Living in Two Worlds,* Lothrop, Lee & Shepard Books, New York, 1986.

Rosenstiel, T.: "Utah Couple Win Guardianship of Navajo Boy," *Los Angeles Times,* Oct. 30, 1987.

Rosenthal, D., P. H. Wender, S. S. Kety, F. Schulsinger, J. Welnew, and R. O. Rieder: "Parent-child Relationships and Psychopathological Disorder in the Child," *Archives of General Psychiatry,* vol. 32, 1975, pp. 466–476.

Rothenberg, E. W., M. Goldey, and R. M. Sands: "The Vicissitudes of the Adoption Process," *American Journal of Psychiatry,* vol. 128, 1971, pp. 590–595.

Rovner, S. "Moral Choices about Genetic Issues," *Los Angeles Times,* Apr. 17, 1983.

Rowe, J.: *Yours by Choice: A Guide for Adoptive Parents,* Routledge & Kegan Paul, Ltd., London, 1982.

Ryberg, H. M.: "Are You My Real Mother?" *Parents,* February, 1974, pp. 56+.

Rynearson, E. "Relinquishment and Its Maternal Complications: A Preliminary Study," *American Journal of Psychiatry,* vol. 139, 1982, pp. 338–340.

Sachdev, P. (ed): *Adoption Current Issues and Trends,* Butterworths, Toronto, 1984.

Salkmann, V.: *There Is a Child for You: A Family's Encounter with Modern Adoption*, Simon & Schuster, New York, 1972.

Sandness, G: *Beginnings: True Experiences in Adoption*, Mini-World Publications, Maple Grove, Minnesota, 1980.

———: *Brimming Over*, Mini-World Publications, Minneapolis, 1978.

———: *Commitment: The Reality of Adoption*, Mini-World Publications, Maple Grove, Minnesota, 1984.

Sanford, M.: *A Look at Adoption*, Lerner Publications Co., Minneapolis, 1978.

Scarr, S.: "The Minnesota Adoption Studies: Genetic Differences and Maleability," *Child Development*, vol. 54, 1983, pp. 260–267.

Scarr, S., and R. Weinberg: "I.Q. Test Performance of Black Children Adopted by White Families," *American Psychologist*, vol. 31, 1976, pp. 726–739.

Schneider, S. and E. Rimmer: "Adoptive Parents' Hostility Toward Their Adopted Children," *Children and Youth Services Review*, vol. 6, 1984, pp. 345–352.

Schultz, A. L., and A. G. Motulsky: "Medical Genetics and Adoption," *Child Welfare*, vol. 50, 1971, pp. 4–17.

"Scientist Says Once-a-Month Pill Shows Promise in Birth Control," *San Diego Union*, Nov. 20, 1982.

*Scott, E.: *Adoption*, Franklin Watts, Inc., New York, 1980.

"Second Baby Produced from Frozen Embryo Reported in Fine Condition," *San Diego Union*, July 7, 1984.

Sector, B.: "Couples Seeking to Adopt a Baby Use Classified Ads," *Los Angeles Times*, May 24, 1987.

Sherman, E. A., R. Neuman, and A. W. Shyne: *Children Adrift in Foster Care: A Study of Alternative Approaches*, Child Welfare League of America, Inc., New York, 1974.

Seglow, J., M. K. Pringle, and P. Wedge: *Growing Up Adopted: A Long-term National Study of Adopted Children and Their Families*, National Foundation for Educational Research in England and Wales, Great Britain, 1972.

"Siblings Need Help When Older Child Arrives," *Adopted Child*, vol. 2, 1983, pp. 1+.

Siegel, B.: "Why One Mother Gave Up Her Children," *Los Angeles Times*, Feb. 27, 1978.

Silber, K., and P. Speedlin, *Dear Birthmother*, Corona Publishing Company, San Antonio, Texas, 1983.

Silcock, B.: "The Legalities of Artificial Insemination," *San Diego Transcript*, Oct. 17, 1984.

*Silman, R. *Somebody Else's Child*, Dell Publishing Co., Inc., 1976.

Silverman, A. R., and W. Feigelman: "Some Factors Affecting the Adoption of Minority Children," *Social Casework*, vol. 58, 1977, pp. 554–561.

*Simon, N.: *Why Am I Different?* Albert Whitman & Company, Niles, Illinois, 1976.

*————: *All Kinds of Families,* Albert Whitman & Company, Niles, Illinois, 1976.

Simon, R. J.: "Black Attitudes Toward Transracial Adoption," *Phylon,* vol. 39, 1978, pp. 135–142.

Simon, R. J., and H. Altstein: *Transracial Adoption,* John Wiley & Sons, Inc., New York, 1977.

Simross, L.: "The DeBolts and Their 19 Children: 'Loving Tough,' " *Los Angeles Times,* Dec. 10, 1978.

Singer, L. M., D. M. Brodzinsky, D. Ramsay, M. Steir, and E. Waters: "Mother-Infant Attachment in Adoptive Families," *Child Development,* vol. 56, 1985, pp. 1543–1551.

*Sly, K. O.: *Becky's Special Family,* Alternative Parenting Publications, Corona, California, 1985.

Small, J. W.: "Discrimination Against the Adoptee," *Public Welfare,* vol. 37, 1979, pp. 38–43.

Smith, D.: "Artificial Birth and Its Effects," *Los Angeles Times,* Dec. 27, 1978.

Smith, D. D.: *A Limb of Your Tree: The Story of an Adopted Twin's Search for Her Roots,* Exposition, Smithtown, N. Y., 1983.

Smith, D. W., and L. N. Sherwen: *Mothers and Their Adopted Children: The Bonding Process,* Tiresias Press, New York, 1983.

Smith, G.: " 'Open' Adoptions on Rise Despite Difficulties," *Los Angeles Times,* May 17, 1987.

Smith J., and F. Miroff: *You're Our Child: A Social/Psychological Approach to Adoption,* University Press of America, Lanham, Maryland, 1981.

Smyth, E. "The Paper Maze to Lost Identity," *San Diego Union,* Dec. 3, 1978.

Snider, A.: "Artificial Embryonation: Fertilizing Female Donor's Egg," *Los Angeles Times,* Aug. 15, 1980.

————: "Motherhood Rated on Happiness Scale," *Los Angeles,* May 9, 1980.

*Sobol, H. L.: *My Brother Steven Is Retarded,* The Macmillan Company, New York, 1977.

————: *We Don't Look Like Our Mom and Dad,* Coward-McCann, Inc., New York, 1984.

Sokoloff, B.: "Should the Adopted Adolescent Have Access to His Birth Records and to His Birth-parents?" *Clinical Pediatrics,* vol. 16, 1977, pp. 975–977.

"Some Foster Parents Expect to Adopt," *Adopted Child,* vol. 5, 1986, pp. 1+.

*Sommer, S.: *And I'm Stuck with Joseph,* Herold Press, Scottsdale, Pennsylvania, 1984.

Sorosky, A. D., A. Baran, and Pannor, R.: *The Adoption Triangle: The Effects of the Sealed Record on Adoptees, Birth Parents, and Adoptive Parents,* Anchor Books, New York, 1978.

Spivak, S.: " 'Test Tube' Fertilization Offers Couples an Alternative," *La Jolla Light,* May 5, 1983.

*Starr, C.: *Vicky,* Faber & Faber, Ltd., Winchester, Massachusetts, 1981.

*Stein, S. B.: *About Handicaps: An Open Family Book for Parents and Children Together,* Walker and Company, New York, 1974.

————: *The Adopted One: An Open Family Book for Parents and Children Together,* Walker and Company, New York, 1979.

Steinhauer, P. D., and Q. Rae-Grant, *Psychological Problems of the Child and His Family,* The Macmillan Company, Toronto, Canada, 1977.

Steinhorn, A.: "On Lesbian Mothers," *SIECUS Report,* January, 1984, pp. 7–8.

Stephens, B.: "Babies: Alternatives for the Have Nots," *Los Angeles Times,* Oct. 10, 1982.

————: "Biracial Child—A Positive Experience," *Los Angeles Times,* July 12, 1982.

————: "Coming to Terms with Infertility," *Los Angeles Times,* May 30, 1982.

"Sterilization Tops Pill as Most Used Contraceptive, Study Finds," *San Diego Union,* Dec. 6, 1984.

Stokolosa, M.: "Birth Control Goes Under the Skin," *San Diego Union,* Nov. 5, 1982.

Stone, H. D., and J. M. Hunseker: *Education for Foster Family Care: Models and Methods for Foster Parents and Social Workers,* Child Welfare League of America, Inc., New York, 1975.

Sugar, M. (ed.): *Female Adolescent Development,* Brunner/Mazel, Publishers, New York, 1979.

*Swope, J. D.: *The Legend of the Bear: A Tale for Children Who Wait To Be Adopted,* The Jess Press, York, Pennsylvania, 1983.

*Taber, B. G.: *Adopting Baby Brother,* Hanover Falls, N. Y., 1974.

*Tate, E.: *Just an Overnight Guest,* The Dial Press, Inc., New York, 1980.

Teasdale, T.: "Social Class Correlations Among Adoptees and Their Biological and Adoptive Parents," *Behavior Genetics,* vol. 9, 1979, pp. 103–114.

Teasdale, T. W., and T. I. A. Sorensen: "Educational Attainment and Social Class in Adoptees: Genetic and Environmental Contributions," *Journal of Biosocial Science,* vol. 4, 1983, pp. 509–518.

"Test Tube Babies," *Living,* vol. 10, 1979, p. 4.

"Thawed Embryo Implanted in Australian Woman," *Los Angeles Times,* May 4, 1983.

"They Said We Were Too Fat to Adopt a Baby," *Good Housekeeping,* vol. 189, 1979, pp. 98+.

Tienari, P., A. Sorri, I. Lahti, M. Naarala, K. Wahlberg, T. Ronkko, J. Pohjola, and J. Moring: "The Finnish Adoptive Family Study of Schizophrenia," *Yale Journal of Biology and Medicine*, vol. 58, 1985, pp. 227–237.

Timms, N.: *The Receiving End: Consumer Accounts of Social Help for Children*, Routledge & Kegan Paul, London, 1973.

Timnick, L.: "Blacks Drop Fight for Baby," *Los Angeles Times*, May 21, 1981.

Tizard, B.: *Adoption A Second Chance*, Open Books Publishing Limited, London, 1977.

———: "Adopting Older Children from Institutions," *Child Abuse and Neglect*, vol. 3, 1979, pp. 535–538.

Tizard, B., and J. Rees: "A Comparison of the Effects of Adoption Restoration to the Natural Mother, and Continued Institutional on the Cognitive Development of Four-Year-Old Children," *Child Development*, vol. 45, 1974, pp. 92–99.

Tod, R. (ed): Social Work in Adoption, Longman Group Limited, London, 1971.

Tomes, N.: "Childlessness in Canada 1971: A Further Analysis," *Canadian Journal of Sociology*, vol. 10, 1985, pp. 37–68.

"The Trend Toward Delayed Parenthood: What Will It Mean," *Marriage and Divorce Today*, Oct. 19, 1981.

Trimborn, H.: "U.S. Couple Fight for Polish Child," *Los Angeles Times*, Aug. 21, 1983.

Triseliotis, J.: *In Search of Origins: The Experiences of Adopted People*, Routledge & Kegan Paul, London, 1973.

Triseliotis, J. (ed.): *New Developments in Foster Care and Adoption*, Routledge & Kegan Paul, Ltd., London, 1980.

"Unwed Dad Allowed to Block Adoption," *San Diego Union*, Oct. 23, 1984.

U.S. Department of Commerce, Bureaus of the Census: *Statistical Abstract of the United States*, U.S. Government Printing Office, Washington, D.C., 1978.

Valenti, L. L.: *The Fifteen Most Asked Questions About Adoption*, Herald Press, Scottdale, Pennsylvannia, 1985.

Valiente-Barksdale, C.: "Recruiting Hispanic Families," *Children Today*, vol. 10, 1983, pp. 26–28.

Van Keep, P. A., and H. Schmidt-Elmendorff: "Involuntary Childlessness," *Journal of Biosocial Science*, vol. 7, 1975, pp. 37–48.

Varna, V. P. (ed): *Stresses in Children*, University of London Press, London, 1973.

Varro, B.: "Don't Expect Perfection in Birth Control," *Los Angeles Times*, Mar. 24, 1980.

———: "Help for the Heartbreak of Infertility," *Los Angeles Times*, Aug. 23, 1979.

———: "Scientific Advances in Fertility," *Los Angeles Times*, Aug. 28, 1979.

————: "The Pill: Controversy Rages On," *Los Angeles Times*, Mar. 21, 1980.

Veenhoven, R.: "Is There an Innate Need for Children?," *European Journal of Social Psychology*, vol. 74, 1974, pp. 495–501.

Veevers, J. E.: "The Social Meanings of Parenthood," *Psychiatry*, vol. 36, 1973, pp. 291–310.

Verny, T.: *The Secret Life of the Unborn Child*, Summit Books, New York, 1981.

Veronico, A. J.: "One Church, One Child: Placing Children with Special Needs," *Children Today*, March–April, 1983, pp. 6–10.

Vieni, M.: "Why Should Physically Handicapped People Want to Adopt?", *Adopting Children with Special Needs*, North American Council on Adoptable Children, Riverside, California, 1976, pp. 43–44.

Viguers, S. T.: *With Child: One Couple's Journey to Their Adopted Children*, Harcourt Brace Jovanovich, San Diego, California, 1985.

Vils, U.: "When Birth Parents Seek Their Children," *Los Angeles Times*, Apr. 23, 1981.

Von Knorring, A., C. R. Cloninger, M. Bohman, and S. Sigvardsson: "An Adoption Study of Depressive Disorders and Substance Abuse," *Archives of General Psychiatry*, vol. 40, 1983, pp. 943–950.

Walter, C. W.: *The Timing of Motherhood*, Lexington Books, Lexington, Massachusetts, 1986.

*Ward, J.: *I Have a Question, God*, Broadman Press, Nashville, Tennessee, 1981.

Ward, M.: "Large Adoptive Families: A Special Resource," *Social Casework*, vol. 59, 1978, pp. 411–418.

————: "The Special Needs of the Adopted Child," *Parents Magazine*, December, 1972, pp. 942+.

*Warren, M.: *Walk in My Moccasins*, The Westminster Press, Philadelphia, 1966.

*Wasson, V. P.: *The Chosen Baby*, J. B. Lippincott Company, Philadelphia, 1939.

Watson, K. W.: "Who Is the Primary Client?," *Public Welfare*, vol. 37, 1979, pp. 11–14.

Waxman, B. F.: "How Do You Know You're Ready?," *Mainstream*, January, 1984.

*Waybill, M.: *Chinese Eyes*, Harold Press, Marshall, Arizona, 1974.

Weathers, O. D., P. L. Campiglia, M. W. Gayle, and E. J. Schwartz, "Update: Adoption Opportunities Projects," *Children Today*, vol. 10, 1983, pp. 20–25.

Weidell, R. C.: "Unsealing Birth Certificates in Minnesota," *Child Welfare*, vol. 59, 1980, pp. 113–119.

Weiss, H.: "On Gay Fathers," *SIECUS Report*, January, 1984, pp. 7–8.

Whelan, E. M.: *A Baby . . . Maybe? A Guide to Making the Most Fateful Decision of Your Life,* Bobbs-Merrill Company, Inc., New York, 1975.

"White Family, Black Child," *Christian Century,* May 6, 1973, pp. 526–527.

"Why a Sudden Drop in Baby Adoptions," *U.S. News & World Report,* July 30, 1973, p. 62.

"White Gay May Keep Black Child," *San Diego Union,* July 27, 1984.

Wieder, H.: "The Family Romance Fantasies of Adopted Children," *Psychoanalytic Quarterly,* vol. 46, 1977, pp. 185–200.

Wilkinson, H. S. P.: *Birth Is More Than Once: The Inner World of Adopted Korean Children,* Sunrise Ventures, Bloomfield Hills, Michigan, 1985.

*Wilt, J.: *The Nitty Gritty of Family Life,* Educational Products Division, Waco, Texas, 1979.

*Windsor, P.: *Mad Martin,* Harper & Row, Publishers, Incorporated, New York, 1978.

Winkler, R. and M. van Keppel: "Relinquishing Mothers in Adoption: Their Long-term Adjustment," *Institute of Family Studies Monograph,* No. 3, Melbourne, Australia, 1984.

Wishard, L., and W. R. Wishard; *Adoption: The Grafted Tree,* Cragmont Publications, San Francisco, California, 1979.

Wolkind, S. (ed.): *Medical Aspects of Adoption and Foster Care,* J. B. Lippincott Company, Philadelphia, 1980.

Wrenn, M.: "Babies Having Babies," *Life,* vol. 6, 1983, pp. 102–112.

Yaeger, D.: "Doctors Make Progress in Treating Infertility, But Costs Are High," *Wall Street Journal,* Oct. 12, 1984.

*Yashima, T., *Umbrella,* The Viking Press, New York, 1970.

Yenckel, J. T.: "Impotence 'Shame' Gets an Airing," *Los Angeles Times,* Mar. 11, 1984.

Yogman, M. W., C. Herrera, and K. Bloom: "Perinatal Characteristics of Newborns, Relinquished at Birth," *American Journal of Public Health,* vol. 73, 1983, pp. 1194–1196.

Zastrow, C. H.: *Outcome of Black Children–White Parents Transracial Adoptions,* R. & R. Research Associates, San Francisco, California, 1977.

Zeilinger, R.: "The Need vs. the Right to Know," *Public Welfare,* vol. 37, 1979, pp. 44–47.

Zimmerman, M.: *Should I Keep My Baby?,* Bethany House Publishers, Minneapolis, 1983.

Index